Europe's Crises

Europe's Crises

Edited by

Manuel Castells

Olivier Bouin
João Caraça
Gustavo Cardoso
John B. Thompson
Michel Wieviorka

polity

First published in 2018 by Polity Press

Polity Press
65 Bridge Street
Cambridge CB2 1UR, UK

Polity Press
101 Station Landing, Suite 300
Medford, MA 02155, USA

This volume was supported by grants from the College d'études mondiales of the Fondation Maison des Sciences de l'Homme and the Delegation in France of the Calouste Gulbenkian Foundation.

ISBN-13: 978-1-5095-2486-0
ISBN-13: 978-1-5095-2487-7(pbk)

A catalogue record for this book is available from the British Library.

Library of Congress Cataloging-in-Publication Data

Names: Castells, Manuel, 1942- editor.
Title: Europe's crises / [edited by] Manuel Castells, [and five others].
Description: Cambridge, UK ; Malden, MA : Polity Press, 2017. | Includes
    bibliographical references and index.
Identifiers: LCCN 2017012651 (print) | LCCN 2017033057 (ebook) | ISBN
    9781509524891 (Mobi) | ISBN 9781509524907 (Epub) | ISBN 9781509524860
    (hardback) | ISBN 9781509524877 (pbk.)
Subjects: LCSH: Financial crises--European Union countries. | European Union
    countries--Economic conditions--21st century. | European Union
    countries--Social conditions--21st century. | European Union
    countries--Politics and government--21st century.
Classification: LCC HC240 (ebook) | LCC HC240 .E8576 2017 (print) | DDC
    940.56--dc23
LC record available at https://lccn.loc.gov/2017012651

Typeset in 10.5 on 12 pt Sabon by
Servis Filmsetting Ltd, Stockport, Cheshire
Printed and bound in Great Britain by Clay Ltd, St. Ives PLC

For further information on Polity, visit our website:
politybooks.com

Contents

Part II: Social Crises

Part III: Political Crises

CONTENTS

Contributors

Guya Accornero is Invited Assistant Professor and Senior Researcher in Political Science at ISCTE – University Institute of Lisbon, Center for Research and Studies in Sociology.

Eirini Avramopoulou is A.G. Leventis Fellow at the British School at Athens.

Joana Azevedo is Invited Assistant Professor at the Department of Sociology, ISCTE-IUL – University Institute of Lisbon, and researcher at the CIES-IUL – Centre for Research and Studies in Sociology.

Olivier Bouin is the Director of the Collège d'études mondiales of the Foundation Maison des Sciences de l'Homme in Paris and of the Network of French Institutes for Advanced Study.

João Caraça is Full Professor of Science and Technology Policy at the Institute of Economics and Management (ISEG) of the University of Lisboa and Senior Adviser at the Calouste Gulbenkian Foundation.

Gustavo Cardoso is University Professor at the University Institute of Lisbon and Associate Researcher at the Collège d'études mondiales, FMSH, Paris.

Noah Carl is a DPhil candidate in the Department of Sociology at the University of Oxford.

Manuel Castells is the Wallis Annenberg Chair of Communication at the University of Southern California; Professor Emeritus of Sociology, University of California, Berkeley; Fellow of St John's College, Cambridge; and the holder of the Chair on the Network Society at the College d'études mondiales of the Fondation Maison des Sciences de l'Homme, Paris.

Sir Paul Collier is Professor of Economics and Public Policy at the Blavatnik School of Government, Oxford University.

Colin Crouch is Professor Emeritus at the University of Warwick, and External Scientific member of the Max-Planck-Institute for Social Research at Cologne.

James Dennison is a Research Fellow at the Robert Schuman Centre for Advanced Studies in Florence.

Geoffrey Evans is University Professor in the Sociology of Politics and Official Fellow in Politics, Nuffield College, University of Oxford.

Sviatlana Hlebik is an economist and mathematician who works in the Economic Studies and Financial Communication Department, Crédit Agricole Carparma, Italy.

Sara Hobolt is a Professor at the London School of Economics and Political Science, where she holds the Sutherland Chair in European Institutions.

Marina Karanikolos is a Technical Officer/Research Fellow at the European Observatory on Health Systems and Policies and at the London School of Hygiene and Tropical Medicine.

Teresa Lago is Full Professor of Astronomy at the University of Porto and a Founding Member of the Scientific Council of the European Research Council (ERC).

Tiago Lapa is Invited Assistant Professor and Associate Researcher in Sociology and Communication at ISCTE – University Institute of Lisbon, Center for Research and Studies in Sociology.

Rachel Loopstra is Lecturer in Nutrition, King's College London and Associate Member of Department of Sociology at University of Oxford.

Martin McKee is Professor of European Public Health at London School of Hygiene and Tropical Medicine and Research Director of the European Observatory on Health Systems and Policies.

Manos Matsaganis is Associate Professor of Public Finance at Politecnico di Milano.

Claus Offe is Professor Emeritus of Political Sociology at both Humboldt University and Hertie School of Governance, Berlin.

Emilio Ontiveros is Professor of Economic and Business Administration at the Universidad Autónoma de Madrid, and Founder and President of Analistas Financieros Internacionales (Afi).

Silvia Pasquetti is Lecturer in Sociology at Newcastle University.

Pierfranco Pellizzetti is former Professor of Global Politics at the University of Genoa and a commentator for the blog il Fatto Quotidiano. it, the newspaper la Repubblica-Genova and the magazine MicroMega.

Aaron Reeves is Associate Professorial Research Fellow, International Inequalities Institute, London School of Economics and Political Science, and Associate Member of Sociology at University of Oxford.

David Stuckler is Professor of Political Economy and Sociology at University of Oxford, Research Fellow at LSHTM, Director of Oxford WHO Collaborating Centre and Policy Pillar for the European Public Health Association.

Daria Gołębiowska-Tataj is Founder and CEO of Tataj Innovation and a Member of the founding Governing Board of the European Institute of Innovation and Technology (EIT).

John B. Thompson is Professor of Sociology at the University of Cambridge and a Fellow of Jesus College, Cambridge.

Michel Wieviorka is Professor at the Ecole des Hautes Etudes en Sciences Sociales and president of the Fondation Maison des Sciences de l'Homme, Paris.

Figures and Tables

Tables

Figures

Introduction: Fading of a Dream?

Once upon a time, there was a dream – that Europeans would unite after centuries of war-making, nationalist confrontation and cultural xenophobia.

The carnage of World War II and the destruction of the productive infrastructure of the continent created the historical opportunity for economic integration and institutional cooperation as a way to supersede the demons of the past and set Europe on a path of shared peace and prosperity. Those who created Europe knew that a direct political process was not possible, and the economic process was a means to achieve political goals in the future. For almost six decades, a process of multidimensional integration proceeded gradually by successive waves, extending the union from the original six founding members of the European Economic Community to the 28 members of the European Union, woven together in a dense institutional network of shared sovereignty between the participating nation-states.

At the dawn of the twenty-first century the European Union, as dreamed by the visionary politicians and technocrats who dared to engage in one of the most remarkable political experiments in history, could be considered a success. It had become the largest economy in the world, with around a quarter of global gross domestic product (GDP), the largest consumer market, the largest repository of non-military science and technology knowledge on the planet, and a decisive share of global finance, with London and Frankfurt among the pre-eminent financial centres in the world. Peace and security appeared to be solidly established among EU members for the long haul, and the remaining European conflicts were ultimately contained by military cooperation with the United States, in spite of some setbacks such as the war that followed the disintegration of Yugoslavia. Prosperity in terms of

1

income, assets and social benefits was the highest on the planet, albeit with increasing social inequality. Democracy and human rights were rooted in the daily practice of European societies, and the institutions of co-governance, however bureaucratic, kept functioning. Tolerance and international solidarity with less fortunate areas of the world were a key component of the ideology of European institutions, albeit not always reflected in practice. The project of preserving and diffusing European values, on the basis of the original project of economic integration, seemed to have been vindicated. A new round of deeper integration was launched at the turn of the century, particularly with the creation of a common currency, the euro, in most of the EU, and the constitution of Europe-wide research and technology institutions, such as the European Research Council (ERC) and the European Institute of Innovation and Technology (EIT). The power of the European Parliament was strengthened to counter the power concentrated in the European Commission. The moment appeared to have come to establish the legitimacy of the European institutions with the promulgation and approval of a European Constitution. While the notion of the United States of Europe was never seriously considered, the creative construction of a supra-national political union made up of a network of nation-states was paving the way for a historically novel form of continental federalism.

However, this process was accompanied by stagnating economic growth coupled with demographic atrophy and an unhealthy emphasis on intra-European politics. And then the process of integration was stalled as it was challenged by the growing salience of anti-EU feelings in many European countries, culminating in the unthinkable: Brexit, the voluntary exit of a member country (the outcome of the UK referendum of 23 June 2016). Suddenly, the European Union became something quite different from a stable institutional construction: its shape and competences could vary, as could its membership. Will the paralysis of the EU mark the beginning of the twenty-first century, as the collapse of the Soviet Union, an unthinkable event at the time, marked the twentieth century's end? Is the European dream fading? Why? How? What are the roots and the potential dangers of disintegration? What are the prospects and consequences of the multiple crises of the European Union in the early twenty-first century?

These are the questions explored and analysed in this volume from an intellectually pluralistic perspective that aims at minimizing normativity to maximize clarity in the analysis and diagnosis of the crises. We use 'crises' in the plural because the rampant crisis of the European Union as an institutional system stems from the convergence of diverse, inter-related and overlapping crises – financial, monetary, industrial, social, political, ideological, moral, geopolitical, migratory – that feed into each other while being distinct in their origins and their development. The tentative answers to these questions are developed in the various chapters of the volume. However, there is a common thread that may explain the contours of the institutional crisis, and therefore clarify the terms of the debate for the eventual overcoming of this crisis.

We start from the assumption that crises of any institutional system can occur when the performance of the system is perturbed and the perturbations become increasingly serious in character, giving rise to the very real possibility that, without taking further action or implementing new policies or regulations, the system may spin out of control and break down. We also contend that such systemic crises are induced by the characteristics and contradictions involved in the process of institutional formation. Concretely speaking, what this means in the context of Europe is that the crises that have plagued the European Union in the last decade stem to a large extent from the flaws in its construction. And these flaws are almost necessary consequences of the political processes that led to its formation. In other words, the decisions that made possible the development of the EU created the conditions for its multiple crises. Of course, these crises are not *only* the result of flaws in the construction of European institutions: there are other factors involved too, in some cases stemming from sources well beyond Europe; but only by understanding the institutional flaws can we understand why these crises occurred as they did in the European context, and why they have (or have had) the characteristics and consequences that they have.

Let us review the argument in its historical specificity (much of the data and detailed analyses in support of this argument can be found in the chapters in this volume).

First of all, any stable political-institutional construction requires some convergence of interests among the actors that build the institutions, as well as some form of common identity among the people involved in the process. In the case of the European Union, there is consensus on the fact that there was originally a defensive project, intended to prevent another war breaking out in Europe, that was later used by a few visionary leaders to put forward a utopian project. This was a project of the political and economic elites without the real participation, commitment and full understanding of most citizens. Every major step of economic and institutional integration was intended to make irreversible the process of European unification, with the creation of the common currency, the euro, being the most blatant expression of this strategy of the '*fait accompli*'.

European construction started as a defensive project aimed at superseding past wars and preventing future wars. It therefore had to involve the traditional warring nations, France and Germany above all, and the powerful American ally in deterring the Soviet Union in the future – NATO was a necessary complement to the European Union. However, the integration had to start with the economy, the most obvious necessity after the devastation of the war. Integrated markets required broader economic integration that proceeded by leaps and bounds to reach some partial monetary and financial integration.

The utopian project included political integration and cultural integration, as the assertion of European values – whatever their meaning – was an intrinsic part of the project. The tension between economic integration and political/ideological integration was a permanent feature of the European Union and a permanent source of conflicts, primarily between the nation-states that were economically interested but politically aloof vis-à-vis the project, the UK and Scandinavia, on the one hand, and the major continental powers, France and Germany, on the other hand.

This difference in interests took a paradoxical twist in the decision to enlarge the EU towards the East. The interests of the two major nation-states, Germany (after re-unification) and the UK, converged in favour of enlargement but for opposite reasons. For Germany, it was a way to reconstruct its traditional geopolitical hinterland as part of the European project without raising fears of hegemony. For the UK, opposed to political integration, the more nations that joined the EU, the more difficult it would be to create a joint political decision-making body, thus weakening Brussels vis-à-vis the autonomous logic of markets that were becoming increasingly integrated globally. Ironically, it was the enlargement towards the East, and the subsequent migration of workers from Eastern Europe to the UK, that in part fuelled the anti-EU sentiments that found their dramatic expression a decade later in Brexit.

The result of these diverse strategies of integration was the construction of a complex network of nation-states with very different economies and cultures, whose full integration would prove hazardous. Thus, an economically strong EU was managed by a politically indecisive EU, without a common foreign policy, and hindered in joint decision-making by contradictory interests that could only be conciliated by a shift of executive power to the European Commission. The increase in efficiency was achieved at the cost of a crisis of legitimacy, as citizens around the continent resented the dependence of their lives on decisions taken by anonymous Eurocrats, barely controlled by the European Parliament. The shift of local and national power to European Union power, with the increasing transfer of sovereignty, created over time a 'democratic deficit' of representation in the EU countries.

In the context of a widespread crisis of the political legitimacy of representative democracy in many parts of the world, the distance between citizens and their representatives increased in the European Union. There was a growing gap between citizens and the decisions taken by the Council of Ministers away from the control of national parliaments. There was a gap between citizens and the European Parliament, whose composition and competences only indirectly reflect national constituencies. And, even more important, there was a gap between the powerful bureaucracy of the European Commission (sometimes symbolized by Presidents of the Commission who see themselves as Presidents of Europe), on the one hand, and citizens and the media in every country, on the other. In situations of normal institutional life, the tensions induced by the democratic deficit are tolerable. However, when there is any crisis of some significance (financial crisis, geopolitical crisis, migratory crisis, etc.) the distrust of European institutions accentuates the crisis of legitimation and ultimately may induce social unrest and political separatism.

Furthermore, the notion of a European identity has remained elusive. If we understand by 'identity' a set of values that provide symbolic meaning to people's lives by enhancing their feeling of belonging, it is difficult to discern the existence of a strong and distinct European identity. A self-defined European identity is indeed present in the minds of many citizens, particularly in contrast to 'others' (to the United States, to Asian cultures, to Islam, etc.), but largely as a rejection of the 'others' rather than as a specific identity that is valued and embraced in and for itself. Moreover, what surveys show is that even when self-identification as being European is stated, it is a weak identity, and it tends to be replaced by local, regional or national identities when the identity boundary has to be asserted in a situation of crisis.

This is precisely our argument. As long as there is smooth functioning of the fundaments of everyday life, work and livelihood in all dimensions, to have a European passport is an added value that is generally enjoyed and supported. But in the event of a crisis that requires solidarity between Europeans at large, the weakness of European identity gives way to the prevalence of national interests protected by the nation-state. Why bail out the Portuguese, said one-fifth of the Finnish electorate, by using 'our savings'? Why prevent the collapse of Greek banks, said the majority of Germans and Dutch, if they are responsible for their irresponsible behaviour? And why do Germans have the right to control our finances, answered the Greeks, if their only interest is to save German banks from their irresponsible lending? In sum: European identity, thus European solidarity, stops at the line (and the cost) of sharing the pain of crises that affect 'the other Europeans'. Moreover, many Europeans feel that the institutions of the Union are biased in favour of the dominant economic powers in the EU.

In a historical perspective, when nation-states had to construct their national identity, they used the powers of the nation-state to support their institutional projects. But in the case of the EU, the attempt to impose an identity to fulfil the European project triggered strong resistance that threatened the entire construction.

In short, in the absence of a crisis in the everyday life of citizens, the European project muddled through to become part of their experience. But when crisis hit, national identities quickly reasserted themselves to overrun a project identity that was, in any case, largely confined to economic and political elites. Furthermore, because of the democratic deficit in the European institutional system, every crisis deepened the crisis of political legitimacy, and fractured societies between 'the cosmopolitans and the locals', between North and South of Europe, and for many, between 'us and the others'.

There was an attempt to sanction the strategy of integration from above by a European Constitution to be approved by citizens. But the fiasco of the French and the Dutch referendums, when proposals to ratify the treaty establishing a Constitution for Europe were rejected by significant margins, stopped the legitimation strategy. The establishment of powerful mechanisms of integration, such as the euro, the free circulation of capital, goods, services and people, or the elimination of borders, were left to treaties approved by national parliaments under the control of mainstream parties, governed by the established political class.

The alliance of the visionaries of the European project and the economic and political elites favoured by European integration succeeded in accelerating the process of integration, adopting measures that were extremely difficult to reverse, such as the creation of the euro. Many economists at the time considered it an aberration to establish a common currency encompassing national economies vastly different in productivity and competitiveness, without a common fiscal policy and without integration of the diverse banking systems. But the real motivation behind the decision to create the euro was to integrate the economies, markets and policies, to bind together the participating nation-states with an economic glue that would be difficult to break, however imperfect it may have been and whatever the cost.

The global financial crisis of 2008 derailed the project because there were no institutions able to manage the crisis at the European level. In fact, in order to save the euro, Germany and the European Central Bank imposed tough policies of fiscal austerity that were able to contain the debt crisis temporarily, but with a high social cost in terms of the suffering of citizens in southern Europe and elsewhere and an even greater cost in terms of the political legitimacy of European institutions, to the point that Mario Draghi, the European Central Bank, and even Angela Merkel had to soften their stand on austerity policies after staunch resistance emerged from different quarters of the Union.

But it was too late. The price paid for the materialization of the European dream by the imposed unification of economic policies was the deepening crisis of legitimacy of the European project. Furthermore, the economic and social costs of the crises stemming from this forced integration were unevenly distributed between countries, between regions and between social classes and age groups within countries, fracturing any sense of pan-European solidarity and generating feelings of resentment among those who suffered most.

The tensions and flaws built into the European integration process created institutions that were crisis-prone, and their weaknesses were exposed when crises hit. In some cases these crises were of Europe's own making, while in other cases the crises had a broader international character, or were precipitated by processes that began outside of Europe; but in all cases it was the weaknesses in institutional design, stemming from the process of European integration, that gave Europe's crises their distinctive character. The financial crisis of 2008 stemmed initially from large-scale defaults in the subprime mortgage market in the US, but as the crisis spread it quickly brought the euro under stress and exacerbated the weaknesses that were already part of the eurozone. Moreover, the austerity policies designed by Germany and the European Commission to save the euro aggravated the economic and social crisis in Europe, particularly in the poorer countries of southern Europe and in the poorer segments of the population. The geopolitical crises with Russia and with the Middle East wars diverted resources and brought the whole of the EU into international confrontations that were only relevant for some of its members. And the refugee crisis, resulting in part from foreign intervention in Iraq and Syria (with the participation of some European countries), broke the solidarity among Member States and antagonized large segments of national populations, seeding xenophobia and anti-European sentiment throughout the territory of the Union.

Yet the crisis of the euro, and its impact on austerity policies, was the result of a flawed monetary and financial construction that resulted from the determination of a minority of countries, led by Germany, to make the integration deeper and irreversible, creating the conditions for a federal Europe – against the explicit opposition of the UK, Scandinavia and Eastern Europe. A similar argument could be developed on a number of European policies, including agriculture, trade and immigration. For instance, the Schengen agreement eliminated borders inside the Union without strengthening the controls at the external borders of the EU, thus creating institutional vulnerabilities that were brought into stark relief by the refugee crisis of 2015 – a crisis that also exposed the inability of European governments to act together in a concerted effort to assert the proclaimed European values in practice.

In sum: the ambition of the European project was belied by the weakness of European institutions, ultimately dependent on the dominant elites of the most powerful countries. The interests of these dominant elites shaped decisively the lives of European citizens via the impact of European legislation and institutional decision-making. In the absence of a strong European identity and under the conditions of the democratic deficit and the crisis of political legitimacy, the EU was unable to manage its crises as a single institutional entity and was unable to respond effectively and flexibly to the multiple fires that began to flare up inside the Union. Rather than dealing effectively with crises, let alone anticipating them and preventing them from arising in the first place, it found itself faced with increasingly severe internal social and institutional fractures. Brexit was perhaps the most dramatic expression of these fractures, epitomizing the potential reversibility of European unification. And the redesign of the European Union in the so-called 'Union at different speeds', as debated in the Bratislava informal summit in September 2016, was a sign of a new-found political realism that seemed to accept the fading of a dream in the interest of preserving what could be saved in terms of economic benefits and social stability.

The research presented in this volume explains the whys, hows and whats of the contradictory process of unification of Europe, both in its successes and its failures, as well as its consequences in the form of multiple, intertwined crises. Any future attempt to re-enact the European dream will have to consider first the European reality, coming to terms with the findings of our and similar inquiries in the hope of saving the project of a shared Europe, at peace with itself and its neighbours, as a key condition for a better world.

Part I

Economic Crises

Chapter 1

The End of European Integration as We Knew It: A Political Economy Analysis

Olivier Bouin

This paper presents a political economy perspective on the European integration process over the past sixty years. It analyses the very singular process that has been implemented for building up the European Union – a process that has been a strange mix of utopia, pragmatism, ideology and compromises. The central question of this paper is whether this complex process has delivered the promise of creating a sustainable, inclusive and efficient economic model for Europe. The first section looks at the systemic implications for the European building process of the increasing reliance on market-based solutions. The second section analyses the economic and social outcomes of European integration with a special focus on the convergence of economic performance across member countries. The third section focuses on the impact of the Economic and Monetary Union – by far the most audacious integrative step undertaken by European countries since the Treaty of Rome – on the future of Europe. The paper ends with concluding remarks on the plausibility of the end of the European integration process as we knew it.

The choice of building the European Union relying on market forces

In this section, we will briefly discuss how the building of the European Union and the unfolding of its integration path have privileged the economic route, initially as a second best in the minds of the most pro-European leaders but increasingly as the main engine of European integration.

Chronologically, the economic route has been used because political integration and federalism were not possible. The failure of the

11

Communauté européenne de Défense in 1950, the limits of the idealistic federalist visions à la Spinelli and the lack of national political will in Europe had created a political context in which the founding fathers considered that economic integration – first trade, then financial or monetary integration – would lead to cumulative integration, known as the 'positive chain reaction' generally attributed to Jean Monnet.

Economic growth would be triggered by many positive factors. Larger internal markets would create economies of scale and would reduce transaction costs. Trade liberalization would better specialization and significantly reduce national opportunistic behaviours. A better allocation of resources – labour and capital – would lead to productivity increases that would support steady economic growth. The sheer size of the growing European economy would offer protection against destabilizing external shocks. All countries would benefit from the economic prosperity – the least favoured countries would be helped by structural funds to help catch the European bandwagon.

All this would lead to a convergence of national economic results, which would in turn reduce heterogeneity among European nations. Such a decline of heterogeneity would lower the cultural and political oppositions at the nation-state level towards a more integrated Europe. It would create the conditions for the production of European public goods, leading to further systemic integration and the final stage of political integration.

This narrative about the succession of integration steps can be considered the positive side of the chain reaction attributed to Monnet and present in the minds of his many followers (including European Commission presidents Walter Hallstein and more recently Jacques Delors and Romano Prodi). And, in all fairness, this narrative has been a powerful principle of action, because the European Union to a large extent delivered much of its good spillover effects between 1957 and 1985 (see the next section).[1]

But this positive chain reaction strategy has been critically and increasingly questioned on two grounds: the first dealing with the effectiveness, legitimacy and sustainability of such an integration strategy,[2] the second

---

[1] The large EU structural funding – mostly available for material and social infrastructure investment – kept playing a positive role in the catching up process of Southern European countries after the 1980s and of Central and Eastern European countries after the 1990s.

[2] A very significant amount of literature has looked at this issue. For recent contributions, see Meunier et al. (2015) who introduced the notion of 'failing forward'. In previous versions of this paper, I proposed the football metaphor of the 'kick and rush' to depict the European integration strategy. It is an indication of how doubtful I am about the possibility of proceeding with European integration as we saw it developed over the

considering the economic and political end point of the European integration process.

On the first question, a darker version of the chain reaction progressively gained importance in Europe as many of its member countries increasingly faced economic problems (the slowing down of economic growth since the mid-1980s, economic transition to a post-industrial system) and social hardships (rising unemployment and income inequalities). This darker version of the chain reaction can be described as follows: when some economic integration created (or was not able to avoid) economic and social imbalances and disruptions across Europe, the response to these problems would be more integration. Integration would continue to proceed with new initiatives because there would be no other (less costly) alternative. At stake would be a possible *remise en cause* of the entire European building process. An extreme – and rather cynical – version of such a building strategy is the reference to the half-built house (Bergsten 2012) that goes as follows: one begins constructing a house knowing that it will be too costly to stop – one has no alternative other than to finish building the house. Many authors since the end of the 1990s have been pointing out the increasingly negative and forced nature of the integration process and its consequences for the overall sustainability of the European construction (Scharpf 1999).[3]

As far as the second question is concerned, there is a very significant uncertainty about where the European integration process will lead its member countries. This uncertainty is to some extent instrumental to the process as most countries have a divergent view of what should be the end point of the entire process. This uncertainty can be observed at two levels. The first is fundamental beyond the scope of this paper: the equilibrium point between European integration and national sovereignty. The euro-federalists also have never given up their dreams to build a federal Europe (United Nations of Europe) and a strong ally has been the European Commission that has always pushed – with some ups and downs – for more Europe, with the ultimate aim of some degree of

---

past decades. A nineteenth-century English football tactic recycled by twentieth-century European politics is certainly not the safest strategy to lead Europe well into the twenty-first century.

[3] Because of the power of intimidation of the TINA (there is no alternative) argument, national governments and public opinion have been constrained to support further European integration and to accept intrusive European regulation and supervision. The emergence of the so-called 'democratic deficit' of Europe is in part rooted in this forced integration strategy pursued by the European Commission with the consent of most European leaders. Other significant factors explaining the 'democratic deficit' are the lack of a positive European identity (Castells, this volume) and the complex – and too many non-transparent – European decision-making institutions (e.g., Commission, Council, Parliament, etc.).

political integration. In that perspective, the referendum on the UK membership of the European Union in 2016 (and obviously its very striking outcome) has made very clear that for some member countries the objective was not at all more Europe but less European integration.

The lack of clear and shared adhesion to a joint integration objective has been a constant problem in the European building process. But as the integration process unfolded and the loss of sovereignty became more and more visible and problematic (touching upon increasingly key 'regalian' missions of the nation-state), the *qui pro quo* about the end point of the European integration became destabilizing enough to almost derail the entire process with the exit of a key EU member.[4]

Yet there is another troubling uncertainty or disturbing hidden perspective in the European building process. As we mentioned before, the European integration process has predominantly relied on an economic agenda and on economic forces, ever since the early 1950s and the creation of the European Coal and Steel Community. Social matters were not prominent in the Treaty of Rome and with the exception of the founding of the European Social Fund (the first structural fund to be created by the European Community) in 1960 and the signature of the European Social Charter in 1961, social policies were not put at the forefront of the European agenda. However, the general policy orientation of most national economies in the 1960s and in the 1970s (and therefore in an aggregated way at the European level) was a mixture of social democratic welfare state with some degree of Keynesian macroeconomic intervention to regulate cycles of mixed economies. The fruits of economic growth to be gained from European economic integration would be redistributed to the weak and the needy.

The progressive change of orientation at national levels towards more liberal, free market and private property based economic systems at the end of the 1970s/early 1980s changed the overall perspective. These national changes were reinforced by the pro-market approach supported by the European Commission. The Single European Act of 1986 that transformed the 'Common Market' into a 'Single Market' marked that change. It was the beginning of a new phase in the economic integration promoted by the European Commission. It was in the zeitgeist since, in 1985, the so-called Washington Consensus started a long cycle of liberalization, deregulation and privatization at a global scale (developed

---

[4] The Five Presidents' Report released in June 2015 favoured a deepening of integration – section 3 and 4 are respectively about the Financial Union and the Fiscal Union. Even though it applies to the eurozone members (and thus not to the UK), the overall objective and its implications for eurozone members and non-members seem to be clear: Europe is heading towards more integration in the coming years.

economies, developing economies and after the fall of the Berlin Wall post-socialist economies were to be subject to this implacable policy shift).

In this global context – even though the creation of the Single Market was accompanied in the mind of President Delors by a strong social pillar – it resulted in a radical but implicit change of perspective. Even though the social pillar was to be built and was high on the agenda of Presidents Delors and Prodi (with, for example, the revised European Social Charter in 1996), these efforts delivered little. The European Commission increasingly leaned towards more liberalization and deregulation. Lobbyist or vested interests obtained gradual deregulation of key markets including commodities that were not supposed to be exposed to market forces such as money, land and labour (see Polanyi 1944).

On paper, some European leaders were continuing to promote a social market economy but the change of policy orientation (away from Keynesian policies towards more austerity policies and away from a regulated version of capitalism towards a widely deregulated version of capitalism) impacted significantly the building of the European project.[5] The freeing of capital movements in 1998, the massive deregulation supported by the Amsterdam Treaty in 2000 (with the famous article 133 on qualified majorities), the Maastricht Treaty creating the Monetary Union in 2002, the Bolkenstein directive on Services in 2005, to name only a few milestones, changed the very nature of the European project. The end point of the European economic integration changed progressively from a social market economy (whether of Beveridgian or of Bismarckian origin) into a capitalist market economy (in the 1990s) into a capitalist market society (in the 2000s).[6]

It is ironic that social democrats such as Presidents Delors and Prodi did not see the sea change coming, that helping the economic genie to get out of the bottle would have systemic effects not only on economic structures and income distributions but on the type of social systems that would emerge and prevail for the decades to come. The strengthening of market forces in the late 1950s had a very different magnitude and meaning than the one that took place after 1985. Some European leaders

---

[5] Several heads of government in Central and Eastern European countries strongly supported such a pro-market and deregulation approach after their entry in the EU (e.g., Poland, Czech Republic, Estonia) and thus contributed to the strengthening of the shift towards reduced state intervention and an increasing private sector.

[6] Reference to the analyses of the embedding of market economies (à la Polanyi) as well as to the strong affinities between private property and market coordination (Kornai 1990) is here helpful. One can conclude from Kornai's analysis that in a dynamic economic system, market deregulation tends to favour private property and that privatization of state-owned enterprises tends to favour market coordination mechanisms.

may have considered that it would be possible to keep markets regulated, rein in unfair competition and promote social policies in the new globalization era, but in retrospect the widespread acceptance of market domination and of massive deregulation[7] led to the 'financializing' of the economy and the marketization of society. These were far off target and were never sold as end points of the European integration process. Much of the opposition at the national level against Brussels stems from the change in the very nature of the economic systems and societies that resulted from the implementation of regulatory reform and macro-economic policies over the past thirty years.

Has the EU institutional building path consistently produced economic results conducive to further *positive* EU integration?

Over the past three decades, hundreds if not thousands of scholars have studied the various (explicit and implicit, short-term and long-term, political and economic) objectives of the European construction, the strategies of the various European actors (national administrations and parliaments, corporations, political parties), the European decision-making processes (the changing and complex interplay of EU Commission, EU Parliament, EU Council, EU courts), the implementation process (with a micro/or macro historical perspective, focusing on the role of key individuals or the bureaucracy, the stops and gos). But surprisingly very few have actually measured or quantified the (positive) economic impact of the European integration process on member countries.

In a recent study, Campos et al. underlined 'the dearth of evidence' because 'studies on the benefits of membership itself are few' and the 'majority of these (few) papers warn about the fragility of their own estimates' (2014: 2).[8] This is all the more surprising since, as we have seen in the previous section, the most important driver of the European construction was supposed to be the economic benefits for the member countries. One would have expected European national and Commission leaders to have handy a lot of empirical evidence to back the discourse in favour of an ever deeper integration. This is not the case and one could machiavelically ask why. Is this because the economic benefits have not been (or still are) not as strong as expected, even though it should be recognized that European leaders have never given any kind of

---

[7] Which ironically in the European case did not lead to fewer regulations, but more pro-market regulations.

[8] They list only three studies between 1989 and 2011!

quantification of these benefits to justify the major integrative steps (e.g., Single Act, Economic and Monetary Union).

So far studies have shown that the economic benefits from EU membership are positive but not considerable, nor evenly distributed across time. Campos et al. (2014) mentioned that the cumulative impact of GDP per capita of EU members could range from 5 per cent to 20 per cent.[9] According to their own work, based unfortunately on a rather disputable methodology of counterfactuals, their conclusion is that 'per capita European incomes in the absence of the economic and political integration process would have been on average 12 per cent lower today, with substantial variations across countries, enlargements as well as over time' (2014: 4). We will discuss later in this section some specifics of these results but as a first comment the overall gains can be considered as relatively limited given the magnitude of the regulatory, institutional and structural changes that have been at play.

But let's put aside for a moment the discussion on the magnitude of the quantitative economic gains related to EU membership and focus on what we should consider structurally relevant to judge whether the EU integration path and institution building process is producing results that are conducive for further positive integration. Here two interconnected dimensions matter: the ability to deliver sustained convergence of economic results among EU member countries and the growing homogeneity of national preferences.

On the first dimension, obtaining a sustained convergence of economic *results* among EU member countries is difficult given the growing divergence of economic *structures* among EU member countries. Not because the divergence of economic structures (simply put: more manufacturing and high-value industry-related services in central Europe, more financial services and high-level education in the UK, a mix of the preceding in the Nordic countries, more tourism and high-value agro-food industries in Southern Europe, labour-intensive manufacturing and services in Eastern Europe and the Balkans) is a problem *per se*, but because trade liberalization and monetary integration suppose that each country is able to develop an equilibrated sustainable path based on its structural comparative advantages.

There is no obvious answer to this question. However, the major shifts in the economic structures registered in all European countries over the past 30 years indicate clearly that (beyond any consideration regarding the macroeconomic management of the economic transition) there have

---

[9] Their paper presents a short discussion of the few studies conducted between 1995 and 2012.

been winners and losers during the various phases and over the past thirty years.[10] The resulting divergence in the overall economic performance across EU member countries calls for fiscal transfers among EU members in order to mitigate the negative impact of EU membership on selected countries. This question (of key political economy importance) has emerged as a crucial one for the future cohesion of Europe, mostly because increasingly divergent economic *structures* tend to react more and more differently to exogenous/external shocks as well as to the strengthening of the endogenous forces of integration themselves.

This relates to our second dimension, i.e. the rising or decreasing homogeneity of preferences across EU members. Recent literature (Spolaore 2013) considers that the reduction of cultural heterogeneity in Europe is needed to accept the production of non-rival goods (e.g., defence, infrastructures) at the European level and thus a prerequisite for accepting further integration. The question of homogeneity of preferences is interesting because it goes beyond the traditional analysis of the national resistance to the European project and of the lack of European sentiment in Europe (see Castells and Hobolt, this volume). It places the emphasis on a dynamic socio-cultural process that would create the positive conditions to support the deepening of the European construction.

The relationship between these two dimensions gives a fresh take on the overall dynamics of the European construction and its possible impasse at some advanced point in the integration process. The story could thus go as follows. The deepening of European integration increasingly reveals the very nature of the structural comparative advantage between EU members up to a point that it overstretches the capacity of all nations to benefit from EU membership. The resulting absence of a sustained convergence of economic *results* among EU member countries then feeds a growing *heterogeneity* of national preferences that in turn will go against the political acceptance of fiscal transfers across EU members. The absence of such fiscal transfers would further undermine the overall capacity of the EU integration to move towards a positive pursuit of its construction. The mounting social dissatisfaction at national level could even lead to the heightening of conflicts and tensions among member countries and vis-à-vis the EU Commission, paving the way for some

---

[10] Even though the significant EU structural funds have had a sizable redistributive effect across member countries and to some extent attenuated the effects of economic specialization, they could not compete in magnitude with the structural changes demanded by trade, financial and monetary integration. The European structural and investment funds available for the 2014–20 period (amounting to a significant €351.8 billion) will represent for the largest beneficiaries (i.e., Central and Eastern European countries) only between 1.5 to 2.5 per cent of their annual GDP.

outcomes unthinkable for the EU integration promoters: (a) the forced exit of a member (when a Grexit was contemplated in 2012–14), (b) the voluntary exit of another (with the Brexit voted by the British electorate in 2016), or (c) the slow disintegration (in the etymological sense) of the EU building process.

The remainder of this section will look at these two dimensions with the longest perspective possible, i.e. from the beginning of the European project over the past sixty years of EU building since the Treaty of Rome. Three main periods will be identified: (i) 1957–85 as the first period of trade liberalization and EU enlargement, (ii) 1985–1999 as a period characterized by a strong acceleration of the EU integration process, with the Single European Act and the various deregulations promoted by the European Court of Justice, and (iii) 2000–15, with the launch of European monetary integration as a further big step towards full European integration.

On the economic and social levels, we will concentrate on three indicators of particular interest – GDP per capita, employment and productivity – to assess the situation. More sophisticated indicators of individual and collective well-being would need to be taken into consideration as they become increasingly available. However, they do not provide enough historical distance to follow the past sixty years of European integration and they still pose serious analytical problems (see Adler and Fleurbaey 2016). As a very rough proxy for the homogeneity of preferences,[11] we will look at the national approval rates of European membership over the past thirty-five years. After all, it represents a rather solid indicator of citizens' overall appreciation of the EU construction (even though or because it includes the 'noise' produced by national political discourses blaming Brussels for radical reforms and severe adjustments).

Increasingly heterogeneous economic results. . .

At the economic level, the results can be interpreted as follows. During 1957–85, the first period of European integration is characterized by fast and robust economic growth triggered by a solid increase in factor productivity and low unemployment. Significant catching up from the lowest performing economies at the beginning of the period (e.g., Italy in the 1960s and 1970s, Ireland after 1973, Greece after 1981) took place, leading to some convergence in terms of GDP per capita among member countries.

---

[11] More theoretical and empirical work needs to be done on this key issue.

During the 1985–99 period, the deepening of market liberalization and the enlargement of the EU (Spain and Portugal in 1986, then Austria, Finland and Sweden in 1995) did not bring any further convergence among EU member countries (see figure 1.1). Income differences across EU members remained stable but in a context characterized by the slowing down of economic growth, rising unemployment and domestic inequalities, most notably since the early 1990s (figure 1.2). During that period, the EU increasingly failed to become a growth engine for its members mostly due to a steady decline in factor productivity growth. The economic performance was rather dismal compared to the United States and was comparable with that of Japan (which in the mid-1980s started to be a structurally sluggish economy) (see figure 1.3).

European economic performance was limited in spite of the upbeat growth assumptions underlying the economic integration process. To a large extent, the growth model based on the gains from an integrated single market proved exaggerated. There are two possible explanations for that: (i) a significant overestimation of gains from economies of scale and cuts in transaction costs (see Eichengreen 1995, recognized *ex-post* by more market-oriented analysts such as Marsh 2013) and/or (ii) because large EU member countries (that account for most of the EU GDP) had already reached optimal sizes (Moss 2005).

The last period (2000–15) is by far the most interesting. As we will see in detail in the following section, this period needs to be split into two different sub-periods: (a) 2000–8, which corresponds to the first phase of the eurozone monetary integration, and (b) 2008–15, which corresponds to the double-dip crisis affecting many European countries of the eurozone. The first eight years of the European monetary integration clearly offered the opportunity for Spain, Greece and Ireland (and to a lesser extent Portugal) to resume the catching-up of the most developed European economies (see figures 1.1 and 1.4). The growth rates of the GDP per capita for Greece and for Spain were respectively three times and twice the average obtained by the EU12 member countries. This fast and significant catching-up process unfortunately proved artificial and short-lived. Comparable positive results were achieved by these countries in terms of rising employment rates (see figure 1.5), which indicated that economic growth was benefitting large segments of the population.

During the pre-crisis period, the eurozone countries still grew at a slower pace than the United States and large resource-rich countries such as Canada and Australia, but by a much reduced margin (respectively 0.5 and 1 percentage point compared to a 2 percentage point deficit between 1992 and 1999 as shown in figure 1.3). In spite of the spectacular buoyancy of the Southern countries of the eurozone, the EU growth engine

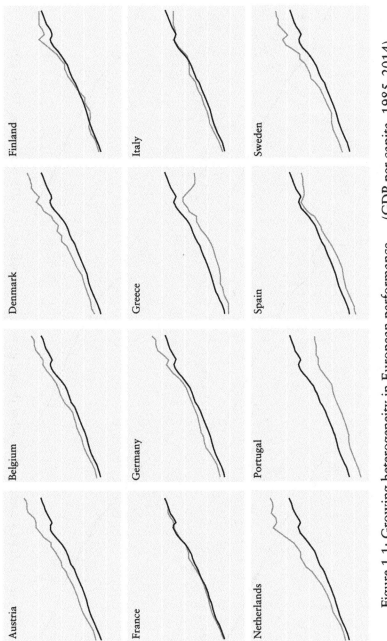

Figure 1.1: Growing heterogeneity in European performance. . . (GDP per capita, 1985–2014)

Source: OECD

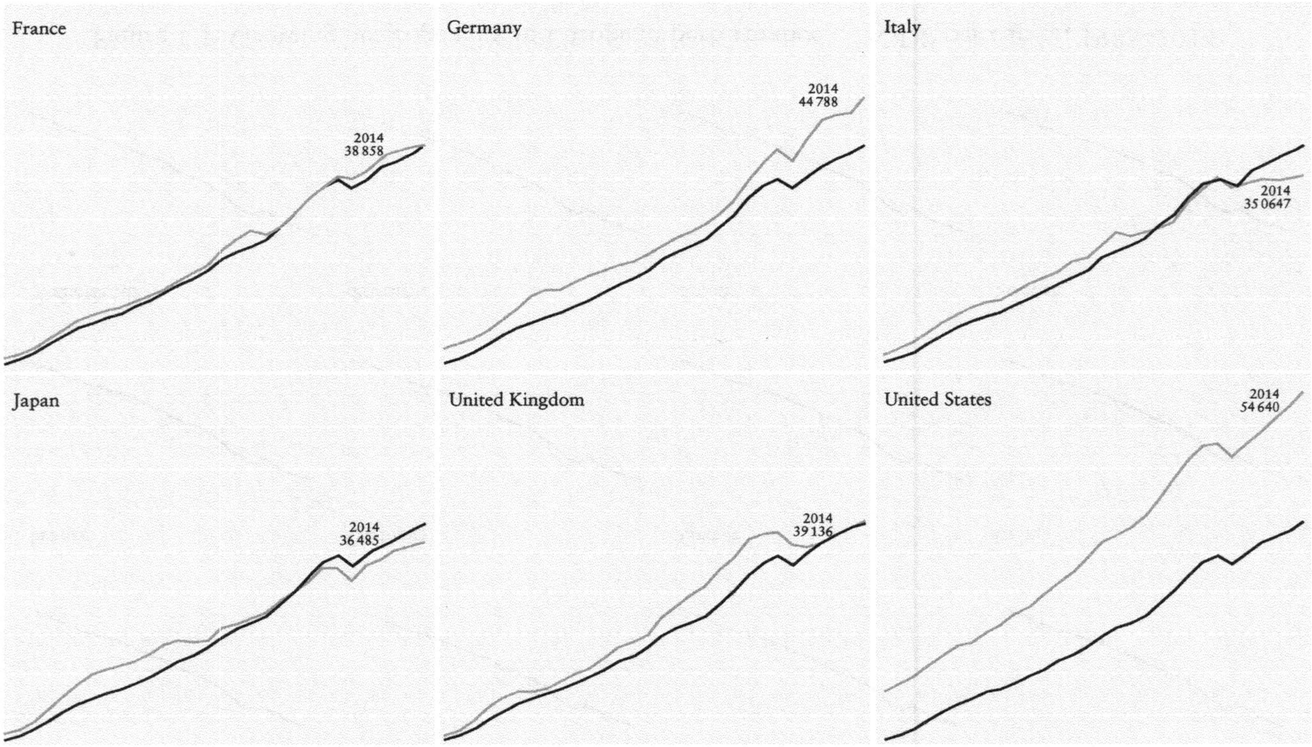

France
2014
38 858

Germany
2014
44 788

Italy
2014
35 0647

Japan
2014
36 485

United Kingdom
2014
39 136

United States
2014
54 640

Figure 1.2: In a context of a rather dismal growth performance... (GDP per capita, 1985–2014)

Source: Eurostat

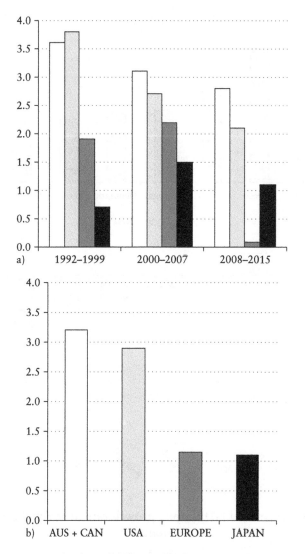

Figure 1.3: . . .and increasingly so since 1992 (real GDP per capita growth rate, per cent)

Source: OECD

remained limited. In fact, the eurozone benefited from a much more limited real GDP boost than expected with the cuts in trade transaction costs, the ending of competitive devaluations and the lowering exchange rate and interest rate uncertainty.

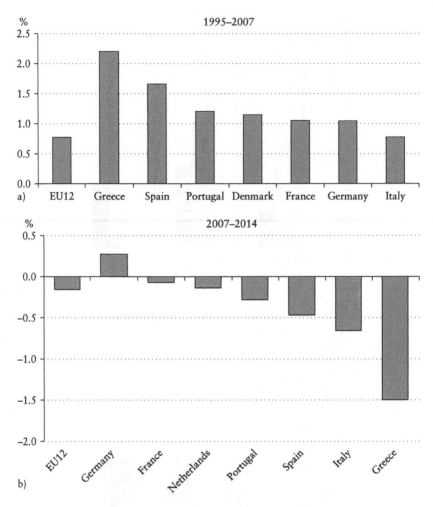

Figure 1.4: Annual GDP/capita growth rate in selected European countries

Source: Eurostat

The economic results of the last period are dreadful. The eurozone has undergone a double-dip recession (mostly due to strong economic adjustments, real internal devaluation and drastic austerity measures) and has hardly grown in terms of real GDP per capita over the period. This is in sharp contrast with the performance of other developed regions in the world that renewed with growth performance comparable to the

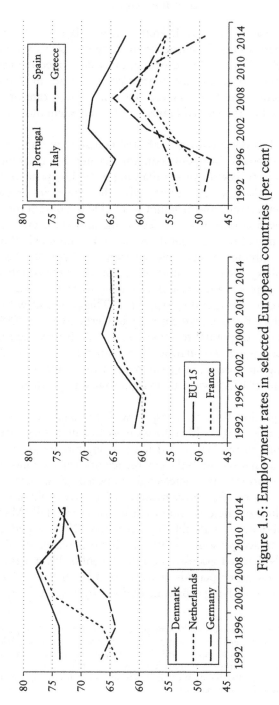

Figure 1.5: Employment rates in selected European countries (per cent)

Source: Eurostat

pre-crisis levels (see figure 1.3). Even the sluggish Japanese economy succeeded in outperforming the eurozone over the past seven years. Because of these terrible years for the eurozone, most developed countries have grown much faster over the past quarter century. Since the launching of the euro, the eurozone has achieved half the growth rate of a control group composed of the United States, the United Kingdom, Switzerland and Sweden.

During this lost decade for growth, the eurozone has also been characterized by extremely divergent economic results among its members.[12] If Germany was successful in maintaining a modest positive GDP per capita growth (along with Austria), all other countries fared poorly. France, the Netherlands and Belgium were able to contain the recession but the Southern countries of the eurozone suffered significant losses (in the magnitude of 0.5 per cent decrease in the annual GDP per capita for Spain and Italy) to considerable hardships (1.5 per cent decrease for Greece). The sharp decline in employment rates in these countries (down 10 percentage points in a few years!) also demonstrates the strong impact of the double-dip recession they registered. This contrasts with the continuing growth of the employment rates in Germany since 2008 (with a gain of 4 percentage points) to almost reach an all-time high of 75 per cent of its working-age population. The 20-percentage point difference in employment rates between Germany and the Southern countries of the eurozone in 2015 is twice the margin that was prevalent before the 2008 crisis.

As the integration became massive (with the passage from external trade and internal market liberalization to full monetary integration), economic results in the last period have strongly reduced homogeneity across European nations with the emergence of clear winning and losing nations.[13] The former have increasingly imposed on the latter a drastic asymmetric austerity with scarce fiscal transfers that could have softened the hard landing of these economies after their free fall. Many of the countries experiencing a double-dip recession (2008–9 and 2012–13) were forced to accept some politically costly sovereignty losses that spurred a hotly debated discussion on the benefit of EU integration.

Based on these three periods characterized by different dynamics of integration and underlying economic philosophy, the resulting economic

---

[12] Which is all the more ironic since the major reason for achieving European Monetary Union was to obtain *greater convergence of economic performance* (Delors Report, 1989, p. 11, original emphasis). We will discuss the issue in the following section.

[13] Central and Eastern European nations have also been strongly hit since 2008 with a double-dip recession affecting most economies in spite of their growth potential to catch up with leading European economies.

Table 1.1 Three phases of European integration process

	1957–85	1985–2000	2000–15
EU underlying economic philosophy	Social market economy	Capitalist market economy	Capitalist market society
Economic results (GDP per capita, productivity and wages, employment)	Convergence	Convergence	Convergence then divergence
Perception of EU (benefits of EU membership)	Positive and homogeneous	Declining and heterogeneous	Increasing heterogeneity

results and perception of the EU can be summarized as presented in table 1.1. After almost three initial decades of sustained economic growth, significant catching up and convergence between member economies, followed by two decades of slower growth but still converging economic results across the EU, the last period (i.e. since 2008) has wiped out part of the economic gains accumulated by some countries and created an unprecedented polarization.

Accelerated economic and monetary integration in a context where fiscal transfers are scarce has produced more heterogeneity across EU countries and – in many countries – tensions about the benefit of EU membership. This has been reinforced by the gradual transition of the EU model towards a capitalist market society, a transition that has never been explicated, nor supported by public opinion in most member countries. The model of incremental integration seems to have reached a critical – and possibly turning – point in its history, as the increased differentiation of economic results and the increased competition amongst countries has created a level of heterogeneity that makes it difficult – if not impossible – to collectively agree and support the only transformations that would save the integration process, i.e. more fiscal transfers and more coordination of policies.

... resulting in degraded national perception of EU membership

It is interesting to see how these increasingly diverging economic results have impacted the perception of EU membership at the national level.

The first observation is that there has been a somewhat deteriorating perception of the benefits of EU membership over the past quarter century (see figure 1.6 for the period 1983–2010).[14] When looking at a sample of eight countries, only two (Denmark and the Netherlands) kept a substantial net positive appreciation margin when assessing whether their countries benefited from the EU (respectively 60 and 40 percentage points). For the other six countries, the net positive appreciation margin decreased significantly over the years. This trend is particularly spectacular in the Southern countries of Europe (here including France) where the margin dropped in the 10–20 percentage points range, which is on average one third of what it was ten or fifteen years earlier.[15] The case of Germany is less straightforward because of the impact of reunification on the German perception of the EU – right after the reunification the German sentiment was that the EU was not supportive enough of the considerable effort undertaken by the country. Between 1995 and 2007 though, the positive appreciation for the EU doubled and the net positive appreciation reached 20 percentage points right before the 2008 crisis. That margin disappeared in three years as Germans considered that their country was penalized by the EU treatment of the crisis by not being tough enough on debtor countries, not requiring them to make severe adjustments and being too accommodating with unsustainable deficits. Beyond this rather negative trend, what is also worrisome is the growing disparity of appreciation of the benefits of EU membership.

One could argue that the assessment of the benefits of EU membership captures many other dimensions of the European project (e.g., enthusiasm or deception regarding the advances of the European political integration, concerns about the democratic deficit in the EU integration path). But there is a very striking symmetry between changes in the perception of the benefits of EU membership and the country's past and current economic situations. In short, the more economic and social hardship the country has experienced or is going through, the lower the appreciation of the benefits of EU membership. The message contained in figure 1.7 is absolutely unambiguous. The five eurozone countries (Italy, France, Portugal, Spain and Greece) whose populations believe by spectacular margins that their economies are doing

[14] Unfortunately, Eurobarometer stopped polling national public opinions on their assessment of the benefits of EU membership for their own country in 2011.
[15] In France and in the Netherlands, the two referenda organized in 2005 on the adoption of a European constitution resulted in massive rejections (respectively 55 per cent and 61 per cent 'no' votes) that were interpreted as a sign of a strong popular defiance regarding any further European integration.

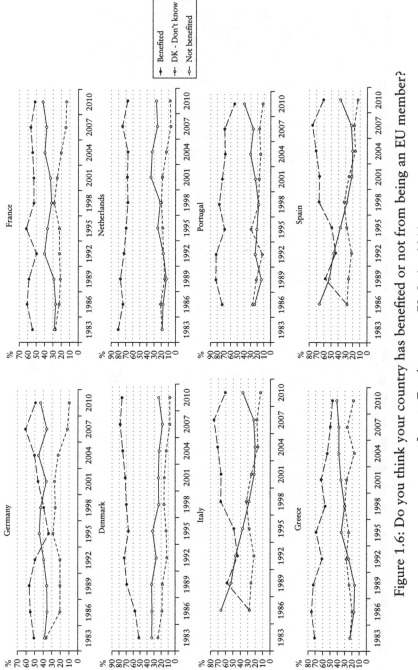

Figure 1.6: Do you think your country has benefited or not from being an EU member?

Source: Eurobarometer 79, Spring 2011

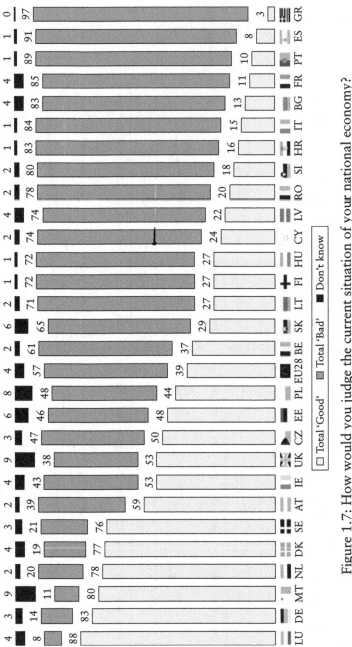

Figure 1.7: How would you judge the current situation of your national economy?

Source: Eurobarometer 85, Spring 2016

☐ Total 'Good'   ☐ Total 'Bad'   ■ Don't know

badly[16] are those that have seen the steepest decline in the appreciation of the benefits of EU membership. On the contrary, Denmark and the Netherlands, which – as seen above – have maintained in the past years a very high level of positive assessment of the EU have almost 80 per cent of their populations believing that their national economy is doing well. In this 2016 poll, Germany stands slightly above (at 83 per cent) and ranks number two, only after cosy Luxembourg.

This symmetry has a name: (perceived) causality. In the minds of many Europeans whose countries struggled in the most recent period, the deterioration of the country's economic situation is seen as a direct consequence of EU policies. The EU is blamed for insisting too much on drastic austerity packages as well as for not being able to launch a virtuous growth cycle and for not supporting more fiscal solidarity across EU member countries. This growing heterogeneity in the perception of the benefits of EU membership – resulting in some cases from the growing negative reaction towards the EU – is another strong signal that more EU integration will be extremely difficult to negotiate among member countries and/or to implement. Because of their current economic situations, most countries will have a very different and potentially conflicting view of what the priority policy responses and integration moves (if any) should be. For example, some countries will argue for more fiscal transfers and others will campaign for a fiscal union that will enact larger sovereignty transfers in the management of fiscal policies. The increasing (real and perceived) heterogeneity among EU countries will prove in the years to come a formidable test to the capacity of the EU to collectively act for the cohesion of the Union.

The far bridge of the European Monetary Union

The European Monetary Union represents an extremely interesting case when we consider the entire institutional building process of the EU: (a) it has been one of the most audacious reforms undertaken in terms of EU integration (with the Treaty of Rome in 1957 and the Single European Act of 1985), (b) the success of this major integrative step is key to any further development of the EU project (leading to more positive integration, or alternatively to some forced/imposed integrative measures to save the process, or possibly to a partial or a complete disintegration of

---

[16] These five countries are at the very bottom of the ranking with only 3 per cent (Greece) to 15 per cent (Italy) of their respective population considering that their national economy is doing well compared to 84 per cent to 97 per cent of them judging that it is doing badly.

the EMU or of the EU). It is therefore necessary to understand precisely what have been the dynamics at play and at stake in the past decade. Is this a crisis of the euro? A crisis of the eurozone? A crisis of the European construction? Or a crisis mixing these three levels? The analysis of the most recent period is crucial to understanding the perspectives for all three (euro, eurozone, European construction) but most importantly, given the scope of the paper, we will concentrate on the future of the overall European construction.

Given its contextual origins, the European monetary union . . .

Three factors point to the fragile initial situation of the eurozone but two additional elements explain the inner dynamics of it and its expected results. Let us quickly start with the first three factors in order to concentrate on the two main elements that seem to capture the dynamics of the eurozone over the past fifteen years.

First, the creation of the European Monetary Union is a result of complex political decisions (see Marsh 2011 and James 2012 for extremely detailed and fascinating presentations of the intra-European discussions and negotiations that led to the approval of the Delors Report in 1989, then to the Maastricht Treaty in 1992, then to the Stability and Growth Pact in 1997, prior to the formal launch of the euro in 1999). If we refer to the Werner Plan back in 1970, the European nations had long struggled with the issue of more monetary coordination and monetary integration. Monetary sovereignty was so central to the definition of the nation-state that even pro-European leaders had been very wary of the advancement of such a significant integrative move.

As mentioned in the conclusion of the Hannover Summit in June 1988, 'the European Council recalls that, in adopting the Single Act, the Member States confirmed the objective of progressive realization of Economic and Monetary Union'. The Delors Report released in April 1989 was at the same time bold and cautious. Bold because it introduced the idea of '*a single currency*, while not strictly necessary for the creation of a monetary union, might be seen – for economic as well as psychological and political reasons – as a natural and desirable further development of the monetary union' (Delors Report 1989: 15). Cautious because it was not introducing any specific dates for the finalization of the process even though the proposed timing of the first stage was 1 July 1990 when the Directive for the full liberalization of capital movements would come into force (p. 28).

This bold plan for the EMU has been realized even faster than its promoters (President Delors and a group of presidents of European central banks and key monetary institutions) had hoped for. Europe's major 'exogenous' shock at the end of 1989 – the fall of the Berlin Wall and the consequential rapid German reunification in 1990 – positioned the Monetary Union as a European priority. It is often said that the French President François Mitterrand agreed with the German Chancellor Helmut Kohl on the rapid German reunification on the premise that it would be 'counterbalanced' by a European Monetary Union. Pushing forward with monetary union was an instrumental way for some countries (led by France) to avoid the ruling (or the 'diktat') of the European monetary zone by the much-feared German Bundesbank.

Overall, it is much less the economic rationale for the EMU (e.g., less volatility, lower transaction costs, higher trade and investment) that prevailed than the political plan supported simultaneously by those aiming to avoid the ruling of Europe by reunified Germany and by those willing to create a new cycle of European integration.[17] These underlying nationally motivated political motives criss-crossed the entire preparation of the Maastricht Treaty and the later stages of the process and in some ways impeded concentration on the crucial requirements for the success of the future eurozone as an optimal currency area (see below).

Secondly, pre-conditions (the so-called 'four convergence criteria') established by the Treaty of Maastricht for entering the eurozone were not met by a majority of applying countries in 1998.[18] In its *ad hoc* April 1998 Report, the European Monetary Institute (EMI) showed that only five countries (France, Ireland, Luxembourg, Finland and Portugal)[19] out of the twelve candidates applying to the eurozone were meeting the four convergence criteria. Most countries were over or above (and in some cases way above) the government budget deficit to GDP (3 per cent) and the public debt to GDP (60 per cent) criteria. The EMI, though, considered that the trends were positive in most countries, banked on the continuation of the budgetary rigour and projected that

[17] The idea of pushing forward with monetary union was seen by europhile politicians and technocrats as a means of driving (or forcing) further political unification, a move that was in line with the chain reaction strategy described in the first section. EMU is a very good example of what I have called the 'kick and rush' approach to European integration.

[18] It should be recalled that in 1996 only two countries (Ireland and Luxembourg) out of twelve candidates applying to the eurozone were compliant with the convergence criteria and that, as a consequence, the introduction of the euro (that was planned for 1997) had to be delayed by the European Council in December 1996!

[19] France was able to meet the '3 per cent of GDP' budget deficit criteria in 1997 thanks to the one-shot payment by France Telecom of a pension scheme arrangement representing 0.45 per cent of GDP. Portugal just met the '60 per cent of GDP' debt criteria in 1998 based on the EMI forecasts (down from 65 per cent in 1996).

most countries would meet the criteria in the near future. Only one country out of the twelve applicants – Greece – eventually did not enter the eurozone in 1999 because it was way off target on the four convergence criteria. It was, however, accepted into the eurozone in January 2001, even though most indicators had not sustainably improved. This initial lack of seriousness in enforcing the Maastricht criteria as well as the initial lack of control (here referring to the absence of sanctions on France and Germany in 2003 for exceeding the 3 per cent deficit threshold – 'the two then united to make sure that they wouldn't face sanctions for doing so – effectively destroying the rules (known as the "growth and stability pact") altogether', as Stacey (2011) put it, considerably undermined the foundations of the eurozone and contained in germ some of its future woes.

Thirdly, the financial regulatory context in which the launching of the euro took place was not ideal. In the United States, massive financial and banking deregulation took place in these years and radically changed the way banks and financial institutions operated. To mention only two major reforms, one could highlight the 1999 Gramm–Leach–Bliley Act that repealed the Glass–Steagall Act completely and the 2000 Commodity Futures Modernization Act that prevented the Commodity Futures Trading Commission from regulating most over-the-counter derivative contracts, including credit default swaps.[20] At the global level, the limits of the prudential regulations defined in the Basel I agreement reached in 1988 by the Committee on Banking Supervision (and enforced by law by the G10 in 1992) were becoming increasingly clear in terms of capital requirements, disclosure requirements and supervisory review. At the European level, the European Commission issued the Financial Services Action Plan (FSAP) in 1999 to complete by 2005 the legal framework enabling the effective exercise of market freedoms in financial services throughout the European Union. As some critics put it, the 42 measures of the FSAP were a product of political compromise rather than a desire to produce the best possible rules for Europe. Many key issues (again prudential assessment, supervision, investor protection) were left unaddressed and the European Commission had to intervene almost every year after the Markets in Financial Instruments Directive of 2004 to try to strengthen the European regulatory provisions.

These three factors have clearly undermined the functioning of the eurozone since its beginning and have their share in the uneasy start

---

[20] See Sherman (2009), which also mentions the 2004 system of voluntary regulation proposed by the Securities and Exchange Commission (SEC) under the Consolidated Supervised Entities program, allowing investment banks to hold less capital in reserve and increase leverage.

of the eurozone. However, they do not constitute the core of the 'real economy' dynamics that were at play in the eurozone and that led to the crisis and its uneasy resolution.

... produced significant heterogeneous real economy effects in the eurozone member countries ...

The core objective of the eurozone was to create an effective monetary integration to reduce transaction costs (to fully benefit from internal trade liberalization and from better productive specialization) as well as to reduce interest rate and exchange rate volatility amongst member countries. Without entering into a detailed presentation of the analytical rationale for monetary integration, one can use Feldstein's (1997) peda-gogic presentation of the 'trade-off between the reduced costs of trade and the adverse macroeconomic effects of precluding interest rate and exchange rate variations'. His approach helps clarify the implications for member countries of the creation of the eurozone using the theory of optimal currency areas (OCAs) developed by Robert Mundell. In brief, in order for an OCA to offset the macroeconomic losses by trade gains, four key factors need to be taken into account: (1) homogeneity of the countries within the monetary union, (2) flexibility of domestic prices and wages, (3) mobility of the labour force and (4) responsiveness of fiscal transfers (1997: 35).

Without going into much detail here, Feldstein (1992, 1997) and Krugman (1993)[21] forcefully pointed out that the eurozone would be a beneficial OCA only for *some of* its member countries and that it would endogenously produce turbulences and conflicts within the monetary zone. The inner heterogeneity of eurozone countries, the limited mobility of the labour force across countries in the eurozone, the almost non-existent fiscal transfers are three of the major explanations behind their predictions of a very complicated future for some countries and thus for the cohesion of the eurozone. Here again in a few words, renouncing an independent monetary policy at the national level (interest rates and exchange rates) would not offer any more possibility to compensate for the strong dynamics and economic consequences of international productive specialization whose effects were to be maximized thanks to the massive internal and external trade liberalization undertaken in the

---

[21] These three articles provide an excellent discussion – though a discomforting one given their predictive dimensions of the future woes of the eurozone – of the arguments in the EU context.

mid-1980s.[22] For Feldstein (1997), the clear conclusion was that 'the countries of the European Union do not constitute a natural monetary union and that forcing a single currency in the area would raise cyclical unemployment in response to adverse demand shocks'.

Krugman (1993) analysed some of the lessons that could be drawn from Massachusetts (a state that underwent massive industrial restructuring in the 1980s) for the EMU. He pointed out that some of the dynamics at play in a monetary union include increased regional specialization, instability of regional exports, pro-cyclical capital movements and divergent long-run growth (pp. 242–3). He warned that the Single Market and the EMU would 'combine to make American-style regional crisis more common and more severe within the European Community. And it is immediately apparent that Europe will have a problem if its starts to experience American-style regional slumps without American-style fiscal federalism . . . Some kind of policy reform will be necessary if the increasingly unified European economy is not to pay an even higher price for that unification than the US does'. Unfortunately, as mentioned by Spolaore (2013) in his overview of the European construction, 'the anti-functionalist argument that integration can lead to specialization and more heterogeneity (e.g., Krugman and Venables 1996) *received much less attention in Brussels*' (2013: 136, emphasis mine).[23]

We have presented in the previous section the increasing heterogeneity in the economic performance of eurozone member countries in the past decade. We will here only quickly illustrate one example of the strong 'real economy' effects of the monetary integration that led to these aggregated results. Following Krugman's (1993) case of increasing regional specialization in the automotive industry in the US, it is striking to see a similar phenomenon at play immediately after the introduction of the euro. As a 2008 expert report put it:

> . . . while the German share of manufacturing employment in the EU has remained broadly unchanged over the past decade [. . .] the German share of employment in the automotive industry has increased, especially since 2000. In 2006, the share was over 5 percentage points larger than in 2000. These figures, therefore, indicate a shift in the location of employment in the automotive industry in the EU over recent years, most especially from the EU15 countries, excluding Germany, to a few of the new member states [. . .] Other data indicate that German auto-

---

[22] As theorized since the 1940s on the basis of the Hecksher–Ohlin and Stolpe–Samuelson theorems.

[23] The fact that this is only mentioned in a footnote in Spolaore's article is very telling: this strand of cautious thinking (while not being an anti-European one) was completely disregarded by European political leaders and analysts.

motive producers have been foremost in expanding production in the new member states. (Loire and Ward 2008: 6)

After the introduction of the euro, the European car industry became increasingly regionally specialized under the domination of German carmakers and at the expense of France, Italy and Spain.

The cumulative 'real economy' effects after the introduction of the euro can also be seen in the rapid increase in the German trade surplus vis-à-vis the EU17 right after 2000. It jumped from 1.6 to 4.7 per cent of GDP between 1999 and 2007, representing more than €120 billion of accumulated gains over the period! The size of the overall German monthly trade surplus was multiplied by four over the period from a range of €4 billion per month in 1999 to €16 billion in 2007![24]

Such 'real economy' effects after the introduction of the euro have made the eurozone significantly more fragile. The de-industrialization in most (Southern European) countries led to an external trade deficit that fuelled in most cases a balance of payments crisis that in turn raised spreads on international financing, these higher costs of funding leading to an even slower growth. These 'real economy' effects have been combined with those related to the public/private indebtedness crisis that go as follows: low real interest rates thanks to the alignment of almost all European interest rates to the low German interest rate in 2000 led to indebtedness of states that were running a high public deficit and uncontrolled indebtedness of the private sector[25] that produced a hangover of bad assets that in turn produced higher risk premiums and less lending, leading to slower growth.

This 'real economy' effect was all the more painful and disruptive in Europe because it took place in the absence of institutionalized fiscal federalism in the eurozone. In federal states (as diverse as the USA, Germany, India and Brazil), budget transfers represent around 50 per cent of the federal fiscal budget. With a total fiscal budget in the range

[24] It is beyond the scope of this paper to study the evolution of the German trade surplus but it is extremely interesting to note that after benefiting immensely from the intra-eurozone trade between 2000 and 2007 (which then steadily declined because of the long recession in most eurozone countries), Germany immensely benefited from the undervaluation of the euro (provoked by the recession in most eurozone countries) to accumulate trade surpluses globally. In 2015, the surplus vis-à-vis the eurozone (2.2 per cent of German GDP) accounted for only a quarter of its global trade surplus (8.8 per cent of German GDP) which was the largest trade surplus in the world!

[25] De Grauwe (2010a) considers that private debt overhang was a key aspect of the eurozone crisis: 'While the government debt ratio in the eurozone declined from 72 per cent in 1999 to 67 per cent in 2007, the household debt increased from 52 per cent to 70 per cent of GDP during the same period. Financial institutions increased their debt from less than 200 per cent of GDP to more than 250 per cent'.

of 24–28 per cent of GDP, this means annual transfers in the magnitude of 12–14 per cent of GDP. In the case of Europe, the budget stands at 1 per cent, less than one tenth of states where solidarity-enhancing fiscal mechanisms are at play. The Delors Report (1989) was aware of this important caveat. It indicated that 'historical experience suggests that in the absence of countervailing policies, the overall impact on peripheral regions could be negative. Transport costs and economies of scale would tend to favour a shift in economic activity away from less developed regions, especially if they were at the periphery of the Community, to the highly developed areas at its centre. The EMU would have to encourage and guide structural adjustment which would help poorer regions to catch up with the wealthier ones. A step in this direction was taken in February 1988 when the European Council decided to double the size of structural funds in five years. But this was way too little to compensate for the huge 'real economy' effects in most eurozone countries.

... that transformed into a crisis of the eurozone made inevitable and worse by a series of wrong responses and policy mistakes

Against that background, the chances of eurozone success looked very slim at the beginning of the period. However, the crisis was made not only inevitable but worse by a series of policy mistakes and wrong responses almost everywhere in the eurozone.

Firstly, peripheral Southern countries made their share of policy mistakes. They wasted most of the 'free lunch' period they had between 2000 and 2007 when their real growth rate was much superior to the real interest rate thanks to the near disappearance of risk premia on national and private debts issued by the countries or their financial institutions. Instead of undertaking painful adjustments in labour markets and in social welfare (as was done in Germany, Sweden and Denmark) as well as financing key infrastructure projects that would improve their factor productivity, these countries (governments, banks and entrepreneurs) squandered that unique opportunity. Growth was mostly spurred by non-exportable sectors fuelled by private indebtedness. The vulnerability of this growth model materialized with a balance of payments crisis and a private debt crisis. It should be noted that such inadequate structural and economic polices were implemented by left-wing as well as by right-wing coalitions.[26]

---

[26] See Aznar (CR) then Zapatero (CL) governments in Spain; Barroso and Santana Lopes (CR) then Socrates (CL) in Portugal; Simitis (CL) then Karamanlis (CR) governments in

Secondly, as the crisis developed in 2008–9 (because of the US-imported crisis of the subprimes but also because of the accumulated public/ private indebtedness and increasingly real economy depressive effects in the eurozone), inadequate responses arrived from the more successful countries (e.g., Germany, Netherlands, Finland and Austria). In these countries, the lack of popularity for solidarity fiscal transfers forced governments to hold firm positions vis-à-vis the troubled countries of the eurozone. These responses were to some extent encouraged by the international organizations that considered that significant budgetary cuts and real economy adjustments would be needed in troubled countries to restore growth perspectives, confidence and thus international financial flows. As we have seen in the previous section, the cut in domestic demand – i.e., decrease of real wages + reduction of public spending requested of troubled countries in exchange for support – was considerable in some countries. Between 2008 and 2012, the purchasing power cut ranged from –4 per cent (Italy) and –8 per cent (Portugal) to –12 per cent (Spain) and –26 per cent (Greece).

Thirdly, there was a strong lack of ability in Europe to foresee the eurozone crisis even though warning signals had accumulated before the eruption of the crisis (e.g., large Balance of Trade or Balance of Payments imbalances, rapid de-industrialization of some European regions/countries, explosive real estate bubbles, skyrocketing private indebtedness). European politicians and technocrats were very complacent about the performance of the eurozone in the 2000–7 period during which it registered its fastest growth rate (but not on a solid, sustainable and virtuous basis). On top of that, they did not use the first years after the launching of the EMU to complete the institutional setting up of the eurozone and to prepare for possible harder times.

The lack of effective economic policy coordination and control mechanisms at the eurozone levels (including the functioning of the Stability and Growth Pact that was rather inefficiently amended in 2005[27] and the uneasy start of the European Central Bank in 2002–7 period) certainly played a role in this rather patchy start of the eurozone. As De Grauwe (2010b) highlighted, 'there is no mechanism to ensure convergence of members' competitive positions, and thus to prevent major trade

Greece. The only short exception could be the short-lived Amato (CL) second government soon to be replaced by Berlusconi (CR) governments in Italy. France would be an interesting case of procrastination under Chirac's (CR) presidency. (CR) stands for Centre-Right and (CL) for Centre-Left.

[27] The amendment of the Stability and Growth Pact in 2011 was approved 'to allow it to better consider individual national circumstances and to add more economic rationale to the rules to be complied with' (in the European Commission's own wording).

imbalances. [. . .] There is no mechanism to resolve crises caused by these imbalances and divergent competitive positions. Consequently, eurozone crisis management is ad hoc, time-consuming, and hindered by a lack of credibility'.

These fault lines were laid bare during the debt crisis of 2008. They fuelled strong communication and institutional hesitations at the beginning of the crisis at the European level as well as in some cases inadequate policy responses. We cannot detail in full the various policy mistakes in the response to the debt crisis, the banking crisis[28] and the real economy crisis, but one needs to mention the following during the period 2008–12.

The response to the crisis by the European Central Bank was initially more conservative and less effective than that of the US Fed or of the Bank of England. In a detailed analysis prepared for the European Parliament, Claeys (2014) concluded that

> the ECB adopted measures that were mainly directed at ensuring the provision of liquidity and repairing the bank-lending channel, through changes to its usual framework for the implementation of monetary policy. By contrast, the Fed and the Bank of England quickly pursued unconventional monetary policies by implementing quantitative easing programmes that appeared to have a positive impact on financial variables and also on the real economy.

There have been costly analytical confusions between solvency crises (Greece) and liquidity crises (Italy) as well as between public debt crises (Greece) versus private debt crises (Spain and Ireland). For instance, the insistence of creditors to refuse any deep restructuring of the Greek debt until early 2012 created strong systemic uncertainty about the management of the crisis by institutions (the ECB, the IMF), by national creditors and by international private banks. This systemic uncertainty severely impacted other indebted countries (Ireland, Spain, Portugal, Italy) and created a risk averse environment that has depressed investment and consumption and as a result cut growth prospects in many countries of the eurozone.

The creation of relevant financial instruments has been hesitant, revealing the existing conflicts among the various stakeholders of the eurozone. In 2010, two temporary rescue programmes were started, the European Financial Stabilization Mechanism (EFSM) and the European Financial Stability Facility (EFSF). Together with massive financial support from

---

[28] In this volume, Ontiveros gives an excellent account of the transformation of the debt crisis into a severe and costly European banking crisis (with, among other negative consequences, the very harmful credit crunch for the real economy in most eurozone countries).

the International Monetary Fund (IMF), these facilities provided funds to Greece, Ireland and Portugal in 2010 and 2011. Under the Securities Market Programme, initiated in May 2010, the ECB bought around €220 billion of Greek, Irish, Portuguese, Italian and Spanish government bonds. But most empirical literature, cited by Claeys (2014), noted that 'it had a positive but short-lived effect on market functioning by reducing liquidity premia and reducing the level as well as the volatility of European government bond yields'. The eurozone had to wait until 2012 to start dealing appropriately with the right financial and monetary instruments and the right scale of intervention.

Finally, the insistence on drastic austerity packages to fix the troubled economies of the eurozone ended in a rather counterproductive way. Some fiscal adjustments were absolutely needed in some countries after the first few years of permissive profligacy after the launch of the euro. However, drastic budgetary austerity (jointly promoted by the IMF and the eurogroup) proved as wrong as its initial theoretical justifications.[29] The self-inflicted recession of 2012 was mostly due to the cumulative deflationary effects of national budget adjustments in the eurozone. It hardly opened the way to a better understanding of the relation between growth forecasts and fiscal consolidation, as shown with the 'Fiscal Compact' and the 'Six Pack' directive (named after a collection of six legislative measures) that came into force in December 2011 to ensure that EU governments respect the requirements of economic and monetary union and do not run excessive deficits.

The eurozone reached a turning point in 2012 that saved the day . . .

2012 can be considered as a major turning point in the management of the crisis by the eurozone. Several major events took place that indicated a significant adjustment of both instruments and policies, most notably at the monetary and banking levels. One key event was the long-awaited Greek debt restructuring. Zettelmeyer et al. (2013) provide an in-depth analysis of this first episode of debt restructuring in Europe since World War II that set 'a new world record in terms of restructured debt volume and aggregate creditor losses'. They recall that 'after a €200 billion debt

---

[29] The Blanchard and Cottarelli paper published by the IMF in June 2010 provided much of the justification based on an econometric analysis of fiscal multipliers. This very influential paper was later highly criticized for understating the recessive impact of budgetary cuts. Olivier Blanchard and Daniel Leigh released in January 2013 an IMF paper with the evocative title 'Growth forecast errors and fiscal multipliers'.

exchange in March/April 2012 and a buyback of a large portion of the newly exchanged sovereign bonds in December, the amount of Greek bonds in the hands of private creditors was down to just €35 billion – just 13 per cent of where it had stood in April 2010, when Greece lost access to capital markets'. Private creditors had to undergo a significant 'hair cut' of 65 per cent on average with the strong support of the IMF and the approval of the heads of governments of the EU member countries. It gave a clear signal that the eurozone was entering a credible phase of stabilization.

The almost simultaneous launching of the Very Long-Term Refinancing Operations in December 2011 and February 2012, then of the Outright Monetary Transactions programme in September 2012 and the creation of the European Stability Mechanism in October 2012 considerably changed the monetary situation for the eurozone.[30] Firstly, these instruments helped create the much-needed lender of last resort for the eurozone. Secondly, the magnitude of possible interventions to combat the liquidity crisis and to support indebted countries was so formidable that it produced a significant credibility impact.[31] Thirdly, the ECB under the presidency of Mario Draghi (which started in November 2011) was showing its strong willingness to make use of these new tools in order to help refinance the banking system, reduce systemic uncertainty and provide monetary stimulus to reignite economic growth in the eurozone. If we add the launching of the Banking Union in 2012 (transferring responsibility for banking policy from the national to the EU level), the Bank Recovery and Resolution Directive in 2013 (to effectively deal with unsound or failing credit institutions), and the strengthening of the European Systemic Risk Board (macroprudential oversight of the EU financial system), one can conclude that a lot has been (rather successfully) done in order to keep the eurozone together and consolidate the euro as a major global currency.

But the quantitative easing of the ECB under Mario Draghi's presidency (in spite of repeated German scepticism if not opposition) has not been enough to restart the eurozone growth engine. In spite of zero interest rates and very low spreads, several countries in the eurozone are still in the vicious circle of fiscal adjustments and low economic growth.

---

[30] See Claeys (2014) and Micossi (2015) for very detailed and interesting analyses of ECB policies since its foundation.

[31] Interestingly, the Outright Monetary Transactions programme (that allows the purchase by the ECB of unlimited amounts of government bonds of Member States subject to a European Stability Mechanism) has not been used, but its announcement had a significant impact on government bond yields of the EMU Member States because it demonstrated the determination of the ECB to maintain the integrity of the euro area.

The EU doctrine has not really changed and Brussels still pushes hard for the respect of budgetary targets under the framework of the Stability and Growth Pact. Some flexibility has been introduced in January 2015 with a new directive, but the budget orthodoxy prevails, with tighter supervision and increasing transfers of fiscal sovereignty (under the preventive arm of the Stability and Growth Pact).

... without however forging ahead sustainable political and economic solutions

More economic coordination is called for, but beyond the prolongation of the hard budget constraint at the national levels, not much has been put forward in terms of fiscal federalism, automatic fiscal transfers, tax harmonization or eurobonds for European infrastructure or environment-friendly direct investments. The much trumpeted €315 billion Investment Plan for Europe (also known as the Juncker Plan) launched in November 2014 is in fact a $21 billion guarantee fund of the European Commission that will not change anything. The combination of the resources unavailable under the European Regional Development Fund, the Cohesion Fund and Horizon 2020 for Science for the period 2014–20 amounts to €60 billion a year or 0.4 per cent of the European Union total GDP. The European Union and the eurozone do not have the direct fiscal resources, nor the project to leverage and/or to coordinate infrastructure, green or modernization investments of Member States.

In brief, much has been done and huge amounts have been invested since the 2008 crisis to save the core engine of the economic systems, i.e. banks and financial institutions throughout Europe. Beyond that very understandable priority, much less has been attempted and achieved in terms of fiscal and social policies. This would require greater political willingness from the European decision-makers and a higher level of consensus among Member States. In the current period marked by overall economic stagnation, and given the rising heterogeneity of Member States, any deepening of the European integration on contested issues such as fiscal and social policies sounds unfeasible and unrealistic.

The Five Presidents' Report entitled 'Completing Europe's Economic and Monetary Union' and released in June 2015 fell short of proposing concrete steps. While acknowledging that 'divergence created fragility for the whole Union' (p. 4), the document is very much in the European Union building tradition. This is an ambitious document, at times precise and technical on reforms that can be undertaken or correspond to the mainstreaming of the European Commission and key Member States

(Banking Union, Capital Markets Union, Macroeconomic Imbalance Procedure, European Fiscal Board, Competitiveness authorities, etc.) and at times vague or full of wishful thinking on less consensual areas ('stronger focus on employment and social performance', 'the exact design of euro area stabilizers requires more in depth work', etc.). This latest example of the piecemeal, pragmatist and ideological European building process fell short of expectations and did not create any of the much-needed positive vision and momentum for the eurozone and for the European Union. One year later, the British referendum prompted the European leaders to propose a new vision for Europe, thus implicitly burying the one-year-old opus.

In the absence of any major concrete initiative undertaken by the European leaders (Commission, Parliament or Council), the short-term future of the eurozone will be a combination of (a) continuing austerity in many eurozone countries with additional real wage adjustments and public spending cuts to obtain a (non-cooperative) competitive deflation but with limited growth and reindustrialization prospects, (b) possible opting out of the eurozone for Greece or Portugal if things get worse, although letting small players out would put the pressure on larger – too big to bail out – ones (Italy) and would mean high depreciation costs for debt holders and a possible severe economic recession, (c) insufficient but stronger coordination and solidarity with higher public budget transfers mostly obtained through the ECB quantitative easing and expansionist policy.

As a concluding word on this section, the euro has been saved (it is now a well-established global currency), the eurozone has survived thanks to much more decisive actions after 2012 (with a crucial role played by ECB's president Mario Draghi), but the European integration process has been so significantly weakened that a positive vision for a further deepening of the Union sounds unrealistic: there is no consensus among antagonized Member States on why (and how) the common house construction should be completed.

Conclusions

What have we learned from this economic policy analysis of the European integration process over the past sixty years?

- The incremental process for European integration (the famous 'chain reaction') has been increasingly dominated by private sector actors and market forces (thanks to the massive deregulation spurred by the

Single Act in the 1980s, then the Economic and Monetary Union in the 1990s).

- This strong departure from a social market economy model praised by most European citizens (although differently because of different Bismarckian or Beveridgian welfarist traditions or of recent transition to capitalist market economies) indicates that some 'forced integration' occurred, progressively widening the democratic deficit of the European Union building process.
- With the Single European Act and Economic and Monetary Union, the integration process has reached a point where any further deepening would require additional transfers of sovereignty on fiscal, social and political levels and has moved closer to the ultimate goal of political federalism that is definitely not an objective for many Member States.
- Simultaneously, the Single Act and Economic and Monetary Union have created strong heterogeneity inside the European Union (far from the anticipated convergence effects) that renders almost impossible any consensus for anything beyond the improvement of the current state of affairs. The lack of consensus in Europe negates the possibility of producing commons at the European level of co-operating for non-rival goods.
- Radical integrative steps without the proper institutional (regulatory and supervision) settings are not productive, particularly when a complex decision process delays timely policy responses.
- The European integration process as we knew it came to an end and cannot be furthered anymore on the same grounds. Many analysts such as Spolaore (2015) now underline that 'further steps towards European integration should be taken only when they are economically beneficial and politically stable *on their own merits* and openly in the eyes of the European population'.
- In order to recreate some economic and political convergence and momentum, high priority would need to be given to policies that produce positive externalities among member countries (such as infrastructure development or environmental protection) or that increase overall factor productivity (rather than uncoordinated regional/national competitiveness policies).
- Political union would need to be pursued only by countries that are explicitly willing to move towards European federalism. It should not be an implicit by-product imposed out of necessity.

Based on this rather severe critical account, it seems legitimate to conclude this paper by wondering whether European integration has been such an economic big deal. We have seen earlier that the track record of Europe over the past quarter century has not been that great. Europe has not really created the conditions for delivering long-term sustainable growth for its member countries and offering strong prospects for the twenty-first century.[32] In addition, one can ask what is the track record of Europe in terms of protecting its member countries (and their citizens) from destabilizing exogenous shocks, from the negative sides of globalization, from an extreme reliance on the invisible hand of the market. Here again, the results may not be that impressive. Beckfield (2006, 2009) warned that regional integration, not globalization, was associated with the rise in income inequality in Western Europe and with the changes to the welfare state in the advanced capitalist countries of Western Europe. Busemeyer and Tober (2015) concluded that

> the process of European integration could in the long term contribute to transforming European countries towards a more liberal variety of capitalism. [...] Those hoping that EU policies could potentially balance out the negative side effects of European and global economic integration on the viability of national welfare states will be disappointed. The current institutional and political setup of the EU certainly does not seem to be an effective counterweight against the ubiquitous trends towards rising inequality.

Given the importance of these issues for the future of Europe, it seems highly advisable that more research should be undertaken and more informed public deliberation should take place prior to any further integration step in Europe.

As a final word, the European integration process has achieved the remarkable task of preventing wars and conflicts between its Member States (even in growing number as enlargement took place), but it may not have been as positive at the economic level as we might have expected (or as we might have hoped for). If this statement holds some truth in it, the process of building a European Union may thus be regarded in history as unfinished business or as a huge missed opportunity – it would have failed to fulfil its promise because of its excessive reliance on second-best (political and technocratic) strategies that increasingly

---

[32] Here the debates before the British referendum on Brexit are extremely interesting. No one (not even in the Remain camp – see, for example, the many balanced articles in the *Financial Times* on the question) considered that leaving the EU would be tragic for a leading country like the United Kingdom. This may signify that if a leading country is in reasonably good economic shape (as is the case with the UK), it may fare just as well outside the EU. This reasoning may not be true though for countries that are in poor economic shape and/or are still lagging behind the European leading countries (such as Greece or Portugal and new Member States from Central and Eastern Europe).

proved unable to create a positive spiralling of popular support in favour of more European integration through inclusive growth, environmental protection progress and social cohesion.

Acknowledgements

The author would like to thank John Thompson for his purposeful comments, the participants in the 'Crisis of Europe' workshops in June and December 2015, as well as the group of high-level scholars who attended my presentation at Princeton University in March 2016 for helpful discussion.

References

Adler, M. and Fleurbaey, M. (eds) (2016) *Oxford Handbook of Well Being and Public Policy*. Oxford: Oxford University Press.
Beckfield, J. (2006) European integration and income inequality. *American Sociological Review* 71: 964–85.
Beckfield, J. (2009). Remapping inequality in Europe: the net effect of regional integration on total income inequality in the European Union. *International Journal of Comparative Sociology* 50(5–6): 486–509.
Bergsten, C. (2012) Why the euro will survive: completing the continent's half-built house. *Foreign Affairs*, September/October.
Blanchard, O. and Cottarelli, C. (2010) Ten commandments for fiscal adjustment in advanced economies. Washington, DC: International Monetary Fund. Available at: http://blog-imfdirect.imf.org/2010/06/24/ten-commandments-for-fiscal-adjustment-in-advanced-economies/
Blanchard, O. and Leigh, D. (2013) Growth forecast errors and fiscal multipliers. IMF Working Paper 13/1. Washington, DC: International Monetary Fund.
Busemeyer, M. and Tober, T. (2015) European integration and the political economy of inequality. *European Union Politics* 16(4): 536–57.
Campos, N., Coricelli, F. and Moretti, L. (2014) Economic growth and political integration: estimating the benefits from membership in the European Union using the synthetic counterfactuals method. Discussion Paper No. 8162. Bonn: Institute for Labor Studies.
Claeys, G. (2014) The (not so) unconventional monetary policy of the European Central Bank since 2008. Paper prepared for the European Parliament. Brussels: Bruegel.
De Grauwe, P. (2010a) Fighting the wrong enemy. *Vox*. Available at: http://www.voxeu.org/article/Europe-s-private-versus-public-debt-problem-fighting-wrong-enemy
De Grauwe, P. (2010b) How to embed the eurozone in a political union. *Vox*. Available at: http://www.voxeu.org/article/eurozone-needs-political-union-or-least-elements-one
Delors Report (1989) *Report on Economic and Monetary Union in the European Community*. Brussels.

Eichengreen, B. (ed.) (1995) *Europe's Post-war Recovery*. Cambridge: Cambridge University Press.

European Monetary Institute (1998) *Convergence Report*. Frankfurt am Main.

Feldstein, M. (1992) Europe's Monetary Union: the case against EMU. *The Economist*, 13 June.

Feldstein, M. (1997) The political economy of the European Economic and Monetary Union: political sources of an economic liability. *Journal of Economic Perspectives*, 11(4): 23–42.

James, H. (2012) *Making the European Monetary Union*. Cambridge, MA: Harvard University Press.

Kornai, J. (1990) The affinity between ownership forms and coordination mechanisms: the common experience of reform in socialist countries. *Journal of Economic Perspectives* 4(3): 131–47.

Krugman, P. (1993) Lessons of Massachusetts for the EMU. In: Torres, F. and Giavazzi, F. (eds) *Adjustment and Growth in the European Monetary Union*. Cambridge: Cambridge University Press.

Krugman, P. and Venables, A. (1996) Integration, specialization, and adjustment. *European Economic Review* 40(3–5): 959–67.

Loire, P. and Ward, T. (2008) Employment, skills and occupational trends in the automotive industry. Annex Report for the European Commission, Groupe Alpha/Alphametrics, Paris, Cambridge, Brussels.

Marsh, D. (2011) *The Euro – The Battle for a New Global Currency*. New Haven, CT: Yale Univeristy Press.

Marsh, D. (2013) *Europe's Deadlock: How the Euro Crisis Could Be Solved – and Why It Won't Happen*. New Haven, CT: Yale University Press.

Meunier, S., Jones, E. and Kelemen, D. (2015) Failing forward? The euro crisis and the incomplete nature of European integration. *Comparative Political Studies* 49(7): 1010–34.

Micossi, S. (2015) *The Monetary Policy of the European Central Bank (2002–2015)*. Brussels: Center for European Policy Studies.

Moss, B.H. (2005) Introduction: The European Union as a neo-liberal construction. In Moss, B.H. (ed.) *Monetary Union in Crisis: The European Union as a Neo-liberal Construction*. Basingstoke: Palgrave Macmillan, pp. 1–26.

Polanyi, K. (1944) *The Great Transformation*. New York: Farrar & Rinehart.

Scharpf, F.-W. (1999) Negative and positive integration in the political economy of European welfare state. In: Marks, G., Scharpf, F.-W. and Schmitter, P. (eds) *Governance in the European Union*. London: Sage Publications, pp. 15–39.

Sherman, M. (2009) *A Short History of Financial Deregulation in the United States*. Washington, DC: Center for Economic Policy Research.

Spolaore, E. (2013) What is European integration really about? A political guide for economists. *Journal of Economic Perspectives* 27(3): 125–44.

Spolaore, E. (2015) Monnet's chain reaction and the future of Europe. *Vox*. Available at: http://www.voxeu.org/article/monnet-s-chain-reaction-and-future-Europe

Stacey, K. (2011) Who originally broke the EU fiscal rules? France and Germany. *Financial Times*, 6 December.

Zettelmeyer, J., Trebesch, C. and Gulati, M. (2013) The Greek debt restructuring: an autopsy. *Economic Policy* 28(75): 515–63.

Chapter 2

Making Sense of the Greek Crisis, 2010–2016

Manos Matsaganis

Anti-climax

In the early hours of 24 May 2016, as the eurogroup meeting drew to a close, the Greek finance minister agreed to rush through Parliament the entire list of 'prior actions' demanded by creditors and enshrined in the bailout agreement of August 2015 – the third of its kind since the Greek crisis began six years earlier.

This time, the familiar menu of spending cuts, tax hikes and structural reforms went further than usual: it included an automatic mechanism to balance the books without prior parliamentary approval every time the projected fiscal deficit deviated by more than 0.25 per cent of GDP from its ambitious target (a primary surplus, not counting debt servicing costs, of 3.5 per cent of GDP from 2018). In spite of strong IMF support, the Greek government failed to get the country's European creditors to pledge debt relief, even in the milder form of 'reprofiling' (i.e. reducing interest and extending maturity). Any discussion of what was tantalizingly but vaguely promised to Greece in November 2012 was now put on hold until 2018 – that is, after the current Economic Adjustment Programme has run its course, and with the German federal elections (scheduled for October 2017 at the latest) conveniently out of the way.

In effect, the anti-austerity coalition government ruling Greece since January 2015, led by the radical left SYRIZA, with the nationalist right ANEL ('Independent Greeks') as a junior partner, had signed up to permanent harsh austerity, coming on the heels of the deepest and longest recession in European history (over a quarter of GDP lost since 2007), and placing the economy under close international supervision for many years to come. All of this and more in exchange for a commitment on the

49

part of creditors to keep funding Greece, allowing it to remain a member of the euro area (at least for the time being). A rather ignominious conclusion to the adventure that catapulted a hitherto marginal political force from irrelevance to prominence on the simple promise 'to end austerity with a single Act of Parliament on Day 1 from taking power' (as Alexis Tsipras, then opposition leader, had announced on live TV on the eve of the January 2015 general election).

In sharp contrast to the events of 5 May 2010, when the huge demonstration against the first bailout deal then debated by Parliament turned violent, leading to the deaths of three persons as protesters set fire to the bank in which they worked, six years later the mood in Athens was far more subdued. While labour unions and the anti-EU left did turn up to protest, joined as is customary by hooded youths in full riot gear, the masses mobilized by the anti-austerity bloc in 2010–15 mostly stayed at home. Numbing resignation reigned.

It looked as if the dream of a quick fix to the hardship and humiliation of recent years, a dream with undertones at once noble and ugly, had been shattered for good. For many Greeks, the morning after the intoxicating experience of the anti-austerity rising felt like a hangover. As they strove to make sense of events, all around them things looked depressingly familiar, only worse. With a quarter of the workforce out of work, firms struggling to survive, and younger educated Greeks emigrating in droves, prospects appeared unmistakably grim.[1]

This essay is an attempt, no doubt highly subjective, to make sense of the Greek crisis. It focuses on the interplay of a constellation of factors, firmly located in the country's political economy,[2] some of which – hopefully the most significant – are discussed below.

The greatest of all recessions

When the international financial crisis hit Europe (in 2008), several periphery economies were undermined. Some countries were forced to accept a full bailout in return for massive fiscal consolidation and structural reforms, supervised by the European Commission (EC), the International Monetary Fund (IMF), and the European Central Bank (ECB), collectively known as 'the Troika'. That was the case for Greece (May 2010), Ireland (December 2010) and Portugal (May 2011). Others,

---

[1] The story of the Greek crisis and the ascent of the anti-austerity coalition has been told in Matsaganis (2014, 2016).
[2] Bouin (this volume) offers a broad analysis of the eurozone crisis from the perspective of political economy.

on the Eastern fringe, having run early into balance of payments difficulties, had to apply for more limited financial assistance, which also came with close surveillance and austerity. That involved Hungary (October 2008), Latvia (December 2008) and Romania (May 2009). As for the more robust economies of larger Member States, such as Spain and Italy, they were subject to softer forms of conditionality.

Nevertheless, not all periphery countries have been equally affected. Economic, social and political effects of the austerity and the recession were adverse everywhere, but remained on a significantly lower scale in Ireland and Portugal (and Spain and Italy). Moreover, both Ireland (December 2013) and Portugal (June 2014) successfully exited[3] their 'Economic Adjustment Programme', while Greece's desperate attempts at an early exit (October 2014) and renegotiation (February–July 2015) backfired.

As an indication of the severity of the crisis, the size of the Greek economy in 2008–15 shrank by as much as 25.9 per cent. None of the other south European countries had recovered to pre-crisis levels either, but at least the size of the contraction there was considerably lower: –5.6 per cent in Portugal, –4.3 per cent in Spain, –7.3 per cent in Italy. As for Ireland, its GDP in 2015 was 11.9 per cent *higher* than it had been seven years earlier.[4]

Furthermore, current trends painted a gloomy picture, setting Greece apart from other Member States. Whereas the EU economy registered a positive rate of growth over the last two years (1.4 per cent in 2014 and 1.9 per cent in 2015 relative to the year before), with Ireland outperforming the rest (5.2 per cent and 7.8 per cent respectively), Greece plunged into recession once again (–0.2 per cent) in 2015, after a timid recovery (+0.7 per cent) in 2014.

As for Greece's relative living standards, having peaked at 85.4 per cent of the EU-15 average in 2009, they plummeted to 65.8 per cent in 2015, and are currently projected to fall further to 64.9 per cent in 2016 – a level unseen since the early 1960s.[5] The Greek crisis has put in reverse the process of convergence with the rest of Western Europe that had seemed to gather speed with the adoption of the common currency in 2001.

---

[3] Hungary (November 2010), Latvia (January 2012), Romania (June 2011) also exited their balance-of-payments (BoP) financial assistance programmes.
[4] Eurostat online database.
[5] Eurostat AMECO database.

Starting conditions

Part of the problem was, of course, that Greece had more ground to cover, in the sense that fiscal imbalances were larger to start with. For instance, in 2009 its budget deficit stood at 15.6 per cent of GDP, compared to 10.2 per cent in Portugal and 13.7 per cent in Ireland.[6]

The Greek crisis hit the headlines in October 2009, when the socialist government, fresh from its electoral triumph earlier that month, announced that earlier fiscal data had been misreported. The general government deficit as a share of GDP for 2008 was corrected from 5.0 per cent to 7.7 per cent (later revised to 9.4 per cent, then 9.9 per cent), while the estimate for 2009 was raised from 3.7 per cent to 12.5 per cent (finally settled at 15.6 per cent).

The figures stunned public opinion in Europe and shocked markets worldwide. Coming not long after the onset of the international financial crisis, and coinciding with sluggish growth everywhere, the Greek case assumed unanticipated dimensions. Markets, until then oblivious to country risk, treating the entire eurozone as a single undifferentiated entity, overreacted by increasing spreads (that is, interest rate differentials from German government bonds) and lowering credit ratings. This turned a fiscal crisis into a sovereign debt one, threatening to bring down the entire edifice of Europe's monetary union. Almost at a stroke, Greece effectively lost access to the international financial markets, no longer able to service its debt except at prohibitive costs.

The political implications were equally fatal. The Greek saga was decisive in reinforcing the perception that the eurozone crisis really was the fault of irresponsible governments violating the pacts they had vowed to respect (in the case of public deficit: 3 per cent of GDP, as enshrined in the 1992 Maastricht Treaty which led to the creation of the common currency, and later in the Growth and Stability Pact). Never mind that the fiscal woes of Ireland (erstwhile known as the 'Celtic Tiger') only started when the government decided to issue a broad guarantee to Irish banks, or that in both Ireland and Spain public debt as a proportion of GDP was below 40 per cent (against the 60 per cent ceiling agreed first at Maastricht then under the Stability and Growth Pact). Nor that the standard view among *mainstream* economists has in the meantime shifted towards a more nuanced understanding that the eurozone crisis

---

[6] In Ireland, the cost of bailing out failed banks (2.7 per cent of GDP in 2009) rose to 21.8 per cent of GDP in 2010. See IMF (2014a).

was primarily due to external not fiscal imbalances.[7] In spring 2010, as Greece's EU partners debated whether to circumvent the Maastricht Treaty's 'No bailout' clause and on exactly what terms, the conviction set in almost everywhere in Europe (and beyond) that Greece was not to be trusted, and should never have been allowed to join the eurozone in the first place.

Nonetheless, in the narrow terms of fiscal consolidation alone, the 'Greek Programme' was an unsung triumph. While politicians and the media in much of the rest of Europe were busy reproaching profligate Southerners, much-maligned Greek governments were engaged in belt-tightening of unprecedented dimensions. The size of deficit reduction in 2010 (almost 5 per cent of GDP), was the biggest in a single year in any developed country.[8] The primary balance went from −10.2 per cent in 2009 to +1.2 per cent of GDP in 2013, in the midst of the deepest recession in living memory (IMF 2015: 66).

The nature of the 2010 bailout

As hinted above, the run up to the Greek crisis seemed to have been scripted by a fully paid-up ordoliberal (as the current economic orthodoxy in Germany and elsewhere has come to be known, with its near religious insistence that *Pacta sunt servanda*, its narrow focus on fiscal deficits, its unshakeable faith on the magical properties of austerity, and its fixation on 'beggar-thy-neighbour' competitiveness). For all the grudging respect paid to George Papandreou, the then PM, and George Papaconstantinou, his finance minister, for their desperate efforts to clean up the mess, the prevailing view in Brussels and Berlin was that the Greeks had it coming.[9] And when the systemic nature of the eurozone crisis became plain for all to see, making further procrastination suicidal, and forcing European leaders to set aside the 'No bailout' clause and move from 'You are on your own' to the May 2010 Memorandum of Understanding, the

---

[7] See Baldwin et al. (2015) and Baldwin and Gros (2015). Note that external imbalances in Greece, with the current account balance reaching −14.9 per cent of GDP in 2008, were far larger than elsewhere.

[8] 'No other OECD country has achieved such a fiscal improvement in a single year over the past three decades' (OECD 2011: 12).

[9] Mark Blyth, in his erudite attack on the ordoliberal orthodoxy, comes quite close to acknowledging that Greece's vulnerability in 2010 was due to 'special structural problems' and hence largely self-inflicted: 'Leaving aside all the often-repeated stories of endemic corruption and dubious early retirements, of which there are many, Greece has a weak tax-collection capacity and an even weaker political will to enforce collection, so revenues have never balanced expenditures' (2013: 63).

consensus was that its terms had to be punitive. In technical jargon, the austerity measures and structural reforms had to be 'frontloaded', partly to reassure the markets and partly to ensure that the 'Programme' was completed before fatigue set in, and before popular opposition undermined its implementation (Sandbu 2015; Papaconstantinou 2016).

Was it all inevitable? Could the Greek government have negotiated harder? And what about the country's European partners? Could they not simply take stock of reality, ugly as it was, offer Greece debt relief, and move on?

The notion that the 2010 bailout was an international conspiracy, that the Papandreou government sold Greece to foreigners, and hence he should be tried for high treason, was a founding myth of the anti-austerity bloc (across the spectrum: from the neo-Nazis of Golden Dawn to the anti-globalizers of the extra-parliamentary left). But the prosaic truth is that in May 2010, the Greek government could do little more than choose among two bitter alternatives. It could accept international aid in return for an austerity programme, as it actually did. Or it could default, and exit the eurozone (and, quite conceivably, the European Union as well) then and there.

Counterfactual history is a notoriously arbitrary game to play. But even so, it seems likely that the consequences of the second option would have been catastrophic for all Greeks (except for those with savings accounts in Switzerland). A unilateral default in 2010 would have relegated Greece to the status of a pariah state, cut off from the rest of the world, its people facing untold hardship. After all, during the 2001 *corralito*, Argentina was at least self-sufficient in food. Greece in 2010 was a net importer of tomatoes.

As far as the terms of the bailout deal were concerned, and the intransigence of Germans and other Europeans, two considerations seem to have played a crucial role. The first was 'moral hazard' – that is, the concern that, coming after such a blatant violation of the rules of the game to which all Member States had signed up (not to mention the cover-up of real statistics carried out by the centre-right governments of Kostas Karamanlis, 2004–9), debt relief to Greece would really open Pandora's box, providing all other eurozone governments with a clear incentive to go on a spending spree, then send the bill to their fellow Europeans. Most people would find that concern to be rather legitimate. In fact, no union can survive anything of the sort. So, the thinking went, the 'rescue' of Greece had to be painful to Greeks.

The second consideration was mostly unconfessed. It was all very convenient for politicians in northern Member States to shrug off the eurozone crisis as if it were a simple story of lazy and corrupt southerners living beyond their means. But it is impossible to have 'feckless debtors' without 'reckless creditors'.[10] Greek governments (and firms and consumers) had been undoubtedly unwise to borrow and spend huge amounts of money, as if there was no tomorrow. But the other side of the coin was banks in core countries who had been unwise enough to throw those huge amounts of money into loans to Greeks and other south Europeans. As a former head of the Bundesbank actually said at the time, the Greek bailout 'was about something altogether different: it was about protecting German banks, but especially the French banks, from debt write offs'.[11]

In other words, politicians in creditor countries had the option of taking the high road of acknowledging, then explaining to voters, that 'the European rescue of Greece' was actually also, if not primarily, the rescue of over-exposed commercial banks in France, Germany and elsewhere with European taxpayers' money.[12] As we all know, they chose to keep quiet about all that, and take instead the low road: the path of least resistance, reverting to the same tired (but so effective) clichés of 'lazy and corrupt southerners', etc.

Failed forecasts

In the meantime, not many imagined just how painful the austerity medicine would turn out to be. The 'Economic Adjustment Programme' in Greece (and, later, in Ireland and Portugal) assumed a fiscal multiplier of 0.5: a deficit reduction of €1 would lead to an output loss of €0.50, which is unpleasant but manageable. The Troika expected – or, at any rate, forecast – economic activity in Greece to contract for two years, by 6.5 per cent (in 2010–11), and unemployment to rise by three percentage

---

[10] In the words of Kenneth Dyson: 'Talking about creditors and debtors without implicit judgements about moral worth is very difficult. Creditor-state elites are open to harsh moral critique for their failure to act as responsible stewards of the system from which they benefit disproportionately. They risk hypocrisy in overlooking the role that their own reckless bankers play in creating moral hazard, for instance in mis-selling credit to the financially illiterate. [. . .] Above all, creditors need debtors' (2014: 95–6).

[11] See the interview of former Bundesbank head Karl Otto Pöhl in the German weekly *Der Spiegel*: 'Bailout Plan Is All About "Rescuing Banks and Rich Greeks"' (*Spiegel Online*, 18 May 2010).

[12] Mabbett and Schelkle have shown that one of the consequences of the Greek bailout agreement was that it bought time so that foreign banks could limit their exposure to Greek bonds. As a matter of fact, consolidated foreign claims of banks declined from $236 billion in December 2009 to $119 billion in December 2011. French and German banks also withdrew, but not as fast as others, so their relative share actually increased over the period (2015: 518).

points to almost 15 per cent, before the country returned to growth in 2012 (IMF 2010a). As it turned out, GDP continued to decline for *four* years after the bailout, by a cumulative 21 per cent (in 2010–13), while unemployment rose by *seventeen* percentage points, peaking at 29 per cent of the workforce[13] in February 2014. In October 2012, the *Financial Times* reported that two IMF economists, Olivier Blanchard (Economic Counsellor and Director of the Research Department in 2008–15) and Daniel Leigh, had concluded that the fiscal multiplier was between 0.9 and 1.7, rather than 0.5 as originally assumed (Blanchard and Leigh 2013).

As might have been expected, the news that the Troika had got it wrong seemed to vindicate anti-austerity economists (and others) world-wide, who had long argued that the obsession with balanced budgets risked making the recession deeper and longer. But in Greece, the sudden endorsement of Keynesian economics looked a bit suspect. Clearly, counter-cyclical demand management is often the appropriate response to a temporary downturn, requiring an expansionary fiscal stance (i.e., higher spending and/or lower taxes). But, by the same token, it also dictates a *restrictive* fiscal stance (i.e., lower spending and/or higher taxes) during a boom. Needless to say, not a trace of fiscal rectitude was to be seen in Greece in the run up to the crisis, when the economy was seriously overheated. Amidst the widespread euphoria of credit-fuelled prosperity, latter-day Keynesians were conspicuous by their absence. As for the political left in opposition, since the restoration of democracy in 1974, it never once failed to denounce budget bills brought to Parliament as being 'against growth, and against the people', implicitly – and sometimes explicitly – demanding higher government spending and lower taxes (i.e., higher fiscal deficits).

Even though popular, the notion that the depth (and length) of the recession could be attributed to fiscal consolidation alone was hardly convincing.[14] Developments in Ireland or Portugal showed that austerity was painful but did not cause the economy to collapse. What accounted for such differences from one 'Programme country' to another?

---

[13] Eurostat monthly unemployment figures, not seasonally adjusted.

[14] In what remains one of the earliest and most thoughtful studies of the political economy of austerity in Greece, Iordanoglou (2011), an academic economist and former leader of the student resistance to the military regime of 1967–74, pointed out that the time profiles of fiscal consolidation and GDP change were out of synchronization: the fiscal expansion of 2009, when the deficit skyrocketed, did not avert the onset of the crisis; the widely acclaimed fiscal consolidation of 2010 made the recession only slightly deeper; the more relaxed fiscal policy of the first three quarters of 2011 failed to prevent the economy from plunging. Political uncertainty, mounting and distortionary tax pressure, and a massive credit crunch, with liquidity drying up as a result of non-performing loans and deposit flight, all played a role.

Generally, the effects of fiscal consolidation on output depend on the savings rate, the average tax rate and export performance (Alcidi and Gros 2012). Specifically, the lower the savings rate, the lower the (effective) average tax rate, and the lower the degree of trade openness in terms of exports, the higher the fiscal multiplier. Let us briefly examine each of these three factors in turn.

Low savings

The savings rate did fall throughout most of Europe pre-crisis, and the creation of the euro itself was an important part of the story. As interest rates converged, the boost to the economy was more pronounced in the South, where they had been highest. Both governments and households had an incentive to borrow and spend – and, by and large, they did. In countries like Ireland and Spain, governments were 'virtuous' insofar as they avoided large deficits, but a bit less so in that they actively promoted (or failed to prevent) a housing bubble. In Greece, while net private savings also declined, it was the 'public sector borrowing requirement' that went up more steeply. The spending spree peaked under the conservative government of 2004–9 which, having inherited from the previous government a budget deficit of 5.7 per cent of GDP, bequeathed one eventually estimated at 15.6 per cent of GDP.

But a profligate government pre-crisis is only part of the explanation for the role of savings in the length and depth of the recession in Greece under austerity. Between early 2010 and mid-2012, savings in Greek banks in accounts held by Greek residents declined by one third (from over €240 billion to below €160 billion). That was partly due to good economic reasons: households dissave in a recession in order to soften the effect of falling income on consumption. But the other part of the explanation was political: lingering uncertainty as to the place of Greece in the euro area.

Political instability at home fed alarmist talk abroad about an impending Greek exit from the euro area, and was fed by it. Just as European policy makers pressed Greek governments to engage in massive fiscal consolidation, they were seen by the markets to entertain the idea that the euro area might be better off without Greece. The Deauville declaration of October 2010, when Angela Merkel and Nicolas Sarkozy sanctioned a bail-in of private investors, effectively warned those considering buying Greek bonds that they risked losing their money. This sent spreads skyrocketing and killed the notion that the Greek crisis might be contained. Eventually ECB head Mario Draghi famously pledged to do 'whatever it takes to preserve the euro' (July 2012). But not before the ambivalence had destroyed investors' confidence in the capacity of the Greek economy to weather the storm.[15]

Low tax take

Greek corruption has become one of the most popular explanations for lack of progress in fighting tax evasion.

All we know on the subject – which is not much – confirms that tax evasion really is higher in Greece (and Italy) than it is in Ireland and Portugal (and Spain). In particular, it is known to be pervasive among the self-employed. A recent study found that the true incomes of the liberal professions and other own-account workers applying for a mortgage in Greece pre-crisis were on average 92 per cent higher than reported to the tax authorities (Artavanis et al. 2016). This suggests a rate of income under-reporting of 48 per cent, broadly in line with our own estimate of 38–43 per cent (Matsaganis et al. 2012).

Quite rightly, the issue of tax evasion was flagged by international organizations[16] as key to the success of the Greek programme *ex ante* (and as one reason for its failure *ex post*). Armed with the conviction that fighting tax evasion was a matter of political will and administrative capacity, the Troika applied pressure to the Greek government to create the office of 'General Secretary of Government Revenue' at the Ministry of Finance.

Results were below expectations. Political interference with, and opposition to, the new office confirmed there was little appetite for effectively combating tax evasion among politicians of all hues. But problems ran deeper than allowed by standard explanations of inefficient and corrupt tax administration. To see why, we should turn our gaze to the US – the country where Al Capone was jailed for tax evasion, not mass murder. Notwithstanding the professionalism and uprightness of the IRS,

---

[15] Speculation about Grexit made a spectacular comeback in December 2014, when it became clear to all that another political crisis in Greece was imminent. Protracted and acrimonious negotiations between the newly elected government and the country's lenders plunged the economy back into recession. Bank deposits, having climbed back to nearly €180 billion in July 2014, dwindled to €130 billion in June 2015 and forced the government to impose capital controls.

[16] The IMF: 'Advancing tax administration reform is a crucial priority to limit risks of revenue shortfalls, and also to increase fairness in sharing the adjustment burden' (2010b). The European Commission: 'Fiscal consolidation was held back by a less than successful fight against tax evasion' (2011). The OECD: 'If Greece collected its VAT, social security contributions and corporate income tax with the average efficiency of OECD countries, tax revenues could rise by nearly 5 per cent of GDP' (2011).

the most reliable estimates point to a *higher* rate of under-reporting of business earnings by the self-employed in the US (57–59 per cent) than in Greece (Slemrod and Yitzhaki 2002; Slemrod 2007).

What the evidence suggests is that the key determinant of the size of tax evasion may not be the efficiency and probity of the tax administration, but the structure of the economy and the labour market. Self-employed workers evade taxes everywhere, no more in Greece than in the US. What really makes the difference is the relative share of self-employment. In the US, the self-employed make up 8 per cent of the workforce. In the euro area as a whole, the figure is 15 per cent. In the south, it is above average (Italy: 23 per cent; Portugal: 20 per cent; Spain: 17 per cent). In Greece, it is 31 per cent. Other things being equal, almost irrespective of competence and/or corruption, tax compliance will be lower the higher the share of self-employed workers.

In other words, the structure of the economy (and of the labour market) places significant limits on how much progress can realistically be achieved on that front. This is not to deny that fighting tax evasion and improving tax administration should be a priority. It is to argue that, unlike what many seem to believe, fighting tax evasion is not so much an issue of political will or administrative capacity, as it is a structural one.

The growth regime

In 2000–7, exports of goods and services had grown in volume by 27 per cent (compared to 62 per cent in Portugal and 49 per cent in Ireland). Under austerity, as domestic demand plummeted, most Greek firms proved incapable of switching to international markets – either because their products were of poor quality, or because they were sold at high prices, or both. In 2009–13, exports grew by 8 per cent (relative to 17 per cent in Portugal and 19 per cent in Ireland). The poor performance of exports[17] revealed the structural flaws of Greece's growth regime.[18]

The Troika's main solution for engineering an export-led recovery was 'internal devaluation' (i.e., policy-driven compression of wages via labour market deregulation, including a drastic cut in the minimum

---

[17] See IMF (2014b). Arkolakis et al. (2017) estimated that the poor performance of Greek exports was responsible for a third of the decline in GDP in 2007–12.

[18] A 'growth regime' is 'the central set of techniques, encompassing policies and the institutions they support, used by the core actors in the economy – governments, firms and organized producer groups – to secure higher rates of economic growth'. See Hall (2015). The author explains that he uses this term 'because these regimes are not always animated by the strategic vision implied by the concept of a "growth strategy" and they are less static than implied by the term "growth model"'.

wage). That was duly implemented, especially in 2012–13. But the reduction in labour costs failed to reverse the decline in employment: in March 2016 the number of workers in employment was 4 per cent lower than it had been in March 2012 (when the minimum wage was cut), and 21 per cent lower than its pre-crisis peak (in May 2008). It seemed clear that massive fiscal consolidation had been achieved *in spite* of a low-performing economy, rather than on the back of a new dynamism. Eliminating the twin deficits, fiscal and external, had been accomplished by simply moving the economy to a lower equilibrium.

The disappointing export performance of Greek firms raised awkward issues for both sides of the austerity divide. To start with, it hinted at a deeper malaise, resistant to the Keynesian-type reflation recipe advocated by critics of austerity both at home and abroad. Boosting disposable incomes and allowing public spending to grow, desirable though it may be, would merely cause imports to rise, setting in motion once again the vicious cycle that led to the debt crisis in the first place.

But the obsolescence of Greece's growth regime also meant that the conventional prescription of 'austerity plus structural reforms' administered by the Troika was flawed. Sustainable growth was unlikely to spring magically from the ruins of 'creative destruction'. As for lowering labour costs, it was implausible to expect it to ensure the survival of struggling firms while the tax burden grew, energy and other costs remained high, and credit became increasingly scarce.

What is more, the focus on labour costs deflected attention from the full range of factors that prevented significant productivity improvements, and caused Greek firms to lose ground in international markets. These included a regulatory environment and public bureaucracy that pile up costs and stifle business growth; a banking sector hostile to newcomers, in symbiotic relationship with established firms; a mismatch between the formal skills embodied in job seekers fresh out of education, and the softer ones sought by firms; an entrepreneurial culture that stresses opportunism, improvisation and immediate gain, at the expense of strategic management and long-term commitment; and exceptionally low average firm size, coupled with an aversion to networking and cooperation between firms.

In terms of low firm size, Greece really stands out. In 2014, small and medium-sized enterprises (defined as firms with fewer than 250 employees) accounted for as much as 86 per cent of all employment in the non-financial business sector, topping the EU league. The overwhelming majority of all workers in that sector (59 per cent) – far more than in any other European country – were employed in small firms (with 1–9 employees), and in micro firms of self-employed workers (European

Commission 2015). And while in theory (and sometimes in practice, as the experience of La Terza Italia has demonstrated[19]), small and medium firms can be high-tech, innovative and export-oriented, the empirical evidence shows that in Greece most such firms are actually low-tech and catering for the domestic market (Kastelli and Zografakis 2017).

Addressing the sluggish growth in productivity and the loss of international markets is an arduous task at the best of times. It requires the sort of sustained effort and broad support for reforms that has always been in short supply in the adversarial climate of Greek politics. With hindsight, the long years of political stability and fast growth before the crisis was the ideal time to try. But as we all know, those years were wasted. The odds of such an endeavour under the harsher conditions of austerity, notwithstanding brave talk by PM George Papandreou ('We either change or sink'), were considerably longer.

Structural reform as practised in Greece was certainly part of the problem. Labour market deregulation had the intended effect of depressing the earnings and weakening the position of workers in private firms (though it left virtually intact the privileges of labour market insiders). But product market liberalization, although potentially more promising,[20] was pursued with less determination, failing to break the stranglehold of business interests over large parts of the Greek economy.[21]

All this pointed towards an emerging growth regime based on lower wages and lower skills. This was likely to prove contentious on social and

[19] See Regini (2016). The classic works in this tradition are Bagnasco (1977) and Trigilia (1986). See also Piore and Sabel (1984) on flexible specialization.

[20] Barnes et al. (2011) have estimated that moving to the OECD average in terms of labour market regulation could raise real GDP per person in Greece by 6 per cent, while a similar move in terms of product market regulation could add as much as 22 per cent. As argued in a recent IMF report (2016: 121): 'Product market reforms should be implemented forcefully, as they boost output even under weak macroeconomic conditions and would not worsen public finances. In contrast, narrowing unemployment benefits and easing job protections should be accompanied by other policies to offset their short-term cost; alternatively, they might even be grandfathered or be enacted with their implementation deferred until a (suitably defined) better time arrives'.

[21] On the trials and tribulations of attempts to reform product markets in Greece, see Katsoulakos et al. (2017). As argued by Ioannides and Pissarides (2015): 'Labour market reforms have been given greater priority in Greece than product market reforms, mistakenly in our view. Whether this was because successive Greek governments found it easier to reform labour markets than product markets or because the Troika insisted on them is a moot point' (p. 364). In contrast, Hassel (2014), having approvingly remarked on the 'intuitive understanding of where political veto points are rooted in the Greek political economy' as revealed in 'anecdotal evidence gathered from conversations with German policy-makers', goes on to explain that 'economic adjustment programmes, for instance in Greece, contain measures on labour market deregulation, not because there is an expectation that these measures will improve competitiveness, but because policy-makers in the Troika believe that the protection and compensation mechanisms must be broken for the effectiveness of financial transfers' (pp. 30–1).

political grounds, and questionable on economic grounds. The notion that Greece might improve its export performance by wresting back traditional industries lost to emerging economies in the 1970s and 1980s looked hardly plausible.

As for the alternative strategy, aiming for a high-skill high-wage equilibrium, it was not just difficult to reconcile with fiscal consolidation – it was also incompatible with the defence of vested interests so dear to Greek political elites. Successive governments failed to elaborate (let alone put in practice) such a strategy, and passively resisted some of its elements when these were actually proposed by the Troika. In the frantic scramble for fiscal savings, and in a political culture obsessed with loss aversion, the search for a higher equilibrium was quietly pushed aside, if ever seriously considered at all.

The battle of ideas

As now seems clear, the old growth regime created a certain sort of prosperity, spread widely though unequally. That gave rise to a broad coalition of political, social and economic actors[22] in its support: business interests lobbying politicians for access to lucrative public procurement contracts; labour unions in state-owned enterprises happily extracting rents; middle-class professionals accustomed to evading taxes; all cheered on by a chorus of sensationalist media.[23] Perhaps the real paradox of the Greek crisis was the resilience of that coalition in defence of a growth regime destined for extinction.

The opposing coalition was soon to prove a poor match. It rested on an assortment of progressive modernizers, leftist reformists, moderate greens, centrist liberals – all minor political traditions in a country like Greece. Furthermore, the social coalition they were meant to inspire (of honest hard-working public officials, of ingenious entrepreneurs hoping to succeed through grit alone and of sensible labour unions keen to protect the interests of workers without endangering the dynamism of the firms on which their livelihood depended) by and large failed to materialize.

---

[22] As Lucio Baccaro and Jonas Pontusson (2016: 200) have put it, 'growth models rest on and are supported by clearly identifiable "social blocs", that is, coalitions of social forces, typically straddling the class divide, that can legitimately claim to represent the "national interest"'. See also the paper by Hope and Soskice (2016) in the same volume.

[23] For a vivid account of the gradual shift in attention on the part of Greek policy makers away from firms producing tradeable goods towards the sheltered non-tradeables sector, see Doxiades (2013). For an analysis of how interest groups, far from being the servants of political parties, as the standard view had it, eventually became their masters, distorting decision making and preventing policy adjustment, see Iordanoglou (2013).

Would-be reformers were eventually defeated – but not before they put up a decent fight, especially in the realm of ideas. They argued that the Greek growth regime was indefensible on economic, environmental, social and political grounds. Austerity was not the cause of the Greek crisis, but its inevitable effect. Denouncing austerity as a neoliberal scam, or as yet another German ploy for world domination, was pathetic (though electorally successful). The progressive option in 2010 was to try to win the hearts and minds of Greek citizens with a home-grown programme aimed to restore fiscal balances while protecting vulnerable groups, tackle the clientelism and corruption at the root of the fiscal crisis, and lay the ground for a sustainable recovery.

In spite of appearances, that option had impeccable progressive credentials: it drew inspiration from a famous response to another crisis, in the late 1970s, when Enrico Berlinguer, the Italian Communist Party leader, openly rejected rampant consumerism and widespread waste, welcoming austerity as an occasion to transform his country (Berlinguer 1977). But a programme of renewal *via* equitable austerity in Greece in the 2010s never made it to the main political arena.

The rest is history. The austerity programme that was eventually adopted was not put together by a reforming government with a popular mandate, but was dictated by international agencies widely viewed as unaccountable; and it reflected the preferences (and prejudices) of the prevailing orthodoxy, not those of a progressive coalition for national renewal. The 'Greek programme' was rightly seen as externally imposed – bitterly resisted by most, reluctantly accepted by some, but never owned with any conviction by political actors at home. The resulting loss of national sovereignty was widely experienced as humiliating, and fed a nationalist-populist backlash which soon poisoned domestic politics. While the country's creditors demanded more austerity, the recession morphed into a social crisis, which caused political unrest, and in turn made the recession deeper than it might have been.

Social costs

The anti-austerity coalition that won the January 2015 general election had amassed considerable political capital by denouncing the country's 'humanitarian crisis' (its preferred term for the social situation in Greece) when in opposition. But closer inspection pointed to a more nuanced picture.

The social impact of the recession and the austerity really was significant. The employment rate fell from 61.4 per cent in 2008 to 48.8

per cent in 2013, undoing in five years the progress of the previous two decades and more (it had stood at 53.7 per cent in 1992). By 2015, it had merely returned to its 2012 level (50.8 per cent). For those still in employment, average gross earnings of all employees in 2014 were 8.4 per cent below their 2000 level and 25.4 per cent below their pre-crisis peak (in 2009). Low pay especially affected the overlapping categories of newly hired and young workers (median reported earnings down by 34.2 per cent and 34.8 per cent respectively in real terms in 2010–14). In contrast, the median earnings of those who kept their job with the same employer declined less (9.6 per cent). Because of the rising tax pressure, earnings losses were even more pronounced in net terms.

As median incomes tumbled, the relative poverty rate went up by less than might have been expected (from 20.1 per cent in 2009 to 23.1 per cent in 2012, falling to 21.4 per cent in 2014). Still, the severe material deprivation rate almost doubled, from 11.0 per cent in 2009 to 21.5 per cent in 2014 (when the EU-28 average was 9.0 per cent). Both rich and poor ended up with far less income at the depth of the recession than they earned pre-crisis, but losses were greater at the bottom of the distribution. As a result, inequality went up (measured by the S80/S20 income quintile share ratio: from 5.6 in 2009 to 6.5 in 2014).

Income losses might have been less painful if the victims of the recession could at least rely on the public provision of health care and other vital social services. In fact, given the extent of waste and inefficiency before the crisis, it would not have been impossible to cut costs, and at the same time maintain an adequate quantity and quality of service. As it turned out, the opposite happened: funding cuts were often indiscriminate, reforms were disruptive and/or imposed higher user costs, suppliers reacted to payment arrears by withholding supplies, industrial action contributed to the general unreliability of public provision, and some public sector workers reacted to wage cuts by reducing effort. As a result, the cost of adjustment was passed on to users of public services.

The 2015 change in government hardly made a difference to all that. The much-awaited social programme of the anti-austerity coalition proved something of an anti-climax. Legislation on 'immediate measures to fight the humanitarian crisis' actually boiled down to three modest schemes of social assistance, for a limited number of beneficiaries (Matsaganis 2017). The resources set aside to pay for these schemes amounted to a small fraction of the previous government's policies, rightly criticized as inadequate.

The welfare state

In principle, a well-designed system of social protection should be able to mitigate the social effects of an economic crisis. In practice, it is probably fair to say that the depth and duration of the Greek crisis, including mass joblessness, would have posed insurmountable challenges to any welfare state, even the most advanced. But the configuration of the Greek welfare state, in spite of rising social spending pre-crisis, was so dysfunctional that it rendered it particularly unfit for the challenge. When the crisis hit, there was little to prevent the hundreds of thousands of families suffering losses in terms of jobs and/or earnings from falling into poverty. The welfare state generally failed to support the living standards of vulnerable groups.

In relative terms (as a share of GDP), expenditure on social protection grew to 31.6 per cent in 2012, i.e. well above the EU-28 average (28.6 per cent). But in absolute terms (per head of population, in fixed prices), social spending peaked in 2009. In 2012–14, as the cuts in social protection under fiscal consolidation took effect, social spending fell faster than GDP. Not all policy areas fared equally. Pensions expenditure continued its upward trend to reach 17.9 per cent of GDP in 2015 (from 14.6 per cent in 2009), as the effect of rising numbers of pensioners more than offset that of nominal benefit cuts (which were certainly non-negligible). More than had hitherto been the case, the growth in pensions spending crowded out other components of Greek welfare.

In other words, as the demand for social protection rose because of the recession, its supply fell because of the austerity.[24] The diminished capacity of the welfare state to respond to increased need can be seen most clearly in the area of income support for the unemployed. Between 2010 and 2014, as the number of jobless workers doubled (from 624,000 to 1.27 million), the number of unemployment benefit recipients *decreased* (from 226,000 to 155,000). As a result, the coverage rate fell dramatically, from 36.2 per cent to 12.7 per cent of all jobless workers.[25]

Was this inevitable? By benefiting large sections of the electorate,

---

[24] Dølvik and Martin, among others, have argued that 'the gaps in the eurozone's economic governance institutions left it without the instruments to cope with the crisis' (2014: 386). Nevertheless, as pointed out by Starke et al. (2014: 234): 'In highly developed welfare states, much of the stabilization happens behind the backs of political actors when automatic stabilizers are "quietly doing their thing"'. As shown by Dolls et al. (2012: 289), 'automatic stabilizers in Eastern and Southern European countries are much weaker than in the rest of Europe'.

[25] It is hard to reconcile this evidence with the claim of Blanchard et al. (2014: 20) that, under IMF advice, unemployment benefit coverage in Greece "expanded"'.

social programmes help create coalitions in favour of the *status quo* (Pierson 2001). In Greece, social protection pre-crisis was so fragmented and wasteful that it left considerable scope for simultaneous progress on efficiency as well as equity. Nevertheless, since 2010 policy makers have done little to mend holes in the social safety net. The rationing of resources (now scarcer than ever) by political influence, rather than by need for social protection, has reaffirmed itself as the guiding principle behind the exercise of social policy in Greece. Defenders of the *status quo*, from labour unions in public utilities to professional associations (judges, engineers, medics) with good connections to the political establishment, have been quite successful in deflecting losses. As a result, the bulk of fiscal consolidation has fallen on less powerful categories (private sector employees, own-account workers), leaving little space for policies aimed at protecting the real victims of the recession (the unemployed, the poor).

Concluding remarks

Where does the anti-austerity bloc fit in all that? Mostly in denying the significance of anything structural as a possible explanation of the crisis, in favour of a simple narrative of 'corrupt elites vs. the pure people'. In particular, the meteoric rise of Greece's radical left from the margins of the political system to ruling party captured the imagination of many progressives worldwide, filling them with hope that change is possible. (It also incidentally proved beyond doubt that Greek democracy, for all its failings, works largely as intended.)

At the time of writing, with a quarter of the workforce out of work, the economy once again in recession, and capital controls still in force, prospects for an early exit from the Greek crisis looked grim. While anti-austerity economists and policy makers emphasized debt relief and fiscal expansion as keys to recovery and job creation, it seemed highly unlikely that Greece could move to a sustainable growth path without the kind of reforms that SYRIZA and its allies had made their political fortune out of resisting.

Acknowledgements

My research on the political economy of the Greek crisis originated in the fall term 2014–15, when I was a visiting scholar at the Center for European Studies, Harvard. Receipt of a Fulbright Foundation scholarship that made it possible is gratefully acknowledged. Earlier versions of this essay were presented at seminars and conferences at Harvard, Yale, Wellesley, Varese, Cagliari, Moncalieri and Paris. I thank participants for comments and suggestions, in particular Deborah Mabbett, Andrew Martin, Waltraud Schelkle and Vivien Schmidt for extensive discussions. Special thanks for detailed comments on previous drafts are due to Olivier Bouin, Manuel Castells, Michel Wieviorka, and to my Greek colleagues Christos Genakos, Chrysafis Iordanoglou, Vassilis Pesmazoglou, Dimitris Sotiropoulos and Panos Tsakloglou. The usual disclaimer applies.

References

Alcidi, C. and Gros, D. (2012) Why is the Greek economy collapsing? A simple tale of high multipliers and low exports. CEPS Commentary (21 December). Brussels: Centre for European Policy Studies.

Arkolakis, C., Doxiadis, A. and Galenianos, M. (2017) The challenge of trade adjustment in Greece. In Meghir, C., Pissarides, C., Vayanos, D. and Vettas, N. (eds) *Crisis in the Eurozone: Policy Options for Greece*. Cambridge, MA: MIT Press.

Artavanis, N., Morse, A. and Tsoutsoura, M. (2016) Measuring income tax evasion using bank credit: evidence from Greece. *The Quarterly Journal of Economics* 131(2): 739–98.

Baccaro, L. and Pontusson, J. (2016) Rethinking comparative political economy: the growth model perspective. *Politics & Society* 44(2): 175–207.

Bagnasco, A. (1977) *Tre Italie: la problematica territoriale dello sviluppo italiano*. Bologna: Il Mulino.

Baldwin, R. and Gros, D. (2015) What caused the eurozone crisis? CEPS Commentary (27 November). Brussels: Centre for European Policy Studies.

Baldwin, R., Beck, T., Bénassy-Quéré, A., Blanchard, O., Corsetti, G., de Grauwe, P., den Haan, W., Giavazzi F., Gros D., Kalemli-Ozcan S., Micossi S., Papaioannou E., Pesenti P., Pissarides C., Tabellini G. and Weder di Mauro, B. (2015) Rebooting the eurozone: step I – agreeing a crisis narrative. CEPR Policy Insight no. 85. London: Centre for Economic Policy Research.

Barnes, S., Bouis, R., Briard, P., Dougherty, S. and Eris, M. (2011) The GDP impact of reform: a simple simulation framework. Economics Department Working Paper No. 834. Paris: OECD.

Berlinguer, E. (1977) *Austerità occasione per trasformare l'Italia*. Rome: Editori Riuniti.

Blanchard, O. and Leigh, D. (2013) Growth forecast errors and fiscal multipliers. IMF Working Paper 13/1. Washington, DC: International Monetary Fund.

Blanchard, O.J., Jaumotte, F. and Loungani, P. (2014) Labor market policies and IMF advice in advanced economies during the Great Recession. *IZA Journal of Labor Policy* 3(2): 1–23.

Blyth, M. (2013) *Austerity: The History of a Dangerous Idea*. Oxford: Oxford University Press.

Dolls, M., Fuest, C. and Peichl, A. (2012) Automatic stabilizers and economic crisis: US vs. Europe. *Journal of Public Economics* 96: 279–94.

Dølvik, J.E. and Martin, A. (eds) (2014) *European Social Models from Crisis to Crisis: Employment and Inequality in the Era of Monetary Integration.* Oxford: Oxford University Press.

Doxiades, A. (2013) *The Invisible Divide: Institutions and Attitudes in the Greek Economy.* Athens: Icaros (in Greek).

Dyson, K. (2014) *States, Debt, and Power: 'Saints' and 'Sinners' in European History and Integration.* Oxford: Oxford University Press.

European Commission (2011) *The Economic Adjustment Programme for Greece* (third review, winter 2011). European Economy Occasional Papers no. 77. Directorate General for Economic and Financial Affairs. Luxembourg: Office for Official Publications of the European Communities.

European Commission (2015) *Annual Report on European SMEs 2014–2015: SMEs start hiring again.* Luxembourg: Publications Office of the European Union.

Hall, P. (2015) How growth regimes evolve in the developed democracies. Paper presented at the 22nd International Conference of Europeanists, Paris, 8–10 July.

Hassel, A. (2014) Adjustments in the eurozone: varieties of capitalism and the crisis in Southern Europe. LEQS Paper No. 76/2014. LSE 'Europe in Question' Discussion Paper Series. The London School of Economics and Political Science.

Hope, D. and Soskice, D. (2016) Growth models, variety of capitalism and macroeconomics. *Politics & Society* 44(2): 209–26.

IMF (2010a) *Greece.* Country Report no. 10/110. Washington, DC: International Monetary Fund.

IMF (2010b) *Greece.* Country Report no. 10/227. Washington, DC: International Monetary Fund.

IMF (2014a) *Ireland.* Country Report no. 14/165. Washington, DC: International Monetary Fund.

IMF (2014b) *World Economic Outlook Database* (October). Washington, DC: International Monetary Fund.

IMF (2015) *Fiscal monitor – Now is the time: fiscal policies for sustainable growth* (April). Washington, DC: International Monetary Fund.

IMF (2016) *World Economic Outlook: too slow for too long* (April). Washington, DC: International Monetary Fund.

Ioannides, Y.M. and Pissarides, C.A. (2015) Is the Greek debt crisis one of supply or demand? *Brookings Papers on Economic Activity* Fall, 349–73.

Iordanoglou, C. (2011) The bailout agreement: a post-mortem. *Athens Review of Books* 24 (December) (in Greek).

Iordanoglou, C. (2013) *State and Interest Groups.* Athens: Polis (in Greek).

Kastelli, I. and Zografakis, S. (2017) Industrial competitiveness and the search for a sustainable path out of the crisis: lessons from the Greek experience. In Hanappi, H., Katsikides, S. and Scholz-Wäckerle, M. (eds) *Evolutionary Political Economy in Action.* Abingdon: Routledge.

Katsoulakos, Y., Genakos, C. and Houpis, G. (2017) Product market regulation and competitiveness: towards a national competition and competitiveness policy for Greece. In Meghir, C., Pissarides, C., Vayanos, D. and Vettas, N.

(eds) *Crisis in the Eurozone: Policy Options for Greece*. Cambridge, MA: MIT Press.

Mabbett, D. and Schelkle, W. (2015) What difference does euro membership make to stabilization? The political economy of international monetary systems revisited. *Review of International Political Economy* 22(3): 508–34.

Matsaganis, M. (2014) The catastrophic Greek crisis. *Current History* 113(761): 110–16.

Matsaganis, M. (2016) To the brink and back in Greece. *Current History* 115(779): 108–13.

Matsaganis, M. (2017) The impact of the Great Recession on child poverty in Greece. In Cantillon, B., Chzhen, Y., Handa, S. and Nolan, B. (eds) *Children of Austerity: Impact of the Great Recession on Child Poverty in Rich Countries*. Oxford: Oxford University Press.

Matsaganis, M., Leventi, C. and Flevotomou, M. (2012) The crisis and tax evasion in Greece: what are the distributional implications? *CESifo Forum* 13(2): 26–32.

OECD (2011) *Economic Surveys: Greece*. Paris: Organisation for Economic Co-operation and Development.

Papaconstantinou, G. (2016) *Game Over: The Inside Story of the Greek Crisis*. Athens: Papadopoulos.

Pierson, P. (2001) *The New Politics of the Welfare State*. Oxford: Oxford University Press.

Piore, M. and Sabel, C. (1984) *The Second Industrial Divide: Possibilities for Prosperity*. New York: Basic Books.

Regini, M. (2016) Mediterranean capitalism: a narrow path between the core eurozone economies and the deregulated ones. *Sociologia del lavoro* 19: 25–43 (in Italian).

Sandbu, M. (2015) *Europe's Orphan: The Future of the Euro and the Politics of Debt*. Princeton, NJ: Princeton University Press.

Slemrod, J. (2007) Cheating ourselves: the economics of tax evasion. *Journal of Economic Perspectives* 21(1): 25–48.

Slemrod, J. and Yitzhaki, S. (2002) Tax avoidance, evasion, and administration. In Auerbach, A.J. and Feldstein, M. (eds) *Handbook of Public Economics*. Amsterdam: Elsevier.

Starke, P., Kaasch, A. and van Hooren, F. (2014) Political parties and social policy responses to global economic crises: constrained partisanship in mature welfare states. *Journal of Social Policy* 43: 225–46.

Trigilia, C. (1986) *Grandi partiti e piccole imprese*. Bologna: Il Mulino.

Chapter 3

The Consequences of Crisis for the European Banking System

Emilio Ontiveros

Introduction

From the outset, a crisis initiated outside of Europe revealed the enormous limitations of the European Monetary Union. The inability of European authorities and institutions to manage the crisis, at least as quickly and pragmatically as it was managed in the US financial system where it originated, exacerbated its effects.

The crisis in the eurozone was essentially of a banking nature. The trigger was the 'American contagion', the extent of the lack of confidence in banking assets. Especially affected were banks with substantial real estate assets. In the beginning, the crisis was not just a crisis of public finances. The initial conduits of contagion were the interbank markets. The initial manifestation was a 'credit crunch'. The bank wholesale funding markets were blocked, especially for those banks belonging to the periphery of the currency area. Lending to small and medium enterprises (SMEs), those more dependent on bank financing, dried up. Financial fragmentation was dominant in the eurozone, questioning one of the basic principles of any monetary union. The regions with the most banking-oriented financial systems would suffer the impact of a foreign crisis more severely than the epicentre.

The combination of these banking problems with subsequent tensions in government bond markets, especially in the weakest peripheral economies, fuelled a 'diabolical loop' with serious consequences, to the point of questioning the viability of the currency area, or at least the capacity of the smaller economies to stay in it. The solutions rested on extensive rescue packages that weakened the financial position of the treasuries involved, and a radical change in the ECB's monetary policy from the summer of 2012. This did not prevent the crisis from spreading, with slowing economic growth in the monetary area, large increases in unemployment and widening inequality in income distribution.

The implementation of inadequate macroeconomic policies, especially those centred on severe and highly pro-cyclical fiscal austerity, did nothing but exacerbate actual economic deterioration and hamper financial restructuring. Interbank activity contracted, while defining the road to the Banking Union intensified pressures towards concentration inside the peripheral banking systems (Berges and Ontiveros 2014).

The result, nine years after the emergence of the crisis, is a European banking system that has not been able to reignite finance to SMEs, while some doubts still persist on the soundness and financial stability of some European banking systems.

Regarding SME finance, it is true that the horizon of 'Capital Market Union' by President Juncker tries to mitigate this overdependence on bank financing instruments and institutionally diversified financial systems in Europe, though it will not be easy to realize such a purpose in the short term. In terms of banking soundness, the eurozone will continue to be vulnerable to episodes of instability in some banking systems, prolonging the crisis convalescence. Recent developments at banks in some countries (Italy, Portugal or even Germany) are a reminder that such a convalescence is here, and will not be over soon.

The financial system before the crisis

The severity of the financial crisis in the eurozone, as well as the vicious circle that developed in the sovereign debt markets, can be mostly attributed to the institutional structure of the financial system.

Traditional literature on banking systems distinguishes between financial systems highly biased towards the banking channel (*banking-oriented*) as a mechanism for financing the economy, compared to systems more biased towards directly channelling funds through capital markets (*market-oriented*). The eurozone financial system is a clear example of the banking-oriented model, in contrast to the US, as the paradigm of a market-oriented financial system. Total banking assets in the eurozone amount to three times GDP, while in the US the ratio is less than one. In the European currency area, banks provide more than 70 per cent of external financing to businesses, while capital markets supplied the remaining third. In the US, however, those proportions are reversed (Berges and Ontiveros 2014).

More indicators are not needed to illustrate the differential importance of the size of banking systems in the eurozone and understand the significance that banking crises have for the real economy or simply the difficulties of this sector to perform the tasks of financial intermediation, essential in any economy.

Besides that, the overall European banking system was overleveraged (or undercapitalized), and the overall equity was unable to absorb the shock brought about by the 2007 crisis. It is striking to note that not only the periphery banks have a low capital or equity ratio (capital plus reserves). Prior to the sovereign debt crisis, the banks in the South and in the North of the eurozone had very similar equity ratios (as a percentage of assets). This fact has been illustrated in De Grauwe and Ji (2013) to show the incentive for banks to issue debt instead of equity, especially for banks from countries with low public debt and good credit rating. Indeed, when the sovereign debt crisis emerged and fragmentation appeared in the bond market, the difference in equity was against the banks from the North. In 2012, De Grauwe and Ji (2013) show that banks in the northern eurozone have capital ratios that are, on average, less than half of the capital ratios of banks in the eurozone's periphery. The reason: 'northern eurozone banks profit from the financial solidity of their governments and follow business strategies aimed at issuing to much subsidised debt' (p. 1). This reflects the 'too big to fail' syndrome, according to Admati and Hellwing (2013), the main proponents of higher capital ratios at banks. As De Grauwe and Ji (2013) expressed, 'Large banks profit from an implicit guarantee from their governments that will not allow these institutions to fail. As a result of this guarantee, banks can issue . . . cheap debt . . . to avoid issuing equity that does not profit from government guarantees' (p. 2).

The evolution of financial systems during the crisis has not been homogeneous. When measured as assets relative to GDP, the banking system contracted slightly between 2008 and 2014 in two of the larger economies, Germany and Spain, as is reflected in figure 3.1. It remained broadly unchanged in Italy, while it increased in France and the Netherlands. The size of the financial industry over the same period contracted in Austria, Belgium, Cyprus and Ireland, while it tended to increase slightly in Greece, mainly due to a contraction in GDP. Over the period 2008–14, the share of the banking industry tended to decline across most countries. Only in Spain, Portugal and Greece did it remain broadly unchanged or increase slightly over the period, while it remained broadly unchanged in the rest of the smaller economies (see figure 3.2).

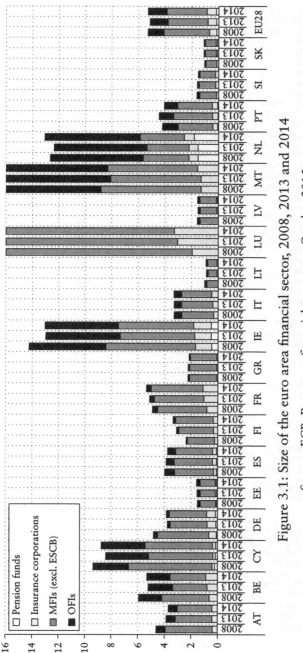

Figure 3.1: Size of the euro area financial sector, 2008, 2013 and 2014

Source: ECB, Report on financial structures, October 2015

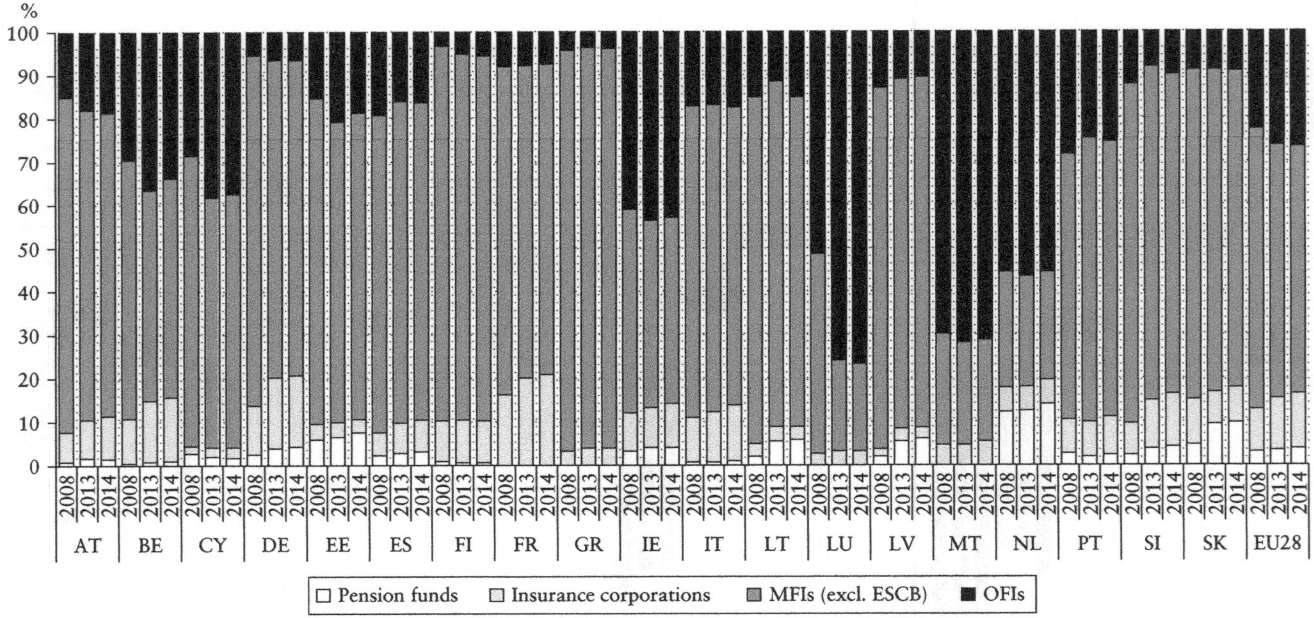

Figure 3.2: Composition of the euro area financial sector, 2008, 2013 and 2014

Source: ECB, Report on financial structures, October 2015

The context of the crisis

To understand the severity of the financial crisis in Europe, it is necessary to put it in the context of trends that developed in the previous decade. In the years preceding the crisis, the financial systems in the main developed economies had significantly grown in size and had become increasingly interconnected. The dynamic of financial innovation was very intensive, and the dominant assumption was that 'The Great Moderation' – the long period of macroeconomic stability in most advanced economies that began in the mid-1980s of the last century – would not end the adaptive orientation of monetary policies, translated into low interest rates and incentives for private debt. Banks also found sources of generation surplus by investing in long-term debt while relying on short-term finance, with the attendant problems of maturity transformation. There were significant financial incentives to innovation, as well as the creation of complex financial products. Financial integration progressed, not only within Europe but also with growing global projection. As a corollary to the above, risk-taking by banks, including systemic ones, sharply increased.

Supervisors were behind that dynamic, without enough control in many cases. It was largely the result of too much complacency about the ability of financial markets to stabilize without intervention. Even Alan Greenspan, the president of the Federal Reserve, admitted the desirability of self-regulation of financial operators. Now we have sufficient evidence about the inadequacies of regulations and policies to identify and calibrate the risks of such dynamics by the authorities in key financial systems. The supervisory institutions maintained a fundamentally domestic focus, while cross-border banking, integration and interdependence advanced.

Despite the fragmentation generated by the crisis, the interdependence between financial systems in the eurozone remains important, especially among the four big economies (Germany, France, Italy and Spain), reflecting largely the size of their banking systems. Some of the eurozone economies eventually became heavily dependent on external financing, defining a savings gap and consequently a deficit in the current account of the balance of payments. Much of that debt was inside the eurozone: in fact, the net financing position was balanced in the area as a whole.

The meaning of the crisis

Banks and sovereigns: a diabolic loop

The emergence of the crisis also revealed the links between banking and risks of public debt, especially in the eurozone where the consequences for the real economy were more pronounced. For that reason, the impact of the recession was particularly adverse on public revenues and on public budgets deficits; in addition, many governments had to commit large amounts of public funds to support the banking system. In this context, the application of budgetary austerity measures deepened the recession; the loss of household wealth and unemployment were rising to unknown heights.

Until the summer of 2012, when the president of the ECB warned of his willingness to intervene in financial markets in order to reassure the integrity of the eurozone, interest rates on the public debt of Spain and Italy exceeded more than seven basis points than that of Germany – a situation not very much expressive of integration and, to a greater extent, of neglect about the attention to some public debt markets which, unlike what happened in the US or UK, assumed that European institutions were unwilling to defend the most vulnerable economies. The ECB had remained passive until that moment. The statement by Draghi – 'I will do whatever it takes' – to correct the financial markets, marked a turning point in the management of the crisis in the eurozone, at which point the ECB's policies were close to those applied by the Federal Reserve and the Bank of England. They were actions no longer aimed at effectively managing the crisis, but to save the euro from collapse. Besides interest rate reductions, the ECB began to implement quantitative easing decisions, buying public and corporate debt.

Financial fragmentation

A financial market is considered fully integrated when agents, regardless of their nationality or residence, have access to it on equal footing, a condition violated manifestly during the crisis. The ECB (2016) assumed a key role in strengthening financial integration. In their own words, 'financial integration fosters a smooth and balanced transmission of monetary policy throughout the euro area. In addition, it is relevant for financial stability and is among the reasons behind the eurosystem's task of promoting well-functioning payment systems'.[1]

---

[1] For further details of indicators and metrics about the financial integration of Europe, see Baele et al. (2004).

The global financial crisis was preceded by a long period of strong growth of cross-border financial transactions and high correlation in asset prices that could be considered expressive of an increase in the degree of financial integration. This took place in a context of under-estimation of price and solvency risks as the proper extent of the crisis became apparent. Money markets, meanwhile, reached a high degree of integration thanks to the role played by the Trans-European Automated Real-time Gross Settlement Express Transfer System (TARGET). Also in the public debt market before the sovereign debt crisis, the bonds issued by different governments reached similar interest rates.

The financial fragmentation that developed in the eurozone, especially between 2007 and 2012, was the clearest symptom of crisis mismanagement, until the ECB decided to act. In 2012 the ECB warned that public debt markets were questioning the viability of the currency area and showed a willingness to act accordingly. The definition of the horizon of the Banking Union, in particular the allocation to the ECB's monitoring mechanism, and the implementation of the OMT (Outright Monetary Transactions), avoided the worst outcomes that tempered the prices of Spanish and Italian bonds, and stock prices of banks. It was the implementation of this last policy that restored the financial stability in the area.

The crisis was a major setback in the dynamics of financial integration. Fragmentation was especially visible in the wholesale funding markets, where banks tried to raise finance from other financial institutions, and in the public debt market. A simultaneous process generalized the movement of 'back to home' in most financial institutions. The result was a new national compartmentalization of the financial activity of unknown dimensions long before the birth of the single currency: a result that seriously questioned integration in the monetary area.

As the ECB (2016) said, the re-integration trend that followed substantial financial fragmentation associated with the financial and sovereign debt crises between 2007 and 2011 took off when the European Banking Union and the European Central Bank's OMT framework was announced in the summer of 2012. It continued when two important pillars of the banking union started to operate, the Single Supervisory Mechanism (SSM), which was assigned to the ECB in 2014, and the establishment of a Single Resolution Mechanism (SRM) in late 2015. Also, further measures from ECB monetary policy very much supported this trend. Figure 3.3 shows the overall development of euro area financial integration since the 1990s, as reflected in a price-based and quantity-based cross-market indicator of overall financial integration (called financial integration composites, or FINTECs).

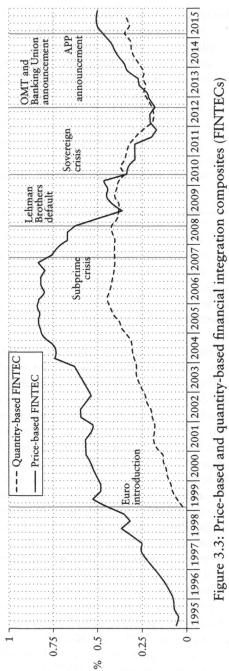

Figure 3.3: Price-based and quantity-based financial integration composites (FINTECs)

Source: ECB and ECB calculations.

Reactions to the crisis

The crisis made a virtue of necessity and intensified the dynamics of integration in some areas. The most notable case was the acceleration of plans for the creation of the Banking Union. It has also acted as a leading factor to correct the excessive degree of banking in the continent and, consequently, the provision of a specific agenda for the creation of a Capital Markets Union (CMU).

Legacies of the crisis

The legacy of the crisis, is, however, still visible in terms of structural deficiencies. Most importantly, the persistence of high non-performing loans (NPLs) underlines the need in several euro area countries to take further steps to tackle this problem in order to free up capital and boost bank credit expansion (ECB 2015). This helps to explain the cost-cutting efforts by euro area banks.

Virtue of necessity: the Banking Union

The severe incidence of the crisis in some banking systems of the eurozone periphery accelerated plans to advance the realization of a more consistent financial architecture within the monetary union. It was in June 2012 when the main objective was defined: to break the link between sovereign debt and the banking system. The special virulence of the Spanish crisis was an important determinant of that decision, as was the role of the IMF who presented an integral view of the problems of the Spanish banking system. As Véron (2016) highlights, 'it was the first public authority to articulate a clear vision of the Banking Union as an essential policy response, building on its longstanding and pioneering support of banking policy integration in the European Union. EU institutions, including the ECB, did not generally have the skills, nor the experience and the mandate that would have enabled them to offset the national authorities' shortcomings. The IMF was thus in a position to make a major positive difference'.

From the foundations of a 'single rule book', the Banking Union defined a single monitoring and resolution mechanism of the banking crisis. The latter has been subject to the tensions that had been observed during the crisis, in particular the reluctance of the central economies, notably Germany. It is also the case with the third pillar, the European Deposit Insurance Scheme (EDIS), designed to mutualize resources in order to protect banking deposits in the eurozone.

The first pillar of the Banking Union is the Single Supervisory Mechanism (SSM), which transfers key supervisory tasks on banks in the euro area, and other participating Member States, to the ECB. In November 2014, bank supervision in the euro area was transferred from the national competent authorities (NCAs) to the SSM, comprising the ECB and the NCAs of the participating countries. The European Banking Authority (EBA) coordinated national supervisors and gave those powers to the ECB, while preserving its responsibility for the development of the 'single rule book'. Supervision in the Banking Union is performed under a dual scheme: directly by the ECB to the 'significant banks' (123 so far), and indirectly by the NCAs (under coordination with ECB) to the remaining banks (around 4,500).

The foundation of the Banking Union, although late, has been a breakthrough in the necessary strengthening of monetary union. Still, there are essential aspects pending fulfilment, such as a common fiscal backstop reinforcing the Single Resolution Fund, as well as a common EDIS. In the absence of such backstop, there is a risk that in a crisis, national authorities themselves would have to support banks established in their jurisdictions, leading to the re-emergence of the sovereign bank risk loop and financial fragmentation.

The Capital Market Union

On 28 January 2015, the European Commission announced its project to create a Capital Markets Union (CMU) with a target horizon set at the end of 2019. European authorities are committed to achieving a basic objective of a sound economic policy: linking economic growth with channelling savings to productive uses. That should mean financial systems in which there are more financing and investment options, and better returns for investors and savers.

It is assumed that the best way to achieve this is the creation of a single capital market to enable further sharing of risks across borders, creating deeper and liquid markets and diversifying sources of financing of the economy. All of this should strengthen financial integration and enhance the growth and competitiveness in the medium term.

The CMU aims to create a single market for equity for all EU Member States (this is an important difference from the Banking Union in which only eurozone countries are participating, at least in the initial setting) by removing barriers to cross-border investment and lower costs of funding within the EU. The premise is that well-functioning capital markets will facilitate the mobilization of private financing, reducing the dependence on the banking sector.

For the purpose of serving a greater role in direct finance to companies, the European Commission and the ECB agree. Both are based on the diagnosis that the crisis has had a differential severity in the eurozone, and its management has been slower and more complex, precisely because of this lack of alternative channels to bank financing, from the bond markets, to the various forms of equity or various routes of asset securitization.

The contraction in bank credit was indeed the most explicit signal of the crisis in the eurozone. Its persistence and severity for several years after the crisis emerged, compared to the speed with which the US overcame it, can to a large extent be attributed to such a credit contraction. Business financial asphyxia, especially in SMEs, and prolonging low rates of economic growth and employment continue to contrast with the results observed in the US, the epicentre of the crisis.

A lower dependence of companies' finance on bank debt would help to better resist crisis episodes. But diversification of funding sources is also necessary for business development, to finance the birth of companies and the growth of those of smaller dimension. It is necessary for start-ups, with higher risks but also a greater chance of growth or productivity contribution, to find funding for their projects, even if this funding did not have banking origin. Likewise, a single capital market to remove any barriers to cross-border investment could result in lower financing costs for smaller companies.

Additionally, another basic aim of CMU is to facilitate financing to infrastructure projects that make up the other major objective of the Juncker Plan. To this end, the European Commission intends to ease some of the restrictions on investment in certain types of infrastructure in the regulation of insurance companies and pension funds.

Regulatory amendments are equally necessary to enable savers to have more options in mobilizing savings, specifically to increase the preference of individual investors for equity markets, also very low compared with the US. In fact, the proportion of individual investors in the EU among all shareholders is below half of what it was in the 1970s. The lack of confidence in those markets requires increasing transparency and harmonizes standards of accountability of listed companies.

Action may also be necessary in the taxation of the EU, harmonizing capital income or reducing disincentives associated with double taxation. Regulatory differences on insolvency proceedings are another area to homogenize. Last but not least, the development of capital markets requires macro prudential structures, both at the national and EU levels, that must be able to adequately react to episodes of instability in the capital markets.

In order to set up a clear and credible 'road map', the European Council defined to the Commission a series of short-term priorities among which are impulses to financing through venture capital funds, as well as supporting new modalities of 'crowd funding' and other alternative finance vehicles that can help support small and high growth businesses, all this while preserving the very necessary investor protection. In fact, the role of non-bank intermediaries is growing after the crisis, largely because of 'convalescence' and regulatory adaptation of commercial banks.

It will certainly take time before bank-based finance stops being dominant in Europe, especially for small businesses. However, that horizon of further development and integration of capital markets is a reference. It is obvious that the most favourable impact from major funding possibilities would take place in the less diversified financial systems. Now it would be beneficial if national authorities assume the intensification of issuer and investor education in the capital markets, the full knowledge of their rights and obligations.

The resulting financial system

The economic and financial crisis in the eurozone has had important consequences. The horizon of 'secular stagnation' is no longer a hypothesis. The persistent underscoring of its inflation target has forced the ECB to maintain and even increase its expansionary monetary policy, with historically low interest rates that do not facilitate obtaining the profitability rates that commercial banks were used to. Along with this, regulatory pressures and a more demanding supervisory scrutiny add to the difficulties that banks face to extract value from a business that is also hurt by the low growth environment, as well as the persistence of large volumes of nonperforming assets.

Against this, the reactions of banking systems continue to advance towards concentration, the formation of institutions of higher than average size in order to generate sufficient economies of scale. Regardless of whether those decisions are sufficient, it is probably the case that the resulting banking map is not necessarily less prone to new crises, as systemic risk increases with concentration. Additionally, higher levels of concentration increase the market power of the new large banks, reducing the bargaining power of families and SMEs.

Long convalescence

Eight years later, the whole eurozone banking system is far from normalizing its activity. Health remains weak in some national banking systems. The main legacy of the crisis in terms of non-performing loans (NPLs) remains important in virtually all countries. In the overall eurozone banking system there are more than €900 billion of NPLs, of which €360 billion are held by Italian banks.

The medium-term future does not favour stability in the banking sector, as is reflected in the equity markets with falls to levels well below the book value of many banks. Bank stocks have not recovered the huge losses they suffered during the crisis. The consequences of economic policies in the eurozone and the very low growth accompanied by deflationary fears play a very important role in explaining this. Low interest rates do not favour the traditional bank profitability, nor does the relatively low rate of financing activity in a context of very low growth and high unemployment in the eurozone, threatening banks not only in the periphery, as was the case in 2012, but also in some core economies.

The reaction to the expansionary monetary policy of the ECB presents many banks with a difficult problem: intermediation margins have narrowed significantly and the cost structure is difficult to decrease at a similar pace. That helps to explain the very adverse reaction of the German banking employers' association, which attacked the ECB's decisions, accusing the institution, as the German finance minister has declared, of 'confiscating' the savings of Germans.

In fact, the problem of the banks is that their total costs represent an important part of its revenue – close to 75% – a ratio that reveals the need to accommodate the cost structure in a business model where operating income is about half of what it used to be before the crisis.

German banks are those most penalized by the application of negative interest rates at the marginal deposit facility. The entirety of German banking represents more than one third of the excess deposits at the ECB, representing a cost of €780 million a year. That penalty for the maintenance of idle resources is a symptom of the contradictions that the German economy (and its authorities) is facing. The excess savings, systematic surplus in the current account, the reluctance to increase public investment, constitute a downward pressure on interest rates, and also present a problem for the normalization of economic activity in the eurozone. If the German authorities assumed the need for increased public investment, especially in infrastructure, it would help alleviate the problem of lack of profitable destinations and to facilitate the eurozone exit from the current impasse. While austerity continues to prevail, the vulnerability of such banking-oriented and inefficient financial systems will continue to present problems that are no longer only local.

Banking concentration

The financial crisis that erupted in 2008 has put additional pressure on banks to deleverage and consolidate, particularly in those countries that were more severely affected by the financial crisis. The number of credit institutions has been declining at a steady pace for the euro area and for the EU as a whole. This trend raises questions about the efficiency and the degree of financial inclusion, as well as doubts about the risk of incurring the problem of 'too big to fail', to avoid the taxpayers funding the costs of banking crises.

On a non-consolidated basis, the overall number of credit institutions in the euro area declined to 5,614 at the end of 2014 from 6,054 at the end of 2013. From a longer perspective, the net decrease over the period from 2008 to 2014 is 1,160 credit institutions (–17.1 per cent). The country that experienced the largest drop was France (–167), though strong declines were also recorded in Spain (–61), Cyprus (–44), Germany (–40) and Finland (–35). Taking a medium-term perspective, since the onset of the crisis, Greece, Cyprus and Spain have recorded the largest relative decrease, due to the restructuring and consolidation of the banking industries in the context of the crisis.

With data from ECB (2015), market concentration, as measured by the share of the total assets held by the five largest credit institutions or by the Herfindahl index, has broadly continued on an upward path at both the euro area and at EU level. This increase in market concentration primarily reflects the decline in the number of credit institutions, as is reflected in figures 3.4 and 3.5.

Requirements for a stable financial system: adequate regulation and supervision

There is an absolute consensus about the financial nature of the crisis which began eight years ago: Europe is still convalescing. Avoiding similar episodes in the future requires taking the necessary actions to neutralize the destabilizing potential of the financial system. This requires at least two types of action, one analytical and another aimed at strengthening institutions and regulations within the EU.

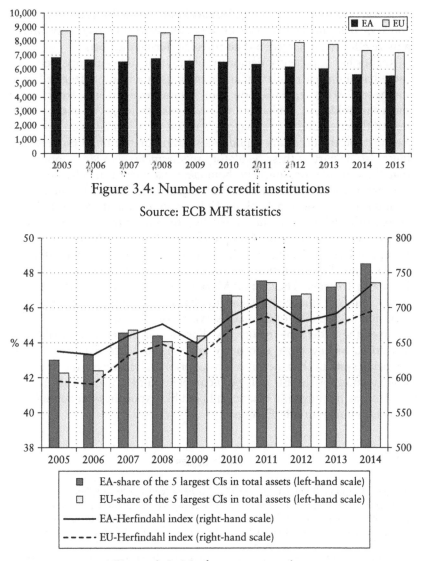

Figure 3.4: Number of credit institutions

Source: ECB MFI statistics

EA-share of the 5 largest CIs in total assets (left-hand scale)
EU-share of the 5 largest CIs in total assets (left-hand scale)
——— EA-Herfindahl index (right-hand scale)
- - - - EU-Herfindahl index (right-hand scale)

Figure 3.5: Market concentration

Source: EU Structural Financial Indicators.

Before the crisis, most standard macroeconomic models did not incorporate credit or banking instability. This made such models inappropriate for the analysis of financial crises and macroprudential policies. Many groups in the economics profession are now addressing this significant shortcoming, and relearning the lessons from Hyman Minsky, and clearly conclude that financial markets must be subject to close regulation and to a more effective supervision than revealed during the crisis.

Reality has sufficiently demonstrated that the deregulatory trends or those based on self-regulation are pernicious in a highly integrated environment. A strict regulation on bank capital requirements, sufficient so that shareholders of banks are those who take major losses in the resolution of the crisis and not taxpayers, is necessary. Clear rules on risk management, on the necessary liquidity and transparency of all proceedings, must also be part of these regulatory requirements. No less important is that these regulations must be homogeneous internationally, especially in those financial systems with a high degree of global interconnection.

Initiatives to create a Banking Union and a Capital Markets Union, as recently defined, are necessary but require extensive specification to complete all its parts. Completing the Banking Union requires a European Deposit Insurance Scheme and a broader and faster extension of risk mutualization inside the monetary union: in the end, a common European Treasury. The Capital Markets Union has to establish a transition towards a financial system less banking oriented, while ensuring inclusion and defence of financial services consumers.

Given the undeniable reality that Europe will suffer additional financial crisis, having more rigorously analysed and effectively supervised financial systems has become a top priority. However, the financial strengthening of the EU will be incomplete until a true fiscal union is in place, as the most important and credible exponent of economic and monetary integration in Europe.

References

Admati, A. and Hellwig, M. (2013) *The Banker's New Clothes: What's wrong with Banking and What to Do about It*. Princeton, NJ: Princeton University Press.

Baele, L., Annalisa Ferrando, A., Hördahl, P., Krylova, E. and Monnet, C. (2004) Measuring financial integration in the euro area. ECB Occasional Paper No. 14. Frankfurt am Main: ECB.

Berges, A. and Ontiveros, E. (2014) Austerity and financial instability. In Bilbao-Ubillos, J. (ed.) *The Economic Crisis and Governance in the European Union: A Critical Assessment*. London: Routledge.

De Grauwe, P. and Ji, Y. (2013) Strong governments, weak banks. CEPS Policy Brief, no. 305, November.

ECB (2015) *Report on Financial Structures*. October.

ECB (2016) *Financial Integration in Europe*. April.

Véron, N. (2016) The IMF's role in the euro-area crisis: financial sector aspects. *Bruegel*, Policy Contribution Issue no. 13.

Chapter 4

The Financial Crisis and the Restructuring of the Italian Banking System

Sviatlana Hlebik

Introduction

The banking system in Europe plays a very important role for the majority of European countries, particularly for small and medium-sized enterprises (SMEs) and 'the non-financial corporate sector', as banks remain the main source of credit.

With Italian banks in the spotlight again, this chapter introduces some insights on the subject of reform and restructuring of the Italian banking sector. Of course, as we already know, Italian banks are not the only ones that have problems. However, there is particular concern about the profound weakness of the Italian banking sector due to the recession, a consequence of businesses going bankrupt and the vicious circle between sovereign risk and the banks. To better understand what has happened recently, and above all to understand what is going on in our times, it is helpful, firstly, to focus on the historical background of the country in question. This can explain how the country came to use a particular bank structure, which is often connected with political-institutional aspects.

Actual European banking landscape

The main challenges of the banks in Europe are now linked to very low profitability (net interest margin) and difficulties related to the incidence of non-performing loans on bank assets which, for some countries such as Italy, are at particularly high levels.

To understand the current European landscape, it is appropriate to focus on some key aspects regarding risk, solvency performance and the lending function of European banks.

Lending. The fundamental question about the role of European banks in the real economy remains. Currently, and since as early as 2014, a small trend in the growth of European bank loans is being observed. The loan to total asset ratios show an increase in loans compared to a growth in assets, which suggests that the banks are directed towards their traditional role. European banks show significant exposure towards entities that do not belong to the banking and financial sector.

Loans to the private non-financial sector, as seen in figure 4.1, have increased since the end of 2013. Despite being sluggish towards the middle of 2016, considering low interest rates (figure 4.2), a recovery in growth is expected. However, since 2011 GDP trends are decoupling within the eurozone: while Germany and France have fully recovered from the 2008–9 global crisis, creating the most favourable economic conditions for credit quality (see figure 4.3), Italy is stuck in a low growth scenario. Despite the trend in growth for loans to non-financial businesses (see figure 4.1b) since the end of 2013, by 2015 loans for the building sector declined. 2015 shows the most marked decrease in the manufacturing sector as well. Toward mid-2016 loans to businesses decreased by 1.2 per cent compared to the previous quarter.

The poor quality of assets remains the main problem in the Italian banking system, i.e. the high share of non-performing loans (NPLs). NPLs are loans that might not be repaid, mainly due to the economic crisis. With the current situation of very weak growth and with so many firms in difficulty, NPLs are strongly impacting Italian banks. The referendum on Brexit, in which British citizens decided to leave the European Union, further aggravated the situation, immediately lowering expectations for growth due to the increased volatility of financial markets.

Coverage ratio. Non-performing loans concerning households or businesses that are no longer able to pay the instalments are the most difficult to recover. The coverage ratio (which is how a bank's ability to absorb potential losses from its NPLs is evaluated) shows improvement in measuring the ability of the bank to absorb potential losses derived from non-performing loans. Therefore, a reduction in coverage ratio means increasing potential risks. We notice non-uniformity among European countries. For example, France, Italy and Spain have higher coverage ratios than the average in the rest of Europe, which indicates that the banks are more prudent. The larger-sized banks had higher coverage levels. Up to mid-2015, lower-sized entities were at the lower end of the classification, but by December 2015 they had reached the same level as medium-sized banks.

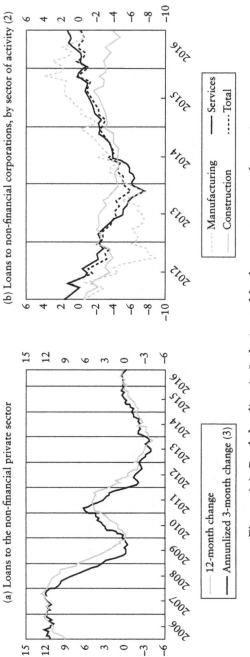

(a) Loans to the non-financial private sector

(b) Loans to non-financial corporations, by sector of activity (2)

Figure 4.1: Bank lending in Italy (monthly data, percentage changes)

Source: Banca d'Italia 2016a

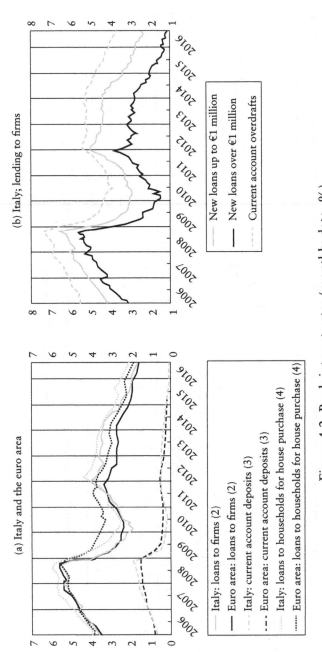

(a) Italy and the euro area

(b) Italy; lending to firms

Italy: loans to firms (2)
Euro area: loans to firms (2)
Italy: current account deposits (3)
Euro area: current account deposits (3)
Italy: loans to households for house purchase (4)
Euro area: loans to households for house purchase (4)

New loans up to €1 million
New loans over €1 million
Current account overdrafts

Figure 4.2: Bank interest rates (monthly data, %)

Source: Banca d'Italia 2016a

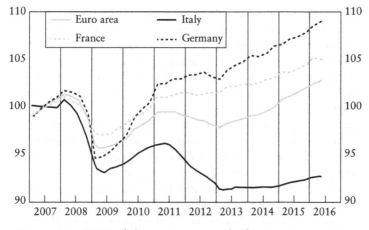

Figure 4.3: GDP of the euro area and of its main countries
(quarterly data, 2007 = 100)

Source: Banca d'Italia 2016a

Asset quality. The issue of asset quality in European banks is still acute, although the incidence of non-performing loans to total loans is on the decrease. The most critical issue is in Italy, which has significantly more NPLs than the other countries under examination. Spain is not far from the European average, and Germany is among the countries with the best portfolio. The size of the entity does not favour small banks, which, despite efforts in recent years, still have a very large gap compared to larger banks, as through securitization a large proportion of NPLs have been sold, freeing up their budgets.

Solvency: financial solidity. During 2016, European banks have continued to strengthen capital. Financial solidity is represented by (CET1 and TIER1) Tier 1 common capital ratio and is measured as a bank's core equity capital compared to its total risk-weighted assets. Note that, compared to 2015, when improvement was due particularly to the increase in capital, in 2016 the reduction of asset risk is being seen. Interestingly, small banks, which in 2014 were less solid (CET1 13.15 per cent) than the medium-sized banks (CET1 13.70 per cent), have made a greater effort over the past two years, resulting in the strongest band (CET1 15.63 per cent) of the EBA sample in mid-2016. The French and German banks on average are more solid than the credit entities in Spain and Italy. Another important consideration concerns the business model of the banks. In the period before the crisis, commercial banks performed better in terms of capitalization (TIER1), while at the epicentre of the

91

crisis those performing best were the cooperative banks. In the after-math, savings banks have managed to improve significantly (e.g., they have performed better than the commercial banks in Italy). Further, it is important to note that as long as default risk does exist and exposure to EU government has zero risk weight, the ratios of the regulator cannot accurately embody the real risk of banks (see, e.g., credit spreads and Greece bankruptcy).

Efficiency. Regarding efficiency, the big commercial banks in Europe are the more efficient, while the small ones are less so. German entities are the most efficient in Europe, followed by France and Italy, while the Spanish banks are below the European average.

Profitability. In 2016 the profitability indicators are still very low. Regarding net interest income: medium-sized banks are leading followed by the large-sized banks. Currently, the returns on equity (ROE) indica-tor that measures the ratio between net profit and net assets of the French and Spanish banks is slightly higher than the European average (about 7 per cent), whereas German and Italian banks (3 per cent and 2 per cent ROE, respectively) are among those with the lowest levels of profitability in Europe (in fact only Portuguese and Greek banks show an average negative performance, –5 per cent and –16 per cent, respectively). Small banks, which typically have very volatile ROE over time, were the best performing in 2016.

As for the differences in business models, on an average European level, the commercial banks are no doubt the best performers. However, in the various national contexts, there are different dynamics. For example, in France both in the pre-crisis period and in the aftermath of bank profitability, there is no significant difference between the various business models. For example, in Spain in 2014, savings banks performed better than commercial banks, while in Italy the cooperative banks were doing well and savings banks had very low profitability, sometimes even negative.

The roots and evolution of banking in Italy

Italy has always been a country of small business, even today. Micro enterprises are prevalent, with an average of 3.9 employees per company (Istat 2016), and these companies make up about 95 per cent of the business network. This has impacted the evolution of the Italian banking system, explaining the peculiarities of Italian banks regarding their spe-cialization in the SME sector.

Currently in Italy there are essentially only private banks, which mainly follow traditional banking activities. From the late nineteenth century until World War I, the rise in private banks drove down public participation by 20 per cent, after which, for two decades, public presence grew continuously. Surely financial instability was one of the principal reasons for this evolution.

It should be noted that from 1930 until the 1990s banking regulations involved a large number of state-owned banking entities with a relatively small number of branches. These were closely connected with the area in which they were located. The Banking Act of 1926 also made it difficult for others to get on the scene. The events of this period heavily influenced the future development of the country. The Italian crisis of the 1920s (1927–9) was concurrent with the collapse of Wall Street and had major consequences. The situation became even more critical when the banks continued to finance and increase their holdings in major companies, which were in financial trouble, and then took control of them. In this way, the banks themselves were at risk of bankruptcy. The main problem was centred on the three largest banks.

These banks, following the German model, were mixed banks, meaning that they were involved in both traditional and investment banking. In 1933, the Institute for Industrial Reconstruction (IRI) was established to deal with the banking and industrial crisis. Consequently, with the law of 1936, banking supervision was reinforced and the system reorganized, separating commercial banks from investment banks. Involvement in companies held by banks was also reorganized. It should be noted that for sixty years, the rules of the banking world went unchanged. The public property of many banks guaranteed the separation between banks and industry and attributed control and funding to the state.

This model aimed to stabilize the banking sector, given the fragility of the period and the difficult phase of recovery after the war, by financing growth and alleviating stress for SMEs applying for credit. With World War II, industrial plants were destroyed and the IRI was split in two. Following the rescue of the government during the Great Depression, public banks accounted for more than 80 per cent of the banking sector. Since the 1990s, with privatization and liberalization, the situation began to change radically, impacting the structure of the Italian banking system. Savings banks and 'public law credit institutions' were turned into SpA (joint stock companies), and in twenty years the number of branches more than doubled, dramatically increasing banking competition. Banking functions were separated from the social and cultural development of savings banks. In this way savings bank SpAs (joint stock companies) were created to do business; meanwhile, foundations held the shares for charity like a non-profit entity in the cultural, scientific or research spheres.

In 1993 the universal banks were introduced to a management model with which came a de-specialization of credit intermediaries. In fact, bank activities and services expanded, giving banks the opportunity to raise funds and grant loans in various forms, and operate in all financial markets. Mergers and acquisitions resulted in reducing the number of banks and redistribution of market shares. Regarding the bank results, the Amato reform helped performance in terms of increasing non-interest earnings; however, it should be emphasized that the efficiency indicator, i.e. cost to income, could not achieve better results than they had before the reforms. Probably, as discussed in Ayadi et al. (2010), the fact is that the savings bank no longer existed in its original form and could have worsened some clients' credit funds. It should be noted that the recent financial crisis of 2007 led to the nationalization of many European banks, including some in the UK and Ireland. In contrast, there are still public banks in Germany and Spain, while with the reform of the 1990s Italian banks became exclusively private entities. From the nineteenth century in Italy there were intermediaries who specialized in various areas. Italian banks were either limited liability companies or cooperative banks (Banche Popolari or Banche di Credito Cooperativo (BCC)). Both 'Banca Popolare' (1860) and Banche di Credito Cooperativo (1883), based on the German model, were established in Europe at the end of the nineteenth century. Based on ethical and Christian motivation, they began to spread very rapidly, increasing their market share.

Among the particular characteristics of the previously mentioned banks, their proximity to the territory with social mutual benefits where credit was distributed mainly to shareholders should be emphasized. Regarding profits, they could not be distributed freely, e.g. they were limited to 70 per cent (according to the Consolidated Law on Banking, annual net profits had to be allocated to legal reserves; it has now been changed to 20 per cent). Following a series of reorganizations since the early 1990s, the statute of cooperative banks (BCC) has been modified, and acquisitions and mergers have been made with the 'Banche Popolari.' Making cross-country comparisons, some exceptions should be noted due to the stock exchange listing of some popular Italian banks. In recent years, the reform has often been spoken of because of some large cooperative banks which are no longer local but were listed on the stock exchange and operating as SpAs.

According to cooperative banks data in 2007, the Bank of Italy accounted for about 30 per cent of private loans and almost a quarter of total assets (Tarantola 2010). The Banche Popolari and BCC are very important since by working locally in the district they provide a credit facility to small and medium-sized enterprises and households, especially in more backward areas. This is one of the reasons for the entity's difficulties with traditional business and especially for cooperative banks that have to adapt to changes in the European context, and technology and deterioration in the economic environment. The crisis has drastically increased bank problems, which in turn have a negative impact on bank profits. The Italian banking sector is in trouble because of non-performing loans and many BCC exhibit particular problems because of the additional issue of low capitalization (Barbagallo 2016).

The main problem is the difficulty of adapting to the new environment, both domestic and international.

The impact of the recent financial crisis

Comparing the Italian financial system with other countries, it must be said that Italian banks in the early years of the crisis, i.e. before the arrival of the sovereign debt crisis, were less affected. This was due primarily to the fact that the banking system was distinguished by traditional business models with a wide network of branches and to a lesser extent there was some risky investment banking. Note that Italy did not have to address the problems related to the bursting of the speculative bubble. In fact, despite the acute phase of the crisis and the deep recession that Italy has suffered since 2008, Italian banks could obtain a stable deposit (funds) from families and the loans and investments were much higher than average compared to European banks. There was also another strong point in Italy's favour: the indebtedness of the private sector was lower than all other major countries. At the beginning of the sovereign debt crisis, the countries of the eurozone differed significantly. Germany had the most robust economy, public debt was contained, and by 2010 it had already achieved GDP growth rates comparable to the pre-crisis period. In contrast, the PIIGS countries (Portugal, Ireland, Italy, Greece and Spain) were the most vulnerable, and presented difficulties relating to the non-sustainability of the public debt and lack of growth.

Following the outbreak of the 2008 crisis, governments intervened with financial aid to banks in order to protect financial stability in Europe. Altogether, state aid amounted to 8 per cent of GDP, of which only 3.3 per cent has been recovered. Figure 4.4 shows that fiscal cost and recovery rate were minimal in Italy.

To understand the reasons why European banks were particularly highly impacted during the crisis, attention must be paid to the evolution

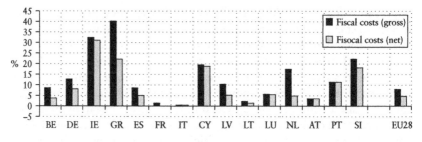

Figure 4.4: Fiscal costs and recovery rates over the period 2008–14
(percentages of 2014 GDP)

Source: ECB 2016

of the funding structure. As market financing was much cheaper before the crisis than through deposits, an imbalance between customer loans and ordinary customers' funding accumulated. Many banks tended to increase their assets, generating high earnings while increasing leverage to dangerous levels. Under these conditions, a bank unable to refinance its debt on the market found itself in great difficulty if investors lacked confidence in them. The crisis revealed the problem, which, particularly after the Lehman bankruptcy, became increasingly serious and was identified as a huge solvency crisis.

As a result, banks have had to revise their strategies, focusing on the liabilities to obtain affordable loans. Some banks are letting go of risky trading assets and investment banking and are trying to focus on traditional, less risky bank business. It is important to note here that the new banking regulation Basile3 will impact the banking system.

The legislation, in addition to the capital intended to help the banks rebound, provides for the introduction of two instruments: short-term liquidity coverage ratio (LLCR), which was introduced in 2015 and became a compliance regime in 2018, and net stable funding ratio (NSFR), which should improve medium- to long-term asset-liability matches once it begins on 1 January 2018. One of the main criticisms of the previously mentioned legislation is that since the perimeter of regulation is limited only to banks, this could spur further growth in non-regulated activities such as the shadow banking system.

Banking crisis reforms

Banca Popolare Etruria and Lazio, Banca delle Marche, Cassa di Risparmio di Ferrara and Cassa di Risparmio di Chieti were in the spotlight in Italy in 2015, an unprecedented year for Italian banks and savers, which ended with these four historical local banks being rescued. These four banks accounted for a total of about 1 per cent of the Italian market in terms of deposits. Italy was planning to intervene through the Deposit Protection Fund, which according to the Bank of Italy supervisor Mr. Barbagallo was set up specifically to manage the crisis in an orderly way. Despite the argument that in Italy guarantee schemes are private, the European Commission believed that this tool could not be used as it is subject to European rules on state aid.

The European Union directive that influenced the rescue of the four banks was published in the Gazzetta Ufficiale on 4 May 2014. A year and a half has passed since the Save-banks decree, and as an alternative the government called on private banks in Italy, which had put emergency resources in place, to carry out the rescue.

Banks in difficulty were relieved of all bad loans that were transferred to another special purpose company that takes care of the management and recovery of bad debts. The healthy and unhealthy parts of the four banks' balance sheets were separated and current accounts were transferred to four new banks which carried the same name as the old banks, preceded by the word 'New'. These new entities were provided with fresh capital from the three main banks in the Italian banking system (Intesa Sanpaolo, Unicredit and Ubi), which have lent about €3.6 billion in the rescue package. This money, through the resolution fund, has helped recapitalize the four banks in difficulty, without the use of public funds.

The aim of the intervention was to ensure business continuity; in fact, the banks themselves have begun to operate without losses to customary depositors and bondholders. However, the investments of shareholders and subordinated bondholders of the four banks are worth nothing. Savers are ready for the opportunity to gain a higher return on their investment, but do not know how to estimate the risks.

The investors, attracted by high dividends, did not know which direction to take, but it should also be pointed out that in some cases people did actually make a profit. In confusing the concepts of price and value, a large hole in the budget was created, for which many have been called to account for. Bank administrators went against the regulations and constructed self-referential systems without effective management. At the beginning of 2016, the first cases for damages against the directors, who were in charge of the four banks, and the assessment of liability of the auditing firms – professionals at an international level called to audit the banks – were announced.

Monte dei Paschi di Siena (MPS)

According to the results of the stress test on the leading European banks, 'Monte dei Paschi di Siena passes the test in the baseline scenario but obtains a negative result in the adverse scenario' (Banca d'Italia 2016b). To note, the stress test has a number of limitations such as an annual static approach, not taking into account long-term developments in the disposal of non-performing loans and profitability. Further, it is important to highlight that that capital loss is not due to the 2009 crisis. Its core capital has been fully offset since 2009 when a €1.9 billion Tremonti bond was issued and since 2012 when the equity burden was covered by a €3.9 billion Monti Bond.

Given that, following the decision of the European Commission and the ECB, the recapitalization of the Italian banking system using state resources has not been allowed, banks have to find alternative solutions to strengthen their capital and repair balance sheets, above all to improve credit quality. The plan proposed by MPS could be a possible example. MPS has imposed a radical restructuring plan that goes beyond the ECB's requirements. The credit institution has reacted to stress tests that show the MPS capital weakness.

The stock market crash does not allow for tapping the capital market on acceptable terms. The plan covers the 2016–19 period and is to divest non-performing loans (those which have deteriorated to 33 per cent of their gross value), increase recapitalization and raise the collateral on other impaired loans still on the balance sheets. It is expected that the project would authorize capital increases on the market.

The plan is based on the following main points: (1) the valorization of the existing customer base, with an acceleration of the digitalization process with particular focus on traditional retail and small business customers; (2) a working model focusing on efficiency by closing about 500 branches and cutting about 2,600 full-time jobs; (3) improved risk management with the complete separation of the commercial division from the credit division; and (4) a strengthened asset and liquidity position that will have positive impacts on liquidity ratio and capital. The success of the operation is very important for Italy as this could relieve pressure on the country's entire banking system.

Unicredit

Another case is Unicredit, which is in a different situation, although after the presentation of stress test results which highlighted deficiencies in terms of solvency, the question of possible capital increase emerges. The new CEO is putting together a group revision strategy that will examine all the main areas in order to strengthen and optimize the group's capital allocation, improve risk management and reduce costs. In addition, in order to increase efficiency, it is intended to create a series of synergies and cross-selling of strategic assets.

Atlante fund

One of the initiatives to address the difficulties of the Italian financial system has been the creation of the Atlante fund. The main purpose for which it was established was the recapitalization of banks in crisis and the securitization of non-performing loans. The participants are voluntary, so the initiative has a source of funding contributions from loan banks, banking foundations, insurance companies and Cassa Depositi e Prestiti. This fund has largely been used to recapitalize northern banks, namely Veneto Banca and Banca Popolare di Vicenza. Atlanta 2 appeared during the summer on the anniversary of the explosion of the crisis at MPS (Banca Monte dei Paschi di Siena).

Banca Popolare di Vicenza and Veneto Banca

Currently a possible merger between Banca Popolare di Vicenza and Veneto Banca is being considered. The shareholder fund Atlante aims to create a joint management committee of the two banks, and define two business plans to make the banks safe, even through extraordinary corporate transactions on assets. These plans must ultimately be submitted to the ECB, which aims to prevent fragile entities remaining in the banking sector. Consequently, in this case it is first necessary to dispose of non-performing loans, increase cover and, if need be, seek an additional increase in capital.

Cooperative Credit Banks

At the beginning of 2015 an Italian decree-law, which was turned into law, required that public banks with assets above €8 billion be transformed into joint stock companies. Despite a banking reform project being on the cards for a long time, it caused a shockwave in the world of cooperative banks. Furthermore, the decree-law of 14 February 2016, no. 18, called for 'Urgent measures concerning the reform of cooperative banks, the guarantee of the securitization of those in trouble, and the taxation regime concerning crisis procedures and asset management.' The project consists of the creation of one or more joint-stock parent

Table 4.1   Insolvency reforms (2007–2016)

2007: Enlargement of the scope of the enterprise insolvency regime, coordination of reorganization plan and liquidation plan, registration of professionals to assess insolvency plans, restrictions to the liability of the creditors' committee.
2009: Reduction of the powers of the court; increase of powers of the insolvency administrator and the creditors' committee. Contents of the insolvency administrators' report, preparation of the liquidation plan.
2012: Easier use of restructuring agreements and rescue plans; provisions for bridge financing and temporary stay of creditor actions; protection against avoidance actions; reorganization plans with continuity of the business. Possibility of entering the reorganization process without a plan (*concordato in blanco*), improvement of the provisions to disclaim executory contracts.
2015: Competing plans in reorganizations; specific timeline for the completion of tasks by the insolvency administrator; more flexibility in the sale of assets (shorter delays, use of experts, less auctions, assignment to creditor, payment by instalments); financial restructuring agreements.
2016: Out-of-court enforcement of secured claims in commercial lending relationships; reduction of delays in auctions; reform of security interests over movables; use of electronic communications in insolvency.
Rordorf proposal (2015): Reorganization of the insolvency law, including the harmonization of the common phase of all procedures; concentration of insolvency jurisdiction in the Enterprise courts and the largest civill courts; acceleration of the treatment of enterprise crisis by means of the *'alert procedure'*.

Source: Garrido 2016

companies which individual cooperative banks join through a deal. Above all, risks, assets and administration were taken into consideration.

This is an important change. The reform of the BCC aims to reduce the fragmentation of the sector and to overcome the structural weaknesses arising from their business model, which is particularly sensitive to the economy of the territory. Ending this discussion on the current Italian reforms, it should be stressed that the state will not put in more money and not repay the bank losses. So it will become even more important to know and understand where and in what to invest and to endorse. It is another lesson to be learned, to prevent the availability of high-risk instruments to small savers from occurring again (for more detail, see Lanzavecchia and Tagliavini 2016).

Resolving insolvency reforms

Apart from the reforms concerning the restructuring of the banking sector itself, a series of procedures were introduced, aimed at making insolvency proceedings more efficient (see table 4.1).

The reforms undertaken in 2015 have improved the position of creditors in bankruptcy proceedings, allowing them to present alternative plans, and allowing creditors to participate more actively in the sale of assets, whereas the last reform, the 'Martian pact', is an innovative measure that avoids lengthy judicial procedures, reducing them by six months (Carpinelli et al. 2016). Another benefit of the reform is the facilitation of access to finance for SMEs.

Conclusion

The financial crisis and the new banking regulations have greatly affected European banks, leading them to revise their business models. Earnings during the pre-crisis period were marked by the highest leverage, were funded at low cost, and had high risk propensity.

The Italian banking sector is still burdened by high levels of non-performing loans. As has been discussed in Italy, many reforms have been made which are aimed at managing the problems inherited from the crisis. The ECB and the European Commission require drastic reduction of non-performing loans in a short time. Another fact to note is that the time acceleration on the disposal of non-performing loans, during the period of difficulties, in order to make growth in capital through new subscriptions, could have a negative impact on bank capital.

The reform of cooperative banks should be completed by the end of 2017. It will involve the arrival on the scene of joint-stock company cooperative banking groups with assets of at least €1 billion; more than 50 per cent of these will be regulated by the BCC. Under the new rules, the parent company will have 'proportionate to risk' powers to monitor banks participating in the cohesion contract that sets out the criteria of risk in terms of liquidity and capital for each BCC. Between the parent company and members there is also a joint guarantee of bonds. Note that this combination could reach a scale so as to be part of the largest banks directly supervised by the ECB. The fact that the BCC represents more than 70 per cent of all credit institutions in the country indicates the importance of this reform for the Italian banking system.

It is interesting to note that bank strategies have changed. The activities that provided an opportunity for the high pre-crisis profits for a number of reasons (macroeconomic and financial market conditions, etc.) began to lose more and more appeal.

Looking to the future, the stability and sustainability of the banks will depend on how they manage to adapt to changes and the environment. In addition, a transformation is taking place towards the most digitized banks which are taking on a significant number of investments in technology. The major challenge for banks are the financial technology companies, also known as FinTech, companies which use technology integrated multi-platform offering. Some of them already carry out both lending activities and consultancy advice, providing an alternative source of lending to that of banks.

In conclusion, a loan, like any debt, is the present value of future income. As the economy is shrinking, loans are defaulting. Yet now the private sector is decoupling: either a firm is bankrupt or it is alive and fast growing in a zero leverage financial strategy. Now the instability is shifting from the private sector towards the public sector: how can public debt be repaid in a scenario where the fiscal budget is shrinking and there is high expenditure on interest payments on the debt?

Finally, I would like to suggest: whether globalization and excessive financialization of the economy (perhaps combined with the failure of strategic governance vision) have not accidentally prompted an irrational and often contradictory pattern, which in some cases may have distorted the primary function of the banks, which (at least for retail banks) should be the backing of the 'real' economy and in particular to SMEs and small savers.

Acknowledgements

The author is grateful to Riccardo Biella, Alberto Lanzavecchia, Luca Mazzucchelli, Gianluca Rusconi and Giulio Tagliavini for their precious comments. The views expressed in this paper are those of the author and not necessarily of the organizations with which she is affiliated.

References

Ayadi, R., Llewellyn, D., Schmidt, R., Arbak, E. and de Groen, W.P. (2010) *Investigating Diversity in the Banking Sector in Europe: Key Developments, Performance and Role of Cooperative Banks*. Brussels: Centre for European Policy Studies.

Banca d'Italia (2016a) Bollettino Economico.

Banca d'Italia (2016b) *Results of the 2016 European Stress Test*. Available at: https://www.bancaditalia.it/media/approfondimenti/2016/stress-test-2016/ note-stress-test-2016.pdf

Barbagallo, C. (2016) Misure urgenti concernenti la riforma delle banche di credito cooperativo e altre misure in materia bancaria. Camera dei Deputati VI Commissione permanente (Finanze) Dipartimento Vigilanza Bancaria e Finanziaria Banca d'Italia. Rome. Available at: https://www.bancaditalia.it/ pubblicazioni/interventi-vari/int-var-2016/Barbagallo-010316.pdf

Carpinelli, L., Cascarino, G., Giacomelli, S. and Vacca V. (2016) The management of non-performing loans: a survey among the main Italian banks. Banca d'Italia Questioni di economia e finanza No. 311. Available at: https://www. bancaditalia.it/pubblicazioni/qef/2016-0311

ECB (2016) Economic Bulletin.

Garrido, J. (2016) Insolvency and enforcement reforms in Italy. IMF Working Paper no. WP/16/134, August.

Istat (2016) Report Risultati economici delle imprese. Available at: https://www. istat.it/it/files/2016/10/Report-Risultati-economici-imprese-2014.pdf

Lanzavecchia, A. and Tagliavini, G. (2016) Consultazione Pubblica su 'Disposizioni di Vigilanza in Materia di Gruppo Bancario Cooperativo'. Banca d'Italia. Available at: https://www.bancaditalia.it/compiti/vigilanza/normativa/consult azioni/2016/gruppo-bancario-cooperativo/Proff-Lanzavecchia-Tagliavini.pdf

Tarantola, A. (2010) Concluding remarks to the OECD-Bank of Italy Symposium on Financial Literacy, Improving Financial Education Efficiency. Available at: http://www.oecd.org/daf/fin/financial-education/45486368.pdf

Chapter 5

European Science and Technology in a Time of Crises: ERC, EIT and Beyond

João Caraça, Teresa Lago and Daria Gołębiowska-Tataj

Science and technology

We owe to Erwin Schrödinger the illumination and comprehensibility of the earliest stages and the origins of science. In his wonderful little book *Nature and the Greeks* he explains how the ancient Greeks invented the concepts of *nature* and *science* (the way of understanding nature) (Schrödinger 1954). There was no limitation on the subjects discussed by Greek philosophers, and the separation of knowledge into disciplines or water-tight divisions had not yet arisen. Many diverse sciences thus sprang up in the world of kingdoms and empires until the epistemological cut of modernity in the seventeenth century, which transformed nature from the plethora of myths and allegories of the past into a description in mathematical language. The triumph of modernity was associated with the effectiveness of the introduction of a symbolic language to represent the order of nature, capable of separating beings from the rules they obey, i.e., ontology from epistemology.

The dominant assumptions of modern scientific reasoning—determinism, reductionism and dualism, meaning, respectively, 'conservation of information', 'use of mathematical language', and 'separation between subject and object', are today being seriously questioned, mainly because the pre-eminence of complexity is pervading everything.

But contemporary science is no longer the science of Galileo and Newton. The success of modern science in the eighteenth and nineteenth centuries provoked also a distinctive evolution in the structures of knowledge, originating conflicts and delimitations which finally fed back into its core. Departing from its first main object, the discovery of the *laws of nature*, scientific research became more and more concerned in the twentieth century with the *production of technology*: thus 'technoscience' was born. The scientific efforts conducted in World War II and its wake led to a first grand transformation of science (the US investment in R&D was of the order of 0.5 per cent of GDP by 1946), with massive channelling of public funds being predominantly directed to stimulate *technology-driven research*. The appropriate balance in funding between *curiosity-driven research* and *technology-driven research* is far from being settled today at national or international levels, giving rise to pertinent questions about the capacity to attract to fundamental science bright young people willing to solve intricate, sophisticated problems.

The social image projected by science also suffered a big transformation in the second half of the twentieth century. The central image of a scientist is no longer that of the scientific researcher who doubts and interrogates nature, but rather that of the expert or consultant who knows and uses practical solutions and implements measures to solve the problems of the community. Science has left the seclusion of university space and now it has to endure the constraints of public space to be legitimated. In fact, all major themes of the present, in areas that range from the oceans to climate change, from transportation to public health, from growth and development to inequality and social exclusion, from the use of resources to the management of large systems and cities, all involve technoscience deeply and thoroughly (Caraça 1999). With seven billion people now living on this planet, there can be no return to the past.

At the end of the 1990s Europe was voicing worries about the widening of the gap in performance with respect to US science and technology. By then, the notion that the knowledge-based economy was the central factor of growth, competitiveness and employment, was consensual. And the admission that research and innovation were at the core of the new economy prompted the need to define a new strategy towards the future.

At the Lisbon European Council in 2000 the EU announced the ambitious goal of becoming by 2010 the most dynamic and competitive knowledge-based economy in the world. One of the projects launched at the Lisbon Council was the European Research Area (ERA), a means to establish a reference framework for research in Europe, as it was recognized that the EU was lagging behind the US and Japan in research and innovation performance. Expenditure in R&D (GERD) in the EU was 1.9 per cent of GDP by then, compared with 2.7 per cent in the US and 3.1 per cent in Japan.

Two years later, in the Barcelona European Council of 2002, the EU tasked itself with increasing the European research effort to 3 per cent of its GDP by 2010, with the provision that two-thirds should be funded through private investment (2 per cent) and one-third from the public sector (1 per cent). Why this target? The most reasonable explanation is that the 3 per cent value is a modern European myth, born in the period the French nationals call 'les 30 glorieuses'. In fact, this figure appears for the first time in the 1964 document entitled 'Réflexions pour 1985', published by the French Commissariat Général du Plan. In this important report it was stated that by 1985 (the 20-year horizon then), France should devote to R&D at least 3 per cent of its GDP – the level of the US science and technology indicator in 1964. This 3 per cent mirage has haunted science and technology policy in Europe ever since.

But the analysis of the funding of this US expenditure is very revealing: in 1964, the Federal government financed 65 per cent of the total (down from 75 per cent in the early 1950s). The private sector invested a little more than 30 per cent (nearly 1 per cent of US GDP, and it took 15 years – until 1980 – for the US to balance the R&D expenditure funding between the public and private sectors).

The competition with the US and Japan was fierce around the turn of the twentieth century. The Union was dreaming of regaining geopolitical pre-eminence and the euro was knocking at the door. But in science and technology Europe could only count on the Framework Programmes, on the JRC, on an ERA still in its infancy and on a collection of national research policies very loosely coordinated. The Open Method of Coordination, heralded then with pomp and circumstance as the main future policy vector in science and technology, would later be proven to be no more than an illusion. Europe was skirmishing against windmills. And the Union was lacking research manpower – well-trained, highly-qualified, entrepreneurially-oriented, truly committed people to reach out and connect to the multipolar world that was in the waking. By the turn of century, 400,000 scientific personnel of European origin were working in US institutions.

But europhoria was rampant. A couple of financial bubbles exploded before the crises initiated in 2007–8, reminding us that the world continued to be dangerous. The EU Lisbon Strategy meant that more new technology was needed for Europe to become more competitive. The co-ordinators of the Framework Programmes were instructed to continue that trend. The pressure was mounting and the European Commission responded, laying out two new initiatives. They had very different objectives and targets. They gave rise to two new European institutions: (i) the first (following a bottom-up approach) led to the creation of the European Research Council (ERC); (ii) the second (more top-down in character) led to the establishment of the European Institute of Innovation and Technology (EIT).

For nearly a decade the scientific community had nurtured the ambition to see established in Europe a new funding structure for supporting the best basic research. Numerous debates took place in different fora and at various levels, from groups of scientists to research organizations and high-level officials. The expectations ran high when in 2005 the European Commission proposed the establishment of IDEAS – the frontier research programme within the 7th Framework Programme.

The arguments for establishing the ERC were championed by Commissioners Philippe Busquin and, later, Janez Potocnik. On the other hand, the EIT was the culmination of a process launched by José Manuel Barroso, then President of the EC, to install in Europe a network of institutes devoted to technology and innovation following the US example. But in 2010 Europe was nowhere near the value of 3 per cent of GDP, in terms of the indicator of total research expenditure.

ERC: a European success story in funding scientific research

The first years

By July 2005 an ERC Scientific Council was assembled: it was composed of twenty-two academics and researchers selected independently of their nationality or expertise from a list of nearly 300 nominations received from approximately forty organizations representative of the scientific community in Europe (ERC 2005).

The first meeting took place in Brussels in mid-October 2005. Reassurances were given of the Commission's commitment to guaranteeing the autonomy of the Scientific Council, and to ensuring that it would work independently and free of political or extraneous interests. Also, and equally importantly, the full support of the Commissioner and of the few designated officers to assist the Scientific Council on the EC complexities and legalities was guaranteed. The Commissioner further challenged the Scientific Council members to start working immediately on the preparation of ERC, even in an informal way, while the political negotiations on the Framework Programme and its specific programmes were taking place, as they were expected to be concluded towards the end · of 2006. The launching of the IDEAS programme was expected to take place in early 2007. Guaranteed its autonomy and freedom, the challenge was accepted and the appointed Scientific Council set in motion its preparatory work, committed to coming up with creative ideas and stimulating proposals, and determined to maximize the ERC's scientific objectives and impact. It was agreed to elect very soon a Chair and two

Vice-chairs for the Scientific Council. Fotis Kafatos, a molecular biologist, was elected the first president.

The ERC was 'taking off'; informally and also voluntarily, as the work of the Scientific Council members would not be remunerated, except for the travel expenses which were to be covered by the European Commission; only much later (in 2011) were they entitled to an honorarium for meeting attendance. The Scientific Council members were enthusiastic and full of dreams. They were to establish in Europe the structure they would have wished to see much earlier in their own careers.

Therefore 2006 became a hectic and decisive year in the preparation of the ERC as the unique pan-European funding organization designed to support the best science and scholarship. Considerable effort was invested to lay the foundations for the operational phase, addressing both key operating principles but also very practical questions. It was clear that the decisions they made would have a very significant influence over the style and culture of operation of the ERC from the outset, and thus on its achievements in the longer term.

It was agreed that besides the regular report to the Commission the ERC should simultaneously embrace an appropriately high standard of transparency to assure communication, with key stakeholders and the scientific community, on the deliberations, activities and achievements of the programme. A high level of confidence amongst the scientific community would be decisive for the ERC while aiming to create leverage towards structural improvements in the research system of Europe.

The roadmap had to be designed at the highest level of ambition, adopting the best practice, if significant 'positive contamination' effects on the European research system were to occur. The European Commission would provide the means and be the guarantor of the ERC's autonomy (European Commission 2006).

Once it identified the main challenges for research in Europe – low visibility, drops in R&D investments, fragmentation of research and funding activities – the ERC Scientific Council moved on to establish its overall ambitious strategy. This would involve the definition of the annual Work Programme, the choice of the review methodology, the procedures to control the scientific operations and management and also the communication with stakeholders and the scientific community.

In terms of scientific strategy, several decisions were made: the ERC should complement other funding schemes in Europe, such as the research funding agencies operating at the national level, while encouraging the highest quality research by supporting investigator-initiated frontier research across all fields, on the basis of scientific excellence, frontier research meaning a new understanding of basic research, avoiding distinctions between 'basic' and 'applied', between 'science' and 'technology', and between traditional disciplines, while also ignoring disciplinary boundaries. The only criterion would be excellence in terms of the individual team and of the research project proposed. The ERC would invest in research talent, proposing attractive and flexible grants under the full control of the Principal Investigator.

The nationality of the researcher would be irrelevant, with calls open to all nationalities in the world, the only condition being that the research ought to be carried out in a host organization located in one European Community member or associated country.

The Scientific Council concluded the need for setting up a dedicated structure to support the implementation of the IDEAS programme. Such a structure would hire a limited number of staff with a high level of competence and experience in research in the various fields of knowledge. It would operate lightly in structure and with a high level of efficiency. The Director, even if a Commission officer, would be nominated by the Commissioner after consultation with the Scientific Council, according to the agreed policy.

The ERC Scientific Council also decided to recruit a Secretary-General, a senior person with a recognized scientific profile and eminence in science policy who, working together with the Director of the dedicated structure, ought to ensure that the strategy and work programme established by the Scientific Council were effectively and faithfully implemented. The Secretary-General would attend and report to the Scientific Council. The post for Secretary-General was advertised quickly, with the formal nomination by the Scientific Council taking place in August 2006, after prior consultation with the Commissioner.

Besides setting up an ERC webpage where all decisions and results would be accessible to the scientific community and the public at large, the Scientific Council also made the decision to hold every other meeting in a different member or associated country. This would provide an opportunity for direct contact with the national decision makers and also to organize an open session with the scientific community for exchange of ideas. Frequently such open sessions included presentations by ERC grantees, the most enthusiastic ambassadors for ERC.

The launch of the ERC took place on 27 February 2007, in Berlin, during the German EU presidency. That same year the EC created the 'European Research Council Executive Agency', the dedicated structure to support and manage the research projects and all ERC activity (European Commission 2007). The first call for proposals was published soon after the launching ceremony while a Guide for Applicants and a Guide for Evaluators were made publicly available through the webpage.

The ERC's activities

The ERC grants were designed to be financially attractive to appeal to the best researchers, flexible to be easily adjusted during the execution of the project, and portable so that the grant would be associated with the investigator and not the host institution signing the contract. Administration and reporting became simple and transparent to save the researcher's time for the research tasks.

Each grant would have an associated fixed institutional overhead (20 per cent) and the host institution was not allowed to take any other ERC fund for administration. The evaluation would be by peer review process in two stages, entrusted to twenty-five high-level transversal panels in three broad domains: ten panels in Physical Sciences and Engineering, nine panels in Biological and Life Sciences, and six panels in Social and Human Sciences. The evaluators would be selected from anywhere in the world based on their high level of expertise, and would meet at the ERC's Executive Agency premises in Brussels for the evaluation assisted by a pool of remote referees. Some types of grants would include an interview of the candidate by the panel during the evaluation meeting. Besides being responsible for the evaluation of the proposals, panels would also make funding decisions.

The ERC Scientific Council would remain fully responsible for the evaluation even if it was not directly involved in it, selecting the panel members, being present at the evaluation meetings, and monitoring the quality of the whole process.

The ERC started funding two grant schemes that would run in parallel every year: one, the Starting Grants, for applicants in early stages of a career as independent researchers (from two up to seven years after their PhD) amounting to a maximum of €1.5 million for a period of five years (an additional €0.5 million would be allowed in certain justified circumstances); the other for established researchers with a recognized track record of achievements, the Advanced Grants, amounting to a maximum of €2.5 million for a period of five years (with extra funds up to €1 million in certain justified circumstances). For budgetary reasons, explained below, in 2007 the only grants available were Starting Grants.

Learning from the experience, the Scientific Council introduced in 2010 a new type of grant, the Consolidator Grants, aimed at supporting researchers at a stage of consolidation of their own research team or programme (between seven and twelve years after their PhD), amounting to a maximum of €2 million for a period of five years. In the face of the success of the various calls, the Scientific Council decided to open another type of grant in 2011, the Proof of Concept Grants, to enable

110

ERC-funded ideas to be brought to a pre-demonstration phase through additional funding, up to a maximum of €150,000 for a period of twelve months.

Coherent with its experimental approach, the Scientific Council launched yet another type of funding, the Synergy Grants, to enable a small group of principal investigators and their teams to bring together their complementary skills, knowledge and resources, in order to jointly address transversal research problems too complex to be dealt with by a single team; the funding was up to a maximum of €15 million for a period of six years. However, this grant scheme was not continued beyond its experimental phase (2012).

The global budget of the IDEAS programme for the 2007–13 period was €7.51 billion, approximately 15 per cent of the total budget of the 7th Framework Programme. Its annual structure, however, was not constant over the period, increasing gradually from approximately €300 million in the first year (2007) to over €1,755 billion in 2013. As a consequence, the Scientific Council decided that in 2007 there would be a single call, only for Starting Grants, while the Advanced Grants scheme would be the only one to open in 2008. From then on both schemes opened yearly.

The first call, unexpectedly, brought in 9,167 applications, demonstrating how eager the scientific community was for such a programme. The budget allowed the funding of only 299 grants, leading to an exceedingly low success rate, even for such a very competitive and selective programme. Some adjustments were made to the application procedure (to save researchers' time, a two-phase submission moved into a single-phase submission process with a two-step evaluation) and the resubmission conditions were also narrowed.

From then on, the number of applications stabilized, typically around 4,000 per year for each Starting and Consolidating Grants call, with an average success rate of 11 per cent. The number of applications for the Advanced Grants remained always below 2,400 with an average success rate of 14 per cent.

Over the seven years of the IDEAS programme the level of interest in the ERC remained remarkably high. Globally 30,366 applications for both Starting Grant and Consolidator Grant were received, of which 2,645 were successful. For the Advanced Grants the global number of applications received during that period was 12,756, of which 1,709 were funded.

At a very early stage the Scientific Council made the decision to create a few internal working groups to address specific relevant topics and prepare documents and resolutions to be discussed and adopted by the plenary:

111

- *Open Access Working Group*: The question of Open Access was discussed at a very early stage and even before the first grants were awarded. Meanwhile a working group was set up within the Scientific Council and later on guidelines were given stating that all peer-reviewed publications from ERC-funded projects should be made openly accessible shortly after their publication.
- *Gender Balance Working Group*: Based on the view that women and men are equally able to perform excellent frontier research, the Scientific Council decided in 2008 to set up a dedicated working group to monitor gender balance-related issues within the ERC activities. Considering the gender differences detected in the results of the first three years of calls, the working group drafted the 'ERC gender equality plan 2007–2013', which was endorsed by the Scientific Council in December 2010.
- *Working Group on Strengthening International Participation*: Created in 2009, this working group focused on monitoring and identifying ways to stimulate the participation in ERC calls of researchers from countries outside the EU.
- *Working Group on Relations with Industry*: An outcome of the Scientific Council's view that the ERC's relationship with the industrial and business sector should be carefully considered in view of their relevance as regards the conduct of frontier research but also the demonstration of the ERC's contribution to the European economy.

At a later stage two other Working Groups were set up:

- *Working Group on Widening Participation*: This group aimed at contributing to a truly inclusive European culture of competitiveness in science and focusing on increasing the participation of researchers in ERC calls, namely from the EU's less research-performing regions.
- *Working Group on Key Performance Indicators*: The main role of this group was to develop a roadmap for monitoring and evaluating the ERC's accomplishment of its mission, beyond indicators and targets, in order to support the short-, medium- and long-term policies of the Scientific Council.

The mid-term review and changes in structure

A mid-term review of the structures and mechanisms of the ERC was foreseen since its creation. It was carried out in early 2009 by a panel of independent experts nominated by the Commission. In their report, although recognizing that 'for the first time a truly pan-European, scientifically independent instrument for frontier research has been created thus establishing a new standard of excellence for Europe' and 'the enthusiastic initial contribution of the scientific community in this success' as well as 'the positive spill-over that the ERC has produced in some national systems', they put forward a few recommendations, namely concerning a more coherent organization and the need to amalgamate into one post the roles of the Secretary-General and the Director of the Executive Agency (ERC 2009).

Following the recommendations, a Standing Committee on Panels and a Standing Committee on Conflict of Interest, Scientific Misconduct and Ethics, composed of members of, and reporting to, the Scientific Council, were set up. Another consequence was that after 2013 the President of the ERC would no longer be elected within and by the Scientific Council members but be recruited for the post by the Commissioner, as Civil Service of the Commission.

During the seven-year period of the IDEAS programme, the ERC managed to reach a high status of visibility, becoming a worldwide reference as a funding organization with best practice while supporting the best science and scholarship. Its impact in the international scientific community was repeatedly acknowledged.

Building on this, the EC decided that the ERC would carry on into the 8th Framework Programme, as part of the first pillar 'Excellent Science' of Horizon 2020. A total budget of €13.1 billion was allocated to the ERC for the period 2014–20, significantly higher than in the previous programme, with the ERC representing approximately 17 per cent of the overall Horizon 2020 budget.

Therefore, the prospects for the future are very positive. Demand for the ERC grants also continues to be very high. Clearly Europe was in need of such a truly pan-European scientific independent agency, funding frontier research at a high level of excellence. The hope is that the ERC carries on at full ambition, building to maturity and stability, without losing its original inventive and creative character.

EIT: an impact investment institution fostering innovation and entrepreneurship

The first years

Europe has all-important components of an innovation ecosystem: excellent research, universities and industry. However, these key systemic components have not been sufficient to leapfrog the United States and Japan. The 2000 Lisbon Strategy goal has not been reached and the innovation gap has actually been increasing.

A mid-term review of the Lisbon Strategy has resulted, among other things, in the establishment of the European Institute of Innovation and Technology (EIT), a small, experimental funding instrument, which was set up as one of the EU agencies. Headquartered in Budapest, the role of this new Institute was to revisit the funding model for research and innovation of the Framework Programmes and propose a new approach. The EIT legislation, approved by the highest EU institutions, granted an unprecedented level of freedom to the governing body of this institution in forming novel types of industry–academia partnerships referred to as Knowledge and Innovation Communities, or 'KICs'.

The EIT mandate was to fund the KICs with annual grants for a period of seven to fifteen years. Taking into consideration a rather limited budget of €308 million initially allocated to the EIT for four years (2008–14), the EIT and its KICs were looked upon as a political project and were widely contested for different reasons. Nevertheless, this daring policy experiment has developed a radically new thinking and a novel governance model. As a result, an alternative networked innovation ecosystem has emerged across Europe (Tataj 2015).

The EIT was established amidst the financial crisis of 2008. Its Chairman was elected in the first meeting of the Governing Board, held on 15 September 2008 under the auspices of the President of the EC, the very same day that Lehman Brothers – the fourth largest investment bank in the US – declared bankruptcy. The history of this institution is strictly linked with the struggle of the European Union and its Member States to overcome what has materialized into the most severe crises for European economies since the Great Depression. In concrete terms, this volatility has been demonstrated by the size of its budget. It was the enthusiasm and determination of the first Chairman of the Governing Board, Martin Schuurmans, that enabled the swift launch of the Institute.

Initially, testing new innovation models in the midst of the crisis quickly delivered promising results. The KICs were considered a successful experiment. In 2013 the Council and the Parliament agreed to increase the EIT budget to €2.7 billion. Two years later, during economic stagnation, a revised EIT budget proposed in the Juncker Plan was cut by 10 per cent, with a 40 per cent cut for 2016.

Nevertheless, the EIT with its KIC model of industry–academia transnational partnerships has had a major influence. It shifted the systemic model of funding research and innovation from subsidies to a financial leverage. The main framework for the KIC model was the 'Knowledge Triangle', that is the combination of research, education and innovation (soon translated into the language of EIT as research, education and business). While Framework Programmes established a long tradition of funding industry–academia collaboration, education was a new element to be introduced into the system. Additionally, the EIT has put an emphasis on inducing entrepreneurship in the Knowledge Triangle partnerships.

The education programmes were to be innovation-focused and branded as EIT-label master, doctorate and post doctorate degrees and diplomas. The business-related activities, including technology transfer and commercialization, were to stimulate innovation in large firms, create spin-offs and start-ups, and support innovative firms across Europe. The innovation-related activities were to attract and work with top-class talent coming from partner organizations and from around the world. In business terms these activities were the offering of a KIC to internal and external customers which were both partners in the consortium and future clients or users.

Entrepreneurship in the broadest sense is a catalyst of value creation processes and it was rightly identified as the missing link in the Knowledge Triangle and introduced into all KIC activities. KICs were to become vehicles for entrepreneurship education and for business incubation and acceleration infrastructure across Europe. Entrepreneurship has become an integrator of the Knowledge Triangle, capable of overcoming the silos of industry and academia through entrepreneurship education, support of new business creation, and growth of existing innovation-driven ventures. The Strategic Innovation Agenda (SIA) also introduced an EIT-labelled diploma for educational programmes at the KICs. It also showcased the EIT Entrepreneurship Award for ventures coming out of the KICs and the EIT Roundtable of Entrepreneurs as a way to establish a link between the EIT entrepreneurial community and venture capital industry. This was done with a view that the EIT and the KICs should contribute to fostering an entrepreneurial culture in Europe.

The regulators gave an unprecedented level of autonomy to the EIT Governing Board in terms of leeway to decide on vision and governance. The Board used this freedom to design a radically different Call for Proposals for the KICs and later the EIT Strategic Innovation Agenda, the main document defining the outlook for this institution. The flexibility manifested itself in a number of derogations from the EC rules but maybe more importantly by a declaration of a political will to truly allow the EIT to experiment.

As a consequence, the Institute declared an ambition to become an 'impact investment institute' rather than a granting agency. This manifested itself in looking at the KICs as a portfolio and making grant allocation decisions based on their value proposition and business plan, delivering on promises and weighing a vision for the future by feasibility of delivering promised results and impact. The grant process resembled a venture capital approach where value is defined in economic terms. In the case of the KICs, value was in their ability to deliver solutions to grand societal challenges, drive economic growth and create new jobs. In short, the EIT as defined by its ambitious goals was to become an entrepreneurial institution, a sort of investor in a KIC and a manager of a KIC portfolio rather than a traditional EU funding agency. It was expressed through its mission: 'To become the catalyst for a step change in the European Union's innovation capacity and impact'.

EIT structure and prospects

Consequently, the KICs are not subsidy programmes. The KICs are pan-European private–public partnerships that have brought together research institutes, universities and businesses as well as, in some cases, NGOs and public agencies. They are based on a conceptual framework of a Knowledge Triangle that is a specific type of innovation network, which in their case has around six co-location nodes. Each node is a hub in a local innovation ecosystem and an entry point to the European network. KICs are autonomous, independent legal entities with a seven-year financial commitment of partners. They are managed by a CEO with executive power over all of the KIC's resources, and a governance structure allowing partners to enter and exit the consortia.

Their financial plan reflects (or should reflect) a vision towards financial self-sustainability based on a value proposition and a market-driven business model. It could have a focus on business creation through spin-offs and start-ups or licensing of technology and patents, and offerings of products and services were part of the self-sustainability plan. The viability of the plan is confirmed by the fact that 75 per cent of the KIC funding comes from partners: industry and universities alike.

The KICs were given the freedom to decide on their legal structure, governance model, organization and strategy, which validated the EIT approach to managing and financing innovation. This approach was to empower bottom-up initiative and encourage business thinking expressed for example by the reference to the KIC's business model and business case, private funding (co-investment), effective governance structure, IP rules and operational efficiency.

In 2010 the EIT established the first three communities: Climate-KIC, EIT ICT Labs (later rebranded as EIT Digital) and KIC InnoEnergy. Two more communities were selected in a call launched in 2014: EIT Health and EIT Raw Materials (see table 5.1). Ultimately, a call launched in 2016 led to the establishment of a new KIC, EIT Food, and two calls

Table 5.1   Knowledge and innovation communities, co-location nodes and key partners in 2015

Name	Co-location nodes	Key industry and other non-academic partners	Key academic partners
1. Climate-KIC	London, Berlin, Paris Saclay, Zurich, Eindhoven/ Randstad	Amsterdam Airport Schiphol, Arcadis, Aster, Bayer Technology Services, Birmingham City Council, CEA, Deltares, DGF Suez, Grundfos, Institute for Sustainability, KLM, South Pole Group, Velux A/S	Chalmers University of Technology, ETH Zurich, Julich Forschungszentrum, GFZ Potsdam, Imperial College London, INRA, TNO, Potsdam Institute for Climate Impact Research, Technical University of Denmark, Berlin University of Technology, TU Delft, Université de Versailles Saint-Quentin-en-Yvelines, Université Pierre et Marie Curie, University of Copenhagen, Utrecht University, Valencia Institute of Business Competitiveness, Wageningen University and Research Institute
2. EIT Digital (formerly EIT ICT Labs)	Berlin, Eindhoven, Helsinki, London, Paris, Stockholm, Trento	Alcatel Lucent, BT Group, CEA, Engineering, Ericsson, Intel, Nokia, Oce, Orange, Philips, SAP AG, Siemens, T-Labs, Telecom Italia, Thales Group, TNO, Trento RISE, VTT	Aalto University, CWI, TU Delft, DFKI, TU Eindhoven, Fraunhofer, INRIA, Institute Mines-Telecom, KTH Royal Institute of Technology, Paris-Sud University, SICS, TU Berlin, University College London, University of Twente, UPMC
3. KIC Inno-Energy	Eindhoven/ Leuven, Barcelona/ Lisbon, Grenoble, Stockholm, Cracow,	Alfen, Areva, Bay Zoltan Nonprofit Ltd., CEA, Eandis, EC Grupa, EDF, EDP, ENBW, ENGIE (GDF SUEZ), Gas Natura Fenosa,	AGH University of Science and Technology, Aix-Marseille University, BarcelonaTech, Eindhoven University of Technology, ESADE, Grenoble Ecole de Management, Grenoble

Table 5.1   (continued)

Name	Co-location nodes	Key industry and other non-academic partners	Key academic partners
	Stuttgart/ Karlsruhe	Iberdrola, inno AG, MetalERG, Schneider Electric, Steinbels-europa-Zentrum S'Tile, Novargi, TURON Group, Total	Institute of Technology, INSA Lyon, Instituto Superior Technico, Jagiellonian University, Karlsruhe Institute of Technology, KTH Royal Institute of Technology, KU Leuven, Wroclaw University of Technology Silesian University of Technology
4. EIT Health	London, Stockholm, Barcelona, Heidelberg, Rotterdam	Abbott, Abbvie, Atos, IBV, Ferrer, Grupe SEB, CEA, Sorin Group, Institute Meriuex, Air Liquide, BD, Leo, Novo Nordisk, Philips, Roche, Sanofi, Stochholms Stad, Thermo Fisher Scientific, UMPC, Inserm, inria, Bull, USB, Siemens, Profil, Medtronic, West Midlands, Clinic Barcelona, CERCA	KTH Royal Institute of Technology, Karolinska Institutet, RISE Institutes, University of Copenhagen, Universite Joseph Fourier, Uppsala Universitet, TUM, Imperial College London, University of Oxford, Trinity College Dublin, KU Leuven TU Eindhoven, Universiteit Gent, IESE, Universität Heidelberg, FAU, Newcastle University, KU Leuven, Universidad Politécnica Madrid, IBEC
5. EIT Raw Materials	Espoo, Metz, Wroclaw, Luleå, Rome, Leuven	BMT Group LTD, Atlas Copco Rock Drills AB; Boliden Mineral AB; Geological Survey of Sweden, SGU; Höganäs AB; IVL Svenska Miljoeinstitutet AB, Jernkontoret, Luossavaara-Kiirunavaara AB, LKAB; RISE	Aalto University, Imperial College London, Chalmers University of Technology, KTH Royal Institute of Technology, Luleå University of Technology, Lund University, Kungliga Tekniska Högskolan, Uppsala University, Delft University of Technology Fraunhofer, Wuppertal Institute, Grenoble Institute of Technology,

Table 5.1   (continued)

Name	Co-location nodes	Key industry and other non-academic partners	Key academic partners
		Research Institute of Sweden AB; Sandvik AB, BASF, H.C. Starck GmbH; Heraeus Holding GmbH; Hydro Aluminium Rolled Products GmbH; Recylex GmbH; ArcelorMittal; Maizières Research SA; Arkema France; CEA, Soprema SAS; Suez Environment SAS; VTT, JM Recycling NV, F.J. Elsner Trading GmbH; Inteco special melting technologies GmbH, KGHM Polska SA, EIT+ Sp. z o.o.	Tallinn University of Technology, University of Zagreb, KU Leuven, Graz University of Technology, Vienna University of Technology, Lodz University of Technology; Wroclaw University of Technology

Note: The list of academic partners is not comprehensive but includes the main partners.

Source: Based on Knowledge and Innovation Communities' websites.

to be announced in 2018 will search for new KICs in the fields of urban mobility and value added manufacturing.

Each KIC has a specific focus, legal setup, operational structure and strategy. Climate-KIC aims to develop solutions to mitigate and to adapt to climate change. It enables universities and companies to partner with regions and cities to design proof-of-concept solutions. Its landmark is a Contextual Learning Journey, a crash course in new venture creation. Like other KICs, it has a limited number of co-location nodes in key European innovation hot spots, and it also has established a parallel structure of regional implementation centres (RICs), which are test beds for innovations coming out of the KIC. EIT Digital (formerly EIT ICT Labs) innovates in the area of the future information and communication society. It fosters an open innovation environment and, based on its 'catalyst-carrier model', it tries to accelerate innovation at such incumbents as Siemens, Ericsson and Nokia, to name just a few partners. KIC InnoEnergy tackles challenges related to sustainable energy. Through its 'Highway', it interconnects European start-ups with their potential clients, that is the largest power producers and distributors in Europe. In return for getting the first client, young companies share a part of their equity. Both EIT Health and EIT Raw Materials were selected at the end of 2014. 2015 was for them the year of incorporation, bringing partners together and launching first activities. The former focuses on developing innovations in healthy living and active ageing and providing Europe with new entrepreneurial opportunities. The latter leads experimentation and commercialization activities related to excavation and exploitation of raw materials and recyclables.

While it still may be too early to assess the return on investment (both in economic and social terms), the experimental model of new innovation networks in Europe surely catalysed the change in the higher education system and led to more diversity and focus on entrepreneurship (Blakemore et al. 2013). It has also enhanced strategies of integrating the Knowledge Triangle and forming a next generation of entrepreneurial Europeans (Technopolis 2013). While the impact of the co-location centres may still be too difficult to measure, operational capacity at the local level may be instrumental in tackling increasingly complex societal challenges (Ecorys 2012).

However, the KIC model should continue to be scaled up. The success of the EIT will be measured ultimately by the achievements of the students, graduates and entrepreneurs nurtured in the EIT community, supported with its projects and funds. The 700 people at Innovation Summit INNOEIT in 2015 in Budapest demonstrated a rising power of ideas coming out of the KICs as manifested by start-ups. The EIT is a unique platform for networking, sharing, learning and innovating through solution-oriented action. It may at some point become the European brand for innovation.

And beyond. . .

The world has not been frozen during this period of crises, nor has the EU. But the speed of achievements in the Union has not been comparable to the global thrust of transformation that sweeps through our societies. Brexit can be thought of as an alarm bell warning us that time is out of joint.

By the year 2000 complexity had engulfed the world. *Complexity* (or *interdependence*, in the language of the social sciences) has many discouraging characteristics for societies like ours, which have been used for nearly three centuries to take refuge in science when the storm approaches. The most important feature of complexity is the impossibility of separating the subject from the object, and ontology from epistemology. Thus, unless a new mathematics is invented to describe complexity, we are left in a situation where no unified approach to complex problems exists! Only in certain specific cases are we able to devise schemes that perform adequately according to circumstances. We have been left with an array of 'sciencettes'.

The main task at the beginning of the twenty-first century thus lies in identifying emergent collective patterns and regularities and in trying to make sense of them. No doubt interdisciplinarity and transdisciplinarity enjoy now a revamped status. But science is nowadays undergoing a second grand transformation, in a still quite unclear direction. Some aspects have already emerged though.

This second transformation is prompted by the obsession with market forces and interest in the ceaseless accumulation of capital. The drive we are observing towards the study of neurosciences, coupled with computer sciences and nanoscience may result in an attempt to control even more efficiently and directly the whole (body and mind) of the human being. This new class of science is now being tentatively called 'big data' but can also be designated as an outcome of *control-driven research*. This new objective and attitude will transform research practices and publications enormously.

The only way to anticipate the future is to engage in its preparation, i.e. in making the future happen now. What can we foresee in the 2050 horizon?

Key transformations will most probably result from the work of the forces of globalization, of demography and of knowledge production. This probably means, in the same order: more privatization (with the rise of China); cities becoming political actors in the geopolitical game (with increasing migration); and big changes in labour markets (with new technology). Education will become again a central societal issue.

By the end of the twentieth century, EU total investment in R&D was of the order of that of the US. In 2014, the EU invested 40 per cent less than in 2000. China doubled its R&D investment from 2008 to 2012 (and is approaching a volume of three-quarters of US expenditure). Korea was the highest R&D spender in 2014 (4.29 per cent of its GDP), Israel the second (4.11 per cent) and Japan the third (3.58 per cent). The EU was trailing with a value of 1.94 per cent for the same indicator (OECD

2016). The volume of EU investment in R&D (and its ability to leverage through ERA-NETs and Joint Programming Initiatives) has never been at the level required for a multinational integrated area. In spite of the increases in funding through successive Framework Programmes, even the billions of the present Horizon 2020 correspond to less than 10 per cent of the total public effort in R&D in the EU. This means that in order to be effective in setting the priorities for Europe, its volume ought to be an order of magnitude higher (i.e. be multiplied by a factor of ten).

Cross-country business investments by transnational enterprises are also revealing: EU-based corporations invest in R&D in the US through its affiliates in higher sums than American-based multinationals in Europe (of the order of 20–25 per cent more) (National Science Board 2016). But no one is sure about the meaning of this gap: is strategic R&D performed overseas a complement, or a substitute, of R&D conducted at national levels?

The prospects for the ERC and EIT are good but may waver with divergences and convergences between the European Council, the Parliament and the European Commission in the aftermath of the crises. Will the model adopted by the ERC for funding research – the life sciences model – be adequate to accommodate the impact of big data in the scientific establishment and therefore enable the ERC to still perform a leading role in 2050? And will the EIT, taking stock of large-scale networking activity in Europe, be able to deliver world-leading innovations that elevate Europe's growth in the next 10–20 years? Are the ERC and the EIT, solely by themselves, sufficient to stimulate a European renaissance? The new technologies that will support economic growth after 2030/2040 will be deployed first by the nation that will become the new leader in global innovation. We cannot be sure that this leadership will continue to be an exclusive prerogative of a nation of the Western hemisphere. Leadership requires much vision, boldness and resources.

A special report by the European Court of Auditors states that seven years after its inception, the EIT is not yet fully operationally independent from the European Commission and that this has hampered its decision-making (ECA 2016). And, further, a report by an EC senior innovation adviser argues that policy makers focused too much on the role of research funding, whereas public awareness of science and intelligent governance are just as important factors for innovation (Madelin 2016). The considerable number of European scientists presently working in the US can be seen also as a sign of excellent training in Europe but coupled with a weak institutional and industrial capacity of talent attraction. This calls for significant action both at the EU and national levels.

It is therefore time to think about devising new scientific institutions. And to install them deftly, besides connecting and funding them generously. We cannot tolerate idleness. After all, what will be the power base of the leaders of the new world of tomorrow?

In 2050 we will probably be worrying about the fate of *technology-driven research* (technoscience) in the face of the overwhelming presence of *control-driven research* (big data). But the grand issue will again be the nurturing of *curiosity-driven research*. For we must not forget the tremendous power of great ideas.

'Life is a-changing', really, and science is an essential element of the endless dialogue between humankind and the universe. Science is our way of interrogating the universe, to get answers and keep abreast of change in order to continue living. Maybe we shall have again to transform the language with which we communicate with nature.

References

Blakemore, M., Burquel, N. and McDonald, N. (2013) The educational activities of the KICs of the EIT, Final report for the European Commission Directorate-General for Education and Culture.

Caraça, J. (1999) *Science et communication*. Paris: Presses Universitaires de France.

Ecorys (2012) *Study of co-location centres using the example of the EIT and KICs*. DGEAC.

ERC (2005) European Research Council Identification Committee. Final Report, June 2005. Available at: https://erc.europa.eu/sites/default/files/content/final_report_erc_20062005_en.pdf

ERC (2009) Towards a world class frontier research organisation: Review of the European Research Council's structures and mechanisms. Available at: https://erc.europa.eu/sites/default/files/content/pages/pdf/final_report_230709.pdf

European Commission (2006) Council Decision of 19 December 2006 concerning the specific programme: 'Ideas' implementing the Seventh Framework Programme of the European Community for research, technological development and demonstration activities (2007 to 2013). 2006/972/EC. 19 December.

European Commission (2007) Two new executive agencies bolster European research. IP/07/1930. Brussels, 14 December.

European Court of Auditors (2016) *Special report no. 04/2016*. Luxembourg: ECA.

Madelin, R. (2016) *Opportunity Now: Europe's Mission to Innovate*. EPSC Strategic Note no. 15.

National Science Board (2016) *Science and Engineering Indicators*. Arlington: NSF.

OECD (2016) *Main Science and Technology Indicators Database*. Paris: OECD.

Schrödinger, E. (1954), *Nature and the Greeks*. Cambridge: Cambridge University Press.

Tataj, D. (2015) *Innovation and Entrepreneurship. A Growth Model for Europe.* New York: Tataj Innovation Library.
Technopolis (2013) *Catalysing Innovation in the Knowledge Triangle.* Brussels: European Commission.

Part II

Social Crises

Chapter 6

Austerity and Health: The Impact of Crisis in the UK and the Rest of Europe

David Stuckler, Aaron Reeves, Rachel Loopstra, Marina Karanikolos and Martin McKee

Introduction

Austerity is a massive experiment on the people of Europe. It was imposed in the aftermath of the Great Recessions of 2007, precipitated by the collapse of the housing bubble in the US. In 2009, gross domestic product (GDP) fell in real terms in all countries of the European Union (EU) except Poland; the mean decrease was 4.3 per cent, but losses ranged from 1.9 per cent in Cyprus to 17.7 per cent in Latvia (Karanikolos et al. 2013). Between 2007 and 2010, unemployment increased substantially and rapidly – for example, by 3 per cent in Portugal, Slovakia and Bulgaria, 4 per cent in Denmark, Hungary and Greece, 5 per cent in Iceland, 9 per cent in Ireland, 12 per cent in Spain and Estonia, 13 per cent in Latvia, and 14 per cent in Lithuania. By 2016, economic output had only just returned to pre-crisis levels.

How best to promote economic recoveries is a topic of ongoing debate. During the initial onset of financial crisis, politicians in nations with significant financial sectors, particularly the US and UK, along with Sweden and Germany tended to implement large stimulus packages. These were used to bail out banks, absorbing their debts into the public sector's balance sheet. This dose of government spending prompted commentator Martin Wolfe to claim (quoting Richard Nixon), 'We are all Keynesians now', referring to the argument that government spending should increase during economic downturns to restore growth. In parallel, however, the economic slowdown was leading to job losses and falling incomes, in turn causing drops in consumer spending and associated tax revenues. These forces, when combined with large bailout packages for the financial sector, generated large rises in government deficits

127

(where annual government spending exceeds revenues) and, resultantly, increased national public debts.

There are two broad options to achieve debt reduction: to invest to promote economic growth and thus boost government revenues for debt repayment, or to reduce government spending to free up revenue for debt repayment. The European Commission (EC), European Central Bank (ECB) and International Monetary Fund (IMF) (the so-called 'Troika'), along with leaders of many European nations, placed an explicit priority on the latter approach to deficit reduction. In a letter to Europe's finance ministers on 13 February 2013 the European Union's Commissioner for Economic and Monetary Affairs, Ollie Rehn, wrote that 'when public debt levels rise above 90 per cent they tend to have a negative impact on economic dynamism' (Rehn 2013). Concerns were widespread that high levels of debt could trigger declines in economic growth (Reinhart and Rogoff 2010), as well as lead to costly, unsustainable debt repayments. In theory, deficit reduction can be achieved by either raising taxes or reducing expenditure. When combined these activities are sometimes referred to as 'fiscal consolidation'. In practice, the majority of deficit reduction policies (> 80 per cent) in Europe involved budget cuts rather than tax increases (Reeves et al. 2013a). Consequently, for coherence we refer to these policies as 'austerity'.

An understanding of the consequences of austerity measures is incomplete without investigating the social and human costs associated with their implementation. While there is now an extensive literature on the economics of austerity, much less is known about their impact on health and well-being.

At the time of this writing, in 2016, more than half a decade has passed since the initial experiments with austerity. In the meantime the magnitude, type and form of austerity measures has developed. This review aims to assess: what impacts have these austerity measures had on health and well-being, and what has helped to buffer them?

Political economy of austerity

Before proceeding, it is important to understand the reasons why some nations but not others opted for the path of austerity. To begin, it must be noted that, contrary to popular rhetoric, austerity is not an economic inevitability. All nations suffered economic downturns. Yet only some introduced austerity and, fewer still, deep cuts to their health and social security systems. In one group of 'stimulus nations', including Germany, Iceland and Sweden in Europe, as well as the United States, politicians pursued greater spending into the crisis, not only for the financial sector but by providing support to those who had lost access to jobs, homes and healthcare. A related group of countries allowed their so-called automatic stabilizers to operate, so that total spending would rise in the face of increasing population needs. These stabilizers are programmes such as unemployment insurance on which spending tends to increase automatically during downturns, boosting spending above what it would be in their absence. A final group of austerity countries, such as the UK, Greece, Italy, Spain, Portugal and Ireland, among others, did the opposite and primarily focused on cuts as a way to reduce spending into the recession and beyond.

One cross-national analysis of 27 EU nations showed that the choice of austerity could not be explained by either the severity of the economic recession or the political ideology of the governing party (Reeves et al. 2013a).[1] Nor was there any link between the pursuit of austerity measures and the actual debt-to-GDP ratio in a country, a marker of severity of debt. In contrast, two main predictors of austerity were falls in tax revenues per capita and entering into a lending agreement with the Troika. Thus deeper cuts were observed in Greece, Ireland, Portugal and Latvia – those countries which entered into bailout agreements with the Troika. The most extreme of these is Greece. Figure 6.1 shows the magnitude of austerity in healthcare expenditure across nations, showing how Greece is a clear outlier.

Those nations pursuing austerity measures had options as to where and how much to reduce budgets. Several nations, while pursuing austerity, explicitly protected spending on public services, such as health and education. The heat maps in figure 6.2 (in constant purchasing-power-parity adjusted dollars) show the magnitude of budget cuts during the first wave of austerity (2009–11). Ten European countries reduced spending on social protection during the economic downturn (Bulgaria, Estonia, Greece, Latvia, Lithuania, Luxembourg, Hungary, Romania, Sweden and the UK) and 17 increased it. Of all areas of government spending, housing, community and health budgets tended to experience the largest reductions (apart from 'economic affairs', which artefactually fell after the massive bank bailout packages of 2008).

What is clear is that many countries adopting austerity tended to protect politically sensitive areas of the budget; for example, older

---

[1] Take Austria and Germany, for example. Both experienced recessions of similar size and timing (2008–9), yet Austria saw reduced government spending on health, of US$90.1 per capita, adjusted for purchasing-power and inflation, while Germany saw an increase of US$57.4 per capita.

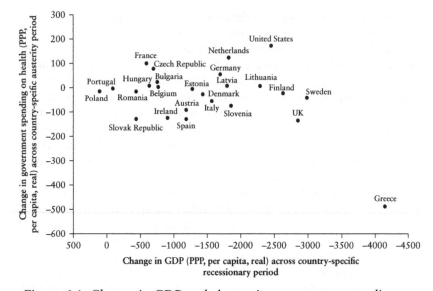

Figure 6.1: Change in GDP and change in government spending on health across country-specific recession and austerity periods

Note: Recession is defined as declining GDP (adjusted for inflation and purchasing-power) in consecutive years. Austerity is defined as declining government expenditure (adjusted for inflation and purchasing-power) in consecutive years. Data on from countries with small populations (i.e., Malta, Luxembourg and Cyprus) excluded from the graphic.
Source: WHO Health expenditure database 2013 edition, Eurostat 2013 edition

persons tend to be among the most likely to vote and are well-organized politically. Thus Estonia was the only nation to make reductions in old-age pensions in the initial period (2009–12), with Greece making cuts in later periods. In contrast, unemployed and disabled persons, who tend to be less well-organized politically, appeared to be an easier target for budgetary reductions. As shown in the heat maps, those aspects of health and social security systems that protect the weak have been most vulnerable to budget cuts across Europe.

It is also important to note that austerity is not a simple yes/no dichotomy. Some countries actually pursued stimulus policies overall but still had elements of austerity. For example, Sweden increased spending in all areas except social protection, where its politicians opted for large cuts to sickness and disability support in this period.

In sum, what these data reveal is that policy makers had a range of

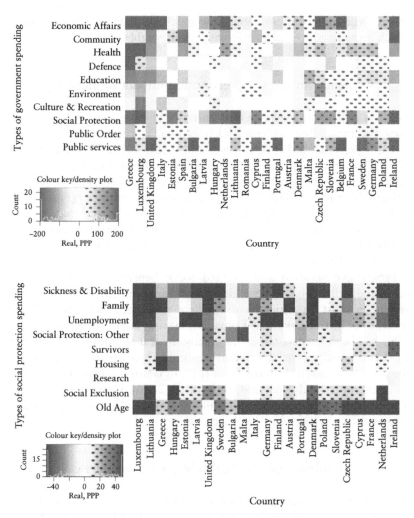

Figure 6.2: (a) Total austerity packages by type of government spending, 26 EU countries, 2009–2011. (b) Budget cuts to social protection systems, 23 EU countries, 2009–2011

Notes: Heatmap depicts reductions in sector-specific government expenditure (constant, purchasing power parity, per capita) across country-specific austerity period for which data are available. Types of social spending ordered from greatest cuts (e.g. sickness and disability benefits) to lowest cuts (dotted, e.g. old-age pensions) overall. Twenty-three countries are provided for which data are available.

choices available to them about how much austerity to pursue, and in which areas to concentrate. Nothing was inevitable.

Evidence on the socio-economic impact of austerity

There is now clear evidence that austerity is regressive, impacting the poor the most, thus widening socio-economic inequalities (Ball et al. 2013; Figari et al. 2015; Schaltegger and Weder 2014; Woo et al. 2013). The full scale of regressivity, however, depends on which areas of the budget are cut. In general, they tend to have greater impact on more vulnerable groups and on deprived regions within countries (Figari et al. 2015; Reeves et al. 2013a). An analysis by the IMF found that, historically, austerity measures that are pursued through spending-based consolidations are much worse than those based on tax-based consolidation (Woo et al. 2013).

Progressive taxation and targeted social benefits could offset these adverse distributional effects. However, changes to the tax and benefit system in most countries have not kept pace with the cost of living (except for in Germany and Romania), leaving many people worse off. Who has been hardest hit varies greatly. In real terms, cuts have fallen hardest on wealthier groups in Portugal and Greece but in some countries the poor have taken the hardest hit (e.g., in Germany, Lithuania, and to some extent Ireland) (Legido-Quigley et al. 2016). However, for vulnerable groups on the margins across all countries studied, these cuts led to greater difficulty affording life's necessities.

Evidence on the health impact of austerity

There is less understanding of the consequences of austerity for health and well-being. A review in the prestigious medical journal *The Lancet* noted that 'public health voices have been largely absent from the debate about how to respond' (Karanikolos et al. 2013). It also pointed out that, in the EU, the Directorate-General for Health and Consumer Protection of the European Commission, despite its legal obligation to assess the health effects of EU policies, has not assessed the effects of the Troika's drive for austerity, and has instead limited EU commentary to advice about 'how health ministries can cut their budgets'.

This lack of evidence is a manifestation of a wider problem in evaluating policy. Social scientists have increasingly called for research to identify wider impacts of economic choices on not just economic phenomena but on social and health outcomes. Layard and Sachs, among others, in the first UN World Happiness Report argue that health measures more closely approximate the economics concept of 'utility', or overall happiness, and are a better barometer of policy success or failure than conventional economic outcomes such as wages or growth (Helliwell et al. 2015). They further find that health status is the strongest statistical correlate of self-reported happiness.

Conceptually, austerity can impact health through two mechanisms: (i) a social risk effect of increasing unemployment, poverty and homelessness and other socio-economic risk factors, while cutting effective social protection programmes that mitigate their risks to health; and (ii) a healthcare effect through cuts to healthcare services, as well as reductions in health coverage and restricting access to care.

The rest of this chapter now turns to understanding the impact on people's health and well-being of austerity measures through these two channels, starting with the indirect effects, on unemployment, homelessness and food security. Where possible, data from across Europe will be drawn upon, as well as more extensive analysis of the UK's austerity measures performed by the authors of this chapter.

Effects on social risk and protective factors

Unemployment and working conditions

Austerity measures have sought to make savings by reducing public sector employment; resulting job losses can be expected to increase depression and suicide rates. Taking the UK as an example, according to the Office for National Statistics, there were over 500,000 public sector job losses between June 2010 and September 2012, of which over 35 per cent were in the North of England (North-East, North-West and Yorkshire and the Humber) (Reeves et al. 2013b). A total of 36,000 NHS jobs were cut during this period, costing over £435 million in severance packages; in total, a further 144,000 public-sector redundancies are expected in 2015–16. The regional pattern of job losses correlates with changes in suicides; a 20 per cent rise was observed in those regions most affected by austerity: the North-East, the North-West, and Yorkshire and the Humber, but a decline in London, where unemployment fell.

Austerity has, in many nations, been achieved by reducing social spending on the unemployed. One means is to tighten eligibility for unemployment insurance. The UK has done this by expanding its punitive policies of 'sanctions' – cutting benefits when an unemployment support recipient fails to meet strict conditions, including evidence of actively seeking work. Several million people have undergone this sanction process in 2014–15. Qualitative research has found that these policies increase risks of hunger and depression, and quantitative studies identify that they increase risks of food insecurity and homelessness (Loopstra et al. 2014, 2015b).

Several policies, while not directly branded as part of an austerity package, have contributed to achieving these reductions. Continuing with the UK as an example, it introduced Work Capability Assessments to screen persons on disability support to assess whether they are capable of work. This system has been heavily criticized following evidence that benefit managers, in pursuit of targets to reduce numbers receiving benefits, focused attention on those who, as a result of their disability, were least likely to be able to meet the conditions, such as scheduling assessments at times when there was no public transport. Those who are deemed 'fit for work' have their benefits cut. A cross-regional analysis found that greater density of Work Capability Assessments corresponded to marked rises in new anti-depressant prescriptions (see figure 6.3) (Barr et al. 2015).

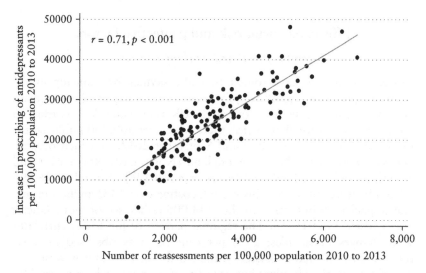

Figure 6.3: Association of work capability assessments and antidepressant prescriptions per capita

Homelessness

Homelessness is a major public health concern, with a significant body of epidemiologic research demonstrating that homelessness increases risks of infectious disease, physical harm, food insecurity, multiple morbidities and premature mortality.

The application of austerity to housing support and subsidies, at a time of rising housing costs throughout much of Europe, has contributed to a growing burden of homelessness and less severe forms of housing insecurity. The European Federation of National Organizations Working with Homeless People (FEANTSA) found that 60 per cent of homelessness organizations experienced cuts in 2011. FEANTSA further argued that the 'need to introduce austerity measures has been used as an excuse by governments not to commit to ambitious homelessness strategies', citing how Poland abandoned its draft strategy during the crisis (FEANTSA 2011).

There is clear evidence of a link between budget reductions and escalating homelessness. FEANTSA's analysis from its membership across 30 EU countries found evidence that austerity measures increased vulnerability of families with children to evictions and repossessions (FEANTSA 2011). In Wales, FEANTSA members reported an increase from 14 per cent in 2010 to 21 per cent in 2011 among adults who cut back on heating to meet housing costs. It also observed large rises in demand for homelessness services, by 20 per cent in Greece, and rising demand for social housing. One of the few quantitative studies, a cross local area analysis of 323 authorities in the UK, found that budget reductions in housing services and emergency housing assistance payments were strongly linked with rising rates of people seeking emergency aid for housing (Loopstra et al. 2016a). These findings are further corroborated by data from a recent survey among local authorities in England, where two-thirds of local authorities reported that welfare reforms over 2010–15 had increased homelessness in their areas (Fitzpatrick et al. 2016). Identified drivers were cuts in Housing Benefit, benefit sanctions and caps to Housing Benefit rates for private tenancies.

Food insecurity

Images of people queuing for food aid recall scenes from the Great Depression, but have now come to characterize many European nations subjected to austerity. In 2016, the UK charity, The Trussell Trust, provided emergency food assistance to over 1 million adults and children, a marked rise from prior to the period of austerity in 2010 (The Trussell

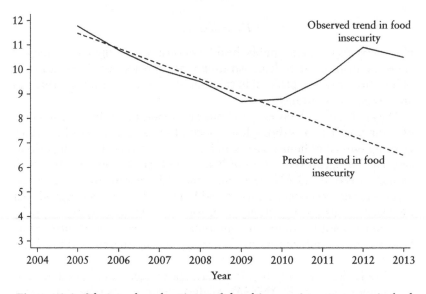

Figure 6.4: Observed and estimated food insecurity over a period of austerity in Europe

Trust 2016). Greek, Spanish and French charities also report marked rises in people seeking emergency food support coinciding with the introduction of austerity measures (Rada 2013; RFI 2014).

There is generally a dearth of comparative data on household food insecurity. One measure employed is from the EU Survey on Income and Living Conditions (EU-SILC), which asks if households are able to afford meat (or a vegetarian equivalent) every second day. As this amount falls well below the general recommendation in European dietary guidelines, self-reports of being unable to afford this basic nutrition on a regular basis is one indication of household food insecurity (Wunderlich and Norwood 2006; Loopstra et al. 2016b).

Across Europe, as shown in figure 6.4 using data from the EU Survey on Income and Living Conditions (EU-SILC), from 2005 to 2010 the proportion of people reporting an inability to afford meat or the equivalent declined by approximately half a percentage point each year (Loopstra et al. 2015a). After 2010, when austerity measures were imposed, this trend reversed, rising from 8.7 per cent in 2009 to 10.9 per cent in 2012, remaining elevated thereafter. This rise has been estimated to equate to approximately an additional 13.5 million people experiencing food insecurity. While unemployment and stagnating wages have been some of the major drivers of rising food insecurity in Europe, cuts to social protection

136

spending have likely exacerbated the impact of these economic shocks on access to healthy diets.

Further analyses of these data indeed highlighted how declining average incomes and rising unemployment within EU countries were associated with rising food insecurity (Loopstra et al. 2016b). These relationships were not inevitable, however; in countries where social protection spending was high, there was not a concurrent rise in food insecurity associated with unemployment and falling wages over the period 2007–12. In short, the effects of recession on population food insecurity were buffered by strong social safety nets.

A relationship between austerity and food insecurity has also been mapped in the UK (Loopstra et al. 2015b). Using data from the Trussell Trust Foodbank Network, the only charity with longitudinal data on rates of usage from their member food banks, the initiation of food banks in local areas over 2010–13 was tied to the magnitude of reductions in spending by local authorities and on benefits in this period. In turn, higher rates of demand for food aid were observed where there were deeper cuts to welfare benefit spending. These findings indicate that austerity measures in the UK contributed to growing demand for charitable food assistance.

Mental health

There is now a large body of evidence on how economic hardship can beget worse mental health. One multi-country study using longitudinal data from health and retirement surveys in the US and 13 EU countries found that job loss among 50 to 64-year-olds, particularly when due to firm closure, was associated with a 28 per cent increase in depressive symptoms in the US and an 8 per cent increase in Europe (Riumallo-Herl et al. 2014). In Greece, one-month prevalence of major depressive episodes increased from 3.3 per cent in 2008 to 8.2 per cent in 2011 and 12.3 in 2013 (Economou et al. 2016). Similar patterns were observed in Australia, England, Spain and the US. In Ireland, patients admitted with an episode of depression attributable to adverse economic circumstances linked to recession had higher suicide risks (but otherwise more favourable mental health outcomes) than patients with depression caused by other factors (Thekiso et al. 2013).

Suicide rates often rise during periods of economic downturn, and the Great Recession was no exception (Norström and Grönqvist 2015; Reeves et al. 2012, 2014, 2015a) As shown in figure 6.5, prior to the onset of recession in 2007, suicide rates had been falling in Europe. Subsequently, this downward trend reversed, rising by 6.5 per cent by

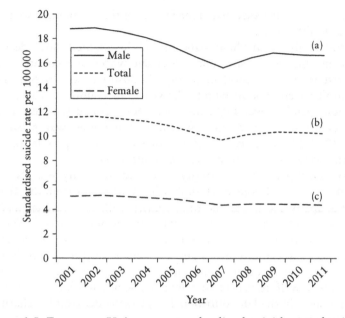

Figure 6.5: European Union age-standardized suicide rate for (b) the total population, and for (a) males and (c) females, 2001–2011

2009 and remaining elevated through 2011. This increase corresponds to an additional 7,950 suicides above what would be expected from past trends between 2007 and 2010. This same trend has also been observed outside of Europe. In the US, where suicides had been on an upward trajectory, the rate of increase accelerated, with an increase over and above past trends of 4.8 per cent, totalling about 4,750 excess suicides between 2007 and 2010 (Reeves et al. 2012). A similar analysis conducted in England found that rising suicides were significantly associated with increased unemployment, and resulted in an estimated 1,000 excess deaths (Barr et al. 2012).

Typically suicide rates rebound after GDP recovers. However, in many European nations, suicide rates remain elevated even where economic recovery appears to have occurred. The reasons are multiple; importantly, several socio-economic risk factors for suicide remain elevated. These include unemployment, unaffordable housing and indebtedness. One cross-national analysis investigated the role of these three risk factors across 20 EU countries, examining the association of suicide rates with rates of unemployment, unaffordable housing and indebtedness at the national level (Reeves et al. 2015a). They found that suicides were most closely associated with unemployment rates, particularly among the working-age population. Suicides were also significantly correlated with rising levels of household indebtedness (Reeves et al. 2016).

There is emerging evidence that economic suicides may be preventable. Some European countries seem to have avoided this association. For example, in Austria the suicide rate has not increased despite rising unemployment during the recession. In those nations with greater degrees of investment in active labour market programmes and unemployment insurance, the impact of job loss on suicide appears to be attenuated (Reeves et al. 2015a, Stuckler et al. 2009). Another protective factor identified relates to people's ability to turn to family and friends for support. This is sometimes operationalized as a concept known as 'social capital', and measured as the degree to which people trust each other in a society. One Canadian study found that high social capital moderated the impact of the crisis on mental health: while financial strain led to deterioration in mental health overall, in communities with high compared to low social capital the effect was milder by a factor of around two for stress and depression (Frank et al. 2014). In Greece, protective factors against depression included interpersonal and institutional trust (Economou et al. 2014).

Suicide – while extensively studied – is just the tip of the iceberg; for each case of successful suicide there are an estimated 1–10 failed suicide attempts (leading to prolonged periods of disability), and between 100 and 1,000 new cases of depression. Although fewer data are available on psychological morbidity, there is evidence of deterioration in mental health in association with austerity measures and accompanying job loss and with housing problems. In the UK, government budget reductions in financial housing support for those in the private rented sector were associated with an increase in the prevalence of depression by 1.8 percentage points compared to those not affected by this policy change, leading to an additional 26,000 people living with depression-like symptoms.

In summary, the available evidence indicates that austerity has exacerbated and prolonged the mental health risks associated with economic downturns.

Pensioners and old-age mortality

One concerning trend is the rise in old-age mortality observed over the last few years in some European countries. In 2015, Italy witnessed the highest mortality rate since World War II; primarily due to an alarming rise among those aged 75–95. In the same year the UK experienced the largest annual rise in the mortality rate for fifty years. The number of deaths in the UK has been rising since 2011 (although with a transient recovery in 2014) after a steady decline from the late-1970s onwards. Like Italy, this rise has been particularly large among the elderly.

Austerity measures appear to have played a role in this rising death rate. Analysis from the UK – which examines changing patterns across local areas – finds that cuts to social care and financial support to elderly pensioners are associated with a rise in mortality among those aged 85 and over (Loopstra et al. 2016c).

Impact on health systems

Financing and efficiency

A European-wide review identified a wide range of responses to economic downturn adopted by countries in the region (Thomson et al. 2014). In response to fiscal pressures, many political leaders responded by reducing public health funding. The largest cuts were seen in Greece, Ireland, Latvia and Portugal. Some countries, however, adopted measures to protect their health systems, at least temporarily, or reduce the extent or impact of budget reductions. These mechanisms, and factors which helped to make health systems more resilient, are outlined in a review of healthcare austerity by Thomson and colleagues (2014) and include:

- policies to boost counter-cyclical public spending on health and other forms of social protection;
- initial adequate levels of public spending on health;
- maintenance of comprehensive health coverage with no gaps;
- absent or relatively low levels of out-of-pocket payments;
- making greater use of comparative information about the cost-effectiveness of different services and interventions, with disinvestment or selective investment where deemed appropriate;
- political will to tackle inefficiencies and to mobilize revenue for the health sector.

The areas most affected by cuts were hospital sectors, administrative costs, and prices of pharmaceuticals, as well as staff numbers and wages.

Coverage and access to care

Key areas of health coverage, such as who is covered, for which services, and to what extent, have seen changes in most European countries during the crisis. These largely focused on increasing user fees, thus placing higher financial burden on patients. A survey of experts has indicated that policy makers often view user fees as a way to raise funding for health system budgets (Thomson et al. 2014), contrary to now extensive evidence that they yield little additional revenue, much of which is accounted for by administration costs, while impacting adversely access to care. During the recession a number of countries in Europe have increased user fees to various services. Among countries which introduced or raised user fees, some also widened exemptions to protect certain population groups, e.g. Portugal. However, despite these protective measures, population surveys indicate steady worsening of access to care among those who feel they need it, with the main reason being financial.

An analysis of responses to the Great Recessions found that it accelerated moves by European health systems to adopt cost-sharing models, including increasing fees paid by patients (so-called 'user fees') (Palladino et al. 2016). Compared with the situation prior to the crisis, researchers found that, in the Survey of Health, Ageing and Retirement in Europe (SHARE) that follows cohorts of people aged 50+, out-of-pocket expenditures grew as well as the proportion of people incurring catastrophic health expenditures. These findings revealed a substantial weakening of financial protection. Only one nation experienced dramatic changes in population coverage. This was Greece, where those losing jobs also lost entitlement to free access to healthcare. However, overall, although the effects were less severe elsewhere, it was estimated that more than 2 million European people faced problems in accessing health care (European Commission 2015).

Understanding the mechanisms by which the application of austerity policies to health systems reduces access is complex, reflecting the diverse nature of the packages that have been implemented. Across Europe there has been an overall reversal in prior downward trends in 'self-reported unmet medical need', whereby people believed that they needed healthcare services but could not access them. These unmet needs had declined by 2 percentage points in Europe between 2005 and 2009 (Reeves et al. 2015b). In 2010 they began to rise, increasing by 0.4 percentage points to 3.4 per cent in 2012 (corresponding to an additional 1.5 million Europeans). This rise in unmet medical need has been particularly pronounced in countries where the share of out-of-pocket payments is high, such as Greece (Kentikelenis et al. 2011, 2014), Latvia (Karanikolos et al. 2016) and Portugal (Legido-Quigley et al. 2016). The latest EU-SILC survey data from these countries show that unmet need increased by 4–6 percentage points when cuts peaked. An American study found that levels of foregone medical, dental, mental health care and prescribed medications increased during recession in working-age adults irrespective of ethnicity or level of education (Burgard and Hawkins 2014). As expected, the impact on those who make most use of health services is typically greatest. Thus, a survey of Greek patients with chronic conditions using primary care services showed that 63 per cent experienced economic barriers in accessing care in 2013 (Kyriopoulos et al. 2014). In the US, half of the respondents from a large-scale representative survey of patients suffering from chronic disease reported that the cost of medication had become a bigger issue for them since the start of the recession, while 13 per cent of patients on prescription medication reported skipping doses or cutting pills for cost reasons (Kalousova and Burgard 2014; Piette et al. 2011).

There is evidence that austerity in healthcare further widens existing socio-economic gaps in access to services, with those on lower income being affected disproportionately, particularly by the rising cost of treatment and medication, unless a country has effective protection systems in place to protect the most vulnerable. Unmet need has progressively increased in Greece between 2008 and 2013 while the inequalities gap has widened dramatically: among the poorest income quintile, unmet need has doubled, from 7 per cent to 14 per cent, while among the richest income quintile it remained below 1 per cent, with the exception of increase in 2011–12 (Kyriopoulos et al. 2014; Karanikolos and Kentikelenis 2016). Inequalities in unmet need can be further widened by job loss: a study from the US found that losing work during the recession increased the probability of unmet need by 4 per cent in richer families, and by more than 6 per cent in poor ones (Huang et al. 2014). Although another study from the US found a decline in unmet medical need in both the insured (from 6.2 per cent to 4.5 per cent) and uninsured (from 17.5 per cent to 16.6 per cent) between 2007 and 2010, the smaller decrease in the uninsured indicates that the gap between the two groups has widened during the recession (Boukus and Cunningham 2011).

Quality of care

One way to assess the quality of care is amenable mortality. This is a subset of deaths which should not happen in the presence of timely and high standard medical care. While amenable mortality has important limitations in terms of selection of causes as well as placing limits on population age, a high rate in comparison with other countries or a reversal of a previous downward trend suggests the presence or emergence of potential weaknesses in care. A recent analysis (authors' calculations) of amenable mortality across the EU showed an increase of amenable deaths of 1.7 annual percentage change in men and 0.8 annual percentage change in women in Greece since 2010. This was largely attributable to increases in premature deaths from ischaemic heart disease and stroke. It also identified a slowdown in the pace of reduction of amenable mortality in a few other EU countries. While it is difficult to establish the exact policies and actions affecting service provision and delivery that lead to increase in amenable deaths, the worsening of access expressed in increasing unmet health need is described above.

Conclusions

The financial crises that began in 2007 confronted many countries with a choice. These nations could either invest to promote economic growth or to consolidate the economy with cuts to spending and tax rises. Each made different choices, with some investing in some areas while cutting others. However, some countries, those subject to conditions imposed by the Troika, had no choice and were forced to implement austerity policies.

Although beyond the scope of this chapter, there is now a growing consensus that austerity slowed, or in some cases, prevented recovery. However, austerity also had important consequences for health and health services. It impacted most those already vulnerable, such as those with precarious employment or housing, or with existing health problems. It was associated with worsening mental health and, as a consequence, increasing suicides. Yet, this was not inevitable. Those fortunate to live in countries with strong social protection systems, such as Sweden and Germany, escaped the worst of the crisis, compared to those with relatively weaker systems, such as Greece.

Looking ahead, the crisis and resulting austerity have accelerated a move to a new model of the economy, one in which power has shifted away from ordinary people and towards those with the greatest control over resources, a group who has emerged from the crisis relatively unscathed, with wealth more concentrated than ever among those at the very top of the distribution. Those without power face a future that is more precarious than ever, with a new term, 'zero-hours contract', entering the vocabulary in several countries, and with the erosion of previous social safety nets (Clarke et al. 2007).

There are many lessons to be learned from the experience of recent years. Some relate to economic policy, as what had become orthodoxy since the 1980s was tested to destruction, forcing a relearning of lessons from the 1930s. Others relate to health and welfare policy, with the natural experiments that have taken place providing new insights into the

143

importance of a strong welfare state. Unfortunately, it is not clear that these lessons will be learnt.

There are also lessons for researchers. At the onset of the crisis, health researchers were working in the dark. While financial data became available within weeks, or in some cases seconds, it took several years to obtain data on health. In these circumstances it was hardly surprising that the balance sheets of the banks (and the incomes of their executives) would be prioritized over the lives of the poor and marginalized. This cannot be allowed to happen again and, while this has stimulated interest in alternative, more timely sources of data, such as trends in Internet searches for 'suicide' (Arora et al. 2016), the research community must advocate for strengthened systems of data collection. It is ironic that Greece's participation in the important SHARE project was terminated on cost grounds just as the crisis was hitting. However, once data did become available, the health research community rose to the challenge, drawing on a wide range of disciplines and expanding the use of innovative studies of natural experiments. This research has also helped to define a new research agenda, now termed the political economy of health that emphasizes the importance of studying the distribution of power, whether visible, hidden or invisible (Hathaway 2016) in society, and the means by which it impacts population health. While the findings from this research will never be able to prevent another crisis, such as that experienced since 2007, they can at least help to ensure that the health consequences form part of the policy debate.

References

Arora, V., Stuckler, D. and McKee, M. (2016) Tracking search engine queries for suicide in the United Kingdom, 2004–2013. *Public Health* 137: 147–53.

Ball, L., Furceri, D., Leigh, D. and Loungani, P. (2013) The distributional effects of fiscal consolidation. IMF working paper WP/13/151.

Barr, B., Taylor-Robinson, D., Scott-Samuel, A., McKee, M. and Stuckler, D. (2012) Suicides associated with the 2008–10 economic recession in England: a time-trend analysis. *British Medical Journal* 345: e5142.

Barr, B., Taylor-Robinson, D., Stuckler, D., Loopstra, R., Reeves, A. and Whitehead, M. (2015) 'First, do no harm': are disability assessments associated with adverse trends in mental health? A longitudinal ecological study. *Journal of Epidemiology and Community Health* 70(4): 339–45.

Boukus, E.R. and Cunningham, P.J. (2011) Mixed signals: trends in Americans' access to medical care, 2007–2010. *Tracking Report* 25: 1–6.

Burgard, S.A. and Hawkins, J.M. (2014) Race/ethnicity, educational attainment, and foregone health care in the United States in the 2007–2009 recession. *American Journal of Public Health* 104(2): e134–e40.

Economou, M., Madianos, M., Peppou, L.E., Souliotis, K., Patelakis, A. and Stefanis, C. (2014) Cognitive social capital and mental illness during economic crisis: a nationwide population-based study in Greece. *Social Science & Medicine* 100: 141–7.

Economou, M., Angelopoulos, E., Peppou, L.E., Souliotis, K., Tzavara, C., Kontoangelos, K., Madianos, M. and Stefanis, C. (2016) Enduring financial crisis in Greece: prevalence and correlates of major depression and suicidality. *Social Psychiatry and Psychiatric Epidemiology* 51(7): 1015–24.

European Commission (2015) *Assessment of the Social Impact of the New Stability Support Programme for Greece.* Brussels: European Commission.

FEANTSA (2011) Impact of anti-crisis austerity measures on homeless services across the EU. FEANTA policy paper.

Figari, F., Paulus, A. and Sutherland, H. (2015) The design of fiscal consolidation measures in the European Union: distributional effects and implications for macroeconomic recovery. EUROMOD Working Paper series EM5/15.

Fitzpatrick, S., Pawson, H., Bramley, G., Wilcox, S. and Watts, B. (2016) *The Homelessness Monitor: England 2016.* London: Crisis.

Frank, C., Davis, C.G. and Elgar, F.J. (2014) Financial strain, social capital, and perceived health during economic recession: a longitudinal survey in rural Canada. *Anxiety, Stress, & Coping* 27(4): 422–38.

Hathaway, T. (2016) Lukes reloaded: an actor-centred three-dimensional power framework. *Politics* 36(2): 118–30.

Helliwell, J.F., Layard, R. and Sachs, J. (2015) *World Happiness Report 2015: Sustainable Development Solutions Network.* New York: United Nations.

Huang, J., Birkenmaier, J. and Kim, Y. (2014) Job loss and unmet health care needs in the economic recession: different associations by family income. *American Journal of Public Health* 104(11): e178–e83.

Kalousova, L. and Burgard, S.A. (2014) Tough choices in tough times: debt and medication nonadherence. *Health Education & Behavior* 41(2): 155–63.

Karanikolos, M. and Kentikelenis, A. (2016) Health inequalities after austerity in Greece. *International Journal for Equity in Health* 15(1): 83.

Karanikolos, M., Mladovsky, P., Cylus, J., Thompson, S., Basu, S., Stuckler, D., Mackenbach, J.P. and McKee, M. (2013) Financial crisis, austerity, and health in Europe. *The Lancet* 381(9874): 1323–31.

Karanikolos, M., Gordeev, V.S., Mackenbach, J.P. and McKee, M. (2016) Access to care in the Baltic States: did crisis have an impact? *The European Journal of Public Health* 26(2): 236–41.

Kentikelenis, A., Karanikolos, M., Papanicolas, I., Basu, S., McKee, M. and Stuckler, D. (2011) Health effects of financial crisis: omens of a Greek tragedy. *The Lancet* 378(9801):1457–8.

Kentikelenis, A., Karanikolos, M., Reeves, A., McKee, M. and Stuckler, D. (2014) Greece's health crisis: from austerity to denialism. *The Lancet* 383(9918): 748–53.

Kyriopoulos, I-I., Zavras, D., Skroumpelos, A., Mylona, K., Athanasakis, K. and Kyriopoulos, J. (2014) Barriers in access to healthcare services for chronic patients in times of austerity: an empirical approach in Greece. *International Journal for Equity in Health* 13(1): 54–61.

Legido-Quigley, H., Karanikolos, M., Hernandez-Plaza, S., de Freitas, C.,

Bernardo, L., Padilla, B., Machado, R.S., Diaz-Ordaz, K., Stuckler, D. and McKee, M. (2016) Effects of the financial crisis and Troika austerity measures on health and health care access in Portugal. *Health Policy* 120(7): 833–9.

Loopstra, R., Reeves, A., Barr, B., Taylor-Robinson, D. and Stuckler, D. (2014) Are austerity measures in England driving rises in homelessness? Evidence from 324 local authorities 2004–2012. *The European Journal of Public Health* 24(suppl 2): cku166-082.

Loopstra, R., Reeves, A. and Stuckler, D. (2015a) Rising food insecurity in Europe. *The Lancet* 385(9982): 2041.

Loopstra, R., Reeves, A., Taylor-Robinson, D., Barr, B., McKee, M. and Stuckler, D. (2015b) Austerity, sanctions, and the rise of food banks in the UK. *BMJ* 350: h1775.

Loopstra, R., Reeves, A., Barr, B., Taylor-Robinson, D., McKee, M. and Stuckler, D. (2016a) The impact of economic downturns and budget cuts on homelessness claim rates across 323 local authorities in England, 2004–12. *Journal of Public Health* 38(3): 417–25.

Loopstra, R., Reeves, A., McKee, M. and Stuckler, D. (2016b) Food insecurity and social protection in Europe: quasi-natural experiment of Europe's Great Recessions 2004–2012. *Preventive Medicine* 89: 44–50.

Loopstra, R., McKee, M., Katikireddi, S.V., Taylor-Robinson, D., Barr, B. and Stuckler, D. (2016c) Austerity and old-age mortality in England: a longitudinal cross-local area analysis, 2007–2013. *Journal of the Royal Society of Medicine* 109(3): 109–16.

Norström, T. and Grönqvist, H. (2015) The Great Recession, unemployment and suicide. *Journal of Epidemiology and Community Health* 69(2): 110–16.

Palladino, R., Lee, J.T., Hone, T., Filippidis, F.T. and Millett, C. (2016) The Great Recession and increased cost sharing in European health systems. *Health Affairs* 35(7): 1204–13.

Piette, J.D., Rosland, A.M., Silveira, M.J., Hayward, R. and McHorney, C.A. (2011) Medication cost problems among chronically ill adults in the US: did the financial crisis make a bad situation even worse? *Patient Preference and Adherence* 5: 187–94.

Rada, A.G. (2013) Child poverty and malnutrition rise in Spain as austerity measures bite. *BMJ* 347: f5261.

Reeves, A., Stuckler, D., McKee, M., Gunnell, D., Chang, S-S. and Basu, S. (2012) Increase in State suicide rates in the USA during economic recession. *The Lancet* 380(9856): 1813–14.

Reeves, A., McKee, M., Basu, S. and Stuckler, D. (2013a) The political economy of austerity and healthcare: cross-national analysis of expenditure changes in 27 European nations, 1995–2011. *Health Policy* 115(1): 1–8.

Reeves, A., Basu, S., McKee, M., Marmot, M. and Stuckler, D. (2013b) Austere or not? UK coalition government budgets and health inequalities. *Journal of the Royal Society of Medicine* 106(11): 432–6.

Reeves, A., McKee, M. and Stuckler, D. (2014) Economic suicides in the Great Recession in Europe and North America. *The British Journal of Psychiatry* 205(3): 246–7.

Reeves, A., McKee, M., Gunnell, D., Chang, S-S., Basu, S., Barr, B. and Stuckler, D. (2015a) Economic shocks, resilience, and male suicides in the Great Recession: cross-national analysis of 20 EU countries. *The European Journal of Public Health* 25(3): 404–9.

Reeves, A., McKee, M. and Stuckler, D. (2015b) The attack on universal health coverage in Europe: recession, austerity and unmet needs. *The European Journal of Public Health* 25(3): 364–5.

Reeves, A., Clair, A., McKee, M. and Stuckler, D. (2016) Reductions in the United Kingdom's government housing benefit and symptoms of depression in low-income households. *American Journal of Epidemiology* 184(6): 421–9.

Rehn, O. (2013) *Letter to Europe's Finance Ministers*. Brussels: European Commission.

Reinhart, C.M. and Rogoff, K.S. (2010) Growth in a time of debt. *American Economic Review* 100(2): 573–8.

RFI (2014) One million French people to receive charity meals. Paris: rfi.

Riumallo-Herl, C., Basu, S., Stuckler, D., Courtin, E. and Avendano, M. (2014) Job loss, wealth and depression during the Great Recession in the USA and Europe. *International Journal of Epidemiology* 43(5): 1508–17.

Schaltegger, C.A. and Weder, M. (2014) Austerity, inequality and politics. *European Journal of Political Economy* 35: 1–22.

Stuckler, D., Basu, S., Suhrcke, M., Coutts, A. and McKee, M. (2009) The public health impact of economic crises and alternative policy responses in Europe. *The Lancet* 374(9686): 315–23.

Thekiso, B., Heron, E.A., Masood, B., Murphy, M., McLoughlin, D.M. and Kennedy, N. (2013) Mauling of the 'Celtic Tiger': clinical characteristics and outcome of first-episode depression secondary to the economic recession in Ireland. *Journal of Affective Disorders* 151(2): 455–60.

Thomson, S., Figueras, J., Evetovits, T., Jowett, M., Mladovsky, P., Maresso, A., Cylus, J., Karanikolos, M. and Kluge, H. (2014) *Economic Crisis, Health Systems and Health in Europe: Impact and Implications for Policy*. WHO Regional Office for Europe.

The Trussell Trust (2016) Trussell Trust foodbank use remains at record high with over one million three-day emergency food supplies given to people in crisis in 2015/16. Salisbury: The Trussell Trust. Available at: http://www.trusselltrust.org/foodbank-figures-top-900000.

Woo, J., Bova, E., Kinda, T. and Zhang, Y.S. (2013) *Distributional Consequences of Fiscal Consolidation and the Role of Fiscal Policy: What Do the Data Say?* Washington, DC: International Monetary Fund.

Wunderlich, G.S. and Norwood, J.L. (eds) (2006) *Food Insecurity and Hunger in the United States: An Assessment of the Measure*. Washington, DC: National Research Council of the National Academies.

Chapter 7

Suffering: The Human and Social Costs of Economic Crisis[1]

John B. Thompson, Eirini Avramopoulou and Silvia Pasquetti

Who pays the price when an economic crisis occurs? Some companies may go bust, some bankers may forgo bonuses and some investors may see the value of their investments fall, but what about all those people who had nothing to do with the decisions and activities that brought about the crisis and yet who find themselves caught up in the economic maelstrom produced by it? What happens to them?

We know that the economic crisis in Europe, precipitated by the financial crisis of 2007–8 and exacerbated by the structural weaknesses of the eurozone and the austerity policies imposed by eurozone leaders, had a major impact on unemployment, poverty and health. The unemployment rate across the EU soared, rising from 6.7 per cent in 2008 to 10.8 per cent in 2013 across the twenty-eight member countries, putting 9 million more people out of work, while in the eurozone it reached 12 per cent. This average rate concealed a great deal of variation from one country to another and among different age groups. The rate was lowest in Germany (5.2 per cent) and Austria (5.4 per cent) and highest in Greece (27.5 per cent), Spain (26.1 per cent), Croatia (17.3 per cent), Portugal (16.4 per cent) and Cyprus (15.9 per cent). The rate in Ireland was 13.1 per cent and in Italy 12.2 per cent (Eurostat 2016b; Caritas Europa 2015: 32). But within these countries, there was a great deal of regional variation too: in Italy, for example, the unemployment rate in 2014 was 8.2 per cent in Lombardy in the north and 23.4 per cent in Calabria in the south (Eurostat 2016a). Between 2008 and mid-2014, 3.4 million jobs were lost in Spain, 1.2 million in Italy and 1 million in Greece, while in Germany the number of jobs increased by 1.8 million (European

---

[1] The research for this article was made possible by the generous support of The Balzan Foundation.

Commission 2014: 16). Youth unemployment (under 25s) was particularly high: in 2013 it was 23.4 per cent in the EU-28 and 24 per cent in the eurozone. Greece had the highest youth unemployment rate at 58.3 per cent, followed by Spain (55.5 per cent), Croatia (49.7 per cent), Italy (40 per cent), Cyprus (38.9 per cent) and Portugal (38.1 per cent) (Caritas Europa 2015: 33). These countries also experienced high levels of young people neither in employment nor in education or training (NEETs). The average NEET rate in the EU was 13 per cent in 2013 (ages 15–24). Italy had the highest NEET rate at 22.2 per cent, while it was 20.6 per cent in Greece, 18.7 per cent in Cyprus, 18.6 per cent in Croatia and 18.6 per cent in Spain (Caritas Europa 2015: 33). The sharp deterioration in labour market conditions led to a marked increase in the percentage of people at risk of poverty or social exclusion.[2] Between 2008 and 2013, nineteen of the twenty-eight Member States saw an increase in the risk of poverty or social exclusion, with the percentage reaching 24.5 per cent across all Member States in 2013. In Greece the figure had reached 35.7 per cent, up from 28.1 per cent in 2008, and in Italy it reached 28.4 per cent, up from 25.3 per cent in 2008 (European Commission 2014: 17, 297, 308, 312). Between 2009 and 2013 an additional 7.5 million people were classified as experiencing severe material deprivation across twenty-seven EU countries, and in Greece the proportion increased from around 12 per cent in 2010 to around 22 per cent in 2014 (Oxfam 2015: 9). The number of people living in households without any income from work doubled in Greece between 2007 and 2012, rising from just over 10 per cent in 2007 to just over 20 per cent in 2012 (OECD 2014: 25).

These are alarming numbers and they indicate that the economic crisis that has engulfed Europe since 2008 has had consequences that are devastating for the lives of millions of people across the continent. They also indicate that, despite some hopeful suggestions to the contrary, the crisis is far from over. In many of the countries that have been hit hardest by the crisis, such as Greece, Ireland, Italy, Spain and Portugal, unemployment rates remain high, inequality is increasing and there are growing numbers of individuals, families and children living in poverty (Oxfam 2015). A new class of poor is emerging – namely, young people leaving school or graduating from higher education and entering the labour market where they find no job, or find only poorly paid, part-time jobs that enable them to generate some income but not enough to survive, forcing them to fall back on the support of family networks or charities,

---

[2] 'People at risk of poverty or social exclusion' is a combined indicator of poverty used in the Europe 2020 Strategy. It combines three separate measures of poverty: people at risk of poverty (a relative income measure), people experiencing severe material deprivation, and people in jobless households.

unable to build the kind of career that many in their parents' generation once took for granted.

The sudden deterioration in life conditions and prospects for millions of people has also had serious consequences in terms of health, both physical and mental. In Greece between 2007 and 2009 there was a significant increase in people reporting that they did not go to a doctor or dentist despite feeling it was necessary, and a significant increase in people reporting that their health was 'bad' or 'very bad' (Kentikelenis et al. 2011: 1457). There was also a significant increase in individuals reporting symptoms of depression in 2008 and 2009, and a significant increase in individuals reporting suicidal thoughts, and the increases were highest among individuals experiencing economic hardship (Madianos et al. 2011: 947–8). Subsequent research found evidence of a substantial increase in the prevalence of suicidal thoughts and suicide attempts between 2009 and 2011, and evidence that vulnerability to suicide was linked to socio-economic variables such as unemployment, job insecurity and loss of income (Economou et al. 2013). Other countries hit hard by the crisis, such as Cyprus and Spain, have also seen significant increases in the incidence of depression, especially among the unemployed (Buffel et al. 2015: 274). Suicide rates, which had been falling in Europe prior to 2007, increased sharply in 2008 and 2009 (Stuckler et al. 2011: 124). Data for 2010 from twenty European countries showed a 10.8 per cent rise in suicide for men and a 4.8 per cent rise for women, relative to suicides expected based on trends over the period 2000–7 (Chang et al. 2013: 3; see also Stuckler et al., this volume).

These numbers paint a dark picture of the deteriorating life conditions of many millions of people who have been hit hard by the economic crisis in Europe: this is a picture in which, for large swathes of the population, real incomes have declined steeply, unemployment has increased sharply, health has worsened and the risks of depression and suicide have increased. And yet, however sombre the picture painted by these numbers, they tell us only part of the story. Numbers are vital indicators and they point to realities that are hard to deny, but they don't tell us what it's like to *live* the realities to which they point. They give us no sense of what it's like to *experience* the impact of economic crisis in the everyday lives of individuals. What does it feel like to be at the sharp end of economic crisis – not the bankers who may have to forgo their bonuses for a year or two while the banking sector undergoes a temporary adjustment before returning to business as usual, but rather the factory worker who loses his job when the factory closes and is unable to find another job, or the office worker whose salary is reduced so low that she is afraid to check her bank account to see how little she is now earning, or the young person who leaves college and enters a job market where there are no jobs to speak of, or the young professional who always dreamt of getting a higher qualification and advancing her career only to find that this pathway is now closed and the dream is dead? These are the people who have paid the real price of economic crisis. Numbers are extremely helpful in documenting the deterioration in their life conditions but numbers alone will never tell us what it's like to live the reality of economic crisis. Numbers cannot express what it means to suffer.

Suffering is a diffuse and complicated concept – not one that readily lends itself to precise definition for the purposes of social science research. For some, the word 'suffering' is inseparably connected with religion, where suffering was understood as a test of the believer's faith. When the term has been used in the social sciences, it has most commonly been in the context of medical sociology or medical anthropology.[3] But the danger of using this concept in medical contexts is that it's too readily associated with illness and physical pain.[4] Of course, illness and physical pain are important sources of human suffering: human beings do suffer a lot when they or their loved ones experience serious illness and physical pain. But we also know that suffering is not linked only to physical or corporeal conditions: suffering can be primarily or even entirely emotional or affective in character, and can even give rise to physical conditions rather than arise from them.

So when we speak here of suffering, we are speaking of a state of being that is primarily affective in character. It is not a discrete emotion but rather a cluster of negative feelings that overlap and often reinforce one another, creating an outlook on the world that is bleak, despondent, filled with sadness and despair. It may also be laced with streaks of anger, frustration, bitterness and resentment, as individuals build into this cluster of feelings their own accounts of how they ended up where they are and who is responsible for their misfortune. Suffering, as we understand it here, is an affective state of being of the individual. It is not just a state of mind, something in the head, but a state of being in which thoughts, feelings

---

[3] See, for example, the work of Arthur Kleinman and his associates: Arthur Kleinman, Veena Das and Margaret Lock (eds.), *Social Suffering* (Berkeley, CA: University of California Press, 1997); Arthur Kleinman, *The Illness Narratives: Suffering, Healing, and the Human Condition* (New York: Basic Books, 1988); and Arthur Kleinman, *Experience and Its Moral Modes: Culture, Human Conditions, and Disorder*, The Tanner Lectures on Human Values, delivered at Stanford University, 13–16 April 1988, available at: http://tannerlectures.utah.edu/_documents/a-to-z/k/Kleinman99.pdf. A more sociological approach to suffering can be found in Pierre Bourdieu et al., *The Weight of the World: Social Suffering in Contemporary Society*, trans. Priscilla Parkhurst Ferguson et al. (Cambridge: Polity, 1999). For a general overview, see Iain Wilkinson, *Suffering: A Sociological Introduction* (Cambridge: Polity, 2005).

[4] The work of Kleinman and his associates does, however, range more widely than this.

and physical aspects of the body – the way an individual carries himself or herself, takes care of himself or herself, his or her state of health and so on – are woven together in the flow of everyday life. In short, to use an old Heideggerian term, suffering is a way of being in the world in which the world is experienced in a certain way: bleak, despondent, filled with sadness and despair.

There are four things to say about suffering understood in this way. First, suffering is intrinsically social – and this is true in several respects. It is social because individuals are always enmeshed in relations with others and suffering is interwoven with these social relations: others may affect an individual's state of being and may be affected by it. It is also social because suffering often has social conditions or causes: it is connected to, and often stems from, social, economic or political processes that extend beyond the circumstances of a particular individual. And precisely because it is often connected to or stems from these broader processes, it is also social in the sense that it is often experienced by many individuals who are also affected, each in their own way, by the same broader processes. For these reasons, it is not particularly helpful to distinguish between 'suffering' and 'social suffering', or between 'psychic' and 'social' suffering, as some analysts have tried to do.[5] So much of what we think of as suffering is interwoven with social conditions and social relations that any attempt to draw a clear distinction here is bound to be artificial. To all intents and purposes, suffering is social suffering, a social state of being: one that is inextricably interwoven with relations with others, often produced by broader social processes and commonly experienced by a plurality of individuals.

A second feature of suffering is that it is relative. Of course, suffering can often feel absolute and totalizing to the individual who is suffering: when you're really suffering you may be absorbed in your world and oblivious to others and the world around you. But for most individuals most of the time, the experience of suffering is a relative matter: you're aware that others are suffering too, that you are not alone and that others may be suffering a good deal more than you. The feeling that 'things are bad, but they're worse for others' is a common feature of suffering: we constantly assess our own state of being in relation to others who find themselves in similar circumstances or share a similar – or even worse – fate. In other words, suffering is most commonly a matter of relative despair.

Third, suffering is a mundane feature of everyday life. It is not a rare and exceptional condition but a common and ordinary one – what

[5] For example, Kleinman et al., *Social Suffering*.

Bourdieu called 'la petite misère' (Bourdieu et al. 1999: 4). It can be precipitated or exacerbated by a sudden change in circumstances like the loss of one's job or the breakdown of a relationship, but even in the absence of major disruptive events of this kind, many people will experience some degree of suffering in the course of their daily lives. But in most cases this kind of suffering remains below the radar of the medical profession because it is not felt – either by the individuals themselves or by those around them – to be sufficiently serious to warrant medical attention. It can easily cross the indistinct boundary between a social state of being and a clinical condition: if an individual is referred to a doctor or a clinic, or refers himself or herself, then suffering becomes a medical matter. But this is the exception rather than the rule. For most people most of the time, suffering is part and parcel of the flow of daily life and is not subjected to the scrutiny of professionals.

Fourth, and despite the fact that it is typically beyond the purview of professionals, suffering matters. It can devastate lives. It can debilitate individuals, destroy their motivation, place great strain on their relations with others and even, in extreme cases, destroy their will to live.

To take suffering as the focus of our attention is not without risks. Many people suffer in one way or another, and as a social analyst it is not always easy to distinguish between forms of suffering that can be linked to broader social, economic and political circumstances, on the one hand, and those that are part and parcel of an individual's personal trajectory through life, on the other. Moreover, the very idea that suffering can have social conditions, that the decisions and actions of some people can have consequences that lead to the suffering of others and that their suffering should be attended to and heard, may well be an idea that belongs to a certain time and place – to our distinctively modern, Western, possibly very recent world (Fassin 2012: 5–10, 21–43). But the fact that this idea may be relatively recent and the fact that suffering may be difficult to study in practice are not compelling reasons to neglect it. Economic and political turmoil really can have devastating consequences for people's lives, and while we need to be attentive to epistemological and methodological considerations, we should not allow them to distract us from the attempt to grasp the lived reality of suffering. We need to put a human face on economic crisis.

For 12 months, between September 2014 and September 2015, we carried out fieldwork at a number of sites in Greece and Italy to explore the impact of economic crisis on the lives of ordinary individuals. One of the authors, Eirini Avramopoulou, is a Greek anthropologist trained in Athens and Cambridge; she did fieldwork in Athens, Volos and Pelion, a mountainous peninsula in southeastern Thessaly, about 350 km north of

Athens. Another author, Silvia Pasquetti, is an Italian political sociologist trained in Florence, Berkeley and Cambridge; she did fieldwork in Parma and Florence – two prosperous northern Italian cities – and in Syracuse and other smaller towns in southeastern Sicily. They each carried out more than 60 interviews – in Greece, around 30 in Athens and 30 in Volos and Pelion, and in Italy, around 30 in Parma and Florence and 30 in Sicily. The sites were chosen to ensure that, in the case of Greece, we interviewed people both in the large metropolitan area of Athens and in a small provincial town and rural region that is some distance from Athens. In Italy we wanted to interview people both in the relatively prosperous north and in the less developed and less industrialized south, where many people worked in agriculture.

In both countries we selected interviewees from different social strata, including upper middle-class professionals (lawyers, doctors, etc.); people in full-time employment in the public and private sectors; people who were self-employed (including small business owners, some of whose businesses had failed); workers who are currently unemployed, who had lost their jobs or who are precariously employed; young people who are not in employment, education or training (NEETs); and pensioners. We ensured that there was an equal representation of men and women and a wide age range, from young people in their late teens and early twenties to pensioners in their sixties and seventies. We also included migrants as well as native Greeks and Italians – a task made easier by the fact that both Greece and Italy have experienced a large influx of migrants in recent years, even before the most recent migration surge from Turkey and North Africa.

The timing of the fieldwork was fortuitous, especially in Greece. The economic crisis in Greece had deepened since the first bailout was agreed in 2010; by 2015 Greece's debt mountain had risen to €320 billion, or 177 per cent of GDP, and GDP had fallen by 25 per cent. Unemployment was running at 26.5 per cent, the highest in the EU, and youth unemployment was over 50 per cent. The first half of 2015 was a tumultuous time in Greece, leading from Syriza's victory in the elections on 25 January to the calling of the referendum on the new bailout offer that was held on 5 July. Capital controls were introduced in late June to prevent capital flight and the collapse of the banking sector, limiting the amount of money that people could withdraw from their accounts. The Syriza government urged people to vote 'No' to the new bailout offer and, indeed, they did, by a resounding majority (61 per cent). But when the creditors then hardened their position and threatened to eject Greece from the euro, the government capitulated and accepted tough new terms as a condition of remaining in the euro. This was a roller-coaster ride through the political economy of crisis, where moments of resistance and outrage on the southern peripheries of Europe were punctuated by the harsh realities of power in the eurozone. While Greece was in turmoil, Italy, with the third largest economy in the eurozone, was struggling to cope with a crisis that had exposed its parlous fiscal position and thrown many thousands of people out of work, and the country was simmering with anger, frustration and fear. Such was the period of our fieldwork.

Our questions were simple: how is economic crisis experienced in the day-to-day lives of individuals in different walks of life? What does it feel like to be on the receiving end of an economic crisis and how do individuals cope? How does it affect their plans, their hopes, their ways of organizing their lives and their relations with others? Our approach was bottom-up rather than top-down, starting not with political elites and the policies they seek to impose on reluctant populations but rather with ordinary individuals living their ordinary lives through difficult and extraordinary times. In this article we present the first findings of our research. Within the confines of an article we cannot examine the lived reality of crisis in depth, explore the complex ways in which individuals in different settings coped with a sudden and dramatic deterioration in their material circumstances, how this affected them physically and emotionally and how they incorporated this new material and symbolic reality into their daily lives, nor can we analyse in detail the differences between Greece and Italy – all of this would require a more extended format; but we can highlight and briefly elaborate a few of the themes that emerged time and again in our interviews. Some of these themes echo the findings of the classic study of Marienthal, the Austrian town that was devastated in the 1930s when its only source of employment, a textile factory, was forced to close (Jahoda et al. 2002). But our research was more wide-ranging and comparative than the study of Marienthal, and of course the circumstances of the economic crisis in Greece and Italy are entirely different from the circumstances of a small town in Austria in the early 1930s. So while we will note the occasional point of similarity, our focus will be on the lived reality of economic crisis in Greece and Italy today.

Anger, disappointment and betrayal

Nikitas is angry.[6] So too are many people in Livaditis, the small village in Pelion where Nikitas now lives. Most of them had voted for Syriza

---

[6] We have used pseudonyms and many place names have been altered to protect anonymity.

and voted No in the referendum, thinking and hoping that it would bring about change and an end to austerity, only to find that the terms they ended up with were even harsher than the terms that had been on the table before the referendum was called. There was a deep sense of disappointment, even betrayal. 'I voted "No"', said Nikitas, 'but what does "No" mean? What the others did but worse?' Nikitas had returned to the village in 1997 after studying in Athens and took out a large loan to renovate his grandfather's tavern, which he now runs. He is finding it very difficult to deal with the crisis and he, like many of his fellow inhabitants in Livaditis, is very angry: 'The people in the village were all paying their bills, it was a matter of dignity for them, but now they can no longer do this and they feel ashamed, they feel angry. I feel very angry too.' He continued:

> We cannot survive, this system is irrational. I am thinking of leaving, maybe to Germany – I have a friend there who owns a restaurant. I also have relatives in England. I think, let's close this place and go to Germany, wherever. Here, you work from day till night and there are days when you don't even make a euro. In any case, I know that the bank will take everything in the end. You are constantly stressed, you feel anxious about everything. You spend your day making calculations. Can you afford to go shopping? Which bills can you pay? How can you get by? I voted 'No' because I think that we are finished with Europe. We didn't belong in Europe in the first place. Europe is supposed to be the Europe of solidarity. What solidarity? If our partners treat us like this, what will our worst enemy do?

Nikitas's plight was made that much more difficult by the fact that, as part of the new bailout agreement in July 2015, the Syriza government had just increased sales tax to 23 per cent and introduced more controls to ensure that taverns, restaurants, shops and hotels paid the tax, and he was directly affected by these new measures. He couldn't increase prices to cover the new tax because the people who frequented his tavern didn't have the money to pay, so he had to absorb the extra cost of the tax himself. 'How am I going to pay what they ask for? I can't make ends meet, I can't live like this. If only I could hope that something would change, that there would be growth, but this isn't happening. It's a deadlock.'

Maria, another elderly resident of the village whose husband, now retired, worked for the public telephone company OTE, also felt a deep sense of anger, disappointment and hopelessness. 'I voted "No" in the referendum and it turned out to be "Yes." They think we are fools. We said "No" to those economic measures that make it impossible for us to survive, but they will pass everything', said Maria, her anger mixed with resignation. 'I no longer expect anything good to come out of this. There is no future for us. In the past, when the war was over, everyone was poor but we knew that better days would follow. Now that we finally managed to build something in our lives, they are taking it away from us and no one expects that better days will come. There is nothing to wait for, there is no hope in Greece.' She pauses, then whispers: 'As much as I want to give you hope, there is none.' Like many interviewees, Maria complained a lot about the current situation and about distant politicians who promised to help and then did nothing in the end – 'they think we are fools.' Yet at the same time, she, like other interviewees, is acutely aware that others are suffering even more:

> I found a person sleeping in the alley behind my son's apartment in Volos. It was winter, several degrees below zero. When I think of him I can't stop crying [she is crying again as she speaks]. He was curled up in a corner and in very bad shape. Next to him there was some milk and a few other things that people had left for him to eat. I asked him where he was from and he told me Georgia. 'I don't have work or money or anything', he said. I went to the police and I begged them to go and take him somewhere. I told him not to worry because they will come to take him. I left for the village – I couldn't stay in Volos. Two days later I read in the paper that he was found dead. This winter again there was a man in the same place wearing sandals and a thin T-shirt, nothing else – it was mid-winter and the temperature was below zero! I remembered what had happened last year and I immediately went to my son's apartment and I found socks, shoes and maybe a jacket, I don't remember exactly what I brought to him. I also gave him a 5 euro note – I don't have money but it doesn't matter. The man thanked me. 'I want to leave, go back', he told me, 'but I don't have a job, I don't have money.' What can we do about these people? If people cannot work, if they cannot eat, they will steal, they will kill, they will die.

Many of the Italian interviewees also expressed feelings of anger mixed with resignation and despair. Some seemed afraid of their own anger, as if they didn't know what to do with it or feared that it would only cause them more harm, leading them to do something they would regret. They didn't experience their anger as a step towards collective action, as something that would drive them into the street to protest with others, but rather saw it as a sign of their own individual failure. To the extent that they directed their anger towards anyone or anything other than themselves, it was towards politicians for their failure to do anything to help or towards asylum seekers who were seen as receiving preferential treatment at the expense of deserving locals. Antonio, a 32-year-old graduate living in Madina, a small town in southern Sicily, son of an unemployed pastry chef and himself precariously employed, put it like this:

> If you're not working in Germany the state helps you out and gives you a job. Here, if you're not working you can die and nobody cares. People commit suicide by setting themselves on fire or hanging themselves or throwing themselves off the balcony – it's news for one day on the TV and that's it. This is really ugly and nobody really helps you fight off these ideas about committing suicide. The state turns its back. The politicians know what's happening, they know what the problems are. The politicians know that we get punched in the face every day but they don't really understand the pain you feel because they've not experienced it themselves – they know it hurts but they don't understand the pain. If one of the senators or members of parliament would live like I live for just one week, they would understand. I would like them to live like an ordinary citizen for a period of seven days, from Monday to Sunday, and to give up all the privileges and pleasures and hobbies they have, give up going to restaurants and going shopping on Saturday afternoon – they would already feel really bad if they weren't able to do these things. Imagine if they had to make calculations about what they could buy at the supermarket or whether they could fill up the car. That's the only way they would understand they have to do more ... I've heard many people saying the right things, Matteo Renzi, Silvio Berlusconi – anyone who wants to get power says the right things ... But then when they get power they make excuses, they speak about obstacles, they say I need to go to Merkel or Mario Draghi to clarify things. There's always something. Then one loses trust in institutions, in politics, in politicians, you don't believe anything anymore.

The feeling of being betrayed by politicians who live in their own world, out of touch with ordinary people and the harsh realities of their daily lives, is evident in both the north and the south of Italy, but it is expressed in different ways and with different intensities. In the north, anger and betrayal is mixed with feelings of disbelief among individuals who, for the first time in their lives, find themselves turning to charities to get help with their electricity bills or to obtain basic staples. In the south the feeling of betrayal is expressed with less surprise, perhaps because the lack of state support is something to which people are more accustomed. In both contexts, the word 'citizen' takes on a distinct double meaning: a frustrated sense of entitlement and an equally bitter sense that 'non-citizens' – whether migrants or asylum seekers – are, by a cruel twist of fate, being privileged over citizens and taken care of by a state that should really be looking after them. Many interviewees, especially those in low-income jobs, precarious employment or unemployed, perceived welfare as a zero-sum game in which they had lost and 'the migrants' had won. Fleeting encounters with asylum seekers provided signs that were interpreted as evidence to support this view: 'I see them in front of the centre [for refugees], near the tobacconist in Via Cotullo, and they have these fancy headphones and new sneakers', explained Antonio. 'And I say to myself: I know they come from places where there is a war but here they seem relaxed, they are taken care of and perhaps that's ok in general – I absolutely don't want these people to be mistreated or sent away, and if we can host them, let's host them. But is it ok when people like me can't have a family or buy a house? The state helps them but it doesn't help us. I'm not racist but this makes me angry.' These are the kinds of sentiments – anger and a sense of betrayal, rooted in the experience of impoverishment – that are easily exploited by right-wing politicians and parties.

Sadness, depression and despair

Aside from anger and a sense of betrayal, the most common sentiments expressed by interviewees were those of sadness and despair. The experience of hardship weighed heavily on individuals who had once hoped for better things. Thomas is a doctor in his early forties in Athens; despite being a relatively well-off professional, the economic crisis has hit him hard. During the interview he broke down repeatedly. While trying to hide his tears, he explained that he had to take the decision to give up his research career – he was specializing in blood pressure research – and become a pathologist instead, even though he had devoted the whole of his professional career to taking all the right steps to become recognized as an academic researcher in Greece and abroad. He feels he had no choice but to 'compromise' and 'be more realistic'; he had to adjust his ambitions to a world in which the dream that he had nourished for so long could no longer be sustained. 'It is a huge blow for my ego. You have a certain recognition in your field, you are writing papers and you are known abroad, and then suddenly your status drops to half a metre off the ground.' He is slowly coming to terms with the fact that he can no longer pursue his ambition and that if he wants to continue doing research, he will have to do it as a hobby. His wife works as a notary and, while she used to earn €5,000–6,000 a month, she can no longer cover her monthly expenses. 'Everything is turning upside down.' For both of them life has been stripped of any positive value and their days are filled with a sense of despondency. But the sadness and depression is not just personal, it is collective. At one point he and his wife were on a trip to the Netherlands and he noticed people smiling in the street. 'Look, I said to my wife, people smile in the street. Why are they smiling? I will never forget this. We walked by and thought, around here, people smile, and in Athens everyone is so depressed. Can you believe the emotional state we have reached?'

Elena is 50 years old and unemployed. She has worked in many different jobs, but during the last few years she was employed as a waitress in a tavern. She got fired because they couldn't pay her anymore. She lives in a small house in Exarcheia, in Athens, with her 18-year-old son. As she spoke, rain was coming in the kitchen from the thin and dilapidated roof. The house was poorly decorated. She explained that she has not paid her rent for a whole year but her landlord was not throwing her out, as has happened to others.

> He also knows that things are tough these days. He asked me if I want to leave. 'You are not paying the rent. Do you want to go?' he asked me and I said 'no, of course not. Where can I go?' I will work in the summer [she still has a summer job as a cook, for two months, on an island in the Cyclades, for which she gets paid cash-in-hand] and I will pay him back. He knows that I will pay him back when I have money. There is trust. What else can we do?

With other bills, she has to find other methods of coping. When she got an electricity bill for €1,000, she was shocked – there was no way she could pay it. So she got a guy to come over and disconnect the meter. 'There are these anarchist electricians that come to your house and do something to the meter with their screwdrivers so that it doesn't record the power that's used', she explained. However, with Cosmote, which runs the mobile phone network, it was more difficult. When she got a €400 phone bill, she offered to pay in instalments but the company refused and cut her off, even though she'd been a customer for 30 years.

While Elena was very hard-up and never had more than €20 or €30 at a time, 'just enough to get something to eat', she appeared to be more concerned about a friend's situation than her own. 'I have a friend who is a *real* victim of our times, a *real* victim of crisis', she explained, constantly stressing the word 'real'. 'Her parents tried to do everything they could in order to provide her with a good life, in order not to let her worry about a thing.' Her father was a businessman and he acquired various properties and then both he and his wife died of cancer, leaving the property to their daughter, who now had to deal with everything on her own – five properties, none of them rented, huge new taxes to pay and no income.

> How do you deal with that? You get depressed, don't you? You get depressed, you suffer from tension, you get anxious and stressed. She's

afraid that she will lose everything she ever had, everything her parents built up through a life of hard work. She constantly tries to find money, to make arrangements and pay taxes and so on, and of course this prevents her from living. It becomes a psychosis.

Elena is on the edge of homelessness, in a small house with a leaky roof where she can't pay the rent or the electricity and where she remains only by virtue of her landlord's goodwill, and yet it is the predicament of her friend, anxious and stressed about losing the properties she has inherited from her parents, that really concerns her. However desperate one's situation may be, the plight of others often seems worse.

Empty time

For individuals who have lost their jobs, one of the challenges they face, apart from trying to pay the bills and ward off the constant threat of depression, is how to fill empty time. When the temporal structures of a working life suddenly fall away, many individuals find themselves struggling to fill their days, which seem to stretch on indefinitely with few features to punctuate the flow – this was a key finding in the study of Marienthal and, in this respect, the life of the unemployed in the twenty-first century is not so different from that of unemployed former factory workers in the 1930s.[7] They also find social interactions with others awkward and painful, which leads them to withdraw from ordinary sites of sociability. The house or apartment becomes both a protective shield and a trap – a protective shield because it allows them to withdraw from painful encounters with others (though the fear of losing their home may make this shield seem very fragile); a trap because, once they withdraw into the home, they may find it difficult to re-engage with others.

Sebastiano is a 61-year-old pastry chef in Sicily. He had taken over his father's pastry shop and built a successful business with several shops until the crisis hit. Prices dropped so low that he could no longer make it work and he was forced to close the business. He and his family moved to Rome to open a shop there but they lost everything; they returned to their town in Sicily empty-handed and defeated ('with our bones broken'). Now he feels sadness and anger mixed together. 'Sadness because we have reached an ugly point, anger because the people who could do

---

[7] 'Cut off from their work and deprived of contact with the outside world, the workers of Marienthal have lost the material and moral incentives to make use of their time. Now that they are no longer under any pressure, they undertake nothing new and drift gradually out of an ordered existence into one that is undisciplined and empty' (Jahoda et al. 2002: 66).

161

something about this don't, because they're fine, they're well paid – I'm talking about the politicians, they don't care. I read the newspapers and I feel sadness and anger when I read about families breaking down and people committing suicide because they can't manage anymore – never good news and the politicians don't care at all.' Now he is 61 and he doesn't know if he will ever find another job, if he will ever earn anything again. 'I don't know if I can live the rest of my life with the worries I have now, paying my bills on time is a struggle, buying a new shirt is difficult . . . all these worries . . .'. He doesn't go out anymore, he stays home and spends his days watching TV.

> I don't like going to the square, I avoid it because people stop and, since I've been away [in Rome], the first thing they ask is, 'when will you open the bakery? When will you open the shop?' So you need to explain things and I don't want to do that, and I don't want to tell them to mind their own business either because some of them were clients and friends and we all know each other. So to avoid all this I don't go out, I stay at home, I'm fine, I watch my TV, I thank RAI for whatever they show [he laughs] and that's it.

In fact he doesn't like talking about this at all, and for the most part he doesn't – 'I don't want to speak about problems because otherwise I make things worse, so I spend my time in front of the TV, in silence. It's tough, even just speaking now feels weird, I usually barely open my mouth, days pass by and I speak only with my son, otherwise I watch the TV and let time pass.'

Sebastiano's son, Antonio, has become the voice of the family in the outside world. While his father spends most of his time at home, Antonio works a couple of days a week – usually as a waiter in a restaurant, sometimes working in the fields or doing odd jobs like painting and decorating. Antonio got a BA in chemistry some years ago, when his father was still running his pastry shops and doing well; Antonio had hoped that after graduation he would find a good job. But he graduated in 2010, just when the crisis was biting hard, and when his father's business collapsed he was left without material support. 'I realized then that the crisis was real, that I had to face reality in my search for jobs. Little by little I saw all the doors closing in front of me – all those doors I'd been planning to knock on. After three or four months I realized that the situation was worse than I could imagine before I graduated. My father had problems too, customers stopped buying his pastries. The climate was very heavy.' What devastates Antonio now is the lack of any prospects for the future, the sense of immobility, of being frozen in time. He is stuck in a situation and he doesn't see how he can get out of it. He battles off feelings of depression. On the days that he's not working, he stays home, 'I go to my room, I close the door, I do something at the computer, I review some chemistry notes to keep the knowledge alive and I try to let the mood pass.' His feeling of being stuck and unable to move forward is exacerbated by the fact that his girlfriend works six days a week as a receptionist at a hairdresser, so he is constantly comparing his own situation with hers; the fact that she is working and he is stuck at home hurts his male pride:

> It's not really a question of jealousy, it's more a question of pride because I've always wanted to make her live well, I always wanted to work and have a family. I'm happy that she has her independence, I'd be happy if she wants to work and have her own professional life, that's all fine. But her work should not be necessary to fulfil our needs. I should be working, I should be the breadwinner. But now she is working and I am not – that's hard. When I don't have anything to do, I start thinking, I have the ability, I have the strength, I have the desire to work, and I can't do anything. My girlfriend is working, my best friend is working, and I'm here in this house, my father is sitting in front of the TV and I'm in this room, and all of this makes me angry, it takes my breath away. I feel like a lion that has been tied up, a lion that is meant to run, to hunt, to provide for its pack, but instead you feel . . . maybe not useless but it's a shame for someone like me to stay still. I could do a lot but there's nothing to do.

And time passes slowly when you have nothing to do:

> There are days when I would like to wake up in the evening so that I can go right back to sleep because I know that that day will last longer than 24 hours, because one hour becomes three hours, it doesn't pass, and so you try to do anything just to pass the time: you go to the gym, you do things in the house, you do the weirdest things – for example, we have a fireplace and sometimes the wood shoots out some sparks so I tell myself that I need to build a screen around it and I try to think of all the different ways I can do that. And anything I do, I do in the slowest possible way. Sometimes I find things like these to fill my day, I start reading, I don't want to spend much time on the Internet or in front of the TV because it makes me very bored and I start thinking about things and I feel heavy. I prefer going out, and go for example to see how things are going on a construction site and if they need something, or go to our garage to see if there is something that needs to be fixed. When I feel like it, I make some phone calls – 'how are you?' 'What's up?' 'Does anyone need anything?' And I try to make the day pass. That's it.

Antonio looks for little ways to fill the empty time, small jobs he can do around the house or somewhere nearby. Seeing his father sitting in front

163

of the TV all day long propels him to look for other ways to pass the time, like going out to check on a building site or calling friends – small things that fill the time but don't add up to anything. 'I try to make the day pass. That's it.'

Apart from the time he spends with his girlfriend and with a good friend of his, Antonio's time is either empty or full of stressful encounters and humiliation. The suffering of his father makes things worse and Antonio is constantly thinking about what the next steps could possibly be. One possible way out of his predicament, he thinks, would be to help his father open another pastry shop, another would be for him to move on his own to a bigger city, but both projects are fraught with uncertainties and anxieties. Opening another pastry shop would be difficult, especially since the family already has lots of debts and the crisis is not over – he's not sure that customers would buy more pastries now than when his father was forced to close his shop. Moving to a bigger city would give him a fresh start, allow him to 'breathe some fresh air', as he puts it, but at the same time he fears what would happen to his father if he were to leave him alone. So when Antonio speaks of his desires for the near future, for the next five years or so, he's stuck: he knows what he wants but he has no practical way of achieving it. He would like to have a stable job, marry his girlfriend and get a mortgage for a flat where they could live together, independently of their parents, but given his precarious state of employment, there's no way he can do this now. Nothing changes. Possible ways out of his predicament are undercut by practical difficulties, anxieties and fears and his days continue as before, doing small jobs around the house to fill empty time and keep depression at bay.

Turning inwards

As the story of Sebastiano and Antonio illustrates, it is common for individuals hit hard by economic crisis to close themselves off from others and turn inwards. In some cases, as with Sebastiano and Antonio, this is because it's simply too painful to have to face one's friends and acquaintances and explain what happened to you and make polite conversation; it's easier and less painful to sit at home in silence. The home becomes a shield – and also a trap. For others, the turn inwards is part of an active strategy to deal with the crisis and possibly to find a personal way out of it. This latter attitude is more common among individuals whose families – either their own family or that of their spouse – have sufficient resources to provide a financial cushion to protect them from the worst effects of economic crisis. A cushion of this kind removes some of the pressure of having to cope every day with hardship and worry about how to pay the next bill, and creates some space to think in terms of personal projects of self-improvement. With a cushion of this kind (however small), individuals are more likely to have the confidence to believe in themselves, to think that they have some control over their lives and can make things better, even if they have lost faith in the idea that parties, politicians and governments will do so.

Monica is a mother of a three-year-old child and lives near Parma in the north of Italy. Now in her early thirties, she worked in a ham factory in her early twenties and then decided to start a degree in civil engineering. Coming from a working-class family, her decision to enrol on a BA degree course that was regarded as particularly difficult makes her feel that she has some control over her future if she is willing to work hard and make sacrifices. She was finishing her studies in 2012 when her husband, who also worked in a ham factory, was fired, and he has been unemployed since then. The birth of their child coincided with the loss of their only salary (except for the money she earns working in a restaurant on the weekends); they could no longer pay the rent on their flat so they decided to move in with her husband's parents. Her husband's parents live in an isolated village about 20 miles away. There are no other children in the village and Monica is obliged to commute to the university while her mother-in-law looks after her child and her husband stays at home. Her parents are retired workers and they have small pensions that barely cover their own expenses, but her husband's parents are wealthier than they are and they own a two-storey detached house where Monica and her husband now live on the second floor. Moving in with her husband's parents has eased the financial pressure. Monica can now focus her energies on trying to improve her situation by finishing her course, improving her skills, getting to know people who could help her and exploiting any opportunities that arise. She has been living for four years in a place that she deeply dislikes – the village is isolated and she would prefer not to live with her in-laws – but she doesn't let this get to her. Although her husband doesn't have a job and she is only working part-time in a restaurant, she remains optimistic and future-oriented.

In some respects, Monica's optimism resonates with the kind of 'forced optimism' of the Renzi government, which came to power in 2014 and, in its public statements, mixed criticism of the austerity imposed by the EU with messages of reform and hope centred on the principle of 'doing one's homework' and taking responsibility for one's own destiny. In this context, 'hope' could mean one of two things. Either hope could be invested outwardly in institutions – in political institutions like the state, political parties, etc., and in the institutions of the economy – towards which one orientates oneself, waiting, watching for signs of improvement, looking for signs that politicians and other leaders are able to make some real difference. Or hope could be invested inwardly, detached from wider institutions and directed inwards towards projects of self-improvement, relying on one's own abilities and efforts to try to change the situation. In the former case, hope is projected outwards but suspended, as one waits, passively, to see if those who have some power can do anything; in the latter case, hope is turned inwards, privatized, and invested in projects of self-improvement.

Monica's hope is of the latter kind. She embraces the 'forced optimism' of the Renzi government but she translates it into the kind of privatized hope that looks for a way out through projects of self-improvement. 'One has to find their own personal path', explains Monica. She elaborates:

> OK, there's crisis, what can I do? I can't find a job, ok, so I can get an education, I can do some training courses, because this is what job centres offer you nowadays – courses. The only downside is that sometimes you have to take the car and drive somewhere to take the course. This is what happened to Michele [her husband], they offered him a course that would enable him to learn a new job and they helped him to get a placement in a company. The only problem is that it's 30 kilometers away and we have to pay for the petrol. But we need to see the positive side because my husband is at home and isn't doing well and this course will be good for him, for sure.

Her husband Michele also threw himself into exercise – he runs a lot, he lost weight and he is now in better shape. So together they focus on how they can improve themselves and their situation, giving themselves small and achievable goals, like finishing a degree (in Monica's case), taking a new course and retraining (in Michele's case) and looking for small opportunities that will enable them to lift themselves out of their predicament. 'So yes, we need to focus on what we can improve, how we can be happy. I think we need to find small goals but we must not give up. There are days when the problems get to you but you need to try not to think about it and focus on what you can do, what you can do better, because at the end of the day there are worse things. Not having a job is a problem but with an illness there is no way out. Perhaps there are no jobs today but there might be tomorrow.'

Nikos, a musician living in Volos in Greece, took a very similar view, falling back on his own inner resources: 'The only solution is to invest in yourself, in what you do, no matter what the consequences are', he explained. 'Crisis makes everybody turn inwards, minding their own business, getting safely inside a cocoon and hiding there because when things don't go well you have two choices: either hitting bottom or moving ahead. Only the strong ones will be able to survive.'

By turning inwards and investing in themselves, these individuals were at the same time turning away from others and from the idea that there might be some collective solution to the crisis. They, like many others interviewed, had given up on the idea that they might be able to improve their situation by some kind of collective action: by privatizing hope and investing their energies in projects of self-improvement, they were at the same time expressing a belief in the futility of togetherness. Sebastiano and Antonio had no faith either in the idea that they might be able to improve their situations through collective action. Occasionally they would mention 'revolts' or 'protests' as they spoke, but these words were always accompanied by nervous laughs and dismissive hand gestures to emphasize their lack of belief in the effectiveness of collective action. 'Each one cries with their own eyes', remarked Sebastiano.

Permanent temporariness

For many people who are unemployed, or precariously employed in part-time jobs that generate small streams of income, planning for the future is an abstract concept that doesn't make much sense – you simply don't have the wherewithal to make life plans. You have to focus on short-term goals and try to figure out how to make ends meet. You focus on the present and live for the here and now. Every solution is just a temporary fix. It is a state of permanent temporariness.

Alexis grew up in Larissa, which is near Volos in Thessaly. He has been living in Volos since 2008. 'The crisis found me in Volos', he said. He studied psychology in Thessaloniki and did his Masters in Athens; he feels lucky because he hasn't been unemployed since he graduated. 'I was one of the lucky ones because I haven't been unemployed. The periods of my unemployment were only from the end of one contract to another.' His father was a fireman but he's now retired and has many debts. 'My father was a victim of the golden era of loans', as he describes it. 'He was working in the public sector and it was so easy to take a loan, many loans. He took a lot.' His father is now in debt for the rest of his life and his children will have nothing to inherit. 'When he dies we'll just refuse the inheritance because it will be an inheritance of debts.' While the situation is very difficult, his family is lucky, explains Alexis, because the three children didn't have to face unemployment (his brother is also a fireman and his sister's husband is in the military): 'we didn't face that situation, which stresses every Greek family: what are we going to do?

167

We have both debts and unemployed children?' Alexis's only worry now is not to lose the family house where his parents are still living. As Alexis recounted the story of his family, the jobs he has done and the impact of the crisis on his life and that of his friends, he surprised himself by the amount of detail he remembered – he remembered every little detail regarding how much money he was earning at each point in time over the past five years. He remembered how much he was earning every month, when he started earning less, each of the different times benefits were reduced, which job paid on time and which didn't, and so on. Suddenly he looked up and said:

> How do I remember all this? This frightens me. Why do I remember my money matters so clearly? I didn't use to care about these things. I remember them because there was a constant discussion about the likelihood of a cutback. I remember myself checking every month to see whether there was a cutback. At some point the salary fell to 30 euros. This is characteristic of the crisis. I don't remember how much money I made in 2008 and 2009, but from 2010 on I can tell you exactly.

When you're earning so little and there's a constant risk that it will be cut further, you can easily become obsessively concerned with the detail of how much you're earning at any point in time, without even realizing that you are.

Even though he was earning very little, Alexis felt fortunate to have any job at all. Many of his friends have the same qualifications as he does but they're unemployed. 'It doesn't matter if you earn less or if you earn very little, you still feel lucky because you have a job. Now you end up working for 480 euros a month and you're still feeling lucky! Before, we would consider this to be disgraceful, but now everybody is running after jobs, any kind of job. In the past we would make fun of these jobs but now if someone hears of a job, he will let you know, he would even apply and hope to get it.' This constant state of running after elusive jobs, of never being settled because every job is temporary and insufficient on its own and the future is always uncertain, is permanent temporariness:

> What I came to realize is that the jobs I do are all temporary. I haven't been left without a job but I live a situation of permanent temporariness. I didn't search for permanence, because I probably wouldn't like it, but there is this precariousness. A project finishes, what am I going to do now? Make applications again. I applied for two jobs yesterday. It has become a routine. Then you wait for them to call you, and you feel lucky if they do. You celebrate. You just manage to survive, you no longer live. You can't plan anything. The situation has become punk, you just live for the moment – and I mean it in the bad sense.

For those on the receiving end of an economic crisis, the horizons of the future collapse into the present. 'You can't plan anything' because you don't know if you will have a job tomorrow, let alone in a year or two years' time. Everything is temporary, and temporariness is permanent.

As a trained psychologist with a precarious but active practice, Alexis has also had the opportunity to observe how others were coping with the crisis. It is quite expensive to see a psychologist, so people would not ask for this kind of help unless they really felt they needed it. In Alexis's experience, he found that people were coming to him because they were finding it more difficult to talk about their problems with friends, who were suffering for reasons of their own. It didn't feel right to burden a friend with problems when they were trying to cope with problems of their own – 'How could I talk about my pain, since the other is in pain too?' So they decide to go to a psychologist instead. Many of the people Alexis saw were suffering from stress, anxiety and panic attacks, often linked to the crisis, but many were also experiencing conflicts in the family or relationship problems. Alexis could see that relationships were coming under a great deal of stress, especially when one or both of the partners were unemployed. But he could also see that people were beginning to come to terms with the reality of crisis and with the fact that it isn't going to go away anytime soon. 'The crisis is not something temporary. It's here to stay and this is the way we'll probably have to live from now on. More and more people are coming to terms with the situation, they now know that things are like this and they will continue to be the same. They realize that crisis is permanent and they have to swallow it.'

Shame and dignity

One of the hardest things for people to cope with is the shame associated with what feels like failure. The sense of shame was particularly pronounced in the case of Sebastiano, the pastry chef whose business in Sicily had failed and whose attempt to forge a new career by opening a shop in Rome had left him and his family penniless. He returned to his town in Sicily a broken man, preferring to stay home and watch TV rather than have to face others and explain what had gone wrong. At the age of 61 he now feels that all is lost. He feels that he will die with the crisis still affecting his life, swallowed by the crisis, and he sees only an end without dignity. 'If one thinks about the situation every day like I do, I always think: is it possible that in every other part of the world people can pick themselves up and carry on with dignity, I don't say get rich but carry on with dignity, while in Italy it is impossible? If there is an end to the crisis it will be after I am gone, another 15 years for sure, and I will be long gone and it will be hard.' Living with the shame of failure is hard, but what really depresses Sebastiano is the prospect of dying without dignity.

Mania too struggles with feelings of shame. She is 70 and living in Athens, and she has an unemployed daughter in her mid-thirties. Ten years ago she lost her husband. She retired in 2007 and had a good pension after working for many years in the public sector – until, that is, the crisis hit. Her pension payments were cut repeatedly, taxes went up and a new property tax was introduced, and suddenly she found herself unable to cope. 'I couldn't keep up. On a practical financial level, I couldn't cope and I found myself in conditions of real poverty.' She was plunging into debt and unable to pay her bills and she was overwhelmed with a sense of shame:

> And then came the shame. The worst feeling was an endless shame and an unbearable sense of no way out. I couldn't cope financially. Some friends helped me out financially – a friend of mine realized I was in a mess and she mobilized people who could help. In some way they gave me a chance to deal with it, to pay off some bills and debts from loans and cards and other things, I don't know what. If I paid my debts and daily expenses I wouldn't have money left for cigarettes, how can I explain that? And I remember that that is how I started feeling something that I can only describe as this: Shame. Shame. Similar to what I feel now because I wrongly estimated my own abilities, lacked perspective and planning in relation to this. I shouldn't have been so immature with regard to my finances, I was to blame, I should have planned ahead. The realization, for example, that I can't help my child out. And this is how things went on, with great grief.

Depressed and overwhelmed by shame, Mania found herself becoming cut off from old friends. New divisions emerged along the lines of who had lost what in the crisis – friendships based on the shared experience of material loss. 'I avoided some groups of friends, some old friends that I knew lived at a different level of comfort. They spoke in theory about all this but they hadn't felt it in their bones.' Even her relationship to her partner was affected, and that was the most painful of all. 'I felt completely devastated when the economic crisis affected my relationship to my partner', she said. 'This was the epitome of degradation, from a person with whom you were so close, thinking that together we can deal with anything life throws at us, and then you split up by getting a letter that reads: I am very sorry, I loved you deeply, I had a wonderful time, best years of my life, but unfortunately I can't cope with the economic stress.'

Alternatives

Not everyone experiences crisis and responds to it like Sebastiano and Mania. Some see crisis as an opportunity to do something different, to forge a new set of relationships and practices that express a different set of values. Vaggelis is one of those. In 2006 he returned to Greece from the UK, where he had studied to become a computer engineer. He never wanted to pursue an orthodox career working in a company: 'I didn't want to work for someone else to make them rich, I didn't want to be part of something that didn't express who I am or work on something that bored me just to survive. I wanted to use my knowledge of engineering but not for something that would be only commercial or profit-driven: I wanted it to have a social dimension.' Vaggelis became one of the founding members of TEM, the Network of Exchange and Solidarity – a local trading system that emerged in Volos in 2010 in the wake of the crisis. The network uses its own local currency, called TEMs, which are used to exchange goods and services. The ethos of TEM resonated with Vaggelis's own beliefs and he threw himself into the project:

> It was a full time job, and it still is. But you don't necessarily make a living doing these things. It can be done but it's not easy. Many of those who are involved in social enterprises like TEM do it in their spare time; they have another job that pays their bills. But that can create problems of its own. I wanted to find a way to make a living out of this job so that I could devote all my time and energy to it. We're now trying to open a repair shop where everybody will learn how to repair their own equipment. We're not going to fix things for people, we're going to help people fix their own things so that they take control of the situation and are not dependent on experts who charge 50 euros for pushing two buttons. This is also a way to help the environment by not throwing things away and to develop alternative economic practices. There is no boss in this organization: everyone will work as a team and be paid the same.

Vaggelis acknowledges that he is fortunate to be able to pursue his dreams by throwing himself into the building of an alternative community like TEM, a privilege that he owes to his parents, as he recognizes: 'I was very lucky because my parents provided me with the opportunity to choose, to look for what I wanted to do with my life. They told me to look for something that makes me feel good and happy. I really thank them for that.' His parents were public sector workers, now retired, and their pensions were cut almost by half, but they managed their situation because they never spent much money anyway – they never wanted to

171

buy expensive clothes and they didn't travel much. They took out a bank loan to buy a house 30 years ago but they managed to pay it back. 'They don't have savings but they don't have debts either.' So Vaggelis's family was not weighed down by debt and his parents were not struggling to pay the bills. That left Vaggelis free to pursue his beliefs, which were focused on the idea of creating a network of exchange that was disconnected from the mentality of debt.

'In general I consider the system of debt to be immoral', explained Vaggelis. 'It's like giving people sweets, or drug dealing. That's how the crisis started. You lend money to people who have internalized the idea that you can buy anything.' It's changing this mentality that matters to Vaggelis, and that's why he invested his energy in creating TEM. Solidarity mattered to him just as much as creating an alternative exchange system:

> We wanted people to change their mentality and be able to envision a more just economy. This network provides people with some financial relief, but it also gives them the opportunity to see things in a totally different way. It's a DIY-economy that doesn't need an authority. People started becoming friends there, they started working together, they started talking about building a shared structure, they started thinking together about how to make things work. It's more than a unit – the unit is just a tool. It's a network of people, a structure of interaction.

Vaggelis, the committed activist, is upbeat about the future. 'Generally, I'm an optimistic person', he explains. 'If nothing extreme happens, like an environmental disaster, I stay positive because there is always an alternative, a solution, even for people who have lost their dreams and values.'

While Vaggelis sees crisis as an opportunity to forge a new set of social relationships and change people's way of thinking, others look for solutions that are more individual in character. Giorgos is 35 and grew up in Athens; his parents and his sister are still living there. His sister studied in Italy and returned to Athens to work. She was doing well in the beginning, but when the crisis hit she became unemployed and she is now living with their parents. Giorgos sensed early on that things were going to get tough and he decided to leave Athens: 'I could smell it. It was in the air. I left early.' He travelled a lot before deciding to buy land in Pelion. He learned how to cultivate the land and how to be self-sufficient after visiting, living and working in various eco-communities around the world. He insists, however, that he is not part of a community – rather, it was as an individual that he decided to buy a small piece of land in Pelion and cultivate it. Other similarly minded people did the same, in their own ways and for their own reasons, but not as part of a collective movement. 'I have my life here, my vegetable garden, my horse, my chickens, my two dogs, a little cat, my fruit trees, I am self-sufficient', he says with simplicity and pride.

> They welcomed us in the village. I was not the first to arrive – there were others before me. In the beginning the locals were curious and even a little suspicious of us, and we were a bit extreme in appearance. But they also helped us a lot. And we didn't want to make problems for them. We managed to create a fairly good relationship. We showed them that we chose their place because we loved it. We were not born and raised here, which also means that we were not bored with it and itching to leave. We chose to come here. Now, there are around ten households here, some live here with their families and the children go to school in the village.

Like Giorgios, some came before the crisis began, but when the crisis erupted and developed from 2008 on, more people arrived and began to cultivate small plots in the surrounding area. They came for their own reasons but they helped one another: 'if someone needs help, we help him. Sometimes two or three people agree to work together and help each other and that's it.' Giorgos produces more than he needs and he sells some eggs, cheese and milk to make some money. He lives a Spartan existence: 'no electricity, I don't pay for the water because it comes from the spring', few expenses, no family. He is alone, largely self-sufficient and content. Rather than trying to forge a career in an economy that was collapsing around him, he chose to return to the soil, leave the urban metropolis where he had grown up and where his family still lives and build a new life on the land that enables him to control, so far as possible, the parameters of his own existence. He lives day-to-day, following the natural rhythms of rural life, and doesn't worry about the future. 'I don't worry about the future because I want to live in the present. Whatever happens, I'll pull through. A couple of years ago I got pneumonia and fortunately a neighbour came by and took care of me and looked after the animals. I was fine.' He didn't vote in the referendum – 'the referendum was a joke'. His world is now his land and his village and he is happy about his life. 'I realized my dream, this is enough for me at the moment.'

Conclusion

We have explored some fragments in the lives of those on the receiving end of economic crisis, those who have found themselves unemployed or underemployed, thrown out of work or thrown into precarious work, struggling to cope with a sudden and dramatic change in circumstances that has forced them to rethink their lives and their relations with others. We have focused on the *lived reality* of crisis – on how individuals experience crisis, on what it means to those who live through it, on their feelings of anger, disappointment and despair, and on their ways of responding to the sudden change in their circumstances. The experiences highlighted here shed some light both on the nature of suffering in general and on the specific kinds of suffering brought about by the economic crisis in Europe. Through the lives of these individuals we get some sense of what it means to speak of suffering as a way of being in the world – not a state of mind but a state of being in which a cluster of negative feelings are woven together, creating an outlook on the world that is bleak, despondent, filled with sadness and despair. We also see what it means to say that suffering is relative: being thrown into hardship sensitizes you to adversity, and from this new viewpoint you see hardship around you as never before. Your situation may be bleak but the plight of others often seems worse. Precisely because suffering is so pervasive in everyday life and assumes so many forms, it generally falls below the radar of the professions, whether these are medical professionals or social services. But as the stories of these individuals illustrate over and over again, suffering matters greatly in the conduct of people's lives. Not only can it be deeply painful and distressing for individuals but it can also envelope them in an affective tissue that shapes their outlook on life, straining their relations with others, sapping their motivation and destroying their self-esteem.

While the experiences recounted here display all of these general characteristics of suffering, they also exhibit some features that are specific to the economic crisis in Europe; let us highlight a few:

1. Suffering in this context is infused with a great deal of anger and resentment towards politicians and political elites, who are seen as distant, untrustworthy, incapable of understanding the lives of ordinary people and condescending towards them ('they think we are fools'). These feelings were particularly strong in Greece in the aftermath of the referendum and the government's capitulation to the creditors ('the referendum was a joke'), but anger and resentment of this kind was strongly present in Italy too.
2. Suffering is often characterized by a deep and pervasive sadness associated with the collapse of dreams and the loss of any sense of hope about the future. Your life seems stuck, frozen in time, and often there seems like no feasible way to move forward.
3. Some individuals turn inwards, withdrawing into themselves and

into their homes, which become both a protective shield and a trap. In some cases they withdraw into silence, cutting themselves off from encounters with others which are simply too painful to sustain, while in other cases they throw themselves into personal projects of self-improvement. But in both cases they are giving up on the idea of collective action as a way of responding to their situation.

4. For individuals who have lost their jobs, filling empty time is one of the toughest challenges. Days seem to stretch on endlessly and individuals struggle to find ways to make the hours pass. Watching television and repetitively carrying out small tasks around the house may help to pass the time but they're also often associated with bitterness and humiliation. While the problem of filling empty time, and of transforming the very meaning of time in the lives of those who have lost their jobs, is certainly not specific to the economic crisis in Europe (it was a key feature of the lives of the unemployed in Marienthal too), it has acquired its own particular inflections in contemporary circumstances.

5. For those seeking work or precariously employed, temporariness has become permanent. You're constantly looking for work and everything is temporary, provisional. You can't plan anything because you don't know if you will have a job tomorrow, let alone in a year or two years' time.

6. Shame and the loss of dignity are among the most painful aspects of suffering – the shame of finding yourself in debt, of being unable to pay your bills without asking others for help, of being unable to face others and explain why your life has collapsed. Shame strips away your dignity, and to be left with no dignity can be the most painful experience of all.

Of course, in highlighting these themes we make no claim to comprehensiveness: there are countless ways in which individuals experience economic crisis, and any attempt to capture this will necessarily emphasize some experiences and emotions at the expense of others. But only by immersing ourselves in the lives of others, entering their worlds and listening carefully to their words, can we grasp the real-life consequences of economic crisis, understand how individuals cope with radical changes to the economic conditions of their lives and see how these changes disrupt their worlds and give rise to experiences that are both painful and debilitating. For many, these experiences may be lived in a personal way, suffered in silence or turned into personal projects of self-fulfilment. But accumulated feelings of suffering and anger can also find expression in collective and unpredictable ways, especially when individuals are given the opportunity to make their voices heard, as in an election or referendum. For political processes of this kind are as much about affect and emotion as they are about reason and interest, and when strong feelings are coupled with deep distrust and growing resentment of established political elites, the results can be particularly disruptive. Political outcomes that may be surprising or even incomprehensible from the perspective of political elites, who typically view the social world from above and are detached from the everyday experiences and feelings of people whose lives are far removed from their own, may be less surprising when they are seen in relation to the lived realities of people's lives. Understanding the suffering of others is an indispensable part of thinking through the impact of economic crisis on people's lives, but it is also essential if we want to make sense of the dramatic upheavals that are shaking the political establishment and overturning many taken-for-granted beliefs in Europe and elsewhere today.

References

Bourdieu et al. (1993) *The Weight of the World: Social Suffering in Contemporary Society*, tr. Priscilla Parkhurst Ferguson et al. Cambridge: Polity.

Buffel, V., van de Velde, S. and Bracke, P. (2015) The mental health consequences of the economic crisis in Europe among the employed, the unemployed, and the non-employed. *Social Science Research* 54: 263–88.

Caritas Europa (2015) Poverty and inequalities on the rise, *Crisis Monitoring Report 2015*. Available at: http://www.caritas.eu/sites/default/files/caritascrisisreport_2015_en_final.pdf

Chang, S., Stuckler, D., Yip, P. and Gunnell, D. (2013) Impact of 2008 global economic crisis on suicide: time trend study in 54 countries. *British Medical Journal* 347: f5239.

Economou, M., Madianos, M., Peppou, L.E., Theleritis, C., Patelakis, A. and Stefanis, C. (2013) Suidical ideation and reported suicide attempts in Greece during the economic crisis. *World Psychiatry* 12(1): 53–9.

European Commission (2014) *Employment and Social Developments in Europe 2014*. Brussels: European Commission Directorate-General for Employment, Social Affairs and Inclusion.

Eurostat Online Database (2016a). Unemployment statistics at regional level, April. Available at: http://ec.europa.eu/Eurostat/statistics-explained/index.php/Unemployment_statistics_at_regional_level

Eurostat Online Database (2016b) Unemployment statistics, August. Available at: http://ec.europa.eu/Eurostat/statistics-explained/index.php/Unemployment_statistics

Fassin, D. (2012) *Humanitarian Reason: A Moral History of the Present*. Berkeley, CA: University of California Press.

Jahoda, M., Lazarsfeld, P.F. and Zeisel, H. (2002) *Marienthal: The Sociography of an Unemployed Community*. New Brunswick, NJ: Transaction.

Kentikelenis, A., Karanikolos, M., Papanicolas, I., Basu, S., McKee, M. and Stuckler, D. (2011) Health effects of financial crisis: omens of a Greek tragedy. *The Lancet* 378(9801): 1457–8.

Madianos, M., Economou, M., Alexiou, T. and Stefanis, C. (2011) Depression and economic hardship across Greece in 2008 and 2009: two cross-sectional surveys nationwide. *Social Psychiatry and Psychiatric Epidemiology* 46: 943–52.

OECD (2014) *Society at a Glance 2014: The Crisis and its Aftermath*. Paris: OECD.

Oxfam (2015) *A Europe for the Many, Not the Few*. Oxford: Oxfam.

Stuckler, D., Basu, S., Suhrcke, M., Coutts, A. and McKee, M. (2011) Effects of the 2008 recession on health: a first look at European data. *The Lancet* 378(9786): 124–5.

Chapter 8

Achilles' Heel: Europe's Ambivalent Identity
Manuel Castells

Introduction: Why European identity is important

After the constitution of the European Central Bank in 1998, the creation of the euro in 1999, and the increasingly tight control of national economic policies by the European Commission, the European Union became, to all intents and purposes, one economy, albeit with dysfunctional internal disparities. Even the economies of EU countries outside the eurozone, such as the UK, Sweden and Denmark, are deeply intertwined with the EU economy at large. Besides the economic dimension, EU countries are entangled in a web of institutional, social and political relationships which have grown in size and complexity over the years, as new countries became associated with the EU, and as the European institutions extended their realm of activity. In spite of this deep intertwining of all the member countries, the European Union ground has been shown to be shakier than Europeans believed, as the crisis within the UK that led to Brexit has clearly shown.

As long as the European Union was a positive sum game, in which everybody won (some in economic terms, some in political terms, others in technological terms, still others in social terms), without sacrificing too much national identity and political sovereignty, crises of transition were absorbed by countries themselves. To be sure, the European Commission has never been very popular, and its bureaucratic arrogance made things worse. Regardless of how much real power Brussels has or will have, the European Union as such, and other supra-national institutions (such as NATO, WTO or IMF), have taken away substantial areas of sovereignty from the European states. Not that nation-states are disappearing. But they have become nodes in a broader network of political institutions: national, regional, local, non-governmental, co-national and international. Europe is governed by a network state of shared sovereignty and multiple levels and instances of negotiated decision-making (Castells 2003). Thus, on the one hand, the unification of Europe is a complex process of economic/technological/cultural transition that creates innumerable problems and resistances, along with new opportunities for economic growth and cooperation. On the other hand, the political system in charge of managing the transition is increasingly disjointed from the social and cultural roots on which European societies are based. In other words: the technology is new; the economy is global; the state is a European network, in negotiation with other international actors; while people's identity is national, or even local and regional in many cases. In a democratic society, this kind of cognitive political dissonance may be unsustainable. While integrating Europe without sharing a European identity was a workable proposition when everything went well, any major crisis, in Europe or in a given country, triggers potentially serious backlash.

The 2008 financial crisis and the misconceived austerity policies spearheaded by Germany and the European Commission reversed the path to prosperity that had paved the way for institutional and cultural pan-Europeanism. Furthermore, the increasing multi-ethnic character of most European countries, and the emergence of new kinds of geopolitical dangers (including nationalism and fundamentalism from the excluded and marginalized of the new economy), has added considerable stress to what was supposed to be an integrated European project for the creation of a successful humankind in this corner of the planet. Yet, the experience of recent years shows that the construction of Europe is an uncertain process that ultimately depends on what Europeans do. The term 'Europeans' is of course the tricky part of the equation. Because, who are they?

The reactions of Northern European countries against the bail out of Southern European countries showed the limits of solidarity when there is not a minimum of common identity (Elliott and Atkinson 2016). The sharp debate on Brexit in the UK, with major resistance against immigration *from the EU* as its central point, showed the limits of socio-cultural integration, and the grassroots resistance to a unified labour market (MacShane 2015). Thus, a shared European identity seems to be a requirement for a sustainable European Union. But what can we understand such an identity to be? And what do we know about the existence or non-existence of a European identity?

What is European identity?

For the sake of clarity, I understand identity as a set of values that provide symbolic meaning to people's lives by enhancing their individuation (or self-definition) and their feeling of belonging to a community of reference. Or course people may have various identities, according to different spheres of their existence: one can feel Portuguese, socialist, catholic, woman, and all these identities can overlap without major contradiction. Which one is dominant depends on the moment in life and on the realm of activity.

European identity would be the set of values that provide shared meaning to most European citizens by making it possible for them to feel that they belong to a distinctive European culture and institutional system that appeals to them as legitimate and worthwhile. What could be the sources of such an identity? (Green 2015). It is essential to know, first, *what is not European identity*. It is not a 'civilization' based on religion, past history, or a set of supposedly superior 'Western values'. European countries have spent centuries (particularly the last one) killing each other, so the notion of a shared history has a sinister connotation (Fontana 1995). Religion (meaning Christianity) is an unthinkable source of common identity since European countries have established the separation between the church and the state, particularly in this historical moment when non-Christian religions (e.g. Islam) are growing fast in the European Union, both among ethnic minorities, and in countries applying for association (Turkey, Bosnia-Herzegovina, Albania). Language, one of the most important sources of cultural identity, is, of course, excluded as a common source of European identity, although I will argue that a certain approach to language is essential in constructing identity. National identity as European identity is also impossible, by definition. Nations and nation-states are not going to fade away.

In fact, they are going to grow and become important sources of collective identity, more than ever, as new, *formerly dominated* nations, come into the open (Catalunya, Euzkadi, Galicia, Scotland, Wales, Wallonie, Flanders, etc.), and as strong nationalist movements assert their rights in the public arena against the submission of the nation to the European state. I start from the assumption that in the foreseeable future, Europe will not be a federal construction similar to the United States. There will be no unified European state, superseding and cancelling current nation-states. Identification with a political construction, such as the state, cannot be a source of identity, thus eliminating the option of 'European nationalism' equivalent to 'American nationalism'. American

180

national identity emerged from a multi-cultural, immigrant nation. But it was because it was an immigrant nation in an empty continent (or forcefully half-emptied of its native populations) that America could combine strong cultural and ethnic identities with an equally strong American identity. Such is not the case of Europe. But if it is relatively easy to know what is not European identity, it is more debatable to know whether there is one and what it is or could be.

What do we know about European identity?

I will differentiate my analysis between two sets of information: on the one hand, the information on self-identification provided by various representative surveys and mainly by the Eurobarometer of the European Commission, the only database that allows for comparison across countries and across years; and on the other hand, the analyses resulting from academic research.

The feeling of European identity in contrast to national, regional and local identities

The available evidence (see Appendix at the end of this chapter) can be summarized as follows:

- There is coexistence between European identity with national, regional and local identities.
- European identity is the weakest among the different territorially-based identities.
- While a majority of citizens feel both national and European, a significant minority feel only national, with just a tiny group declaring themselves mainly European.
- The strength of European identity varies over time. It was gradually increasing until 2008 but national identity became paramount in most countries after the economic crisis.
- There is considerable variation among countries in terms of the relative importance of national identity vis-à-vis European identity. Britons (in fact English but not Scottish, Northern Irish or Welsh) are clearly the most nationalist among all Europeans, and their anti-Europeanism has been accentuated over time, forcing a referendum on EU membership, leading to Brexit. Scandinavian countries display a eurosceptic attitude among the majority of their citizens. Switzerland and Norway are not EU members and are happy to stay so.

181

- Overall, European identity is a weak identity. And its weakness makes it vulnerable to any major disruption in the European Union, be it economic, geopolitical or migratory.

The scholarly debate on European identity

The role of identity in the European Union has been a subject of heated debate since its founding. Let us remember that the European Community was established in the wake of World War II to bring an end to the traumatic violence and nationalist sentiment that had torn the continent apart over centuries, and prompted mass killings and widespread destruction in the twentieth century. Although rooted in an ethical project to end wars within the continent, it was also a *defensive* project to contain nationalism rather than to supersede it. Though the core of the current European Union is built upon the economic foundations established under the Maastricht Treaty, there have been a number of accompanying efforts to build solidarity and reduce barriers among citizens of European states, such as the creation of the Erasmus programme to encourage exchanges among university students, and the border-free Schengen area to facilitate seamless travel within the majority of EU countries. There are also a number of cultural programmes, such as the 'European capitals of culture' that designates one city every year, or the Creative Europe Programme that funds innovative cultural initiatives. Despite these efforts, the notion of a pan-European identity remains fragile, and within the body of scholarship on the European Union, there is little consensus as to the salience of European identity or the factors that contribute to its strength or weakness.

As mentioned above, since 2008 Europe has been particularly challenged by the global financial crisis, which has splintered the economic union. Because the burden of the crisis was distributed unequally across Member States, it introduced a substantial strain and divide between the nations in debt crises, related to financial turmoil, and those who ultimately became responsible for a bailout. This divide is also reflected geographically in the divisions between Northern European states, which came through the crisis relatively unharmed, and Southern states, which are still struggling to recover. Xenophobia is on the rise within a substantial minority of Europeans, who support nationalist far-right political parties that oppose the Union, particularly in France, Austria, the Netherlands, Denmark and Finland. Available evidence shows that the fracturing of the economic base of the European Union has also had downstream effects on European identity.

The findings of academic research conducted on European identity, with a few exceptions, seem to converge with the main conclusions I summarized above on the basis of my own examination of the sources, that is: (1) identification in Europe is divided; the majority of Europeans self-identify as having both a national and European identity, and (2) national identity tends to be favoured over European identity. However, the European identity is not equally shared by all citizens. A number of socio-demographic factors appear to influence whether and how strongly a person will identify as European. In general, these indicators are tied to their experiences of the economic, political and social changes within Europe. Europeans that experience closer transnational relationships over the course of their own lives are more likely to see themselves as European; those who do not are more likely to see the EU as a distant place where business interests are served rather than their own. In terms of demographic indicators, the pro-Europeans are those who have both the opportunity and inclination to travel to other countries, who speak other languages, and who routinely interact with people in other societies (Fligstein 2008: 126). They are among the highest socio-economic groups in society, travel and live in other European countries, and speak second or third languages for work. As youths, they travel across borders for school, tourism and work (Fligstein et al. 2012: 109). They are the dominant material beneficiaries of EU integration. There is a close association between high social status and the feeling of being European. This association is more intense in the case of social elites, so that it would not be fanciful to say that feeling predominantly European, let alone a 'citizen of the world' is an attribute of high social class. This explains the reverse association between feeling exploited and marginalized and feeling national rather than European.

Indeed, those who lack the opportunity or interest to interact with their counterparts across Europe tend to hold on to their national identity, and see the EU as a place that undermines the nation. In fact, the threat of being disenfranchised by globalization in Europe is expressed by the threat of pan-European identity. The people who feel threatened by European integration tend to be blue-collar and service workers, are older, and are less likely to know other languages. They are more likely to remember who was on which side during World War II, hold less favourable views of their national neighbours and have conservative political views that hold the nation as the most important category (Fligstein et al. 2012: 110). In general, men are more likely than women to think of themselves as primarily European; those who identify as right wing are less likely (Fligstein 2008: 145). On a national level, UK citizens are among the most nationalist in their political collective identity, while Germans are among the strongest advocates for more European political union (Fligstein 2008: 136). I dare to hypothesize that Britons remember the wars while Germans are trying to forget them.

Despite these overarching trends, the data suggests that for most Europeans, identity is a fluid and hybrid concept. Overwhelmingly, citizens of European countries are 'situational Europeans', who sometimes view themselves as European and, under the right conditions, place this over their national identity (Fligstein 2008).

In addition to these social indicators, other potential sources of European identity should also be considered. From the perspective of Europeans themselves, survey research has shown that respondents see democratic values (40.8 per cent), geography (26.6 per cent), social protection (26.4 per cent), common history (22.5 per cent) and common culture (21.6 per cent) as most important to a sense of European identity. Interestingly, entrepreneurship and religious heritage were not seen as important (Fuchs and Schneider 2011). The establishment of pan-European media has been identified as a key contributor to the development of European identity. However, the actual framing of Europe within the most-watched media channels in Europe works against these dynamics. Discussion of European issues tends to be filtered through national media: while coverage of Europe has grown, it is often filtered through national debates and self-images rather than European ones (Fligstein 2009; Corcoran 2011; Thiel 2011). Shared memory has also been identified as a potentially important factor in Europe's identity project (Green 2015). The shared experience of World War II, collective remembrance of the horrors of war and a commitment to avoiding another massacre through integration may help establish transnational identification among Europeans, though research on this is largely theoretical (Bottici and Challand 2013).

The economy is sometimes pointed to as a critical factor in the formation of identity, though it appears less frequently in the post-crisis literature than may be expected. Verhaegen et al. (2014) find that the *perception* of economic benefits is significantly associated with whether or not citizens will identify as European, even more than the reality. They find that when respondents perceived their country's economic situation as positive, when they relate the EU with economic prosperity and when they have a positive perception of the financial situation of their household, they are more likely to identify as European. Importantly, they also find that perceived benefits are more important than objective benefits in determining identification.

The case of Greece is a particularly interesting one: in an examination of the Greek response to the crisis in relation to European identity, Dora Kostakopoulou (2014) argues that high levels of Europeanness are not a strong predictor of whether a country will welcome a fiscal union, or be prepared to grant bailouts to debt-ridden neighbours. The presence of a strong collective identity did not make the Greeks less critical of the status quo, and they did not rally behind their national government immediately following the exposure of the country's debt despite the possibility that austerity measures could be enforced by the EU. The rise of the Syriza coalition, and its assurance that Greece will stay a part of the eurozone (despite mild euroscepticism) further bolsters this claim.

Looking further into the future, economic factors may facilitate the process of European identity building due to the changes they are enacting in the Union's demographics: the expansion of the market, changes in demography and rise in skills and education all work in favour of increased European identification (Fligstein 2008: 157).

Culture is seen by many scholars of European identity as more salient than economy in relation to identity formation. In general, European cultural policy has taken a pluralist model that champions local culture by appropriating and redefining it as European: in this mode, diversity takes precedence over unity (Holmes 2009; Tagiuri 2014; Todorov and Bracher 2008). Integration of citizens in the process of identity building is particularly important to the cultural project; Juan Diez Medrano (2009) notes that the top-down approach to European integration has created a mismatch between national leaders' conceptions of the EU and the views of citizens – identity building has been approached as an elite-driven affair rather than a grassroots one.

Yet this effort is not without its successes: the Erasmus programme and other student exchange programmes have been seen as particularly important in encouraging a broader understanding of the shared elements of European culture (Delibasic 2013). There is moderate empirical support for this assertion: one study of Erasmus participants across six countries found significant and positive changes in students' identification as European, as well as their identification with Europe (Mitchell 2015). At the same time, others have argued these experiences can create feelings of alienation among students when they experience barriers, even when they speak the language of their host country. Study abroad has the potential to result in the development of local attachments rather than cosmopolitan ones (Moores and Metykova 2010). This has also been supported empirically: two studies found that Erasmus does not strengthen, and can even have an adverse effect on students' European identity (Sigalas 2010; Wilson 2011). Thus, the ultimate impact of the Erasmus programme on the formation of European identity has remained inconclusive.

Researchers disagree as to whether national/European affiliations have changed over time. Fuchs and Schneider (2011) argue that attachment to Europe has stayed relatively stable and relatively lower than national identification over the past twenty years, while Schlenker (2013) finds there is greater supra-national identification in Europe today than in the past, recognizing major differences from country to country. In general, Eurobarometer indicators show a continuing but relatively slow trend overall towards a dual mode of identification among Europeans (Citrin and Wright 2014). European and national identity appear to be compatible in most cases; several authors used the concept of nested identities integrating various geographic and political levels ranging from hometown to region, nation and eventually Europe. However, in the event of conflict between these modes of identity, national identity will be more salient than European identity (Fuchs 2011; Karolewski 2010). So, European identity is an ambivalent identity while national identity is a strong identity, and local/regional identity appears to be the primary identity in territorial terms.

The rise of nationalism in Europe

Much more about European identity can be understood from examining its converse, nationalism. The rise of the far right in Europe (analysed in this volume by Michel Wieviorka) has been well-studied by researchers of European identity, who explore the ways in which the marginalization of the growing population of immigrants has served to produce a 'felt' understanding of what it means to be 'European' for some EU citizens (Cetti 2014). This dynamic, termed alternately as nationalism, ethnic nationalism and ethnonationalism, is arguably a response to the EU's integration project, the pace and scope of which has produced anxieties about whether the state has lost control over who and how many persons can enter the territory. These anxieties are also used as a political tool by far right parties in order to instil a cohesive sense of 'Europeanness' and to normalize the adoption of a neoliberal pattern of politics (Cetti 2014: 140).

Ethnonationalism appears to be linked to reduced social capital. It also increases the negative social impact of diversity (Reeskens and Wright 2013). There are conflicting arguments as to the actual mechanisms of ethnonationalism: in her study of far right parties in Austria, Croatia and Hungary, Martina Topic (2014) finds that although most rightist parties have strong views on immigration, some generalize their far right views as European, while others ignore or reject the notion of the EU itself in favour of nationalism. Perspectives also differ as to the granularity of the way conservatives in Europe view migrants: Schlenker (2013) finds that European migrants appear to be more accepted than other migrants, with Muslims the least accepted, while Messina (2014) finds that a critical number of Europeans perceive few if any meaningful distinctions among ethnic, linguistic, racial and religious groups defined as 'the other'.

Often, ethnonationalism is posited as a parallel and opposing identity project in contrast with cosmopolitanism (Checkel and Katzenstein 2009; Corcoran 2011; Lapeyronnie 2009). The cosmopolitan European identity project is described as 'rational' or 'non-emotional', while ethnonationalism is seen as affective (Guibernau 2011). Schlenker (2013) finds that cosmopolitanism is linked positively to civic and cultural constructions of European identity, and negatively to ethnic constructions of EU identity. While the EU has not developed the strong sense of political community that would inspire great sacrifice on the part of its citizens, it can establish a sense of institutional and legal order within which they can exercise their liberty (Castiglione 2009: 51).

Lastly, Schlenker-Fisher (2011) finds correlations between the level of respect for cultural diversity at the national level and the extent to which a country tends to identify as European. She uses these findings to differentiate between European countries, categorizing them as liberal (post-national: both national and European identity are embedded; includes Luxembourg, Denmark, Sweden, Finland and Italy), republican (national and European identity are compatible in a limited or conditional way; includes Spain, Portugal, Ireland and the Netherlands), and ethnic (national and European identity exclude one another; includes Austria, Germany, Greece, Belgium, France and the UK).

A fractured Europe? European identity and the economic crisis

There is surprisingly little academic literature on the relationship between the financial crisis and European identity. However, a number of prominent European scholars have commented publicly on the dynamics of the crisis and its impact on European solidarity, and the relationship to identity.

The crisis seems to have inhibited the slow but steady growth in European identification, and even to have contributed to a decline in European identity in some states. After decades of peace, the attractiveness of the union as a mechanism to prevent war seems much less salient to the lives of younger Europeans, who have yet to experience the outbreak of conflict within their borders.[1] Rather, the European Union plays more of an economic role by bolstering the stability and viability of finance throughout the region – at least, it did so until the crisis.

Once the financial shock hit, Europe began to fracture across North/ South fault lines, between benefactors and debtors. For those in the South, Europe appears to have failed them in their moment of need. This has resulted in a turn within many states, notably in Greece, to national political parties that claim they will insulate their citizens from the economic austerity measures issued by the EU. For those in the North, the politics of the crisis seem unfairly weighted against those states forced to pay for the misdeeds of the South, leading to increased dissatisfaction with the project of the EU. There is very little solidarity within or between the two regions, and the response to Europe's banking problems has meant that support for the Union from both financially successful and vulnerable nations has been undermined.

This has contributed to downstream effects on how citizens of the EU identify themselves. According to Fligstein (2014), the number of citizens who sometimes think of themselves as European has decreased in Spain, Portugal, Italy, Ireland, the UK, and to a lesser extent France and Germany. Overall, it appears that the financial crisis shook the economic foundations of the European Union in a way that has had negative impacts on the identification of Europeans with the EU.

The acid tests of European identity

Given the ambivalence of European identity, possibly the most accurate method to observe its strength or weakness is to evaluate the behaviour of citizens in each country when called to help co-Europeans in distress, or when they are consulted on relinquishing a greater share of sovereignty or act together in the event of a common crisis. Indeed, the key criticism to the formation and development of the European Union is that it has been largely a project of the elites, spearheaded by the political with little consultation of their citizens. There was an attempt to fill the EU democratic deficit by consulting citizens in each country via referendum to approve the project of a European Constitution. It triggered a backlash that jeopardized the legitimacy of the European construction. While the first referenda in Spain and Portugal were easily won by the

---

[1] See 'A Crisis Within a Crisis: Europe's Identity Crisis', Public Radio International, 19 June 2012. Available at: http://www.pri.org/stories/2012-06-19/crisis-within-crisis-europes-identity-crisis

pro-European vote, albeit with a very low participation rate (around 40 per cent), this was due to the fact that Southern Europeans always saw the EU as a protective shield against their authoritarian, nationalist demons. Moreover, Catalans and Basques are the most European in Spain (as Scots are in the UK) because they seek the protection of the EU against their own nation-states. Yet, when referenda were organized in France and the Netherlands, a majority of votes rejected the Constitutional Treaty. Instead of accepting the verdict of citizens, the enlightened despots of Europe halted the referenda and let their national Parliaments (controlled by the political class) approve the Treaty. It was never forgotten by large segments of European citizenry. There was even an attempt in the UK to let Parliament override the popular vote, with the support of the court, but it is unlikely that the politicians would take the risk of a major grassroots backlash.

Another key test of European solidarity came during the economic crisis of 2008 onwards, regarding the bailouts of countries such as Portugal and Greece (and in fact Spain as well, although it was not called so for political reasons) that were in fact as much a necessity for the North as for the South (German and French banks would have been the biggest losers in a Greek default) but were perceived by citizens in Northern Europe as an unfair salvation of their profligate Southern neighbours. A case in point was Finland, where a new nationalist party, the True Finns, jumped to 20 per cent of the vote in their first elections on the basis of a very simple slogan 'Do NOT bailout Portugal', because the Portuguese bailout was the one being debated at the time. Indeed, the True Finns have continued to prosper, on a xenophobic nationalist platform, and became partners in government with the Center Party in 2015. The Greek debt crisis induced a wave of criticism in Germany and Scandinavia that forced Merkel to influence the European Commission and the Troika of financial institutions to impose the most astringent conditions on Greece in exchange for its bailout, leading to the collapse of the Greek financial system, and ultimately to a deep political crisis. Similar stories can be documented concerning Spain, Portugal, Ireland or Italy, although in these cases the subservience of their governments facilitated the imposition of German austerity policies, at the cost of a long, painful recession. Thus, if feeling shared identity with one's compatriots is tested at a time of crisis, when togetherness and solidarity are essential to survive the crisis, we can say there is a very weak European identity, in contrast with solidarity behaviour among Germans, French or Greeks. Nation-states are still based on nations who have stronger ties than their states, now taken away by the whirlwind of globalization in institutions of shared sovereignty without shared identity.

The refugee crisis, European solidarity and nationalist xenophobia

The refugee crisis of 2015–16, analysed by Paul Collier in this volume, is driven by war, violence and poverty, and has the potential to revitalize the experiences and collective memory shared by many Europeans of being refugees themselves during World War II. In contrast with widespread xenophobic expressions all over the continent, the images of German and Austrian crowds warmly welcoming refugees arriving at railway stations in Munich and Vienna powerfully capture what the UN Secretary General, Antonio Guterres, has called a 'defining moment' for the European Union.[2] The city governments of Barcelona and Madrid launched a movement to give asylum to the refugees in a concerted initiative of major European capitals, including Paris and London.

The definition of the moment may hinge on the distinctions being drawn between a xenophobic, nationalist Europe and an open, welcoming one. These distinctions are readily apparent within the reaction of state leaders to the EU's refugee policy. Hungary, a key entry point into Europe for many refugees, serves as the primary exemplar of a xenophobic response: the government under Prime Minister Viktor Orban has taken on a strongly anti-migrant rhetoric, encouraging greater xenophobia among Hungarians. The country closed its border with Serbia, and erected fences in order to prevent the flow of refugees from entering or exiting its territory.[3] In one incident, Hungarian police used water cannons on refugees at the Roske-Hergos border,[4] while a Hungarian journalist tripped and kicked refugees, including a little girl, running away from the police.[5]

Xenophobia has also been reflected in the reactions of Central European states to refugee policy. The EU established a quota system, which would effectively mandate each state to take in a proposed number of refugees from Greece, Italy and Hungary, the primary entry points for the flow of refugees from the Middle East. Under the system, France and Germany would take in the bulk of the refugees, with Spain, the Netherlands and Poland following behind. The majority vote calls into question the

---

[2] 'Cheering German crowds greet refugees after long trek from Budapest to Munich', *The Guardian*, 5 September 2015. Available at: http://www.theguardian.com/world/2015/sep/05/refugee-crisis-warm-welcome-for-people-bussed-from-budapest
[3] http://www.bbc.co.uk/news/world-europe-34260071
[4] http://www.bbc.co.uk/news/world-europe-34272765
[5] http://america.aljazeera.com/articles/2015/9/9/hungarian-journalist-fired-for-tripping-refugees.html

sovereignty of the nation-states within Europe – though ostensibly voluntary, the quotas effectively serve as an EU-mandated immigration policy. The Czech Republic, Hungary, Romania and Slovakia voted against the quotas and may refuse to accept the terms.[6] Others, like Spain, accepted a quota of 16,000 refugees and at the time of this writing in Spring 2016 had admitted less than 400. In contrast, Germany, under the leadership of a compassionate Angela Merkel admitted one million refugees in one year.

The migration of refugees into Europe is likely to continue, and has the potential to substantially alter the fabric of Europe.[7] This would clearly have downstream effects on European identity, but what those are exactly is harder to predict. The first influx of refugees have tended to be wealthier, white-collar workers with the resources to leave their countries. The second wave is more likely to be made up of poorer people who may face an uphill battle resettling in a new nation. However, as Gutierres indicates, this may present Europeans the opportunity to forge a positive, rather than negative, European identity.

Yet, overall, Europe has failed to come together in relation to the refugee crisis. National political interests and electoral worries have prevailed over a common policy. And there is no common policy largely because there is little shared European identity.

Conclusion

Identity is clearly central to the future of the EU. Yet available evidence suggests that while most European citizens hold multiple identities, national identity tends to be more salient than European identity, and that the forced integration project, the economic crisis and the growth of immigration have resulted in an identity crisis for Europe.

For a small minority of Europeans, largely members of social and economic elites, the EU is a cosmopolitan project in which transnational and transboundary relationships are only likely to grow. For many others, instead, it is linked to processes of globalization and marketization that have largely excluded them. Recent events have created pulls in each direction: on the one hand, the economic crisis and the rise of xenophobia have created cleavages between European countries and within European nations that seem likely to drive Europeans further apart; on

---

[6] http://www.bbc.co.uk/news/world-europe-34331126
[7] For additional statistics on the influx of refugees, see: http://www.independent.co.uk/news/world/Europe/refugee-crisis-six-charts-that-show-where-refugees-are-coming-from-where-they-are-going-and-how-they-are-getting-to-Europe-10482415.html

the other hand, the refugee crisis has contributed in some countries to greater solidarity for some Europeans, possibly invigorating the collective memory of the catalysing moment that brought Europe together in the first place.

Indeed, it is my hypothesis that it is in the realm of values, of new values, where we could find the seeds of a potential European identity. On the basis of surveys of attitudes, and a review of the literature, I have identified some elements of what I have called a 'European identity project'. This is what appears empirically to possibly carry a broad cultural consensus throughout Europe, besides the values of political democracy and liberty in all its manifestations (which are widely shared values, but not distinctively European). These elements can be identified as shared feelings concerning the need for universal social protection of living conditions; social solidarity; stable employment; workers' rights; gender equality; universal human rights, including gay and lesbian rights; concern about poor people around the world; extension of democracy to regional and local levels, with a renewed emphasis on citizen participation; the defence of historically rooted cultures, often expressed in linguistic terms. If European institutions could promote these values with specific measures, and could accord life and policy with these promises for all Europeans, this 'project identity' would probably grow. But the problem is precisely that some of these aspirations will have to be rethought and adapted in the new historical context, for instance as far as the welfare state or stable employment in a post-crisis economy are concerned. Moreover, the mere enumeration of these values shows that while they are a reasonable wish list, it may not be easy to combine them in a coherent set, beyond their popularity in public opinion. So, these elements of a European project, while they must be materials to work with, cannot be asserted as a finished model to be imposed. In a fully democratic, multicultural, multiethnic Europe, exposed to global flows of communication and information, no project can be imposed from the state. And yet, the problems raised in this chapter are still relevant. While national and local identities will continue to be strong and instrumental, if there is no development of a compatible European identity, a purely instrumental Europe will remain a fragile construction, whose possible, future wrecking would trigger major crises in European societies, and around the world.

Thus, even if there is no clear European identity model, there still can be an identity in the making, that is a process of social production of identity. In other words, it is not possible to create, artificially, a European identity, but European institutions could help the development of a series of mechanisms that, in their own dynamics, would configure the embryos of this shared system of values throughout Europe. It is by engaging in social experimentation, by letting society evolve by itself, but helping to constitute a European civil society, that we could see the emergence of a new, strong European identity in the foreseeable future. Because if a European identity project does not emerge, nationalist resistance identities from retrenched nations will prevail, eventually dooming the European dream.

Bibliography

Bottici, C. and Challand, B. (2013) *Imagining Europe: Myth, Memory, and Identity*. New York: Cambridge University Press.
Brown, S. and Gilson, C. (2013) Symbols, trauma and European identity. London School of Economics, 4 May. Available at: http://blogs.lse.ac.uk/eurocrisispress/2013/05/04/symbols-trauma-and-European-identity/
Castells, M. (2003) *The Power of Identity*. Oxford: Basil Blackwell.
Castiglione, D. (2009) Political identity in a community of strangers. In Checkel, J.T. and Katzenstein, P.J. (eds) *European Identity*. Cambridge: Cambridge University Press.
Cetti, F. (2014) Europe and the 'Global Alien': the centrality of the forced migrant to a pan-European identity. In Radeljić, B. (ed.) *Debating European Identity: Bright Ideas, Dim Prospects*. Oxford: Peter Lang.
Checkel, J.T. and Katzenstein, P.J. (2009) The politicization of European identities. In Checkel, J.T. and Katzenstein, P.J. (eds) *European Identity*. Cambridge: Cambridge University Press.
Citrin, J. and Wright, M. (2014) E Pluribus europa? In Gould, A.C. and Messina, A.M. (eds) *Europe's Contending Identities: Supranationalism, Ethnoregionalism, Religion, and New Nationalism*. New York: Cambridge University Press.
Corcoran, F. (2011) The politics of belonging: identity anxiety in the European Union. In Jakubowicz, K. and Sükösd, M. (eds) *Media, Nationalism and European Identity*. Budapest: Central European University Press.
Delanty, G. (2014) Post-national. *Theeuropean.EU*. Available at: http://en.theeuropean.eu/gerard-delanty/8002-the-europeanization-of-national-identity
Delibasic, I. (2013) The need for a new European identity? *European View* 12(2): 299–306.
Duchesne, S. (2014) Smoke and mirrors. *Theeuropean.EU*. Available at: http://en.theeuropean.eu/sophie-duchesne/7933-European-identity-no-use-for-now
Elliott, L. and Atkinson, D. (2016) *Europe Isn't Working*. New Haven, CT: Yale University Press.
Fligstein, N. (2008) *Euroclash: The EU, European Identity, and the Future of Europe*. Oxford: Oxford University Press.
Fligstein, N. (2009) Who are the Europeans and how does this matter for politics? In Checkel, J.T. and Katzenstein, P.J. (eds) *European Identity*. Cambridge: Cambridge University Press.
Fligstein, N. (2014) Ugly politics of the crisis. *Theeuropean.EU*. Available

at: http://en.theeuropean.eu/neil-fligstein/7903-the-future-of-Europe-and-the-European-identity

Fligstein, N., Polyakova, A. and Sandholtz, W. (2012) European integration, nationalism and European identity. *Journal of Common Market Studies* 50(1): 106–22.

Fontana, J. (1995) *The Distorted Past: A Re-interpretation of Europe*. Oxford: Wiley-Blackwell.

Fuchs, D. (2011) Cultural diversity, European identity and legitimacy of the EU: a theoretical framework. In Fuchs, D. and Klingemann, H.-D. (eds) *Cultural Diversity, European Identity and the Legitimacy of the EU*. Cheltenham: Edward Elgar.

Fuchs, D. and Schneider, C. (2011) Support of the EU and European identity: some descriptive results. In Fuchs, D. and Klingemann, H.-D. (eds) *Cultural Diversity, European Identity and the Legitimacy of the EU*. Cheltenham: Edward Elgar.

Green, S. (2015) *The European Identity*. London: Haus Curiosities.

Guibernau, M. (2011) Prospects for a European identity. *International Journal of Politics, Culture and Society* 24: 31–43.

Held, D. (2014) Touching the fuzzy core. *Theeuropean.EU*. Available at: http://en.theeuropean.eu/david-held/7981-European-identity-a-way-of-solving-problems

Holmes, D.R. (2009) Experimental identities (after Maastricht). In Checkel, J.T. and Katzenstein, P.J. (eds) *European Identity*. Cambridge: Cambridge University Press.

Jolly, S.K. (2014) Strange bedfellows: public support for the EU among regionalists. In Gould, A.C. and Messina, A.M. (eds) *Europe's Contending Identities: Supranationalism, Ethnoregionalism, Religion, and New Nationalism*. New York: Cambridge University Press.

Karolewski, I.P. (2010) *Citizenship and Collective Identity in Europe*. London: Routledge.

Kostakopoulou, D. (2014) Political alchemies, identity games and the sovereign debt instability: European identity in crisis or the crisis in identity-talk? In Radeljić, B. (ed.) *Debating European Identity: Bright Ideas, Dim Prospects*. Oxford: Peter Lang.

Lapeyronnie, D. (2009) Nation, democracy and identities in Europe. In Kastoryano, R. (ed.) *An Identity for Europe: The Relevance of Multiculturalism in EU Construction*. New York: Palgrave Macmillan.

MacShane, D. (2015) *Brexit: How Britain Will Leave Europe*. London: Tauris.

Medrano, J.D. (2009) The public sphere and the European Union's political identity. In Checkel, J.T. and Katzenstein, P.J. (eds) *European Identity*. Cambridge: Cambridge University Press.

Messina, A.M. (2014) European disunion? The implications of 'super' diversity for European identity and political community. In Gould, A.C. and Messina, A.M. (eds) *Europe's Contending Identities: Supranationalism, Ethnoregionalism, Religion, and New Nationalism*. New York: Cambridge University Press.

Mitchell, K. (2015) Rethinking the Erasmus effect on European identity. *Journal of Common Market Studies* 53(2): 330–48.

Moores, S. and Metykova, M. (2010) 'I didn't realize how attached I am': on the environmental experiences of trans-European migrants. *European Journal of Cultural Studies* 13(2): 171–89.

Reeskens, T. and Wright, M. (2013) Nationalism and the cohesive society: a multilevel analysis of the interplay among diversity, national identity, and social capital across 27 European nations. *Comparative Political Studies* 46(2): 153–81.

Risse, T. (2014) Be tenacious and fight! *Theeuropean.EU.* Available at: http://en.theeuropean.eu/thomas-rissen/7985-European-identity-already-exists

Schilde, K.E. (2013) Who are the Europeans? European identity outside of European integration. *Journal of Common Market Studies* 52(3): 650–67.

Schlenker, A. (2013) Cosmopolitan Europeans or partisans of fortress Europe? Supranational identity patterns in the EU. *Global Society* 27(1): 25–51.

Schlenker-Fisher, A. (2011) Multiple identities and attitudes towards cultural diversity in Europe: a conceptual and empirical analysis. In Fuchs, D. and Klingemann, H.-D. (eds) *Cultural Diversity, European Identity and the Legitimacy of the EU.* Cheltenham: Edward Elgar.

Sigalas, E. (2010) Cross-border mobility and European identity: the effectiveness of intergroup contact during the ERASMUS year abroad. *European Union Politics* 11(2): 241–65.

Tagiuri, G. (2014) Forging identity: the EU and European culture. *Survival: Global Politics and Strategy* 56(1): 157–78.

Thiel, M. (2011) *The Limits of Transnationalism: Collective Identities and EU Integration.* New York: Palgrave Macmillan.

Todorov, T. and Bracher, N. (2008) European identity. *South Central Review* 25(3): 3–15.

Topic, M. (2014) European identity and the far right in Central Europe: a new emerging concept or a new European 'other'? In Radeljić, B. (ed.) *Debating European Identity: Bright Ideas, Dim Prospects.* Oxford: Peter Lang.

Verhaegen, S., Hooghe, M. and Quintelier, E. (2014) European identity and support for European integration: a matter of perceived economic benefits? *KYKLOS* 67(2): 295–314.

Wilson, I. (2011) What should we expect of 'Erasmus generations'? *Journal of Common Market Studies* 49(5): 1113–40.

Appendix: Selected data on European identity

All data taken from Eurobarometer: http://ec.europa.eu/commission/index_en

IT	82%	+24
AT	72%	−8
HU	76%	−5
EL	58%	−1
FR	57%	−1
LU	74%	=
EU27	58%	=
DE	54%	=
CZ	73%	−1
UK	34%	−1
SK	73%	−1
IE	59%	−2
LV	39%	−6
ES	58%	−7
PT	64%	7
PI	70%	−7
MT	61%	−8
PL	63%	−9
NL	46%	−10
BE	50%	−11
BG	58%	−11
RO	63%	−12
SE	48%	−13
LT	48%	−14
BI	58%	−15
CY	48%	−16
DK	56%	−19
EE	54%	−19

Question: Q83. Thinking now about the fact that you are European, how important is being European to you personally? Being European...

Answers: Total 'Matters'

Map Legend

- Positive
- Stable
- Negative

EB73.3 March 2010 / EB69.2 March-May 2008

196

People may feel different degrees of attachment to their town or village, to their region, to their country ot to Europe. Please tell me how attached you feel to... the European Union (11/2015)

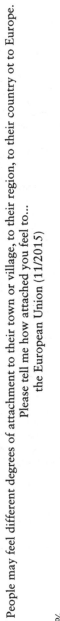
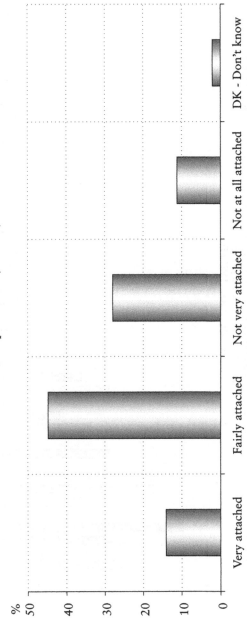

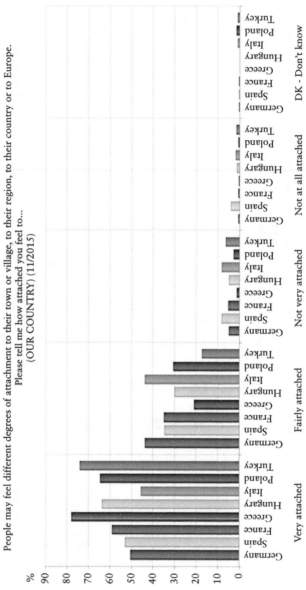

People may feel different degrees of attachment to their town or village, to their region, to their country or to Europe. Please tell me how attached you feel to... (OUR COUNTRY) (11/2015)

People may feel different degrees of attachment to their town or village, to their region, to their country or to Europe.
Please tell me how attached you feel to...
Your city/town/village (11/2015)

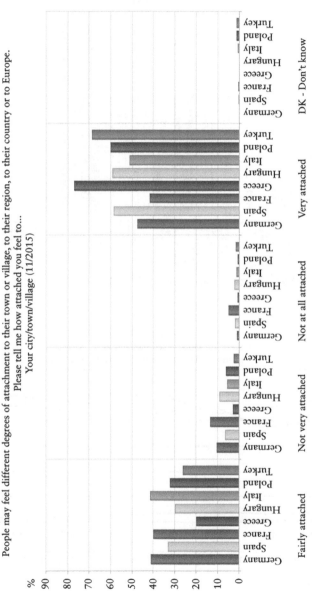

Do you ever think of yourself as not only (nationality), but also European?
Does this happen often, sometimes or never?
09/2006

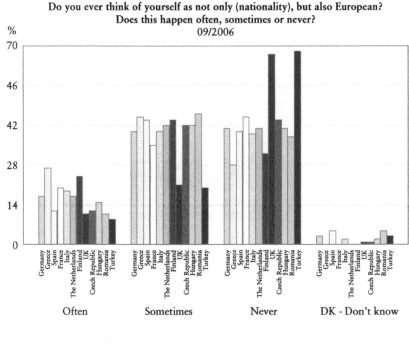

In the near future
Do you see yourself as...?
European Union (from 03/1992 to 05/2015)

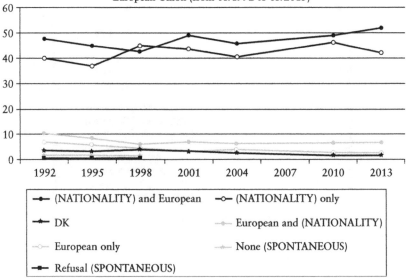

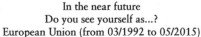

200

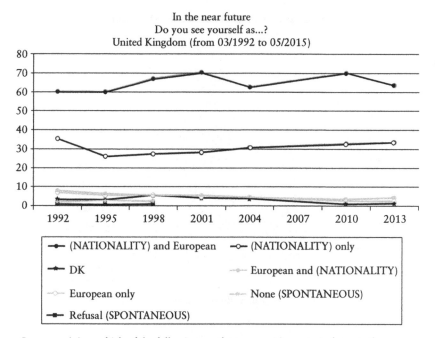

In the near future
Do you see yourself as...?
United Kingdom (from 03/1992 to 05/2015)

In your opinion, which of the following are the two most important elements that go to make up a European identity?

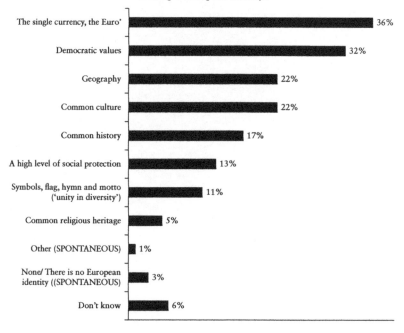

Percentage of mistrust of EU institutions by country

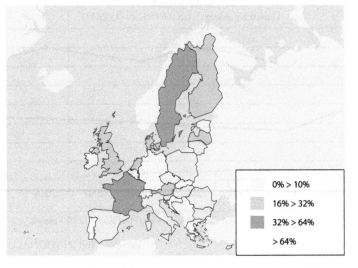

	0% > 10%
	16% > 32%
	32% > 64%
	> 64%

Source: Eurobarometer

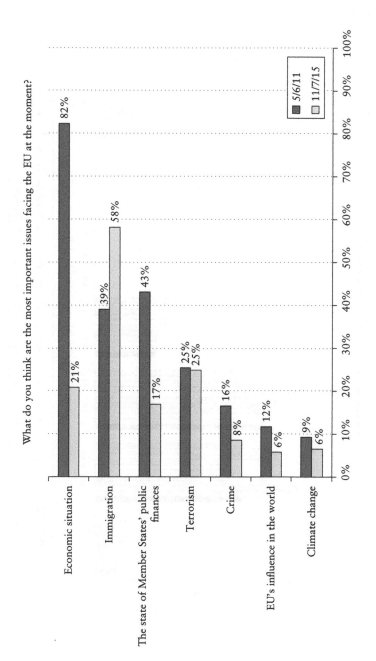

What do you think are the most important issues facing the EU at the moment?

Economic situation — 82%, 21%

Immigration — 39%, 58%

The state of Member States' public finances — 43%, 17%

Terrorism — 25%, 25%

Crime — 16%, 8%

EU's influence in the world — 12%, 6%

Climate change — 9%, 6%

5/6/11
11/7/15

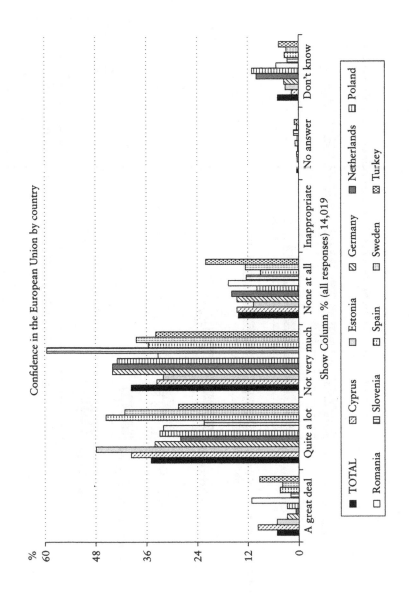

Confidence in the European Union by country

Chapter 9

Europe Facing Evil: Xenophobia, Racism, Anti-Semitism and Terrorism

Michel Wieviorka

Initially, the construction of Europe was based on profoundly humanist, moral convictions. The aim was to preclude any return to war and barbarism, to prohibit nations from killing each other as they had done on two occasions in the previous half-century by bringing them closer together as members of a community. On 9 May 1950 Robert Schuman, one of the founding fathers of the European Community, had declared (this date was to become Europe Day) that henceforth war between the nations of Europe 'was not only unthinkable but materially impossible'.

While this community was ultimately to be political, the founders thought that it was necessary to proceed step by step and begin by implementing economic integration. Thus it was decided to create the ECSC (European Coal and Steel Community), the founding act of European construction set up in 1951 by six countries (Germany, France, Italy, Belgium, the Netherlands and Luxembourg).

Europe was later enlarged and strengthened, becoming in particular not only an economic union but also a monetary one with the euro, and, through various treaties, defining a political structure.

But today the economy seems to be diverging from the founding values and pursuing its own interests and the political project is increasingly seen as managed by a technocracy which is very far from being democratic. This Europe, which had a concern for morals and thought it possible to put economics at the service of ethics or political morals, is today faced with tremendous challenges which compromise its capacity to represent the humanist values which should characterize it. Since the 1980s, and increasingly since the crisis in recent years, the forces of evil are gaining ground, undermining Europe's capacity to assert itself at world level as the continent which was the origin of, and now represents, universalism and human rights

Over the past thirty years, Europe has witnessed the development of forms of racism which are largely new, a scourge which one might have thought would have been eliminated by decolonization and the entry into a new postcolonial era. It has also witnessed the revival, also in another form, of a hatred of Jews, even though Nazism had been a demonstration of the most barbaric criminal type possible. Europe has also become one of the fertile breeding grounds of a terrorism which is also profoundly different from that of the 1960s and 1970s. Furthermore, all these phenomena in Europe have been seen to forge direct or indirect links with the rise of political forces which are anti-European and nationalist and, at the same time, to a large extent racist, xenophobic, anti-Semitic and Islamophobic.

These expressions of evil are in many ways related to the rise of national egos, made much worse by the migrant crisis, especially since 2015, and also by the refusal of the increasingly powerful sovereignist or nationalist forces to implement European solidarity. They are in line with the much broader tendencies to make Europe the cause of the ills to which nations and peoples are subjected; in their own way, they contribute to the endeavours of those who would like their country to leave Europe, or even, where appropriate, the euro, and they almost always contribute to weakening the construction of Europe. They mainly originate within national societies. But these expressions can no longer be analysed, as in the past, in the categories of 'methodological nationalism' so well deciphered by the late Ulrich Beck, who criticized analyses set in the context of the nation-state, and what is known as international relations, alone (Beck 2004). Their analysis implies thinking globally and distinguishing levels which extend from the global to the local, passing through the regional – Europe – and the national.

Racism in movement

Amongst the ideologies that rose rapidly in the Europe of the second half of the nineteenth century, racism appeared as primarily a question of physical or biological inequality: what were presumed to be human races were ranked and classified using very specific criteria (colour of the skin, type of hair, form of bones and skulls, etc.). On the basis of these, the superiority of the white 'race', or the 'Aryans', over other races was asserted and from this point on it became legitimate to dominate or exploit them.

From classical racism to new racism

This racism has not entirely disappeared, but it has considerably declined in Europe, particularly since World War II and in the context of decolonization. It has continued to fuel or accompany the resentment of those who still regret the colonial period. We see it, for example, in top-level football when monkey calls greet a black player on the pitch or when a woman politician who is black is the victim of racist insults. This happened to Christiane Taubira, the French Minister for Justice, who was compared to a monkey in 2014 or, in Italy, when the Minister for Integration in the Letta government, Cecile Kyenge, originally from Congo Kinshasa, was racially insulted by the leaders of the Lega Nord. In both cases, traditional sexism and racism go hand in hand: racism is the reaction to what racists find unbearable, what seems to them to be a reversal of history, namely that those who were formerly racialized and dominated today hold positions within the elite.

This classical form of racism was also associated with a phenomenon which only lasted for thirty or forty years in countries where post-war reconstruction relied massively on immigrant labour, usually employed in unskilled jobs. They were known as 'Gastarbeiter' in Germany, for example, where they came primarily from Turkey or 'immigrant workers' in Belgium and in France, where they mainly originated from North Africa. In a period of growth and full employment, this racism was consistent with rationales of inferiorization and targeted people who were integrated in employment, therefore socially, but who did not participate in the civic, political or cultural life of the host country. These workers were presumed to be there for a limited period of time before going back to their own countries with their savings. When immigration became no longer a matter of labour but one of settlement, everything changed. The United Kingdom was the country where this change took place earliest and most rapidly. Decolonization in this specific case had not meant the end of the Commonwealth and, beginning in the 1950s, large numbers of immigrants from all over the former British Empire settled permanently, very often with their families. Elsewhere in Europe, with the exception mainly of Southern European countries (Spain, Italy, Portugal, Greece), from the mid or end of the 1970s immigration began to change: men, women and children settled permanently in contexts where growth was beginning to slow down and unemployment and vulnerability were developing. At the same time, there was less demand in industry for unskilled labour. At this point, immigrant-origin populations began to be the victims of a racism that was also undergoing change; specialists described it as 'new racism', 'neo-racism', 'cultural' racism or yet again 'differentialist racism' (Barker 1981). The people targeted by this new racism were no longer described in physical or biological terms but much more in cultural terms. They were considered to be so totally different that they would never be able to adapt to the 'values' of the host society or its culture and that henceforth they would constitute a threat to its existence as a nation. With this new racism, it is not so much a question of considering immigrants as inferior to facilitate their exploitation, but instead of keeping them apart, excluding them, preventing immigration and encouraging immigrants and their children to go back. Often this is no longer meaningful for the people concerned who have long lived far from their countries of origin, where furthermore they are often rejected.

Classical racism was concomitant with the development of an open society. It was not opposed to the construction of Europe. New racism, for its part, calls for a closed society and a homogeneous nation. It thus became an element in the rejection of Europe and the rise of nationalisms. There was a place for classical racism in societies which were still highly industrialized: it despised, discriminated and segregated male workers who came on their own with no intention of settling. The new racism in the 1980s and 1990s targeted men, but also women and children, excluded from employment much more than others, unemployed, vulnerable, living in working-class areas where they were accused in one way or another of forming separate communities culturally. New racism constituted an element in the breakdown of community life and was no longer uniquely a tool in the service of a rationale of domination and exploitation.

In the same context, anti-racist campaigns, the progress of national legislation, possibly backed up by legislative and judicial action at the European level where the campaign against racism had long been an important theme, made the more explicit forms or expressions of racism difficult. The phenomenon became 'subtle', veiled and disguised, and a further observation had to be acknowledged. Racism was becoming indirect and institutional; it was no longer expressed directly, although it continued to exist, in particular in the form of discrimination in access to employment, housing, education, health care, etc. For example, in the firm studied by Philippe Bataille in Alès, nobody was openly racist (Bataille 1997). However, in a town which had a considerable immigrant-origin population and for them a very high level of unemployment, the CFDT trade unionists could see that there was not a single immigrant amongst the hundreds of workers in the firm. In fact, the survey showed that as soon as a job became vacant, there was always an employee ready to propose a non-immigrant relative or friend.

In the 1990s, the rising power of the new cultural racism and the institutional avatars of more classical racism extended from the North of Europe to the South; Italy, Spain, Portugal and Greece became countries of immigration, whereas previously they had been countries of emigration. Contrary to the over-hasty arguments of researchers, it became apparent that these changes should not be considered the mark of a simple transition from one form of racism to another but effectively as a reconfiguration in which the dimensions of inferiorization and differentiation are declined in another way. At the same time, references to physical or biological characteristics persist, combined with more cultural considerations which are naturalized or essentialized. After all, if a culture can in no way change, is it not a nature or an essence?

Changes in racism

But other changes in racism continue to make of it a phenomenon subject to permanent change. On one hand, immigration has continued to bring to societies in the throes of an economic crisis newcomers from countries other than the previous arrivals: sub-Saharan Africa, Latin America, Central Europe, the Middle East, Asia. A considerable proportion of these migrants are Muslims, and Islam has gained momentum in many countries in Europe, all the more so as former migrants and their children, subjected more than others to unemployment, exclusion and various social problems, find comfort in this religion, which provides a meaning they have been deprived of in a difficult or impossible integration. Conversions to Islam, involving tens of thousands of individuals every year at the European level, have added to the tendency of this religion to grow. Henceforth, racism targeting fairly spontaneously the migrants and their descendants and already imbued with cultural rejection, has taken the form of hatred of Islam, a religion which was practically non-existent in Europe apart from the UK in the 1970s, to the point that the neologism Islamophobia – a term forged in the colonial period – has made a comeback. The terrorist attacks in New York on 11 September 2001, then in Madrid (March 2004) and London (July 2005) all contributed to the fear and hatred of Islam in Europe. The most recent attacks in France for which Al Qaeda and then Daesh have claimed responsibility (Toulouse in March 2012, Paris in January and November 2015, Nice and Saint-Etienne-du-Rouvray in July 2016) and in Belgium (Jewish museum in Brussels on 24 May 2014, Brussels international airport and Maelbeck Underground station on 22 March 2016), have considerably radicalized the anti-Muslim tendencies. These last attacks have specific European dimensions: Brussels is the European capital city, Maelbeck metro station is close to the main European Union buildings, and the Jihadists were acting not only at the Belgium level, but at a European one, with a clear Brussels–Paris axis.

It is true that hatred of a religion cannot be analytically merged with racism which targets a presumed race, an essence, a nature said to be specific to a human group, and numerous discussions have challenged the amalgamation of the two categories. But this amalgamation does make sense: Islamophobia, while not being strictly speaking a form of racism, belongs materially to the same family. It is the basis, the vehicle or the justification for practices of discrimination, segregation and ethnicizing prejudices and racial violence. In European countries, Islamophobia has made Islam a religion which sets its believers apart from the other members of the national community. It has turned them into enemies, as in the theories based on Samuel Huntington's well-known 'clash of civilizations'. Or at least, as the leader of the extreme-right in the Netherlands, Pym Fortuyn suggested, Islam is culturally backward. He considered there to be a direct continuum from Islam to terrorism and from barbarism to the Jihad. Islamophobia has permitted the deployment of a hatred which does not look like racial hatred, which is 'de-racialized': thus without the risk of appearing explicitly racist throughout Europe, it federates the racist impulses which previously targeted Arabs, and now migrants – the same as those targeted by Islamophobia.

At the same time, European societies have witnessed the development of rationales of fragmentation challenging their capacity to integrate their members. Social inequalities have been reinforced, and are visible, with the formation of ghettoes for the rich, for the middle classes and for the poor – a segregation which owes a lot to the rationales of the housing market and sometimes also to urban planning policies. Cultural and religious differences, which for some groups are national in origin, have been accentuated further especially since, contrary to conventional wisdom, the rise of individualism encourages their spread. Anyone can, as an individual, choose to join a specific minority to give meaning to their existence. Anyone can adopt an 'identity', or even several. Individual subjectivity sustains diversification and from there, cultural and religious fragmentation. From this point on, there are numerous groups, of varying degrees of stability, which are each capable of being a victim of racism specifically targeting them and, on the other hand, of expressing forms of racism towards other minority groups, even of the dominant group. In recent years in several countries in Europe, a number of intellectuals and political leaders, usually conservative or extreme-right, have allegedly been subjected to what they refer to as 'anti-white' racism – or 'racism in reverse'.

Another new development is that within groups targeted by racism, there are rationales of self-racialization which lead to their increasingly asserting a physical identity: Black people, for example, do not only wish to be considered as people with equal rights; they present themselves in the public sphere as being Black to pursue claims or to act more effectively against discrimination. Racism then begins, not at the point where individuals are defined by racial attributes, as was often the case in the past, when it was inferred from these attributes that they determine the intellectual or moral qualities of the individuals and that they are the foundation of their presumed inferiority, but from the point at which individuals and groups don't benefit for some recognition, for instance related to some historical suffering.

This set of developments radically transforms racism, which henceforth is also fragmented and charged with various racial, cultural and religious themes. The phenomenon is no longer mainly a feature of the dominant group; it is also encountered in much smaller fragments within the minorities themselves who are dominated or excluded, and who are victims of racism while being simultaneously perpetrators. It becomes a general category of thought and sometimes of political action. Completely new forms of racism co-exist with more classical expressions, the oldest being today perhaps those which target the Gypsies, a population which has long since been subjected to fear, contempt and racial hatred, particularly in Central European countries but also in Spain and in France.

The return of anti-Semitism

At the end of World War II, there was little space for anti-Semitism. It could no longer be an opinion; henceforth it was a crime which had taken the form of the genocide of the Jews (but also moreover of the Gypsies). While the behaviour of Pope Pius XII towards Nazism during the war was open to criticism, on the occasion of the Second Vatican Council (1962–5) the Catholic Church ended the previously sanctioned teaching of hatred and contempt of Jews and the charge of the Jewish people as 'deicide' (as they were considered to have killed Jesus Christ). Modern anti-Semitism, which appeared in the transformation of religious anti-Judaism towards the end of the nineteenth century and which culminated with Hitler, seemed to be merely residual in Europe at least in the public sphere, even if in the depths of individual consciences it still retained considerable reality, as witnessed by the difficulties of the countries most implicated in the destruction of the European Jews in fully acknowledging the eminently criminal nature of this enterprise. The knowledge of what the Shoah had involved – the term only became the standard reference in the 1980s – forbade any deployment of political forces or the publication of any intellectual discourse based on hatred of the Jews.

But, beginning in the 1980s, this hatred began to re-appear (Wieviorka 2007). The international context was favourable, in particular as a result of the beginning of criticism of the State of Israel, whose military intervention in Lebanon in 1982 had a disastrous impact on European public opinion. In particular, it was on this occasion that Christian militia massacred several hundred Palestinians in the camps of Sabra and Chatila, with the Israeli army doing nothing to prevent them. By forcing Yasser Arafat and the Palestine Liberation Organization (PLO) to leave Lebanon for Tunisia, Israel created the conditions for a change in the strategy of the PLO which resulted in the First Intifada (1987), in which those throwing stones (in the role of David) were the young Palestinians and the State of Israel appeared to be Goliath. From this point on, a space opened up for a renewal of anti-Semitism which often assimilated the Jews of the diaspora to those in the State of Israel.

This space re-opened along two main axes. With regard to the first, the extreme-right movements found in 'negationism' (the assertion that the gas chambers never existed) a useful hypothesis for their propaganda, or else their accusations stated that the Shoah was a 'business' and a source of profit for the Jews. At this time the resurgence of neo-Nazi, neo-fascist and extreme-right parties which took place in several countries in Europe, in Belgium, in Germany, in Austria, in France, etc., found in anti-Semitism one of the components of their ideology and one of the themes which ensured continuity with the past.

The second axis for the renewal of anti-Semitism was due to changes in immigration, in particular Arab and/or Muslim origin immigration. As we have seen, this began as a settlement movement in the 1970s (earlier in the United Kingdom and later in Southern Europe). It originated in societies where there had long existed a certain contempt for Jews who had generally been given an inferior legal status – that of 'dhimmis' (non-Muslim citizens), which also applied to Christians. Amongst these immigrant populations, some could identify with the Palestinian cause, often quite unrealistically but with the profound conviction that the Jews in the diaspora were in no way different from those in Israel. This was consistent with visions expressed by left and extreme-left political forces who were often critical of Israeli policy. We also find the belief that what the Jews in Europe (or in the United States) have succeeded in achieving, a successful integration, a presence amongst the economic, political and intellectual elite (once again frequently something of an illusion) was not possible or not open to immigrants and their children. This feeling also

212

found an echo in left-wing anti-Semitism which, while never as virulent as its right-wing, nationalist and often Christian counterpart, accused Jews of representing money and therefore capitalism, and Israel, their state, of pursuing a colonial policy.

As from 2000, this updated anti-Semitism was activated, so to speak, by strong currents of empathy towards radical Islam, including its terrorist aspects. Its identification with the Palestinian cause then became more remote, and in any event was no longer restricted to this. It became religious and Islamist with the idea that the Jews, and along with them the State of Israel, represented the leading Western force in the land of Islam and that one had to admit that there was an ongoing war between Islam and the West. We find here again a version of Samuel Huntington's 'clash of civilizations' hypothesis. The 'new anti-Semitism' was there, condemned by intellectuals, particularly in France, but also by representatives of Jewish communities observing the rise in anti-Semitic acts. There were attacks or threats to people, property and places of worship, Jewish schools, etc. The new anti-Semitism, unlike that of the previous period, did not insist on the physical attributes which were said to be characteristic of Jews. There is less talk of the 'Jewish race'. Instead it depicts a population which is in essence evil and malicious. It is, however, sustained by material borrowed from other periods and which circulates widely at global level via the Internet, mobile phones, TV satellite dishes and social networks. Some specialists, to emphasize its novelty, have endeavoured to promote a word which differs from anti-Semitism, speaking of 'Judeophobia'.

A fact which is less important, because it is expressed amongst smaller minorities, is that this new hatred of Jewish people has some acceptance amongst black populations, reinforced by arguments specific to these populations, in particular those of Caribbean origin (mainly in France and the United Kingdom), sometimes amongst sub-Saharan populations. Here the Jews are accused of having played a leading role in the slave trade (a false and fallacious hypothesis propagated at the beginning of the 1990s by an academic in New York) and, with the Shoah, of wishing to have the monopoly of historical suffering and not allowing other genocides or slavery to express themselves, which is no less erroneous and fallacious.

Finally, one notices that the propagation of anti-Semitism is more gradual in certain circles, particularly amongst young people, due to the distrust which political parties and actors evoke in most European societies. The crisis of the political systems in Europe undermines their discourse, as it does that of the classical media. It encourages 'conspiracy theories' which suspect and accuse anything resembling 'officialdom'.

Furthermore, the contemporary digital culture promotes anything to do with the circulation of opinions, no matter what these may be, without limitation or reserve, instantaneously, to an audience which is infinite and with a degree of interactivity. Hatred of the Jews finds its place in this culture all the more easily, especially because it has always been based on the idea of causal factors associated with the devil, to use the words of the historian Léon Poliakov. It is exacerbated when Jewish institutions or political leaders recall that anti-Semitism is a crime, and not simply an opinion, and that it must not be condoned on social networks, blogs and other forms of digital media: Jews are then accused of demanding restrictions to the freedom of speech and expression, which is central to contemporary digital culture.

At country level there are considerable variations in the present day expressions of anti-Semitism. It remains fairly traditional in Central Europe where Arab-Muslim immigration or the presence of black populations is non-existent. In Western Europe, it is closer to the new Judeophobia, to use this vocabulary for an instant. In some countries, Jews do constitute a significant population. This is primarily the case in France where there are estimated to be between 500,000 and 600,000 Jews and where anti-Semitism is a living reality; but in other countries the Jewish population is smaller, which does not prevent anti-Semitism from thriving on occasions. Thus, various surveys and European comparisons indicate that anti-Semitic prejudices are particularly virulent in Greece, where there are only 10,000 Jews, or in Spain where the Jewish population constitutes 0.2 per cent of the total population. Therefore the presence of Jews at a national level does not explain anti-Semitism, or has little impact.

Generally speaking, the phenomenon is largely permeated by world-level rationales; it is global. In this instance, hatred of Jews is at the crossroads of tensions specific to the Near and Middle East which are projected onto European soil. It is to a large extent due to the way in which immigration is dealt with in Europe. It is no less largely national, not as we have just seen, as a result of the presence or not of a significant Jewish minority, but for other reasons which refer to the work of the societies in question on themselves: successful integration of immigration or not, colonial past or not, etc. Its evolution does have European dimensions, if only because of the very clear commitment of the European Union and the Council of Europe to combat it, along with racism, moreover. But while racism tends to lead to disintegration and separation, producing possibly violent rationales of rupture, anti-Semitism on the contrary amalgamates or brings together people and groups which otherwise have nothing in common. In any event, it is capable of contributing to extraordinary alliances. Hatred of Jews is indeed characteristic of those on the extreme-right who are also racist and xenophobic, but it is also found amongst migrants and their children who are detested by these same extreme-right sympathizers. It is a characteristic of dominant actors and of others who are excluded or dominated. It is encountered amongst the extreme-right but also, on occasions, amongst the extreme-left. It constitutes a factor for political confusion and amalgamation which can only add to the moral and intellectual crisis in Europe.

Finally, it is important to note the paradox of present-day anti-Semitism. Historically, if we consider the evolution of prejudice over the past century, there has been a decline. Today it tends to be concentrated within restricted sectors of the population. But it is also much more violent than in the past: it can kill and, from this point of view, it constitutes a physical threat which encourages numerous Jews, particularly in France, to leave their country and go to Israel (or other destinations, especially the United States and Canada). It is central to the deadliest radical Islam; we shall return to this point. The different forms of evil, racism, anti-Semitism and terrorism cannot be addressed separately; they maintain numerous and complex relationships.

Europe and global terrorism

A third scourge afflicts Europe: terrorism. Once again, there is nothing entirely new about this and, at the same time, profound processes of change must be taken into account for an understanding of the present-day issues and challenges. It is useful to consider the situation from two perspectives.

The first examines the issue of terrorism in Europe over the past fifty years, with due consideration for the dimensions of this phenomenon which are national on one hand and global on the other, and for the transformations in its historical importance: here events are located in time. The second perspective envisages the social, political and cultural sources of these events on the basis of their actors and their trajectories, and by examining the conditions which have enabled the transition to action. This complementary perspective not only focuses on the global, European and national systems involved. It takes into consideration the individual subjectivity of the protagonists of terrorism and focuses on processes of de-subjectivation and re-subjectivation, even if, as we shall see, we should be wary of simplistic 'sociologizing'.

215

A historical perspective

Over the past fifty years, what we refer to as 'terrorism' (Wieviorka 2004), a term which should be defined more precisely, has moved from one configuration to another.

Classical terrorism

Since the end of the 1960s and until the beginning of the 1980s, the analysis of terrorism lay within the scope of what Ulrich Beck calls, as we said above, 'methodological nationalism'. The phenomenon was in the main internal, set within the framework of the nation-state, or in its extension, referred to as 'international relations'. Internally, it was primarily either extreme-right, of fascist inspiration for example, as was the case in Italy, or else extreme-left, once again in Italy and in Federal Germany. It could also be separatist and regionalist, Basque or Irish for example, attaching political orientations, in particular Marxist-Leninist, to its nationalist meanings. Internationally, terrorism identified primarily with the Palestinian cause, spilling over into Europe with, for instance, the killing of Israeli athletes at the Olympic Games in Munich in 1972.

The conceptualization at the time contended with non-scientific uses of the term and it was not rare for an article or a lecture to begin with a few remarks on the impossibility of proposing a satisfactory definition of terrorism, because those whom some referred to as terrorists, others described as freedom fighters or the resistance. The Cold War did not facilitate the search for a definition that would be legally acceptable at an international level. In the United Nations it was difficult to achieve an understanding between representatives of the Soviet bloc and the West, for example, to know whether one should, or should not use the word 'terrorism' in connection with the acts of extreme violence committed in the name of the Palestinian nation.

From the sociological point of view, and in this context, it was nevertheless possible to suggest a conceptualization in which the phenomenon was seen from two aspects. On one hand, terrorism is an instrumental action, a resource mobilized by actors to achieve certain ends; it is a matter of calculation, strategies, a rational use of means, the main characteristic being the disproportion between the cost of the action and the expected results. On the other, it concerns loss of meaning; the perpetrator of violence may have little connection with the actual population, class, people or nation in whose name he or she speaks. Here, terrorism is all the more violent, and knows no limits or frontiers, when the perpetrator is no longer recognized by those he or she claims to represent. The perpetrator's words are weapons and explosives, whereas those whose cause is being defended, the movement of which he or she is meant to be the ultimate expression, may in no way recognize themselves in these acts. The perpetrator's speech is artificial; it originates in the inversion of the social or national movement whose meaning has been perverted.

Instrumentality and loss of meaning were therefore the two pillars supporting a sociological definition of terrorism.

Global terrorism

In the 1980s, a major change took place. The terrorisms of the previous era declined, disintegrated and often quite simply disappeared, creating space for other possible forms of action. A new era began, that of global terrorism; this was inaugurated outside Europe in the wake of the Iranian revolution, by the attacks in Lebanon in 1982. Terrorist action was no longer contained within the framework of a nation-state and international relations; henceforth it was meta-political, religious, driven to a great extent by references to the Ouma and the Jihad; its space was global with no restrictions. The instrumental dimensions of the action became difficult to define as now the terrorists were often ready, or even wished, to die in action at the same time as they killed. Evaluating the cost/benefit relationship from the point of view of the terrorist actors became problematic when it was a question of taking into consideration the value of a human life. For many people in the world, terrorist action could be meaningful; it aroused a considerable degree of sympathy, in particular amongst Arab and Muslim populations, where the virulent anti-Westernism and anti-Semitism of the terrorists found an echo. It could also have resonance in Europe and in particular in places where changes in the immigration from Arab and/or Muslim countries have, as we had seen, created a permanently settled population.

Global terrorism struck Europe, beginning with France, in the mid-1980s and particularly in 1995 with a series of attacks that were related to a mixture of internal sources (crises in the deprived outer suburbs, anti-Arab racism, exclusion, unemployment) and global rationales (Jihad, Islamist networks extending from Afghanistan to France and passing through Algeria). But it really peaked for the first time with the 11 September 2001 attacks in the United States, known now as 9/11. Furthermore, the perpetrators were not living on American soil. The meaning they attributed to the action was religious and anti-Western and they had succeeded in demonstrating a high degree of rationality in the accomplishment of their action. They had business-class airline tickets, giving them an air of respectability, their weapons being simple cutters; they had thwarted the analyses of American anti-terrorist specialists – an activity which is highly developed and sophisticated in Washington.

At the time, Al Qaeda was structured in pyramidal fashion, similar to movements in the previous period. But already, with the idea of the existence of 'sleeping networks' and local actors who had no need for orders or instructions to take action one day, a new aspect of the global rationale of the phenomenon was beginning to take shape. It was driven by actors who had no need of a chain of command to act at a local level while giving their action a general, global meaning.

After 9/11, three main tendencies differentiated global terrorism. First were the spectacular attacks in numerous cities, including, in Europe, Madrid (March 2004) and London (July 2005). These attacks were carried out by people living in the country in question, but who had no political project other than to express hatred and the feeling of not having a place in society. They had no design on the Spanish or British state; it was mainly a question of doing harm and expressing resentment, as well as criticizing the international policy of support for George W. Bush's 'war against terrorism'. These attacks were committed by organized terrorists, having some connections with Al Qaeda.

Second were the attacks, often described over-hastily as 'lone wolf attacks', carried out by perpetrators apparently acting in isolation, alone or in pairs, like Mohamed Merah (the perpetrator in Toulouse of two killings, one of French soldiers, the other of children and a Jewish teacher in March 2012), the Kouachi brothers (the perpetrators of the Charlie Hebdo murders on 7 January 2015) and Amedy Koulibali (who killed four Jews in a kosher supermarket in Paris on 9 January 2015). Here extreme violence does not seem to be associated with membership of an organization; it is hyper-local, while at the same time its meaning is set in the global and meta-political rationales of radical Islam (or sometimes of other struggles, those of the extreme-right, for example, like that of Anders Breivik in Norway). This image of the 'lone wolf' should not be over-emphasized because police and court inquiries often indicate that there are virtual networks behind the killers, but also actual knowledge of other radical Islam actors, meetings in prison, in the Middle East, in European mosques, etc. It is, on the other hand, more likely if one considers other terrorists who are not Islamists, for example, Anders Breivik in Norway (this extreme-right terrorist killed, single-handedly, 77 people on 22 July 2011) – but some recent news suggests that even Breivik is not really a 'lone wolf' terrorist, and has some connections with extreme-right activists.

Finally, the third tendency or approach at work in this global terrorism is the attempt to construct quasi-States, in the Middle East and perhaps in Libya with Daesh and in sub-Saharan Africa with Boko Haram and the attempt to impose these States by violence, of course, both internally and externally, but also by respecting or initiating ways of life at a local level. The Daesh terrorism, like that of Al Qaeda, and much more than that of Boko Haram, has links with European actors, who find therein a source of inspiration but also concrete possibilities of ideological and physical preparation, and even of military involvement which will enable them on their return to Europe to become operational. The terrorist attacks in 2015, 2016 and 2017 are connected with Daesh, and usually not with Al Qaeda, some of them with an important number of victims (Paris, 13 November, 130 people killed; Brussels, 22 March 2016, 32 people killed; Nice, 14 July 2016, 86 people killed; Berlin, 16 December 2016, 11 people killed). Other attacks had 'only' a few victims (Munich, 22 July 2016, Stockholm, 7 April 2017, 4 people killed; Charleroi, Wurtzburg, 18 July 2016, etc.), some with fewer victims, or missing their target altogether.

Here, Islamic terrorism is therefore diversified, but distinctly global since its meaning is world-wide and its actions even at very local level are set in a symbolism and imaginaries that are global. What makes it so ominous is that while it is a threat that can be materialized all over the world, it is also a threat because it is not a phenomenon confined to a few hot-heads. For many it is meaningful, even if not many of them take action.

The social sources of Islamist terrorism

Islamist terrorism in Europe indicates on one hand that there is a deficit: there is a loss or perversion of meaning, an absence of bearings, frustration, a demand. On the other hand, there is, so to speak, an offer: the input in meaning which radical Islam offers and its promises of martyrdom. If the end point, extreme violence, does demand an understanding of the global rationales in which radical Islam is located, as something absolute, sacred, the point of departure has little relation to this new meaning. It is located in social processes where its quest has been rendered almost crucial for some. Thereafter, chance encounters with actors who could provide the missing references have taken place in places of worship, on the Internet, in prison for delinquency, etc. Public opinion mainly hears about those who take action and actively become terrorists. But for the few who effectively participate in extreme violence, there are many more who become radicalized and go part of the way before turning back or failing. There are thousands of volunteers for the Jihad going to the Middle East from Europe.

In addressing this question of meaning, the best way to proceed is undoubtedly to start with two observations. The first refers to what constitutes the core of Islamist discourse: hatred of the West (and of

Jews); the second observation is the outcome of the work of those who, like Farhad Khosrokhavar, have studied the trajectories of terrorists: at the outset, they are characterized by loss of meaning, the feeling of an existential vacuum, awareness of a total lack of benchmarks to construct themselves as subjects. This loss, this deficit points to weaknesses, voids which are individual but also global because they are encountered in several countries in Europe where Muslims live, in France, in the United Kingdom, in Belgium and in Spain in particular, but also in various countries in the Arab and/or Muslim world and amongst other groups, other actors than those who become radicals or join sects without necessarily becoming members of present-day radical Islamism. But it is true that the most impressive examples are observed when these weaknesses are resolved in the plethora of meanings, the absolute, the landmarks provided by radical Islam.

The sources of de-subjectivation are multiple. The most obvious are connected with the economic crisis, the difficulties of young people of immigrant origin in working-class areas, the dramas of failed integration, the shortcomings in education or yet again the destructuring of the family. On the whole and over and above national differences, these 'problems' invoke the idea of a failure of the West, in particular as regards its responsibilities in decolonization and for the missed opportunity for the marginalized to enter post-classical modernity. In other social and historical contexts, the losses or deficits are dealt with by social movements, associations, NGOs or charitable organizations and are thereby addressed at a political level which may be conflictual, but is non-violent. But here, nothing like this exists: those who become terrorists act from actual situations where no collective action has enabled the expectations or social demands to be turned into an issue for discussion and conflict. The problems encountered have led to non-relations and lack of support, and at one point or another, those concerned have lost their balance and fallen prey to an environment which fosters delinquency, but also anger and possibly violent breakdowns in relations for lack of ground for dialogue – even conflictual – or for a possible negotiation. From this point of view, global terrorism is not the murderous folly of a few religious zealots. It represents the inhuman action of those who, all over the world, and for us here in Europe, in a context of failed decolonization and absence of perspective, have not succeeded in engaging discussions and conflicts which can be institutionalized and enable us to live together.

But the processes which lead to unrestrained violence and, in any event, to radicalization are not restricted to the lack and impossibility of finding a place in society. The most frequent sociological explanations, those which insist on the crisis and consider the Jihadis as those who have been marginalized by change are not adequate. We should be wary of simplistic 'sociologizing'. How can we account for a terrorist trajectory when it starts from a social environment with no problems – a loving family, a middle-class background, no particular difficulties at school, etc., not to mention, if it is a case of Western countries, of young people from Christian families and who have chosen to convert to Islam? In addition to the failures and frustrations described above, there is in fact the loss of meaning. For a number of future terrorists, many are convinced that they have no place in society – whence the utility of elementary sociological explanations. But for some, commitment originates in other rationales, reveals other flaws and, in particular, stresses the lack of bearings offered by society and the environment in which they live. In these instances it is related to the aspiration to an absolute, the desire to confer a meaning to an existence which would otherwise seem without interest. Many potential Jihadis are young people who at the outset are disgusted by the selfishness and futility of the consumer society and the widespread disrespect they see around them, the lack of vision and future prospects that those in politics have to offer them. Yet again, there are others who wish to join the struggle in opposition to Assad, and fight his bloody dictatorship in Syria but who do not wish to fight with Daesh. In some cases, young girls convert to Islam and go to Syria for romantic reasons, to live a love story with a hero who, in their eyes, has no fear of sacrificing his life for his convictions, or for a voyage of initiation. There is considerable variety in the routes which can lead to Islamist terrorism, including where it involves the Muslim faith. This is always very elementary and frequently only becomes clearer at the end of the trajectory, once radicalization has taken place. This is why radicalization is often much more ambivalent than is too often thought.

On one hand, for those who have not found the place they long for in modernity, radicalization is directly linked to present-day individualism. In these instances, radical Islam provides the promise of another life in Paradise, in particular the satisfaction of a sexuality which is repressed or cannot be fulfiled on earth. It also offers the possibility of reversing the self-denial experienced to date into total power. It affords the opportunity of being the hero who terrorizes the society which until then had totally ignored him or her. Killers are keen to publicize their acts, sometimes carrying them out with a camera with which they can transmit their crimes live. In contrast, Islam, then radical Islam, both provide actors with the meaning that society no longer affords them, the perspective of a life built along the lines of a just, and not a futile, world. This helps us to understand when specialists estimate that 20 per cent of the converts attempt to leave France to join Daesh.

The initial de-subjectivation, whether it be associated with a lack of possibilities or a search for meaning is almost annihilated by the meaning provided by the combination of religious references, which in content are in fact very poor, and the resort to unlimited, even pure, violence of which the excesses, the cruelty, the lack of humanity are consistent with the lack or the loss for which they compensate. It always testifies to the implacable hatred of the West, as we noted, but also of Jews and we should stop here. Marc Sageman's research, for example, has demonstrated the extent to which an unbounded anti-Semitism characterized the members of Al Qaeda in the early 2000s and we can easily generalize and extend this observation. Here we have geopolitical dimensions and others, internal to the societies where the future terrorists live.

In geopolitical matters, it is the existence of Israel that is the motive force behind the actors. In this perspective, Israel, backed by the United States, is seen as a Western presence in the land of Islam and as an oppressor of Muslims. The Jews in the modern world are assimilated to the Jewish State – anti-Zionism and anti-Semitism are amalgamated here. Within some European societies, the Jews are seen as benefiting from all the rights, being totally integrated and even stakeholders in the world of the moneyed elites, the media and politics, whereas on the contrary there are no rights for the excluded, the poor, the children of immigrants and those who wish to identify with a just world. The Jews are perceived as being on one side, the right side, and the Muslims on another, the wrong side, in a world of double standards.

The Islamist radicalization of tens of thousands of young people in Europe is the foundation on which trajectories are constructed, some of which culminate in action. It is related to the experience of racism, since this is one of its sources, and to anti-Semitism by which it is wholly permeated. It has no realistic political outlet in Europe, apart from imaginary long-term scenarios such as that depicted in Michel Houellebecq's novel *Soumission*, which seem highly unlikely. This is also why for the time being violence constitutes its main horizon.

The rationales of evil, whether it be a question of terrorism, racism or of anti-Semitism, cannot be understood without reference to a history which goes back more than half a century. The important turn taken in 1973, which can symbolically be associated with the first oil crisis following the 1973 Arab-Israeli, or Kippur, War, was the opportunity for major transformations in Europe in all areas, including economic, demographic, social, cultural, etc., which were beginning to have an impact on the forms of evil in Europe. A further turning point took place ten years later. Like the previous one, it was to a large extent due to global changes at world level and impacted Europe in different ways depending on the countries, their national history, their political culture and the public policies implemented. For example, extreme-left terrorism, which is such a vital force in Italy, is much less so in Germany and not very active in France, and gives way in the 1980s and 1990s to global, Islamist terrorism, which also targeted the United Kingdom, Spain and Belgium. The explanation for the rise of evil is therefore not only to be sought in the European crisis, but in the first instance in the evolutions and history of national societies and in the possible projection on their soil of global, world-level rationales. Europe as a framework for the analysis has therefore now been outlived; at present we have world level at the top, with the nation-state below. The rise of evil cannot be explained uniquely by the most visible crises, those of the political systems, the economy and finance. It is also in large part due to the phenomena of loss of meaning, the lack of benchmarks and perspectives which all lead to a search for meaning. It is therefore also part of a moral and cultural crisis which impacts the different countries in Europe in a variety of ways. For example, concern about Europe varies from country to country and is also dependent on the period examined. It is to a large extent due to the European Union's incapacity to confront specifically the challenges represented by terrorism, racism or anti-Semitism, for example by adopting integrated policing systems or by imposing the harmonization of intelligence services and improving communication between them. To put it in a nutshell: Europe is not the only reason for the rise of the forces of evil we have described, but, on one hand, it is a victim of these forces and, as such, has been weakened; on the other, and this is linked, it does have a heavy responsibility to the extent that it has not provided itself with the means to deal with these forces. This strengthens nationalisms, which promise to be much more efficient, and reinforces the tendencies towards the break-up of Europe as a whole and also of its partial achievements (the Schengen area and the euro in particular).

References

Barker, M. (1981) *The New Racism*. London: Junction Books.
Bataille, P. (1997) *Le racisme au travail*. Paris: La découverte.
Beck, U. (2004) *Der Kosmopolitische Blick oder: Krieg ist Frieden*. Berlin: Suhrkamp.
Wieviorka, M. (2004) *The Making of Terrorism*. Chicago, IL: University of Chicago Press.
Wieviorka, M. (2007) *The Lure of Anti-Semitism*, trans. K.C. Lobel and A. Declerck. Leiden: Brill.

Chapter 10

Europe and Refugees:
Tragedy Bordering on Farce
Paul Collier

Introduction: The EU as a 'Failing State'

Does the EU aspire to be a state? The change of language from 'Community' to 'Union' implied such an aspiration, as does the mantra 'ever closer union' and those iconic symbols of statehood, the euro and Schengen. These could reasonably be interpreted as steps towards the goal of a United States of Europe. But perhaps the goal is far more modest: to build a framework that enables cooperation for mutual benefit among Member States to become routine: the default option. That even after sixty years this existential question cannot readily be answered suggests that deep disagreements have been buried. An analogy is the commitment to 'the nationalization of the means of production and distribution' that used to feature in the constitutions of several of the left-leaning European political parties. While the commitment was long ignored, the process of repeal revealed an existential disagreement. The departure of Britain over the issue of free movement might have provided such a decisive moment. But while it is evident that Britain has chosen the right to restrict movement over membership, it is not evident that other member countries have chosen the right of free movement in preference to continued British membership. Rather, they gambled that insisting on free movement would not induce Britain to leave, and cannot retrospectively change their position. Possibly Brexit has inadvertently put the EU on a state-building course. The loss of a major state in order to retain free movement could be justified if it is an inviolable principle of future statehood more plausibly than by its modest practical benefits.

However, if it is a state in the making, the EU cannot benchmark itself purely on symbols: within its domain of responsibility, a state should be *effective*. State effectiveness is perhaps best judged by resilience. Has the state built a system that limits the risk of crises, and has it built the capacity to manage those crises that, despite such measures, nevertheless arise? On the criterion of resilience, the European Union is not an effective state: rather, it manifests the classic features of state failure. Through prioritizing the symbols of statehood over the practical needs of citizens, the EU has created two major but avoidable crises and then demonstrated a profound inability to manage them. One of these is the economic divergence of Southern Europe from Germany and the UK; the other, which is the focus of this chapter, is the refugee-cum-migration influx.

To characterize the EU as a failing state evidently requires justification. Much of my own work is on failing states and I have come to see them as somewhat analogous to Tolstoy's unhappy families: states can fail in many different ways. However, one common underlying feature is that there is a radical mismatch between the spatial structures of identities and power: typically, identities are more fragmented than power. In the typical African failing state, identities are predominantly tribal. In the EU, identities are predominantly national. Only in Germany, which due to its exceptional history is fearful of its national identity, and Belgium, which due to its language divisions has predominantly sub-national identities, is a larger European identity seriously entertained. This lack of shared identity among citizens of the polity limits the perception of a 'common interest': there is no 'common'. In the absence of a 'common interest', centralized power cannot turn into authority. By this I mean that the cost of enforcing compliance with state commands remains high, dependent upon active enforcement, rather than underpinned by recognition that self-interest is trumped by common interest. This makes centralized power redundant or dangerous. It is redundant if central activity is limited to those actions that each identity group recognizes as being in its own interest: that is, cooperation for mutual benefit. The role of the centre in such an arrangement is that of facilitating cooperation. If, however, the centre asserts that it is empowered to override some of these interests, since its power is not backed by authority it has only three options: repression, open conflict or theatre. Perhaps the closest the EU has come to repression is over the Cypriot banking crisis and the Greek fiscal crisis: in each case, national governments took highly unpopular actions that they publicly opposed, in order to avoid threatened penalties. The more usual form has been theatre: Commission instructions to national governments that have been ignored or finessed. The refugee crisis has been of this form.

The implication is that its institutions should eschew attempting to exercise power. Rather, the EC should recognize that the EU, which it services, is not a state in the making, but is fundamentally a club for the mutual benefit of its members. It should therefore concentrate upon facilitation of the myriad practical opportunities for reciprocal benefit, and from this gradually build habits of cooperation. The EC has had many successes in such activities, but they remain surprisingly limited. For example, all modern economies are overwhelmingly about the production of services rather than goods. Yet Europe's service sector remains largely restricted to national markets: there are no pan-European retail chains equivalent to Wal-Mart in the USA, nor pan-European insurance companies or banks. There is not even pan-European access to national television channels. Ironically, the major national European television services broadcast nightly news coverage across America, but not across Europe beyond their own national borders.

To the extent that Europe had scope for a collective 'mission' beyond reciprocity, it was as a vehicle for *convergence* across the European continent. Due to their recent histories of dysfunctional governance (albeit for different reasons), both Southern Europe and Eastern Europe were significantly poorer than North-Western Europe. By setting basic standards of honest and democratic governance as the entry criteria for membership of a high-status club, until the millennium the EU played a highly valuable role in accelerating political and economic convergence. In the past decade this has gone into reverse. This is not just a matter of a divergent periphery, although that is manifest. Since 2007, Italian per capita GDP has declined by 11 per cent while growing by 11 per cent in Germany. Perhaps unsurprisingly, an anti-EU insurgent party currently leads in Italian opinion polls.

The impetus for this reversal was that the EC was seduced by the notion that it is the proto-government of a proto-state, and so set about accumulating power. What else can the language of '*acquis*', and 'ever closer' imply other than such an ambition? Recall, however, that since at the pan-European level power cannot turn into authority, the menu of power-driven activity is limited to repression, open conflict and theatre. The EC largely lacks coercive power. While it has tried to exercise coercive power over its national governments, through instruments such as fiscal ceilings, its attempts have routinely been ignored, inevitably undermining its credibility. This has left theatre as the only remaining option: the construction of symbols of statehood.

All states use symbolism, but in failing states it is dangerous because it easily gives office-holders the delusion of real power. Other than encouraging such delusions, *pure* symbols, such as flags and anthems, are harmless. But some policy instruments that primarily do real things also carry some symbolic meaning. Tragically, EU office-holders trespassed into this domain. To the extent that there was a strategy behind this, as opposed to pure blundering, it was that the resulting stresses would force the pace of the necessary underlying centralization of power. This was, to say the least, a reckless gamble with the lives of European citizens. Office-holders appear to have justified recklessness on the grounds that in the larger context it reduced risk: most notably, European political integration was the only alternative to renewed warfare. The fanciful nature of this narrative of peace through institutions is illustrated by the following. In 1940 Germany invaded both the Netherlands and Norway: the former is now in the EU and the euro, the latter is in neither. Is Norway more at risk than the Netherlands?

In pursuit of the trappings of statehood, European Union office-holders explicitly invoked the model of Canada, and implicitly may have imagined themselves building a United States of Europe as a counterweight to the United States of America. Canada and the USA had a common currency and open internal borders, and so the United States of Europe should leap directly to equivalent policies: the euro and Schengen. The euro achieved symbolic convergence at an excruciating price in terms of divergent rates of growth and youth unemployment: surveys now find that the youth of Southern Europe has unprecedented levels of pessimism. But the flaws of the euro were complex and very hard for ordinary politicians to grasp. In contrast, the flaws of Schengen were nakedly apparent.

Why border controls are necessary

All states need to control their borders. Border controls are not just about migration; they include the regulation of trade in goods and movements of capital. Without such controls criminality in many forms would escalate. Since the need for controls is evident, all states have them. All high-income countries, and many middle-income ones, will need effective controls for many decades. This is because many millions of people in poorer countries would naturally prefer to live in rich ones. With cheap travel, instant information flows, and large diasporas already resident in Europe, migration in the absence of effective controls would rapidly accelerate to levels that were socially unacceptable to a majority of European citizens. Controlling immigration from poor countries is neither racist nor unethical.

The fear of uncontrolled immigration apparent among many European citizens need not be due to racism. The individual nation-states of Europe are highly unusual in having built shared identities that have enabled generous welfare systems to be seen as in the 'common interest'. Recent pan-European research has found that those earning above median income are less willing to support transfers to those below median income the higher is the proportion of immigrants (Rueda 2014), and the more salient is immigration (Pardos-Pardo and Muñoz 2017). Migrants do not pose a significant wage threat to indigenous workers, but they do pose a significant threat to poor households. Part of the ethical case for migration controls is that those Europeans on above-median income do not have the moral right to sacrifice the interest of their poorer fellow citizens.

A further part of the moral right to impose border controls is that there is no moral 'right to immigrate'. The ethical position is apparent if a non-European case is considered, such as Botswana and Nigeria. Fifty years ago both countries were very poor. Both discovered valuable natural resources, but while the people of Botswana used their diamonds prudently, Nigerians squandered over a trillion dollars of oil revenues. As a result, per capita income in Botswana is now around ten times higher than that in Nigeria. Do Nigerians now have the moral right to migrate to Botswana? If they do, since there are nearly 100 Nigerians for each Botswanan, Botswana will rapidly become predominantly Nigerian, presumably in all respects. As it is, the Government of Botswana maintains very tight controls on the right of foreigners to live and work in the country, and it is hard to see this as morally unjustified. Nor can the moral right to immigrate be inferred from the evident moral right to emigrate. The latter follows from the moral limitations on government: no government has the right to turn its territory into a jail for its population. But freedom to leave one place is not freedom to enter any other particular place. I cannot morally restrain my spouse from leaving our house, but you are morally entitled to prevent her from entering yours.

A final ethical argument for border controls is that, far from being a triumphant exercise of a moral right, the migration of enterprising people from their country-of-origin to richer countries may be a self-serving response that worsens the position of the less capable people left behind. An analogy is capital flight as a response to a macroeconomic disequilibrium: it is privately rational but in aggregate makes the situation worse. Open borders, on this analysis, tempt enterprising and educated young people from poor societies to abandon their responsibilities towards those who need them.

This is not to deny that the disequilibrium of mass poverty alongside mass plenty is grotesque. But the moral imperative is to help poor societies to catch up, not to entice their ablest young workers away.

Schengen

Schengen is not to be confused with the right of EU citizens to live and work in other EU countries. Britain, which is not part of Schengen, has been party to this reciprocal right. Schengen is the physical removal of border controls between participants. Beyond symbolism, this had two substantive effects: anyone (citizen or not) could move between member countries without scrutiny, and entry to the entire area would be determined by the policies and implementation capacities of each of those countries with an external border.

Astonishingly, this vast area was created without either agreement on common external immigration policies or the creation of a common external border police. This gave rise to a classic weakest link problem: the external borders of all were at best as porous as the most generous national immigration policy. In practice, they were yet more porous due to the evasion of controls enabled by the least competent national border policing. But since this weakest link feature was evident *ab initio*, the EC/EU must bear the responsibility. It introduced a system that would inevitably place enormous stress on the weakest national border force without any effective policy to strengthen it.

The lack of a common migration policy created an unseemly incentive for individual governments to sell the right of entry to the zone, an opportunity that was duly taken. For example, Portugal introduced a scheme whereby for €500k of investment in Portuguese property, anyone could get entitlement for themselves and their children to live in the zone.[1] Wealthy Chinese apparently bought these entitlements so that their children could study in prestigious locations such as Paris. The government of Malta sells citizenship at a slightly higher price (€650k); the high value of citizenship evidently not being for residence in Malta. Both have recently been undercut by Hungary which is offering permanent Schengen residence for €360k.[2] Beyond mercenary considerations, some states had remarkably generous rules of entry. For example, Spain adopted a rule that anyone arriving on its territory, notably, people on boats from Africa reaching the Canaries, would receive the right to permanent residence after only 40 days unless expelled. Since there was no capacity for expulsion within such a timeframe, it implied open access to the Schengen area for anyone able to travel illegally by boat to the

---

[1] The official website of the Portuguese Government Tourist Board has full details of this 'Golden Visa' programme, which requires that the property be held for five years.
[2] The Maltese and Hungarian schemes are both widely advertised on the Internet.

Canaries. Ireland had a rule which is estimated to have entitled some 40 million non-Irish people to Irish passports, and hence to residence anywhere in Schengen.[3]

Obviously, a border-free area requires a common external force to police its borders. A real federal state such as the USA has one, but the EU adopted the symbol without the necessary supporting organization. The EC cobbled together a quasi-volunteer frontier force, Frontex, by drawing on various national forces. But it is a proto-agency that would take many years to build into something equivalent to that of Canada or the USA. Currently, it is tiny and barely serious: as explained to me by a high EC official, at Christmas 2015, a time of massive border pressure, the staff of Frontex simply went home for a week's holiday, leaving their posts unmanned. Manifestly, this is state as theatre. As a practical matter, this left border policing and migrant processing in the hands of the national public services of those countries with external borders.

While Frontex fell far short of the Canadian border force, its task was an order of magnitude more demanding. Europe borders on two of the world's most conflict-prone regions: the Middle East and North Africa. Further, adjoining each of these troubled regions are yet larger zones of instability: Central Asia, the Sahel, and the Horn of Africa. The gate-keepers for these enormous populations were Turkey, Morocco, Algeria, Tunisia, Libya, Egypt and Syria. The prospects of all of them being continuously cooperative and effective were negligible.

This made the weakest link problem acute because by 2015 Europe had its very own failing nation state: Greece, easily reachable from Turkey, but also reachable via Crete from North Africa. In 2011 Greece's then Prime Minister, George Papandreou, had warned his fellow European heads of government that the Greek public sector was corrupt to the core. Indeed, it was by falsifying its public accounts that Greece was able to satisfy the conditions for joining the euro.[4] Membership of the eurozone set in train a disastrous boom–bust sequence which is still playing out. By 2015, with its economy having contracted by an astounding 25 per cent, the government in charge of coping with this nightmare, including the reform of deeply flawed public services, was an untested party of the radical left, Syriza.

Hence, at the time when Schengen was formed, it was predictable that any of its members on the Southern border were liable to face an

---

[3] In consequence, post-Brexit the Irish government has been flooded with requests for citizenship from British citizens.

[4] However, the conditions for entry to the euro were not enforced. Only Luxembourg would have met the conditions, requiring the splitting of its currency union with Belgium.

influx from some country in conflict, and that Greece would be in no position itself to meet this challenge. The poignantly named Arab Spring ignited Europe's vulnerabilities. As Libya descended into chaos, the entire Mediterranean border became exposed, with Italy the easiest country to reach. The pressure was contained because Libya's population was small, the sea crossing was substantial, and between it and adjoining countries was the further barrier of the Sahel. Both barriers were surmountable but required significant organization. The more gradual collapse in Syria had a more dramatic effect because it was both more populous and much closer, the easiest country to reach being Greece.

By 2015 around ten million Syrians were displaced from their homes due to spreading violence, and about half of the displaced had crossed into the neighbouring countries of Turkey, Jordan and Lebanon, where their legal status changed from 'internally displaced people' to 'refugees'. International law on refugees was, however, clear that they had an absolute right to shelter in their first country of arrival. The principle that neighbouring countries should be havens for the displaced is important, because such countries are by far the easiest for the displaced to reach, and from which to return to their homes once a conflict ends. However, for it to be practicable, the governments of haven countries should not be expected to bear the financial burden. Usually, such countries will be relatively poor and in no position to meet the costs of shelter, nor to provide employment opportunities to an influx of refugees. In respect of Syrian refugees, it was evident that the principal responsibility for financing them in haven countries, and for generating employment opportunities in situ, rested with Europe, the most proximate part of the OECD. This, Europe singularly failed to do. Indeed, in 2014 the German government actually halved its modest financial contribution, forcing UNHCR to cut its monthly payments to refugees.

Enthusiasm for the symbolic principle of borderless internal travel, combined with negligence towards the external border, left the vast Schengen area predictably dependent upon an ineffective Greek border force adjoining a pool of ten million displaced Syrians. Beyond them lay a further pool of people displaced from other conflicts such as Afghanistan. The lack of border capacity created a further massive problem. If border forces were unable or unwilling to register and screen extra-legal arrivals, and crucially have an effective capacity to return those that were not eligible for asylum, then *refugees would not in practice be distinguished from ordinary immigrants at the point of arrival.* This exposed the Schengen area to the vastly larger pool of would-be immigrants from poor countries around the world. Around 40 per cent of the citizens of poor countries say that they would rather live in rich ones. With the fall in transport costs and the increase in diasporas and information flows, border controls are a major reason why migration from poor countries is not much larger. A breakdown in border controls would therefore place a growing burden on the behind-the-border capacity to repatriate migrants who were not eligible for asylum. In practice, return faces both practical and legal impediments: if migrants destroy their papers, their nationality cannot be established, and many countries are judged not to meet the governance standards required for return even though only a small minority of their citizens are genuine victims of state oppression.

A further consequence was that the Schengen area became hostage to the policy choices of an increasingly unattractive government which wanted opportunities to put pressure on the EU. The Turkish government, headed by an Islamic-nationalist authoritarian facing deep internal political problems, found itself with massive leverage. With two million Syrian refugees in the country, as its policies were varied between encouraging and impeding migration to Europe, the numerical impact was substantial. President Erdogan wanted the prestige that would come from publicly forcing Europe into conceding a range of recognitions, including ultimately full entry to the club. As a result, his government had an incentive to exploit rather than address the practical weaknesses of the Greek border force. The Greek government, which had been required by the German government to implement policies that it regarded as anathema, had a similar opportunity for pressure. Whether the slow pace at which it improved border controls reflected an attempt to exploit this opportunity, or whether the delays were unavoidable given the parlous state of the Greek bureaucracy, cannot currently be determined.

Faced with the reality of porous borders, European governments determined to contain the risk of mass immigration by adopting the Dublin Agreement. This ruled that only those governments that admitted extra-legal migrants had the responsibility to keep them: other countries within the EU had the right to return any migrants who crossed into them to their country of first arrival. In order that the country of first arrival could be known, governments of the countries of first arrival were required to register all migrants. The theory was that this supposedly gave each country an incentive to prevent illegal entry. Instead, governments of the countries of first arrival found an obvious alternative. As long as they neglected to register the migrants and facilitated them to cross the open borders to other members of the Schengen area, migrants could not be returned because they could not be traced back. Migrants had an interest in cooperating: they wanted to try their luck in the most promising Northern countries rather than remaining in the poorer Southern countries of arrival.

Given the above conjunction of initial policy errors and events, and the inability of EU leaders to respond in a timely manner, it was inevitable that the Schengen area would lose control of its borders and consequently experience a massive influx of refugees and immigrants. In the summer of 2015 this happened. Predictably, the Dublin Agreement proved impotent to prevent many migrants from reaching Germany, which, as a result of the misaligned exchange rate, was attractive as the only booming economy within the eurozone.

At this point, Chancellor Merkel took the unilateral decision to abandon the Dublin Agreement. This may have been due to recognition that it was not politically practicable for Germany to send thousands of refugees back to Greece, in effect compounding the acute tensions between the two countries that had been generated by the Greek economic crisis. Or it might have reflected the legacy of German history that made the opportunity of launching a credible narrative of moral superiority over the rest of Europe on the criterion of acceptance of an ethnic and religious minority uniquely tempting. Certainly, the stance was initially popular with a significant part of the German population. Or it might have been humanitarian concern for the manifest plight of the people arriving at Germany's borders. It may even have been a technocratic concern to replenish a declining labour force, although there was a wide array of alternative policies that could have been adopted, and due to the distinctive training requirements for employment in Germany, to date (July 2016) only a negligible number of refugees have gained jobs.

Whatever the motivation, the policy change had the predictable effect of radically increasing the attraction of migration. Since the invitation to Germany came with no safe or legal means of getting there, the only feasible means of transport was to buy places on boats sold by the people-smuggling industry. This industry is a global phenomenon. Not only is the sector illegal and so unregulated, by its nature it does not usually enter into repeat transactions with the same person and so firms have no need to build reputation. Consequently, competition is on the basis of price, driving costs down at the expense of even minimal concerns for safety. Boats are overcrowded and sink not by chance, but as an inevitable consequence of market forces. While the industry was already well-established in the Mediterranean, the massive increase in demand triggered by the invitation from Germany led to a rapid expansion, aided by the arrival of established Latin American people-smuggling criminal syndicates. The industry is estimated to have had a turnover of around €6 billion in 2015.

The massive expansion in the people-smuggling industry had two awful consequences. One was avoidable mortality. Since all of the migrants and refugees embarked from Turkey where they were already in a safe haven, this massive movement of people did not save any lives. On the contrary, thousands of lives were lost due to drowning.

The other was that the exodus of Syrians from the regional havens was highly selective. Fewer than 10 per cent of the Syrians displaced became migrants to Europe. Refugees are not natural migrants: the predominant aspiration of the displaced was to return to their homes, while in the meantime staying within Syrian-dominant communities of exile. Germany was attractive predominantly for the well-educated, as they stood the best chance of getting a well-paid job. Consequently, the exodus was educationally selective: the educated minority moved to Germany, the uneducated majority stayed in the neighbourhood havens. Most evidently, it was financially selective: because a place purchased from a people-smuggler was expensive, it attracted the affluent rather than the most vulnerable. Affluent families raised the quick finance necessary for a place by selling property at distressed prices. Finally, it was selective by age and gender. Travelling by a small boat across open seas was risky: young males were far more willing to take these risks than elderly females or family groups. The educated, young males from affluent families that had sold off their assets in Syria are relatively unlikely to return to Syria once the conflict ends. Unfortunately, this is the group likely to be most valuable for rebuilding the society after war: recent analysis of post-conflict recovery suggests that the loss of human capital is more damaging than the physical destruction (Serneels and Verpoorten 2015). Inadvertently, the exodus may well have inflicted significant long-term losses on the majority who have remained behind.

A final inadvertent consequence was that in Germany some of the young men behaved like massed young men reared in a chauvinist culture are liable to do away from their families. This produced a further tragedy: the compassion that is the natural human reaction to the plight of the displaced turned to fear and resentment. This has dissipated the vital resource on which refugee policy must rest.

The accelerating influx to Germany rapidly ceased to be popular with its citizens. In response, Chancellor Merkel pressured the EC to introduce quotas for other European countries to take some of the migrants. Since no other government had been consulted on the initial unilateral German decision to abandon the Dublin Agreement, the moral force of this pressure was undermined. Faced with resistance from governments in Eastern Europe, the Chancellor initially threatened them with suspension of structural funds (a move which would have been illegal). Instead, the Commission changed its established practice of taking decisions on potentially sensitive issues by unanimity, overriding the opposition of five governments to impose migration quotas totalling 160,000. This turned out to be a further instance of government as theatre, since the quotas were largely ignored.

Meanwhile, the Schengen area itself dissolved into theatre as it was dismantled piecemeal in contravention of the rules. Country after country, both Sweden and Denmark in the North, and Austria and the Balkan countries in the South, imposed border restrictions in a domino effect.

By late 2015 the situation was sufficiently difficult that a very different approach started to gain traction.[5] A joint initiative of the governments of Jordan and the UK, together with the World Bank, convened an international conference, held in London on 4 February 2016, at which a large group of donors belatedly pledged substantial financial support for the haven governments bordering on Syria. They also undertook to create jobs for refugees by encouraging firms to set up production in industrial zones near the camps. The Government of Jordan committed to 150,000 work permits for refugees for new jobs created in the zones, and the European Commission agreed to relax trade restrictions on products made in them. In retrospect, this approach should have been vigorously adopted *ab initio*, rather than as a response to panic.

The German government attended the meeting, but behind the scenes was uncooperative. Instead, in March 2016 Chancellor Merkel again acted unilaterally, striking a deal with President Erdogan of Turkey at the very time when the EC was itself in negotiations with him. The deal introduced the repatriation of migrants who had arrived in Greece back to Turkey in return for an equivalent number of Syrian refugees being taken directly from the camps to Europe. Since by this stage the German population appeared unwilling to accept a further unlimited number of immigrants, a pre-emptive cap on numbers was fixed at 73,000, and the EC established a further voluntary quota scheme to distribute this number around the Schengen area. The theory was that by breaking the link between extra-legal migrant and successful entry to Europe, there would no longer be any incentive to buy an illegal passage.

The strategy had vulnerabilities. Gaining the agreement of Turkey to accept the return of migrants required conceding to President Erdogan of Turkey not only the substantial sum of €6 billion, but promises of visa-free entry for Turkish citizens and a reinvigorated process of Turkish admission to the EU. Visa-free access rapidly led to an embarrassing conflict of interest between the EU and Syrian refugees. President Erdogan announced in Southern Turkey that refugees were being considered for Turkish citizenship, an integrationist step that the international

---

[5] For a fuller analysis of reforming the refugee system, see Betts and Collier (2017).

community should have welcomed. Instead, the EU expressed concern that the refugees would thereby acquire the right to visa-free travel to Europe. Further, the timing of the deal was highly embarrassing since, lest there should be any confusion, President Erdogan announced on the day of the agreement that words such as 'democracy' and 'human rights' were meaningless in the Turkish context. A further vulnerability is that the entire people-smuggling industry could simply switch to the coast of North Africa and ship migrants to Italy instead of Greece. The agreement with Turkey would not cover such migrants and no equivalent repatriation agreement could be negotiated because, whereas Turkey can be deemed to be a safe haven, countries such as Libya cannot. If the end result is a shift of the industry to North Africa the long-term consequences could be massive, since the entire Sahel region, and beyond it huge societies such as Nigeria and DRC, become potential feeds.

The crux of immigration policy

The mass attempts at extra-legal migration to Europe, from North Africa via the Italian island of Lampedusa, and from Turkey via the Greek island of Lesbos, were an existential phenomenon. Here was a manifestly pan-European problem that rapidly aroused deep fears across European populations. Although numbers started off as modest, they clearly had the potential to escalate to unmanageable proportions, threatening cultural cohesion and, hence, the welfare systems that cohesion sustained. What European citizens increasingly asked for was a practical strategy that would reassure them that control of borders would rapidly be restored with sufficient efficacy that extra-legal entry would rapidly cease.

As such, this was a rare opportunity for the EC to take actions that would turn power into authority, building a common European identity. Instead, it did almost precisely the opposite: requiring its member national governments to accept migrants that their citizens did not want. The result was in part more theatre: its rules were ignored and so implied a further loss of credibility. More fundamentally, from the perspective of ordinary European citizens it began to look like an extension of the United Nations, rather than as an invaluable entity for mutual benefit.

In the end, Chancellor Merkel met the expectations of her citizens by a unilaterally negotiated deal with Turkey that reversed her policy of welcome. She promptly recovered much of the massive drop she had suffered in national opinion polls. But the EU was a spectator in this policy reversal. The outcome made Europe look ungenerous: having chosen to define generosity in terms of the number of refugees accepted, Europe slammed the door. It made the EC look unresponsive to citizen concerns and incompetent in execution. Finally, it made the locus of real power appear to be Germany.

It need not have been like this. David Cameron, then British Prime Minister, had recognized a more viable response: generosity defined in terms of practical and financial assistance to refugees and governments in the havens, citizen reassurance in terms of maintenance of effective border controls. The two complement each other: by providing havens that function well enough to preserve human dignity, the influx of would-be migrants can be reduced to a level at which those entering illegally can be transferred to the havens without violating due process. Had the EC devised and promoted this approach from 2014, there would have been no exodus, no rise of the populist right across Europe, and quite probably no Brexit. The EU would have begun to look to its citizens like a valuable protector of European values in dangerous times.

The Syrian refugee crisis was thus an opportunity for the EU to demonstrate its value that ended by demonstrating the opposite. This happened because, although the political structure of its institutions imitates the external trappings of a state, they cannot function as a government. The group of people who collectively hold power of decision do not constitute a coherent political unit such as a political party, or coalition, under the authority of a head of government. Power is diffused between the Council of Ministers, which represents governments and has a rotating chair and an appointed president; and Commissioners appointed by their national government but assigned to head a particular Directorate by the President of the Commission, who in turn is elected by the European Parliament. The President of the Commission has the unenviable task of 'heading' a group of Commissioners who span the entire spectrum of political opinion and national interests. His only room for manoeuvre is to assign those Commissioners from fringe political interests, or minor countries, to the less strategic Directorates. Under normal circumstances, the Directorates for Migration and Human Rights fit into this category. In consequence they have become staffed with people who passionately hold somewhat exceptional beliefs: for example, a senior official of the Migration Directorate explained to me that there was no ethical justification for any border controls. Not feeling under an obligation to meet the concerns of a majority of electors, such office-holders have been more concerned with applying their interpretations of human rights law than of addressing the concerns of most citizens.

The structure is dysfunctional because it is a hybrid of two rival visions. The romantic Federalists want a state; the practical national politicians want a mechanism facilitating cooperation for mutual benefit. In the former, a Council of Ministers has no place; in the latter, a European parliament has no place. Until this existential disagreement is resolved, the EU will lurch from one crisis to another.

Conclusion

The EU needed a strategy to respond to migration and asylum but failed to generate one. This is recognized in parts of the EC, but the pertinent Directorates were in no position to undertake it. Instead, European policy has been set by bypass deals such as the one negotiated secretly between Chancellor Merkel and President Erdogan. A coherent strategy would have two core elements.

As to asylum, the duty of rescue in desperate situations such as the exodus from Syria needs to be rethought. Part of that duty is to ensure that there are proximate safe havens able to take all those displaced from their homes by violence. This requires generous and sustained finance for haven countries. The EU should have provided such support for the countries bordering on Syria. Shamefully, we left Jordan, Turkey and Lebanon to bear the financial burden. But the duty of rescue is not just about safety, shelter and food. Most of the refugees in the haven countries have avoided the camps where shelter and food are free, in preference to the grim opportunities of working illegally in the cities of the haven countries; or they have risked their lives on the boats. What this demonstrates is that the human condition craves autonomy: refugees in the camps are housed and fed, but are stripped of the dignity that comes from earning a living. Hence, part of the duty of rescue is to provide viable employment opportunities to refugees in situ in the havens. As a result of globalization this is entirely feasible. For example, German firms have spent two decades creating many thousands of manufacturing jobs in Poland and Turkey. During the past decade a previously remote Turkish town has become the world's main production centre for synthetic carpets. Jobs can be brought to refugees as long as global firms receive the incentives to do so, and trade regulations are adjusted to ensure easy market access for what refugees produce.

As to migration, human rights law is a grey and unreformed accumulation of rules that is procedurally so cumbersome as to leave substantial opportunities for extra-legal migrants to game the system. The human rights of people who are nationals of countries that are poor but safe, and those of asylum-seekers from conflict areas who have already reached neighbouring safe havens, need to be reassessed. Specifically, as has become evident, if would-be migrants and asylum-seekers are *de facto* able to improve their chances of remaining in Europe by extra-legal arrival on European territory or waters, immigration will escalate uncontrollably, as people-smuggling businesses expand a highly profitable niche. Hence, regardless of the characteristics of the individual, arriving on (or off) the shore of a European island must confer no greater right of entry than had the individual applied from outside of Europe through a legal process.

Our belated actions towards the havens have been driven not by compassionate recognition of our duty of rescue, but by fear and hatred: 'stop them coming here'. The predominant narrative that refugees hear from Europe should be the offer of credible hope that life will improve. That hope should not have been reaching Germany – refugees are not migrants. Hope should mean jobs in the havens bordering on Syria, followed by a return to Syria as order is gradually restored. That is what refugees overwhelmingly want. It is also what the governments of the haven countries want. They would like European firms to bring jobs, shared between refugees and locals. That is why Jordan has offered 150,000 work permits for refugees for new jobs in zones.

The creation of the Schengen area without either a common immigration policy or a common border force, and the inability to respond to the resulting crisis, are sad testimonies to a larger truth. As with the adoption of the euro without the macroeconomic preconditions, a symbol of statehood was elevated above elementary principles of sound policy. The most astounding aspect of these blunders is that they were not the consequence of populist pressures: these were projects of elite romanticism. In aspiring to statehood, the EU has forfeited its opportunity to be a vital force for European cooperation and convergence.

References

Betts, A. and Collier, P. (2017) *Refuge: Transforming a Broken Refugee System.* Harmondsworth: Penguin.

Pardos-Pardo, S. and Muñoz, J. (2017) Immigration and support for social policy: An experimental comparison of universal and means-tested programmes. Working Paper, Department of Politics, Oxford University.

Rueda, D. (2014) Food comes first, then morals: Redistribution preferences, altruism and group heterogeneity in Western Europe. CAGE Working Paper 200, University of Warwick.

Serneels, P. and Verpoorten, M. (2015) The impact of armed conflict on economic performance: Evidence from Rwanda. *Journal of Conflict Resolution* 59(4): 555–92.

Part III

Political Crises

Chapter 11

The Crisis of Legitimacy of European Institutions

Sara B. Hobolt

Introduction

The euro crisis has had consequences not only for the economic governance in Europe, but perhaps more fundamentally for the European Union's political settlement and popular legitimacy. It presented the European Union (EU) with a fundamental challenge: on the one hand, the crisis led to greater public contestation of and opposition to the EU, and on the other hand, the Union has become ever more reliant on public support for its continued legitimacy. The Brexit referendum has illustrated how the lack of public support for the EU can challenge the very foundations of the European project. Moreover, institutional reforms of the eurozone's economic governance are constrained by public opinion as future EU treaty changes need to be ratified by Member States, either by national parliaments or by national electorates in referendums. In the long run, closer fiscal integration in the eurozone is only likely to be viable if it is perceived to be legitimate in the eyes of citizens. This chapter examines the effect of the euro crisis on the accountability and legitimacy of the European Union. It investigates how the crisis, and the reforms of economic governance, have tested the legitimacy of the Union, and how the public has responded.

Historically, European integration has been largely an elite-driven project, supported by a 'permissive consensus' by European citizens (Lindberg and Scheingold 1970). When elites decided on which areas of cooperation would be most beneficial to their countries, their citizens largely followed suit. This consensus has been challenged since the referendums on the Maastricht Treaty in the early 1990s and the increasing politicization of the European integration issue (Hooghe and Marks

2009). The euro crisis, however, led to a step change in the public debate on the EU, as it amplified not only the public salience, but also the redistributive consequences of decisions taken by the European Union (Cramme and Hobolt 2014; Laffan 2014). Furthermore, the attempts of EU leaders to manage the crisis were widely reported in national media (see Kriesi and Grande 2014), and the EU imposed conditionality of drastic austerity measures on Member States in return for credit (see Scharpf 2014). In this way, this crisis starkly demonstrated the impact of decisions taken at the EU level on domestic economies and it highlighted divisions and differences between Member States by focusing attention on the contrast between 'creditor' and 'debtor' status and between North and South. This raises the questions examined in this chapter: what has been the effect of the crisis on the institutional balance in the European Union, how have citizens responded to the crisis, and with what consequences for European democracy?

This chapter is organized as follows. After a review of the debate on the democratic deficit in the European Union, the chapter discusses how the euro crisis, and the institutional responses to it, has exacerbated the Union's accountability deficit and tested the legitimacy of EU governance. The subsequent section looks at the public's response to the crisis across Europe, showing that there has been decrease in trust in EU institutions, but that a majority of citizens still see the EU as the most effective solution to the continent's economic woes. Thereafter, I examine how Eurosceptic parties, on the right and on the left, have increased their electoral appeal due to the crisis, but highlight how the electoral responses to the crisis have been very different in the wealthier creditor countries in the North compared to the poorer debtor states of the South. Finally, the last section concludes that the crisis has increased the public constraint on policy-making in the EU and that such divisions in public opinion make it challenging for the European Union to find common solutions that will solve the EU's legitimacy problem.

The EU's democratic deficit

The 'democratic deficit' has been a central theme in the literature on the European Union for the past two decades. At the core of this concept is the argument that important powers have been transferred from national parliaments to the European level, but without recompense in the form of adequate mechanisms of representation and accountability to the European level (see Føllesdal and Hix 2006 for an overview). As a consequence, the EU is seen to lack democratic legitimacy. The question in

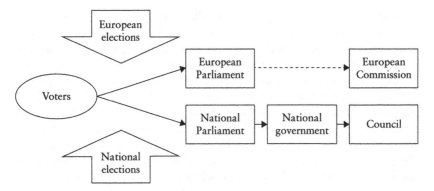

Figure 11.1: Paths of legitimation in the European Union

this chapter is whether and how the European sovereign debt crisis that began in 2008 has exacerbated, or ameliorated, this problem.

The European Union is a hybrid multi-level political system, more akin to a federal system than an international organization (Hix and Høyland 2011). Its core institutional structure is composed of a dual legislature (the Parliament and the Council) and a dual executive (the Commission and the European Council). Similar to other democratic multilevel systems of government, the EU thus provides citizens with two paths of representation to express their preferences and hold policy makers to account, as illustrated in figure 11.1.

As the figure shows, European citizens are represented directly via elections to the European Parliament (EP) that take place every five years. Successive treaty reforms have significantly enhanced the powers of the EP in EU policy-making, establishing it as a co-legislator with the Council in most areas of policy-making (Hix et al. 2007). Indeed, the Union's primary response to the increase in the scope and level of European Union power has been to strengthen the European Parliament's legislative powers, with the aim of improving democracy and accountability in the EU (Rittberger 2005). European citizens are also represented indirectly in the policy-making process through their national government representatives in the Council. The Council of the EU, composed of national ministers, remains the key legislator in the policy-making process, and the European Council is the dominant executive body when it comes to setting the EU's general political direction and priorities.

The constitutional framework of the European Union thus provides clear mechanisms of representation of accountability. Elections at both the national and the European levels allow citizens to control EU policy makers. However, scholars have questioned whether these elections adequately serve to legitimize governance in the European Union. For electoral representation to function, when choosing parties, voters need to use their votes to express preferences that are relevant to policy-making, and parties must subsequently pursue the policies that they have proposed. Studies of EP elections, however, have generally found that despite efforts to enhance the EP's powers, European elections continue to have a second-order nature, which fails to motivate public interest in the elections themselves and, more broadly, in politics at the European level. Accordingly, scholars have concluded that vote choices in EP elections are based on domestic rather than European policy concerns and that they fail to provide a democratic mandate to policy makers in the EU (e.g., Reif and Schmitt 1980; Van der Eijk and Franklin 1996; Schmitt 2005; Føllesdal and Hix 2006; Hix and Marsh 2007). Increasingly, Euroscepticism has also become an important factor motivating voters in EP elections (Hobolt et al. 2009; De Vries et al. 2011; Hobolt and Spoon 2012). Nonetheless, research has shown that the classic model of electoral accountability (sanctioning) cannot be applied to European Parliament elections, since citizens are unable to identify which parties within Parliament are linked with specific policy decisions and outcomes, and thus do not hold Members of the European Parliament to account for poor performance (Hobolt and Tilley 2014). Despite the recent introduction of partisan lead-candidates for the Commission presidency (*Spitzenkandidaten*) in EP elections, the Parliament still lacks a clear government–opposition dynamic that enables voters to choose between clear alternatives, and the link between the EP ballot and executive decisions in the EU remains tenuous (Hobolt 2014b).

As figure 11.1 illustrates, there is an alternative mechanism of accountability in the European Union, namely via national governments represented in the Council. National governments are indeed accountable to national electorates through elections to national parliaments/presidents. However, there are important limitations to the extent to which national governments in the Council are fully accountable to their parliaments, and in turn their national electorates, on decision making in Brussels. First, the actions of government ministers in the Council are largely beyond the control of national parliaments, especially when national governments control a parliamentary majority (Føllesdal and Hix 2006). Ministers in the Council and national bureaucrats in COREPER (Committee of Permanent Representatives) are generally more isolated from national parliamentary scrutiny and control than are national cabinet ministers or bureaucrats in the domestic policy-making process. Second, voters do not use national elections primarily to hold national governments to account for the performance of the EU. Hence, incumbents' positions and performance in the EU generally only play a small role in national election campaigns and vote choices, although there are exceptions to this (see e.g. De Vries 2007). Even to the extent that European integration is becoming a salient issue in the public debate in the framework of national electoral competition, this indirect mechanism of accountability remains tenuous, since most decisions in the Council are made by qualified majority voting rather than unanimity. Hence, EU decisions do not necessarily reflect the positions of individual governments on all matters, and this means that national electorates cannot necessarily punish a national government for a decision made collectively by the Council, since voters have no means of punishing governments of other Member States. In the next section, we turn to the question of how the crisis has affected the pathways of legitimation in the EU.

The crisis and the weakening of representative institutions

How has the eurozone crisis affected the democratic deficit in the EU? To answer this question we need to examine both the changing role of EU institutions as well as the public contestation and salience of the European Union. A key problem identified in the literature on the European Union is not the lack of *formal* mechanisms of accountability and representation, but rather the absence of politicization of European issues and government–opposition competition, which are necessary to make these mechanisms work in practice. Without public deliberations on matters of European politics and party contestation of different policy options at the EU level, it is difficult to envisage a well-functioning electoral democracy at the European level. Indeed, the need for a European public sphere and greater debate about European politics has been emphasized by some of the most prominent advocates for a supra-national democracy (Schmitter 2000; Hix 2008; Habermas 2012). Scholars of European elections have also identified the lack of public interest in and politicization of European politics as one of the key reasons for the weak electoral connection in European Parliament elections (Van der Eijk and Franklin 1996; Hobolt et al. 2009). Since long before the sovereign debt crisis, many have therefore argued in favour of far-reaching institutional reform to achieve greater contestation of European politics in order to create stronger linkages between citizens and their European representatives and thereby increase the accountability and legitimacy of the EU.

In many ways, the euro crisis succeeded in bringing about greater politicization of European issues in national public spheres (Kriesi and Grande 2014), and greater public awareness of the responsibilities and powers of the European Union (Hobolt 2014a). Moreover, since the decisions taken at the European level during the crisis have important redistributional consequences both within and between countries, with identifiable winners and losers, there is clearly a greater potential for more traditional 'left–right' political contestation about the future of Europe at both the domestic and European levels (Hix 2014). Put differently, the crisis has starkly illustrated that the EU has moved far beyond the remit of a 'regulatory state' (Majone 1996), and that there is no longer any neat separation between economics and politics where decisions can be delegated to regulatory agencies without intense public scrutiny (Majone 2012).

Given that these conditions for greater democratic politics – public salience, the emergence of a public sphere, real policy choices that can be contested – appear to be more present than ever due to the euro crisis, many therefore expected to witness the empowerment of European representative institutions engaged in the contestation of pan-European policy alternatives. However, there is little evidence to support this case. Instead, the EU's response has resulted in a weakening of representative institutions and processes, in both the national and European paths of legitimation, identified in figure 11.1. At the European level, a stronger emphasis has been placed on executive-driven politics, with the European Council taking the lead on all core decisions – often with limited input from the European Parliament – and important powers delegated to the European Commission with limited parliamentary oversight. This 'executive turn' in European governance has been justified in terms of the emergency politics of the crisis (White 2014). Representative institutions have played a limited role in the core reforms of economic governance in the EU. Indeed, the European Parliament and the transnational euro-parties have been notable by their absence in the significant decision-making moments during the crisis, while the debate has instead been dominated by national heads of government. Despite the opportunities the crisis has offered euro-parties to present alternative solutions, they have largely failed to shape the debate at a European level, and the discourse has instead focused on the economic imbalance between Member States, rather than policy debates that cut across national borders. While the European Parliament has formally approved some of the key institutional innovations adopted in response to the crisis, including the 'six-pack' regulations establishing the institutional framework of the 'Excessive Deficit Procedure', it has been more a question of consenting to discretionary authority than of playing a central role in the execution of that authority (Scharpf 2014). In a systematic overview of the impact of the crisis on the EU's constitutional balance, De Witte and Dawson conclude:

> This big shift towards executive politics is exacerbated by the simultaneous decrease in power of both the European Parliament and national parliaments, which traditionally served as checks on executive power, ensuring the wishes of the citizenry. While it could have partly legitimized the Union's shift to greater re-distributive decision-making, the EP has played no role of significance in either the ESM or the Fiscal Compact. (De Witte and Dawson 2013: 832)

This leads us to the *national* path of legitimation, where we have similarly observed the weakening of representative institutions and mechanisms of accountability, although the impact of the crisis is highly asymmetric. The constraints imposed by the new measures of fiscal oversight, in particular the requirement that national budgets be assessed by the Commission, make it increasingly difficult, if not impossible, for national parliaments to control their executives. However, such constraints are not equal for all Member States, but primarily affect those countries in receipt of bailouts, often referred to as 'debtor states', and other states with excessive deficits. This means that in effect the parliamentary sovereignty of such Member States has been constrained by the decisions of other Member States in the Council. National electorates in debtor states, such as Portugal and Ireland, may be less willing to sanction their national governments for a decision taken collectively by the Council (see Lobo and Lewis-Beck 2012; Magalhaes 2014). Unsurprisingly, therefore, many of the sacrifices and rescue conditionalities agreed at the European level on Member States were perceived by people as imposed from the outside with limited legitimacy. The new rules governing economic corporation have also significantly limited the policy choices available to elected government in the eurozone. Taxing and spending policies are the main issues in domestic electoral and party politics. Yet, these new mechanisms of eurozone governance heavily constrain the policy promises parties can make to electorates on these issues, and the room for manoeuvre of politicians once elected to office (Laffan 2014). The recurring refrain from national governments to their citizens was 'there is no alternative'.

In summary, the crisis has weakened the primary institution representing citizens directly, the European Parliament, and has instead been dominated by national executives justifying their decisions using the rhetoric of necessity and emergency. It has also reduced the powers of national parliaments and constrained the policy options available to national governments. This intensifies the need for democracy at the

EU level. Yet, serious concerns remain about the Union's capacity for transnational democratic politics. Despite the heightened salience of the European issues, and the increasing evidence of a 'parallelization of national public spheres' (Kriesi and Grande 2014), this has not resulted in truly pan-European debates about different solutions to the crisis, similar to the familiar 'left–right' contestation in domestic politics, which can unite interests across national borders (Hix 2008; Hobolt and Tilley 2014). If anything, the politicization we have witnessed has served to exacerbate conflicts between individual Member States and the union, and between the 'core' and 'periphery' nations (Kriesi and Grande 2014; Scharpf 2014). I look more closely at this tension in the next section, which focuses on the public response to the crisis.

Public opinion and the crisis

How have people responded to the crisis, and the EU's institutional response to the crisis? First, it is clear that European citizens, at least in part, hold the EU responsible for the crisis (see Hobolt 2014a; Hobolt and Tilley 2014). Many citizens blame the EU for the economic downturn. According to a poll conducted in 2012, 83 per cent of Greeks, 47 per cent of Spaniards and 39 per cent of Italians thought that other EU countries pose a 'major threat' to their national economy.[1] This has consequences for politics, and for the pathways of legitimation discussed above, at both the national and EU levels. At the national level, the tendency to attach more responsibility to EU institutions for things that are going wrong may make citizens more likely to absolve their national governments of blame, and this weakens national accountability. While national government still attracts a large share of the blame, it is very plausible that individuals who think the EU is responsible for the crisis are less likely to punish them for the poor economic conditions in elections (see e.g. Lobo and Lewis-Beck 2012; Magalhaes 2014). Indeed, Bellucci, Costa Lobo and Lewis-Beck conclude their overview of national elections during the economic crisis stating that 'the European Union system of multilevel governance may hamper national accountability, as previous research on globalization has suggested. Voters with a heightened perception of EU economic responsibility are less likely to hold their national government accountable for managing the economy' (Bellucci et al. 2012: 471).

[1] PEW Global Attitudes Survey, Spring 2012: 'Now, thinking about some possible economic concerns for the country. Do you think that the power that Germany and other European Union countries have over our economy pose(s) a major threat, a minor threat, or no threat to the economic well-being of (survey country)?'

This raises the question of who is held to account for the economic crisis, if not national governments. The primary mechanism through which citizens can hold EU institutions to account is via elections to the European Parliament. Yet, unlike in national parliamentary systems, the majority in the European Parliament does not 'elect' the EU executive. Even with the introduction of *Spitzenkandidaten* for the role of Commission President in the 2014 EP elections, most citizens were not aware of the link between their vote and the Commission presidency (see Hobolt 2014b). Despite formal procedures of accountability, government clarity of responsibility within the EU is thus largely absent, and this makes it hard for voters to punish specific representatives for the crisis (Hobolt and Tilley 2014). Nonetheless, the tendency to pin part of the blame for the crisis on the EU may have other implications for the European project. Not least, it might lead to lower levels of trust in the European institutions as a whole, as citizens gradually lose faith in the ability of the European Union to deliver results. Lower levels of 'output legitimacy' may gradually erode trust in the institutions of the EU (Harteveld et al. 2013). We do find indications that such loss of trust in the EU has occurred over the course of the crisis. Eurobarometer data, reported in figure 11.2, show that before the onset of the crisis 57 per cent of Europeans 'tended to trust' the EU, but by the spring of 2014 this had dropped by 26 percentage points to 31 per cent. In comparison, trust in the national government and parliament dropped 13 percentage points in the same period. As European economies stabilized in late 2014

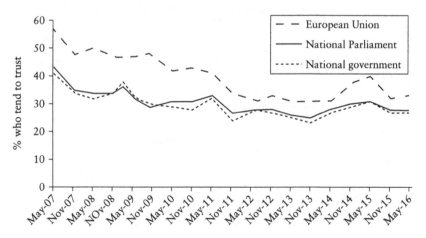

Figure 11.2: Trust in national and European institutions

Source: Eurobarometer, 2007–2016

and 2015, we have witnessed a slight increase in trust, but not a return to pre-crisis levels.

Research has shown that while European citizens are not able to 'throw the rascals in Europe out' in the way that we see in national elections, people do change their minds with regard to the EU institutions themselves (Hobolt and Tilley 2014). Poor performance leads to the institution itself becoming tarnished, and this is exacerbated when people hold those institutions responsible for the poor performance.

Does this evidence of declining trust in the European Union also imply that citizens have lost faith in the EU's ability to handle the crisis? Public opinion data suggest that this is not the case. It is noteworthy that even if trust in the EU has declined quite dramatically, it remains slightly above trust in national governments and parliaments (see figure 11.2). Moreover, we find that support for monetary integration, the euro, has remained high among citizens, especially inside the eurozone, where just under 70 per cent of people favour the single currency. Given that the crisis has not only exposed the fragility of the euro, but has also led to reduced national autonomy in fiscal policy-making, we might have expected a more severe backlash in support for the single currency. Figure 11.3 plots the proportion of citizens who favour the EMU (with a single currency), dividing EU Member States into four groups. First, the *euro debtor states*, that is the eurozone Member States whose economies

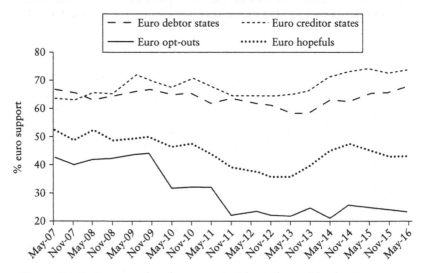

Figure 11.3: Support for the euro, inside and outside the Eurozone

Source: Eurobarometer surveys, 2007–2016.

have faced a particularly severe sovereign debt crisis, the so-called GIIPS countries (Greece, Ireland, Italy, Portugal and Spain) as well as Cyprus. All of these countries, except Italy, have received some form of emergency credit from the eurozone. The second group are the eurozone Member States that have not been in need of special measures, referred to here as *euro creditor states*. The third group, the *euro opt-outs*, represents the countries that have chosen to remain outside the eurozone until now, despite being able to meet the Maastricht convergence criteria, Denmark, Sweden and the UK.[2] The final group is composed of the *euro hopefuls*, which are the remaining nine EU Member States that have an official policy of joining the eurozone when they meet the convergence criteria.

Figure 11.3 shows, not surprisingly, that support for the euro is the lowest in the countries that have voluntarily remained outside the eurozone and the highest inside the eurozone. It also shows that this gap has widened since the crisis: there was a decline in support by euro outsiders during the sovereign debt crisis, however support inside the eurozone has remained high and stable for both debtor and creditor states. The similarity between support in 'debtor' and 'creditor' euro states may be due to the fact that the distributive consequences of the crisis and euro-rescue measures are somewhat unclear within the eurozone. On the one hand, debtor states have suffered most severely from the crisis and have had to accept austerity measures imposed by the EU, but on the other hand it could be argued that these states have received the most tangible benefits from the eurozone in the form of credit, which has effectively prevented them from defaulting on their debt obligations (Hobolt and Leblond 2013).

These data present an interesting puzzle: why do citizens inside the eurozone continue to support the single currency in times of severe economic downturn, not least since this downturn has been exacerbated by design flaws in the EMU itself and the austerity measures associated with bailout arrangements? (De Grauwe 2011, 2013; Scharpf 2014). A primary reason is that the cost–benefit calculation for citizens is crucially determined by whether they are already in the euro or not. For citizens in countries that have already adopted the euro, uncertainty associated with a break-up of the euro appears to outweigh the cost of staying inside. Given that most voters are risk-averse, this implies that they will be willing to bear a certain cost to save the euro (see Hobolt 2014a; Hobolt and Leblond 2013). Moreover, survey evidence suggests that many citizens continue to think that the EU is better equipped than their national

---

[2] In both Denmark and Sweden, the governments have been in favour of adopting the euro, but the electorate rejected the proposal in referendums in 2000 and 2003.

government to deliver effective solutions to the crisis. Since February 2009, the Eurobarometer surveys have asked the following question: 'which of the following is best able to take effective actions against the effects of the financial and economic crisis?'. The options include the national government, the European Union, the United States, the G20, the IMF, other, and none. On average, EU citizens perceived the EU to be the most effective at taking action against the crisis compared to all other options. As the crisis worsened in Europe and the EU started to intervene, more people thought that the EU is best placed to deal effectively with the consequences of the crisis. Except in the euro opt-out states, citizens are more likely to perceive the EU as an effective actor in taking action against the crisis than their national government. This is especially the case in the debtor countries, which were arguably in the greatest need of EU intervention, closely followed by other eurozone states. Interestingly, euro hopefuls also put their faith in the EU to handle the crisis, while the proportion is significantly lower in euro opt-out states. It is notable that across the EU, except in the euro opt-out states, citizens are more likely to perceive the EU as an effective actor in taking action against the crisis than their national government. In euro opt-out states, in contrast, citizens perceive their own national government to be the most effective institution.

In summary, these data show that Europeans inside the eurozone, and in most of the countries hoping to join the euro, have increasing misgivings about the EU institutions; however, they still perceive the EU to be more effective than their national government (and other international organizations) in taking action against the economic crisis. This also suggests that while Europeans are increasingly disillusioned with the European Union, they may – up to a point – be willing to support further economic integration to avoid the more uncertain, and potentially more sinister, consequences of a eurozone collapse. However, the dissatisfaction with both national and European politicians, and the lack of political choice, have also manifested in increasing support for radical, and more Eurosceptic, alternatives on the left and on the right. This is discussed in the next section.

Support for Eurosceptic parties

The clearest indication that voters across Europe have become more concerned about European issues has been the surge in popularity for political parties that proposed radical reform of, or even exit from, the EU. This was particularly pronounced in the eighth direct elections to the

European Parliament in 2014. With the exception of Malta, all EU countries had a Eurosceptic party gaining more than 2 per cent of the popular vote, although with considerable cross-national differences in their level of popularity (see figure 11.4). Overall, 220 of the European Parliament's 751 MEPs represented Eurosceptic parties, accounting for 29 per cent of MEPs (see Hobolt and De Vries 2016). The rise in the 'Eurosceptic' vote was therefore the message that dominated the headlines in the aftermath of the EP elections, and sent shockwaves through domestic political systems. The most striking result was that radical right Eurosceptic parties, which had never been in government, topped the polls in France, the UK and Denmark. A listing of the Eurosceptic parties that fought in the 2014 European Parliament elections is presented in table 11.1 in the appendix to this chapter.

Of course not all Eurosceptic parties are the same. *Euroscepticism* may be broadly defined as a sentiment of disapproval towards European integration, and this classification of Eurosceptic parties includes both 'soft' and 'hard' Eurosceptic parties (Taggart and Szczerbiak 2004). Soft Eurosceptic parties refer to those that accept the idea of European integration, but oppose specific policies or institutional aspects of the EU, such as Syriza in Greece, the Conservative Party in Britain or Fidesz[3] in Hungary. Hard Eurosceptic parties include parties that reject the European integration project as such, and tend to advocate a country's withdrawal from the EU, such as the Freedom Party in Austria and the UK Independence Party in Britain (see Treib 2014; Hobolt and De Vries 2016). The parties classified as Eurosceptic in this chapter belong to both categories and have been included in the list because a significant proportion of their campaign rhetoric and manifesto was devoted to a critique of the EU.[4] Most Eurosceptic parties are found on the fringes of the left–right political spectrum, although a few adopt more centrist positions (such as the British Conservative Party and the Polish Law and Justice party) or reject any left–right classification (such as the Italian Five Star Movement).

While these parties share a critical, or even hostile, attitude towards the European Union, they vary considerably in the nature of their position on the left–right spectrum and therefore also in their views on

---

[3] Fidesz is unusual among Eurosceptic parties, as it belongs to the pro-European EPP; however, its leader Victor Orbán's rhetoric has become increasingly hostile towards the EU (for example, he compared EU bureaucrats to Soviet apparatchiks). Orbán has described his position as 'Eurorealist' rather than Eurosceptic.

[4] The classification shown in the Appendix to this chapter has been cross-referenced with expert judgements in the Chapel Hill Expert Survey, as well as other academic work on Eurosceptic parties (e.g. Treib 2014). See also Hobolt and De Vries (2016).

other issues, such as redistribution, immigration and civil liberties. The left–right positions also translate into differences in the critique of the EU. The right-wing criticism is traditionally centred on nationalism and thus an opposition to the external threats to national sovereignty and to immigration (Mair and Mudde 1998; Mudde 2007). In contrast, critique from left-wing parties of the EU is rooted in an anti-capitalist ideology and calls for greater state intervention and redistribution both nationally and internationally. However, while much divides the radical right and the radical left, they share a Eurosceptic, nationalist and often populist rhetoric that cuts across traditional left–right alignments (Halikiopoulou et al. 2012). In the context of the 2014 European Parliament elections, the concern about threats to national sovereignty and opposition to EU institutions and policies was shared by Eurosceptic parties on both the right and the left, often combined with populist and anti-establishment rhetoric. However, the anti-immigration rhetoric was far more pronounced on the right (especially in Western Europe), while the anti-austerity rhetoric was more pronounced on the left. These themes of opposition to immigrants and the establishment were also central in the campaign leading up to the British referendum on EU membership in 2016 that resulted in a narrow majority in favour of leaving the EU (Hobolt 2016).

As shown in figure 11.4, the majority of Eurosceptic parties are found on the right, often on the far right. The popularity of radical right-wing Eurosceptic parties is particularly pronounced in Northern Europe creditor states: Austria, Denmark, the Netherlands, Finland and the UK. The Eurosceptic right also did very well in Italy and France, as well as in Central and Eastern Europe (CEE), Hungary, Latvia, Lithuania, Poland and Slovakia. Yet, we also saw the success of the radical left Eurosceptic parties in a handful of countries. Interestingly, the Eurosceptic left did well in the countries that experienced the most severe anti-austerity programmes and conditionality associated with their bailout packages, namely in Greece, Cyprus, Spain, Ireland and Portugal, where the parties polled an average of 24 per cent.

These MEP data clearly demonstrate the heightened appeal of Eurosceptic parties in the 2014 EP elections. Moreover, they point to important North–South and East–West differences: in the richer North, the radical right parties performed very well. In the poorer South-West (and Ireland), where the EU had imposed conditions of austerity and structural reform in return for credit, radical left parties did well; whereas there was a notable absence of radical right parties. In CEE, the Eurosceptic parties on the right generally performed well, although voter apathy was more pronounced than vocal Euroscepticism in this part of Europe.

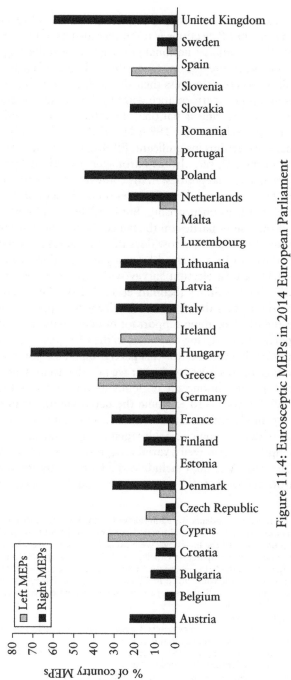

Figure 11.4: Eurosceptic MEPs in 2014 European Parliament

What explains support for Eurosceptic parties in the 2014 EP elections? Electoral behaviour in EP elections is often regarded as a 'protest vote': a protest against the incumbent national government or indeed against the direction of European integration. Since these elections remain 'second order', they allow voters to express their dissatisfaction with the political establishment and policy performance without the constraints that voters feel when they are selecting a national government (Reif and Schmitt 1980; Van der Eijk and Franklin 1996; Hix and Marsh 2007). Yet, this does not render the elections insignificant. EP elections matter, not only for policy-making in the EU, but also as barometers of citizens' preferences and as 'markers' in national politics. In the context of an economic crisis in Europe, the fact that voters endorsed parties on the fringes of the political spectrum therefore seems unsurprising. But it still leaves several questions unanswered: if the rise of parties on the fringes were a protest vote, what were voters protesting against? How does this vary across Europe?

These questions can be addressed by analysing the European Election Study (EES) 2014; a post-election survey with representative samples in each of the 28 Member States (Schmitt et al. 2015).[5] This study allows us to examine the factors that motivated citizens to support Eurosceptic parties across the EU. I examine support for both left-wing and right-wing Eurosceptic parties by analysing responses to the EES question 'how probable is it that you will ever vote for this party?' on an 11-point scale. The distinct advantage of this question is that we are able to measure support for Eurosceptic parties among *all* respondents and not just those who voted in the EP elections.[6] To examine the determinants of Eurosceptic vote choice, we firstly measure individuals' socio-economic position by including a set of demographic variables (gender, age, education,[7] occupation[8] and unemployment) as well a variable capturing individuals adversely affected by the crisis.[9] Second, I include variables that capture individual's ideological attitudes towards the government[10] and the economy.[11] Third,

---

[5] Approximately 1,100 respondents were interviewed in each EU member country, totalling 30,064 respondents. The EES 2014 was carried out by TNS Opinion between 30 May and 27 June 2014. All the interviews were carried out face to face. More information can be found here: http://europeanelectionstudies.net/european-election-studies/ees-2014-study/voter-study-2014, where the EES questionnaire can also be found.

[6] I also ran the models with vote choice in EP elections as the dependent variable (1= Eurosceptic Left/ Eurosceptic Right party) and the same explanatory variables come out as significant in these models.

[7] Age of ending full-time education.

[8] Dummies for respondents in a working-class occupation (unskilled or skilled manual labour) and in a professional/ managerial position.

[9] Loss of income and/or loss of job in the household over the last 24 months.

[10] Disapproval of 'The government's record to date'.

[11] General economic situation over the next 12 months in the country.

I capture ideology using questions on economic redistribution, immigration and combating crime versus civil liberties.[12] Finally, I include various questions that capture attitudes towards European integration[13] and EU policies on trans-national redistribution,[14] fiscal integration[15] as well as approval of EU performance during the crisis.[16] I also include a measure of (objective) knowledge of the European Union.[17]

These predictors of support are best illustrated by plotting the marginal effects that result from a multilevel linear regression model of Eurosceptic party support with random intercepts for political system. In figure 11.5, I show results from separate models for left- and right-wing Eurosceptic parties and for Western Europe – with more established party systems and longer democratic traditions – and post-Communist CEE, with less established party systems and lower salience of EU issues. The figure shows the marginal effects (min–max) of each of the significant explanatory variables on Eurosceptic party support (0–10) (holding all other variables in the model constant). The results show both striking similarities and important differences across support for Eurosceptic parties (left and right) and regions (West and CEE). Starting with the similarities, we can see that people who are economically disadvantaged are more likely to support the Eurosceptic parties: those in working-class occupations, the unemployed and those who have been adversely affected by the crisis. In other words, it is the 'losers' of European integration, and globalization, who are most attracted to Eurosceptic parties. It is also noteworthy that supporters of these parties are generally dissatisfied with the performance of both their national government and the European Union. This suggests that the Eurosceptic vote is a classic protest against the political establishment among those who feel that that mainstream parties have let them down, and those who have suffered most in the crisis.

Turning to the differences, we notice that the ideological motivations for supporting these parties vary considerably across party types and region. When it comes to left–right preferences, it is perhaps unsurprising

---

[12] Opposition to the redistribution of wealth from the rich to the poor in the country; Opposition to a restrictive policy on immigration; In favour of restricting privacy rights to combat crime.

[13] Opposition to 'European unification'.

[14] Disagreement with the statement: 'In times of crisis, it is desirable for [country] to give financial help to another European Union Member State facing severe economic and financial difficulties'.

[15] Opposition to EU authority over the EU Member States' economic and budgetary policies.

[16] Disapproval of 'The actions of the EU during the last 12 months'.

[17] A scale based on correct responses to six factual knowledge questions on the EU and the lead candidates.

259

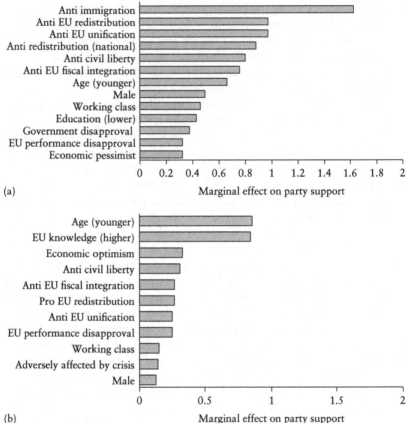

Figure 11.5: The Eurosceptic voter: (a) Support for right-wing Eurosceptic parties (West); (b) Support for right-wing Eurosceptic parties (East); (c) Support for left-wing Eurosceptic parties (West); (d) Support for left-wing Eurosceptic parties (East)

Note: Marginal effect plots based on hierarchical linear models of Eurosceptic party support
Source: European Election Studies 2014 (see Schmitt et al. 2015).

that supporters of right-wing parties in the West are opposed to both redistribution and immigration, whereas support for left-wing Eurosceptic parties in the West is driven by a contrasting set of attitudes: favouring immigration and redistribution from rich to the poor. In contrast, in CEE these ideological considerations were far less significant as a predictor

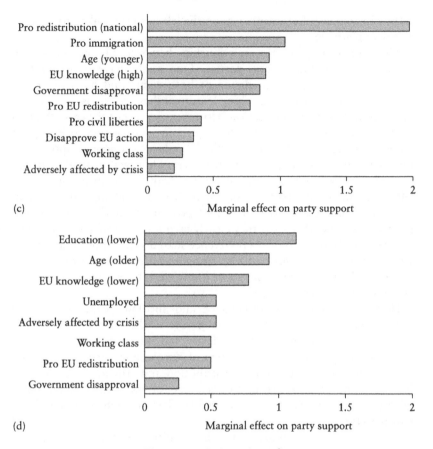

(c) Marginal effect on party support

(d) Marginal effect on party support

Figure 11.5: (continued)

of party support[18] (see figure 11.5b and 11.5d). Figure 11.5a shows that anti-immigration attitudes were the most important driver of right-wing Eurosceptic support, whereas figure 11.5c shows that pro-redistribution attitudes were the key motivation behind left-wing Eurosceptic support. This is of course also a reflection of the rhetoric and policy positions of these parties. Right-wing Eurosceptic parties in the West have often very successfully linked their Euroscepticism to more salient concerns such as immigration (from inside and outside the EU), as most recently illustrated in the British referendum on membership of the EU (see Hobolt

---

[18] But note that pro-redistribution attitudes are a significant predictor of left-wing Eurosceptic party support also in CEE.

2016). In contrast, Euroscepticism on the left has been linked to an anti-austerity platform.

Most interesting is the relationship between EU attitudes and the support for Eurosceptic parties. One might have expected that Euroscepticism is a key predictor of both right- and left-wing party support, given that a distinguishing feature of these parties is their critical position on European integration. However, that is not the case. We find a strong association between Euroscepticism – opposition to European unification and opposition to specific EU policies – among supporters of right-wing Eurosceptic parties in the West. However, general attitudes towards European integration is *not* a significant predictor of support for left-wing Eurosceptic parties, such as Syriza and Podemos. If anything, supporters of these parties are more pro-European than mainstream party supporters. Moreover, they clearly favour greater financial transfers between EU Member States (a preference shared with supporters of right-wing Eurosceptic parties in CEE). Supporters of left-wing Eurosceptic parties in the West are also far more knowledgeable about the European Union than the average voter.

Hence, far from being disengaged and anti-European, the findings suggest that the Eurosceptic left-wing vote in the West is a call for a different Europe with greater solidarity and redistribution across and within European borders. Supporters of Eurosceptic parties in the East also favour greater European redistribution and critical stances on the EU's handling of the crisis. In contrast, supporters of Eurosceptic right-wing parties in the West favour closed borders, less integration and less redistribution.

The final section discusses the implications of this mixed public response to the crisis for the legitimacy of the European Union.

Conclusion

This chapter has examined the pressure that the euro crisis has put on the European Union's already fragile democratic structure. Institutionally, it has further weakened parliamentary institutions at the national and European level by increasing the powers of the executives in the area of fiscal policy-making and by limiting the policy scope of national governments. Politically, the crisis has resulted in a decline in trust in European and national institutions and a heightened electoral appeal of Eurosceptic parties on the left and on the right in both national and European elections (see Hobolt and De Vries 2016; Hobolt and Tilley 2016). Whereas the crisis has increased the salience and debate of the European Union, it has not led to a Europe-wide debate on different policy solutions to the crisis. Instead, it is the question of 'more or less European integration', rather than different policy options for Europe, that continues to resonate most strongly. The outlook for representative politics in Europe is thus highly ambiguous. A key challenge is that the crisis has affected Member States very differently. Some Member States, notably those in receipt of bailout, have felt the crisis most acutely not only economically, but also in terms of the constraints imposed on them by the European Union. Other Member States, notably in Northern Europe, have retained far greater autonomy in terms of fiscal policy-making, but are concerned about the financial burden of bailing out other Member States as well as intra-EU immigration, as demonstrated most starkly in the 2016 British referendum on membership.

These differences are also reflected in in the divergent public responses to the crisis. A decline in trust in the European Union can be found across the EU; however, the preferred solutions are very different. Inside the eurozone, support for a single currency has remained high whereas it has plummeted outside the eurozone. Yet, North–South divisions are increasing inside the euro area. Support for the EU has always rested in large part on the idea that European integration would bring about greater prosperity for all its Member States rather than substantial redistribution between Member States. The crisis has called this basic premise into question not only due to the severity of the economic downturn, but because of the evident need for financial support, at least in the short term, for some Member States. The electoral appeal of Eurosceptic parties in the North calling for less solidarity, contrasted with the demand for more solidarity by parties in the South starkly illustrates the difficulty of any European reforms that demand closer fiscal integration and transfers between Member States.

The decrease in trust in the EU and the support for the Eurosceptic parties is not going to transform, or even undermine, policy-making in the European Union in the short term. However, these developments have deeply affected a number of national political systems, by giving radical parties an important foothold and by signalling to governments that many voters wanted a different direction for Europe. In Britain, the success of the United Kingdom Independence Party in European elections contributed to the decision of the Conservative Party to hold a referendum on Britain's continued membership of the EU that led to the decision to leave the EU (Hobolt 2016). In Greece, people's discontent with their mainstream parties and the austerity imposed by the Troika led to the election of a Syriza-led government, which complicated negotiations with EU partners. In the former case, discontent was driven by a desire for *less* pan-European redistribution and immigration, whereas in the latter case, voters wanted *more* European redistribution and solidarity. The fact that the visions for reform of the EU differ so radically across (and within) nations point to the challenges ahead when it comes to finding common solutions for Europe. More than ever, Europe needs to find common solutions to shared economic, geopolitical and policy problems, yet governments are also increasingly reliant on public legitimacy to implement such solutions.

References

Bellucci, P., Costa Lobo, M. and Lewis-Beck, M.S. (2012) Economic crisis and elections: the European periphery. *Electoral Studies* 31(3): 469–71.

Cramme, O. and Hobolt, S.B. (eds) (2014) *Democratic Politics in a European Union under Stress*. Oxford: Oxford University Press.

De Grauwe, P. (2011) Managing a fragile eurozone. *CESifo Forum* 12(2): 40ä5.

De Grauwe, P. (2013) *The Economics of Monetary Union*, 9th edn. Oxford: Oxford University Press.

De Vries, C.E. (2007) Sleeping giant: fact or fairytale? How European integration affects national elections. *European Union Politics* 8(3): 363–85.

De Vries, C.E., Van der Brug, W., Van Egmond, M.H. and Van der Eijk, C. (2011) Individual and contextual variation in EU issue voting: the role of political information. *Electoral Studies* 30(1): 16–28.

De Witte, F. and Dawson, M. (2013) Constitutional balance in the EU after the euro-crisis. *Modern Law Review* 76(5): 817–44.

Føllesdal, A. and Hix, S. (2006) Why there is a democratic deficit in the EU: a response to Majone and Moravcsik. *Journal of Common Market Studies* 44(3): 533–62.

Habermas, J. (2012) *The Crisis of the European Union: A Response*. Cambridge: Polity.

Halikiopoulou, D., Nanou, K. and Vaslopoulou, S. (2012) The paradox of nationalism: the common denominator of radical right and radical left euro-scepticism. *European Journal of Political Research* 51(4): 504–39.

Harteveld, E., De Vries, C.E. and Van der Meer, T. (2013) In Europe we trust? Exploring three logics of trust in the European Union. *European Union Politics* 14(4): 542–65.

Hix, S. (2008) *What's Wrong with the European Union and How to Fix It*. Cambridge: Polity.

Hix, S. (2014) Democratizing a macroeconomic union in Europe. In Cramme, O. and Hobolt, S.B. (eds) *Democratic Politics in a European Union under Stress*. Oxford: Oxford University Press, pp. 180–98.

Hix, S. and Høyland, B. (2011) *The Political System of the European Union*, 3rd edn. Basingstoke: Palgrave Macmillan.

Hix, S. and Marsh M. (2007) Punishment or protest? Understanding European Parliament elections. *The Journal of Politics* 69(2): 495–510.

Hix, S., Noury, A. and Roland, G. (2007) *Democratic Politics in the European Parliament*. Cambridge: Cambridge University Press.

Hobolt, S.B. (2014a) Public attitudes towards the euro crisis. In Cramme, O. and Hobolt, S.B. (eds) *Democratic Politics in a European Union under Stress.* Oxford: Oxford University Press, pp. 48–66.

Hobolt, S.B. (2014b) A vote for the President? The role of Spitzenkandidaten in the 2014 European Parliament elections. *Journal of European Public Policy* 21(10): 1528–40.

Hobolt, S.B. (2016) The Brexit vote: a divided nation, a divided continent. *Journal of European Public Policy* 23(9): 1259–77.

Hobolt, S.B. and De Vries, C.E. (2016) Turning against the union? The impact of the crisis on the eurosceptic vote in the 2014 European Parliament elections. *Electoral Studies* 44: 504–14.

Hobolt, S.B. and Leblond, P. (2013) Economic insecurity and support for the euro. In Bermeo, N. and Bartels, L. (eds) *Mass Politics in Tough Times: Opinions, Votes and Protest in the Great Recession.* New York: Oxford University Press.

Hobolt, S.B. and Spoon, J-J. (2012) Motivating the European voter: parties, issues and campaigns in European Parliament elections. *European Journal of Political Research* 51(6): 701–27.

Hobolt, S.B. and Tilley, J. (2014) *Blaming Europe? Responsibility without Accountability in the European Union.* Oxford: Oxford University Press.

Hobolt, S.B. and Tilley, J. (2016) Fleeing the centre: the rise of challenger parties in the aftermath of the euro crisis. *West European Politics* 39(5): 971–1010.

Hobolt, S.B., Spoon, J-J. and Tilley, J. (2009) A vote against Europe? Explaining defection at the 1999 and 2004 European Parliament elections. *British Journal of Political Science* 39(1): 93–115.

Hooghe, L. and Marks, G. (2009) Postfunctionalism: a postfunctionalist theory of European integration: from permissive consensus to constraining dissensus. *British Journal of Political Science* 39(1): 1–23.

Kriesi, H. and Grande, E. (2014) Political debate in a polarising union. In Cramme, O. and Hobolt, S.B. (eds) *Democratic Politics in a European Union under Stress.* Oxford: Oxford University Press, pp. 67–86.

Laffan, B. (2014) Testing times: the growing primacy of responsibility in the euro area. *West European Politics* 37(2): 270–87.

Lindberg, L. and Scheingold, S. (1970) *Europe's Would-Be Polity.* Englewood Cliffs, NJ: Prentice-Hall.

Lobo, M.C. and Lewis-Beck, M.S. (2012) The integration hypothesis: how the European Union shapes economic voting. *Electoral Studies* 31(3): 522–8.

Magalhaes, P. (2014) The elections of the Great Recession in Portugal: performance voting under blurred responsibility for the economy. *Journal of Elections, Public Opinion and Parties* 24(2): 180–202.

Mair, P. and Mudde, C. (1998) The party family and its study. *Annual Review of Political Science* 1: 211–29.

Majone, G. (1996) *Regulating Europe.* London: Routledge.

Majone, G. (2012) Rethinking European integration after the debt crisis. University College London, The European Institute, Working Paper No. 3.

Mudde, C. (2007) *The Populist Radical Right in Europe.* Cambridge: Cambridge University Press.

Reif, K. and Schmitt, H. (1980) Nine second-order national elections – a conceptual framework for the analysis of European election results. *European Journal for Political Research* 8(1): 3–44.

Rittberger, B. (2005) *Building Europe's Parliament: Democratic Representation Beyond the Nation State*. Oxford: Oxford University Press.

Scharpf, F. (2014) Political legitimacy in a non-optimal currency area. In Cramme, O. and Hobolt, S.B. (eds) *Democratic Politics in a European Union under Stress*. Oxford: Oxford University Press, pp. 19–47.

Schmitt, H. (2005) The European Parliament elections of June 2004: still second-order? *West European Politics* 28(3): 650–79.

Schmitt, H., Hobolt, S.B., Popa, S.A. and Teperoglou, E. (2015) *European Parliament Election Study 2014, Voter Study*. Cologne: GESIS Data Archive. ZA5160 Data file Version 1.0.0, doi:10.4232/1.5160.

Schmitter, P.C. (2000) *How to Democratize the European Union . . . and Why Bother?* Lanham, MD: Rowman & Littlefield.

Taggart, P. and Szczerbiak, A. (2004) Contemporary euroscepticism in the party systems of the EU candidate states of central and eastern Europe. *European Journal of Political Research* 43(1): 1–27.

Treib, O. (2014) The voter says no, but nobody listens: causes and consequences of the eurosceptic vote in the 2014 European elections. *Journal of European Public Policy* (21)10: 1541–54.

Van der Eijk, C. and Franklin, M. (1996) *Choosing Europe? The European Electorate and National Politics in the Face of Union*. Ann Arbor, MI: University of Michigan Press.

White, J. (2014) Politicising Europe: the challenge of executive discretion. In O. Cramme, O. and Hobolt, S.B. (eds) *Democratic Politics in a European Union under Stress*. Oxford: Oxford University Press, pp. 87–102.

Appendix

Table 11.1 Eurosceptic parties in the 2014 European Parliament elections

Country	Parties[a]	Eurosceptic Left vote %	MEPs	Eurosceptic Right vote %	MEPs
Austria	Freedom Party [R], EUstop [R], Coalition for another Europe [L]	2.1	0	22.5	4
Belgium	Vlaams Belang [R]; PTB-GO! [L]	2.0	0	4.3	1
Bulgaria	VMRO-BND/Bulgaria without Censorship [R][b], National Front [R], ATAKA [R]	—	—	16.7	2
Croatia	Croatian Party of Rights [R]	—	—	c	1
Cyprus	Progressive Party of Working People [L]; ELAM [R]	27.0	2	2.7	0
Czech Republic	Communist Party [L]; Party of Free Citizens [R]; Dawn of Direct Democracy [R]	11.0	3	8.4	1
Denmark	Danish People's Party [R]; People's Movement against the EU [L]	8.1	1	26.6	4
Estonia	Conservative People's Party of Estonia [R]	—	—	4.0	0
Finland	Finns Party [R]	—	—	12.9	2
France	National Front [R]; Left Front [L]; France Arise [R]	6.3	3	28.7	23
Germany	Alternative for Germany [R]; Left Party [L]; National Democratic Party [R]	7.4	7	8.1	8
Greece	Syriza [L]; Golden Dawn [R]; KKE [L]; ANEL [R]; Popular Orthodox Rally [R]	32.7	8	15.5	4
Hungary	Fidesz [R]; JOBBIK [R]	—	—	66.1	15
Ireland	Sinn Fein [L]	19.5	3	—	—
Italy	Five Star Movement [R][c]; Northern League [R]; The Other Europe with Tsipras [L]	4.0	3	27.3	22

Table 11.1   (continued)

Country	Parties[a]	Eurosceptic Left vote %	MEPs	Eurosceptic Right vote %	MEPs
Latvia	National Alliance [R]; Union of Greens and Farmers [R]	—	—	22.5	2
Lithuania	Order and Justice [R]; LLRA [R]	—	—	22.3	3
Luxembourg	Alternative for Democratic Reform [R]	—	—	7.5	0
Malta	—	—	—	—	—
Netherlands	Freedom Party [R]; Socialist Party [L]; CU-SGP [R]	9.6	2	21.0	6
Poland	Law and Justice [R]; Congress of the New Right [R]; United Poland [R]; Right Wing of the Republic [R]	—	—	42.9	23
Portugal	United Democratic Coalition [L]; Left Bloc [L]	18.6	4	—	—
Romania	People's Party – Dan Diaconescu [L]; Greater Romania Party [R]	3.7	0	2.7	0
Slovakia	Ordinary People and Independent Personalities [R]; Nova [R]; Freedom and Solidarity [R]; Slovak National Party [R]	—	—	24.6	3
Slovenia	United Left [L]; Slovenian National Party [R]	5.5	0	4.0	0
Spain	United Left [L]; Podemos [L]; The Peoples Decide [L]	20.1	12	—	—
Sweden	Sweden Democrats [R]; Left Party [L]	6.3	1	9.7	2
UK	UKIP [R]; Conservative Party [R]; Sinn Fein [L]; Democratic Unionist Party [R]	0.7	1	50.6	44
Total MEPs			50		170

Notes:

[a] Only parties with more than 2 per cent of the national vote or 1 MEP have been included. L = Left, R = Right.

[b] VMRO-BND formed a coalition with Bulgaria Without Censorship, a soft Eurosceptic party, and other smaller parties, and their two MEPs joined the Eurosceptic ECR Group.

[c] Croatian Party of Rights dr. Ante Starčević (HPS AS) formed an electoral alliance with three other parties. The HSP AS member sits in the ECR group, whereas the other coalition members sit in the EPP Group. The coalition received 41 per cent of the votes.

Chapter 12

Narratives of Responsibility: German Politics in the Greek Debt Crisis

Claus Offe

To set the stage for an analysis of the role of Germany in the still ongoing and unsettled debt crisis of the eurozone, let me start with a brief review of the phenomenon known as the euro. The euro is the monetary system of the European Union. It is a regime that, together with the Stability and Growth Pact and various subsequently adopted tools to control fiscal policies and the viability of the banking system of Member States, subjects them to a unitary framework of rules with which their monetary, fiscal and trade policies must comply and which also indirectly affects the leeway of their social policies. By joining the Union, all Member States (with the now no longer relevant exception of the UK) have committed themselves to adopting the single currency at some point or to put their national currency into a fixed exchange rate with the euro, as is the case with Denmark. This commitment to the single currency is binding on all members of the group that have adopted the euro, the eurogroup, regardless of the vast differences in their political and institutional traditions, levels of economic development and performance, and economic cultures.

The euro as an ideology

The euro is also what in the Marxist tradition is called an 'ideology': a set of tendentiously mistaken perceptions of socio-economic realities together with false hopes and promises suggested by the appearances these realities bring forth. As is the case with all ideology, its interested proponents, i.e. those who stand to benefit from the ideology being near-universally accepted as a valid belief system, must face the risk of a moment of truth when the constitutive misperceptions become manifest

269

and associated hopes frustrated. For a long time prior to the adoption of the euro regime, experts from outside of the EU, especially from representatives from all schools of economic thought in the US, have voiced serious yet unheeded warnings that this moment would come sooner rather than later.

What were the promises and hopes, invoked by soothing neologisms of euro speech such as 'inclusion', 'cohesion', the 'European Social Model' and the 'knowledge-based economy', which were invested in the single currency? One guiding idea was that of a 'level playing field' that would be created by the pressure applied by the monetary regime on the relatively backward economies in the EU. The euro was thought of as a wholesome modernizing force that would both incentivize and allow productivity laggards, together with transfers they were granted from EU structural funds (less than 1 per cent of the EU budget), to improve their level of economic performance so as to gradually approximate the level of the most advanced European economies. It was also thought to be a device to disempower the harsh stability regime that the German Bundesbank had executed over the economy of Europe and to replace it with a more employment-friendly alternative. The hoped-for modernization effect would be achieved by tying the hands of productivity laggards: as long as countries had national currencies and could run their national monetary policies, they were able to adjust to trade imbalances resulting from their competitive disadvantages by the often-used tool of lowering the external value of their currency, thus making exports cheaper and imports more costly. In other words, they could adjust to and live with inferior levels of productivity by modifying the external value of their currencies. Once they adopt the single currency, this option is precluded. The only way to maintain or even increase competitiveness in international trade becomes that of switching from external devaluation to 'internal' devaluation, meaning the cutting of state expenditures and labour costs. The key economic variable here is that of *unit costs of labour*, which is a measure of economic performance that relates labour *costs* to labour *productivity*. The other indicator of how well a national economy performs is the ratio of sovereign debt to GDP. As the increase in labour productivity presupposes private and public investment (an adequate volume of which is typically unavailable in the short run), the former – wages, pensions, public services – are typically targeted as the action parameter of policies enhancing competitiveness, which also, in addition to decimating overall demand, typically exacerbates domestic political conflict and jeopardizes political stability. Also, the anticipation of declining demand may well undermine medium-term investment. Due to these causal factors, the single currency can make countries

270

economically defenceless within the radically 'open' economy of the EU and its institutionalized factor mobility; this is the plain opposite of a 'levelling' of the playing field of trade.

As far as national economies such as Germany with their more advanced level of productivity (as well as an institutionalized system of wage moderation) are concerned, the single currency tends to serve their *further* relative advancement. As long as they operate with their national currency, they are subject to a mechanism of automatic punishment from which they are freed under the single currency. For as a country increases its export surplus, the external value of its national currency will appreciate, exported goods become more expensive, foreign sales of exported goods stagnate or decline, and the export surplus becomes self-limiting. Yet not so in the case of exports that are paid for in euro, given the fact that not every member of the eurogroup runs a current account surplus in its trade with the world outside the eurozone. Those who do not will indirectly help the high export performers to escape from the self-limiting effect and allow them to win further export surplus (and the attendant levels of domestic employment and economic growth) that they could never achieve on the basis of their own domestic currency. Again, the euro sets in motion a dynamic that, in the absence of adequately sized compensatory counter-action, results in an ever more tilted, rather than level, playing field: the single currency regime favours highly competitive export-intensive economies and punishes productivity and competitiveness laggards.

A second promise of the single currency was the prospect of the playing field not just becoming more level but as a whole *rising* on a scale of prosperity benefiting all members. This optimistic assumption was based on the expectation that a fully integrated market of some 500 million people with the four freedoms of movement (persons, labour, capital, services) in place and tariffs as well as non-tariff trade barriers regulated away would yield a universally beneficial economic 'integration dividend'. As market size increases, so do the economies of scale to be reaped. With an increasing division of labour and specialization among national economies, border crossing chains of production, also facilitated by the Schengen open borders regime, would further enhance productivity. The role of the common currency in this scenario would be that of a guarantor of fixed exchange rates, or rather an arrangement that makes exchange rates obsolete within the eurozone, and hence costs and prices more reliably calculable. While some of this reasoning has become true and while there certainly has been an overall integration dividend (however hard it is to quantify), its distribution has been highly uneven in both space and time. In the middle of the 2010s, the EU has barely recovered from the Great Recession of 2008 and reached, on average, its pre-2008 level of GDP, but overall growth rates continue to decline, the distance between prosperous and backward economic regions within the EU is increasing (as is the income inequality within most Member States) and vigorous new impulses are neither in sight nor deemed likely, according to the growing number of expert voices forecasting an age of 'secular stagnation' (Gordon 2016). Real demand in the eurozone was 2 per cent lower in 2016 than it was in 2008, and total savings by far exceed total investment in the 'real' economy, a phenomenon now commonly referred to as 'savings glut'. These sobering trends all have dismal implications for the tax base of national governments and the prospects of coping with sovereign debt, for the employment situation, and for the stability of the eurozone banking system that suffers from completely unsustainable burdens of non-performing loans.[1]

The two broken promises of the euro currency regime – its failure to create a level playing field and its failure to advance evenly distributed prosperity gains – have deeply divided the countries and regions of the eurozone into camps of losers and winners. The clearest case of the former camp is Greece and of the latter Germany. The interaction between the two is hence the focus of the present chapter.

A third idea associated with the adoption of the euro was that, once established, it would engender a level of confidence of all sides involved – national governments, banks, investors, international commerce, consumers – that would make it permanent and practically irreversible. Irreversible the currency regime has in fact become, not thanks to its satisfactory performance and fulfilled expectations, but because of the incalculable, at any rate giant and prohibitive risks of any serious move to abandon it, be it by individual Member States or the currency area as a whole. There is neither an established and agreed-upon pathway by which a eurozone Member State could exit or be expelled from the eurozone. Also, the complexities of implementing an exit of one country, to say nothing about the abolition of the entire currency regime of the euro, are likely to be immensely time-consuming (as the much easier case of Brexit might help to illustrate) and at the same time calling for an overnight *fait accompli* that is needed to forestall speculative moves. Moreover, who would seriously (as opposed to a mere trope of populist propaganda) opt for exiting from the common currency? Probably not the losers of the regime: they would have to devalue their new national currency in order to regain competitiveness while their burden

---

[1] This burden is very unequally distributed, with roughly a third of it (€360 billion) being shared by the Italian banking system at the end of 2016.

of euro-designated debt would become even heavier as a consequence; also, they would forgo the economic advantages of membership mentioned above. If one member were to exit 'voluntarily', others would be desperate to convince (including pay) that member to desist from doing so as the spillover effects on others, as mediated by speculative moves of banks, would be seen as potentially pernicious in their adverse consequences. And neither would the winners such as Germany consider leaving the eurozone due to the indirect export subsidies they obtain from membership. Thus it seems safe to conclude that the euro is going to stay, if primarily because members are literally trapped in the historically unprecedented arrangement of nineteen states no longer having a central bank of their own while one central bank, the ECB, has no corresponding federal state (yet) (Offe 2016).

Critics of the euro regime have convincingly argued that the sequence taken in building it is exactly the inverse of what a rational designer of monetary integration would have recommended. Such a designer would arguably have started with the integration of fiscal policies of Member States which would have ended in the installation of a European ministry of finance endowed with its own competencies of taxing, spending and borrowing under authorization of the European Parliament. After such integrated budget is established, it could be used to conduct economic and social policies aimed at making the EU fit for the perfectly foreseeable risks of monetary integration. And only after such fitness is assured would the time be ripe for adopting a common currency. Fiscal, economic and social policy competencies lodged at the level of the EU are an indispensable precondition for making true what in their absence remains a frivolous assumption – the assumption that 'one size fits all' and that all eurozone Member States can equally function under a monetary regime that stipulates one and the same *exchange rate*, as well as one and the same *interest rate* for all. As long as the unit costs of labour are not roughly the same among participating economies, the ones with the more favourable cost structure will push others into a structural current account deficit and a rising indebtedness against which they are defenceless. This is the basis of German economic power: unions' wage moderation, the decline of multi-employer wage bargaining and the tight integration of German industry with low-wage CEE countries plus its above-average labour productivity have together bestowed an advantage[2] to the German economy that its players enjoy at the expense

---

[2] The evidence of this advantage is breathtaking indeed: 'Germany's total export trade value nearly tripled between 2000 and 2007. Germany's trade surplus with the rest of the EU grew from €46.4 billion to €126.5 billion during those seven years. Germany's bilateral trade surpluses with the peripheral countries are especially revealing: between

of most other euro economies, particularly the countries of the southern periphery (Kundnani 2014). This advantage has helped to boost the growth and employment performance of the German economy, causing as a further structural divide a massive migration of skilled manpower ('brain drain') from the periphery to Germany, which further undermines prospects of economic recovery of the former.

Seen in this perspective, the euro can be described as a premature and institutionally unembedded creation, the control of which is left in the entirely unaccountable hands of the ECB leadership. On top of the economic damage and inequities it has caused, the euro currency regime had political repercussions which in a number of countries, both in the loser camp and the winner camp, have fundamentally reshaped the configuration of forces at the levels of parties, movements and voter preferences. The questions being asked in protest and with growing mobilization are reciprocal ones. The winners ask why 'we' should share parts of our prosperity gains with the losers, while the latter insist that the former must practise more 'solidarity' and burden sharing. Both are united, however, in their protest and opposition against politically inaccessible European institutions, the Commission and the ECB, who are held responsible for the unfair and unsustainable distribution of gains and burdens. Yet both sides are in agreement, if mostly only tacitly so and contrary to much anti-euro sloganeering in public, that the outright dismantling (rather than fixing) of the currency regime and the wider institutional framework of the euro group and EU would amount to a giant negative-sum game that would severely hurt all participants. And both sides agree that national 'sovereignty' must be reclaimed from 'Brussels'.

Arguably a further factor working in the same direction of maintaining high levels of German export surpluses yet not directly related to the monetary regime is a consistently export-promoting foreign policy that focuses on East Asia (China) and North America, as well as a stability-obsessed neo-mercantilist fiscal policy that minimizes stimuli for ailing European economies abroad and, in addition, implies

2000 and 2007, Greece's annual trade deficit with Germany nearly doubled, from €3 billion to €5.5 billion; Italy's more than doubled, from €9.6 billion to €19.6 billion; Spain's well over doubled, from €11 billion to €27.2 billion; and Portugal's more than quadrupled, from €1 billion to €4.2 billion. German banks played an important role in supplying the credit that drove wage increases in peripheral eurozone countries like Greece, which in turn produced this divergence in competitiveness and trade surpluses between Germany and these same eurozone members' (https://en.wikipedia.org/wiki/Greek_government-debt_crisis#cite_note-Bloom_edit-316). It must also be noted that taking out credit in these countries was irresistibly cheap, as, with the nominal interest rate being the same everywhere, the real interest rate declined with the higher rate of inflation prevailing in the countries of the periphery.

deficient infrastructure investment at home. Observers like Kundnani have seen in recent German foreign policy shifts a tendency to turn away from both European and Atlantic commitments in favour of a foreign and trade policy seeking to develop commercial ties to whatever 'Gestaltungsmächte' ('shaping powers' or 'powerful players') may be available, thereby converting its foreign and trade policy from the proclaimed ideal of the country's foreign policy being that of a 'civilian' and 'normative' power into an indiscriminate 'policy of no red lines'. 'Germany's objectives seemed to narrow from the civilization of international relations to the pursuit of its own prosperity' (Kundnani 2014: 82, 85). German governments develop and cultivate trade relations with virtually anyone who is ready to buy German cars (or tanks). Kundnani portrays a normatively hollowed out export-driven foreign policy that is based on 'economic nationalism', 'export nationalism', shaping a self-image of Germans as 'export champions' (achieving, after all, no less than *twice* the volume of exports relative to GDP compared to China) (Kundnani 2014: 86, 90).

Moments of truth

A moment of truth occurred in the summer of 2015 when the eurozone members had to rescue Greece from imminent insolvency, the possible spillover effects of which were deemed a severe threat to the entire euro currency area. If governments are no longer able to obtain affordable credit which they need in order to fulfil their contractual obligations to employees, suppliers and creditors, and/or if banks can no longer pay by their own means what they owe their depositors, a stage of financial precariousness is reached in which the viability of the currency as a whole is at stake. What indisputably needs to be done is to refinance the state and recapitalize banks. A state in such situation faces the death of its politics. If in a TINA situation ('there is no alternative'; in this case, to submitting to externally set bailout conditions) the choice of actionable policies is reduced to one, politics is reduced to zero. If that happens, a country is disowned of its politics.

Greece's turbulent summer of 2015 provides compelling evidence of how the European institutions have used their power to nullify the results of a democratic political process in Greece. Here is a brief recapitulation of the time line (The Guardian 2015a). On 25 June, the 'Troika' (the supervisory body consisting of representatives of the ECB, the IMF and the European Commission, installed after the adoption of the first Greek bailout programme of 2010) specified its harsh austerity conditions for a renewed (third) Greek bailout programme. In mid-2015, the country had arrived at a truly dismal economic situation, unparalleled in any advanced country during peace time: GDP was down 25 per cent since 2010, unemployment averaged at 26 per cent (with a large part of the unemployed receiving no unemployment and health insurance benefits whatsoever), wages were down by 38 per cent and pensions by 45 per cent. Some 32 per cent of the population were living below the poverty line and the critical ratio of sovereign debt to GDP was approaching 180 per cent. The solvency of Greek banks was threatened by huge amounts of non-performing loans extended to both the public and the private sector (Minenna 2015).[3]

On 27 June, prime minister Tsipras, bravely ignoring the 'death of politics' that had occurred already in his country, called a referendum on the bailout conditions, which was held on 5 July. Sixty-two per cent of voters rejected those conditions as overburdening and unsustainable. On 8 July, Tsipras applied for (by now urgently needed) emergency loans from the European Stability Fund. Contrary to the vote of more than three-fifths of voters, Tsipras had no option but to accept the terms of a third bailout package during the decisive negotiations that took place for 17 hours in the eurogroup on the night of 12 July in Brussels. This package provided for conditions which are even considerably *harsher* than those rejected by Greeks in the referendum. They stipulated further spending cuts (among other things concerning pensions), the raising of indirect taxes designed to achieve a 'primary' budget (the budget net of debt service) surplus of 3.5 per cent of GDP by 2018, large-scale privatization of state-owned assets as well as a detailed schedule specifying which liberalizing reform legislation must pass the Greek parliament within days or weeks, respectively (The Guardian 2015b; European Commission 2015). Moreover, the Greek government 'commits to consult and agree with the European Commission' on every step of this legislative agenda, practically handing over Greek law-making powers to a non-elected body in Brussels. Jürgen Habermas rightly speaks of this exercise of raw power as a 'de facto relegation of a Member State to the status of a protectorate [that] openly contradicts the democratic principles of the European Union' (Oltermann 2015). The two components of this blackmail operation were (a) the Commission dictating the legislative agenda *and decisions* of the Greek parliament (which was given

The following section uses materials from the introductory chapter of Offe and Preuss (2016).

[3] 'According to some estimates, there are around 320,000 families in Greece that are not paying down their mortgages and obviously these bad loans are dead weights for the banking system' (Minenna 2015).

two days to pass the required legislation!) by (b) forcing prime minister Tsipras to perform a clear U-turn[4] regarding the majority will the Greek electorate had expressed – and Tsipras had strongly advocated – just a week prior to the negotiations of 12 July. 'Ten days after 62 per cent of the voters rejected the terms of a harsh bailout package, the country's parliament voted with clenched teeth for an even tougher set of reforms' (The Economist 2015).

How could this brutal act of overpowering the declared will of the Greek people succeed? When submitting to *power* (as opposed to force or coercion), the less powerful party in a conflict makes a *choice* opting for the 'lesser evil' among two or more alternatives which were presented to it by the more powerful player. The latter exploits a condition of asymmetrical dependency for serving its own interests: trivially, Greece depends more strongly on the ECB and the other eurogroup members than these depend on Greece. The logic of the situation was the following: as Greece needed to obtain financial assistance from the EU in order to prevent an imminent meltdown of its banking sector (and, as a consequence, its entire economy), the country's population and its government were given the choice between being politically expropriated (deprived of the 'ownership' of even its legislative agenda, let alone sovereignty) and being instantaneously plunged into an economic disaster. 'Germany wants Greece to choose between economic collapse and leaving the eurozone' (Eichengreen 2015). Or, as prime minister Tsipras put it in the debate of the Greek parliament on 15 July 2015, Greeks had been given a choice between 'waging an unfair battle' and 'handing in their weapons' (The Economist 2015). Yet the negotiators on the other side of the bargaining table had also to worry about the consequences of the latter alternative being realized, that of Greece leaving the currency area, an alternative which left Greece with some minimal leverage.

These worries of eurogroup negotiators were twofold. On the one side, the appearance and subsequent reputational and political damage was to be avoided that negative economic consequences for Greece were caused by the pressure exercised by the majority of eurozone members that sided with Germany (Reuters 2015).[5] As the *Frankfurter Allgemeine Zeitung* (FAZ) warned: 'from the German perspective it is extremely important,

---

[4] ... for the performing of which he was then widely ridiculed in the German media as an unreliable and erratic character!

[5] After the 17 hours of negotiations of 12–13 July, Italian prime minister Renzi is reported by Reuters news agency to have angrily remarked about the behaviour of German negotiators: 'Enough is enough! The German government has to compromise and not humiliate Athens. Humiliating a European partner after Greece has given up on just about everything is unthinkable' (Reuters 2015).

and it is to be feared more than anything else, not to be seen at the end of the day as the one who has kicked Greece out of the eurozone' [author's translation] (2015a: 22). Whatever cruelty was to be performed, the hands of its perpetrator must be seen as free of blood. On the other side, a 'Grexit' (or, even more so, a 'Graccident' in the form of an unregulated implosion of the Greek banking system and economy with all its unpredictable spillover effects) might have consequences that affected, through contagion or a domino effect, other members of the eurozone, thus bringing the entire euro system into jeopardy – an outcome and potential self-inflicted economic damage for which the protagonists of a tough approach to the bailout conditions would have had to anticipate blame. Given this dilemma, and also given the fact that the vast and deepening problems of the Greek economy could not possibly be solved, for legal reasons and because of the statutory irreversibility of the common currency,[6] by simply expelling the country from the eurozone, the actual pressure used against the Greek negotiators had to be *disguised* so as to make the deal look like a voluntary agreement.

It is these two worries that appear to have motivated the German minister of finance to draft and circulate among eurogroup negotiators (as well as leaking to the media), one day prior to the negotiations scheduled for the evening of 12 July, the unprecedented suggestion to resolve on a procedure of a 'temporary Grexit', i.e. the creation of an option for Greece to leave the common currency zone for a period of five (or more) years with the (entirely unrealistic) option of re-entry at a later point (FAZ 2015b). Greece's making use of this option was actually incentivized in Schäuble's proposal so as to make it tempting and to create the appearance of a completely voluntary and worthwhile move. This was done by the promise attached to it of technical, humanitarian and other assistance, as well as other gestures of 'generosity' extended to the country if only it accepted the leave offered to it. Yet had the Greek government actually accepted this poisoned chalice, it would have instantaneously relieved Schäuble and the other negotiators of the two above worries: it would have endorsed the appearance of German generosity, confirmed the narrative of a *voluntary* exit, and insulated the euro system as a whole from the Greek crisis and the menace of spillover effects. Moreover, it would have taught a lesson to whomever might be tempted to emulate the Greek mistake of 'excessive' indebtedness as well as that of voting into office a 'radical' leftist government. It would also

---

[6] The Treaties do not provide for a procedure that allows a country to leave the eurozone without leaving the EU altogether according to Art. 50 TEU. The initiative for the latter step must be taken by the country that wishes to leave, not by the remaining members of the EU.

278

have camouflaged the exercise of power, making its outcome appear as a freely adopted mutual agreement. Yet it would also have been an act, on the part of the Greek authorities, of causing near-suicidal damage to their country, for it would have cut the country off from European structural funds (worth transfers of €5 billion p.a.) and it would have necessitated the adoption of a heavily devalued national currency with the effect of substantially increasing the country's – euro-denominated and hence entirely unsustainable – debt burden. Given this configuration of alternatives, the choice Greek negotiators made was understandably and rationally the option of submitting to the power of blackmail.

In retrospect, this outcome is criticized on two counts: for being *illegitimate* as to its mode of coming into being and for being *ineffective* concerning its promise to solve the problems of the Greek economic, fiscal and debt crises in any durable fashion. As to its legitimacy (its capacity to oblige compliance on normative grounds, that is), the following objections continue to be raised (Truth Committee on Public Debt 2014, 2015). In response to its request for 'stability support' addressed to the European Stability Mechanism on 8 July, the Greek government was offered a third 'Memorandum of Understanding' (MoU) that specified on its 32 pages no less than 48 legislative measures the Greek authorities would have to adopt by which month and year during the period of 2015–17. This 'extraordinarily detailed list' (The Guardian 2015b) implied that legislative powers in the areas of fiscal policy, the financial system, economic policy (including matters such as the mandatory opening hours of milk and bread stores), and the modernization of all major branches of public administration were practically to be ceded to the Commission and agencies (such as the International Labor Office and the OECD) the Commission has endowed in the Memorandum with advisory and supervisory roles. In general, it was stated that the Greek government must 'commit to consult and agree with the European Commission . . . on all actions relevant for the achievement of the objectives of the Memorandum . . . before these are finalized and legally adopted' (European Commission 2015: 4).

Unsparingly, this wholesale usurpation of Greek law-making authorities by EU institutions met with the objection, in Greece itself and far beyond, that it amounts to a massive violation of the democratic principles on which the EU is supposedly built. Moreover, the politically non-accountable EU agencies who have authored the list of conditions that Greece must fulfil in exchange for a loan of €86 billion for a period of three years vindicate themselves, by implication, with the paternalistic wisdom of having established two interrelated truths. First, the truth that the fully compliant implementation of the letter of the MoU will

279

be compatible with *political* stability within Greece; second, that such implementation will be conducive to the *economic* recovery of Greece and its social, economic and fiscal viability. Both of these propositions, however, are being vehemently contested, and for good reasons.

As to the first, it relates to the issue of legitimacy. The MoU is criticized for being in outright violation of the Greek people's sovereignty and self-determination. Given the political will expressed in the referendum of 2 July, it is deemed 'inconceivable that any circumvention of the referendum outcome can ever be "in the interest of the Greek people"' (Truth Committee on Public Debt 2015: 7). Moreover, an implied violation of human rights (such as the right to universally affordable health services) is seen by critics in the specification of the MoU concerning fees to be collected by hospitals. Legitimacy complaints have also been raised concerning the attempted blackmail stemming from members of the ECB Governing Council concerning a discontinuation of the ECB's emergency assistance as well as the threats of a 'temporary Grexit' coming from the German minister of finance. At a level of principle, the question is being raised as to why, in case a debtor turns out to be insolvent and the respective loan 'non-performing', the problem must be solved at the expense of the *debtor*, while the *creditor* (private banks who obviously have entered into a risky lending transaction while having been given reasons to anticipate that they would be bailed out at a third party's expense) does not suffer any damage. To the extent this argument from fairness is valid, it would result in a justified demand for debt repudiation.

Finally, as to the issues of effectiveness, the assumed conduciveness of legislative measures imposed upon Greece (austerity, deregulation, privatization of state-owned assets) to the economic recovery of the country is wide open to question. Being the third MoU since 2010, one might have expected the Commission and its experts to have learned from the plain and evident counterproductivity of the two previous editions of a trade of loans for austerity measures and sacrifice of sovereignty. The above-quoted indicators of the condition the Greek economy found itself in in 2015 should have provided ample evidence of the counterproductive effect of the previous programmes. According to Christine Lagarde, the IMF's Managing Director, 'Greece's debt has become unsustainable . . . Greece cannot restore debt sustainability solely through actions of its own. . . . Greece's debt . . . is expected to peak at close to 200 per cent of GDP in the next two years. . . . Greece's debt can now only be made sustainable through debt relief measures that go far beyond what Europe has been willing to consider so far' (IMF 2015). If that is so, the very term 'debt', used as a designation of the total of funds that have been transferred to Greece by private and public lenders under the expectation that they will be paid back, turns out to be nothing but a mendacious misnomer, invented and used for the purpose of demolishing the economic fates of an EU Member State while buying (at most) three years' worth of time before the issue is likely to be on the table again (Streeck 2014). The widely used cynical slogan is 'extend [transfers] and pretend [it is debt]', a formula that has, for a while, helped to keep domestic protest in creditor countries at bay.

Three features of German power

'Germany is widely perceived to be calling the shots in Europe's sovereign debt crisis management' (Janning 2013). This perception of Germany as the most powerful actor in the EU derives primarily from its economic resources which are, by all relevant indicators, superior to any other Member State in the middle of the second decade of the twenty-first century (Schoeller 2016: 107–13; 2017). The country occupies top positions in terms of its GDP, its credibility in financial markets and the most favourable 10-year bonds yield, the export intensity of its economy and hence its current account surplus. Its sovereign debt relative to GDP, while still violating Maastricht rules, is below the average of eurozone members. Germany is also seen as the most powerful EU actor in terms of its institutional position. As the biggest country in terms of population, it enjoys a *de facto* veto power in the Council. Many observers agree that these power resources become effective through *reputational* mechanisms and informal ways (Watkins 2014: 21, 20).[7] That is to say, German members of European institutions do not have to actually deploy these resources in the making of credible threats and promises. Rather, they can rely on Germany's possession of these resources *being known* to all others and therefore, in line with the 'law of anticipated reaction', do not need to be explicitly activated. 'The essence of Member State power lies in anticipation, in the perception of strength, preference, options and partners of one actor in the eyes of others' (Janning 2013). Germany's power position was far from a 'unilateral power grab'; rather, its 'preponderance since 2011 rests . . .on a tacit recognition by the other states that the investors and the US Treasury see the German Chancellor as executive head of Europe' (Watkins 2014: 13, 15).

A second feature of the peculiar way in which German power resources have been deployed is the tendency to avoid and delay action,

---

[7] Watkins speaks of the 'new, informal polity of post-2011 Europe' with an 'entirely extra-constitutional role of the German Chancellor' (2014: 21, 20).

to maintain rather than change the status quo, to deny the need for collective action, to always declare concessions as an *ultima ratio* and to relate fearfully defensively to the allegedly misguided activism of others. The logic of this pattern is simple: if you are in a position of strength, you can afford to drag your feet and engage in agenda-building through 'non-decisions' and inaction (Schoeller 2016: 79–100). Many commentators and observers have focused on the German government's tendency to refuse to put its political resources to constructive use in a role of leadership. As leadership has both costs and benefits, German political elites, sometimes cheaply and conveniently hiding behind the burdened history of Nazi Germany in Europe, seem to have determined that the costs of leadership – defined as the readiness to solve EU-wide collective action problems through enabling and motivating others to contribute to some common good – exceed its benefits (Kindleberger 1981). If an actor is actively intervening, he is visible as an actor and exposes himself to demands and criticism; if you opt for inaction, procrastination and negative agenda-building through gate-keeping, for an attitude of 'wait and see' and for indifferently 'letting things happen', you are much less visible as an agent causally contributing to the outcome seemingly attributable to the anonymous operation of 'the markets'. As in court cases where a defendant is accused of 'criminal neglect', a *failure* to act is much more difficult to prove and to attribute to concrete agents than overt action, as such attribution of wrongdoing presupposes both the stipulation of a *duty* to act and the specification of *whose* duty it would have been. Consistent inaction makes both of these questions virtually impossible to answer.

In an official address he delivered in Berlin in 2011, the Polish foreign minister Radek Sikorski pointed out that Germany is the biggest beneficiary of the euro and has 'the biggest obligation to make [it] sustainable'. He appeals to the German government that it may recognize and fulfil this obligation: 'I fear German power less than I am beginning to fear German inactivity ... You have become Europe's indispensable nation ... You may not fail to lead. Not dominate, but to lead to reform' (Sikorski 2011). Yet such appeals have consistently fallen on deaf ears in Berlin. The response of German political leaders has been unequivocal ever since: Germany will not be the 'paymaster of Europe', certainly not so under the domestic threat of a rising anti-EU populist right that has made its appearance in Germany, too.

Throughout most of the year 2015 when the need for a third 'assistance package' for Greece became evident, the German government found itself in a complex strategic situation that can be summarized as an asymmetrical deal-making between the majority of 18 eurozone members on the one side and an isolated and acutely debt-ridden Greece on the other. The only shared interest of both sides was to maintain the viability of the currency regime through a negotiated outcome that would prevent spillover effects from the Greek debt and banking crisis to the eurozone as a whole and which could also be expected to provide for a consolidation of the precarious political stability of the country.

What also played a role is the fact that domestic constituencies of the creditor states had grown very sensitive to a perceived transfer of 'our' tax money to Greece and other 'deficit states'. The interest of the Greek side, which was completely isolated from the others, was to obtain concessions which included an (at least partial) debt forgiveness significant enough to generate prospects for the recovery of the Greek public finance, banking system and overall economy. The interest of the other eurozone negotiators was to minimize the volume of their credit assistance and risks involved in the final deal and to maximize, as a conditionality attached, the control over all aspects of the Greek policy and economy. The puzzle was (and remains) unresolved: Is there a way to prevent contagion and eventual breakdown of the currency while still avoiding an outright transfer union as it is explicitly proscribed by Art. 125 of TFEU? For the time being, the deal was one of emergency credit in exchange for a sacrifice of sovereignty. All of these interests had to be reconciled under immense time pressure, as Greek banks were already operating on ECB-provided credit and as adverse reactions from the financial markets concerning other deficit countries were deemed imminent.

All participants in the negotiation must have been aware of the two features of the German role discussed above: German veto power and German refusal to play a leadership role in the sense specified (Schieder 2014).[8] The reason why German negotiators could get away with this set of strategic attitudes, both in relation to their fellow eurozone negotiators and their domestic constituency must be seen, or so I want to argue, in a third feature of German power, namely a distinctively German *repertoire of frames and narratives* concerning the nature of the conflict and the responsibilities of the two sides involved in it. This repertoire served as a powerful means of immunization against critical objections and *blame avoidance*; and provided the good conscience that actors need when engaging in a strategy that is both brutal in its foreseeable impact on others and counterproductive concerning all interests involved.

---

[8] Two candid statements of Chancellor Merkel put the matter in a nutshell: 'Without us, against us can and will there be no decision which is economically viable' (author's translation). 'To me, the concept of hegemony is completely foreign' (Schieder 2014).

Narratives of responsibility

How did the problem on the table come into being in the first place? In social science terminology, answers can be framed in terms of agency theory or, alternatively, in terms of an institutionalist or structuralist theory – in terms of *decisions* that actors take and institutional *rules* that apply to them. Powerful winners will typically be inclined to opt for an agency-focused interpretation of the dismal situation and its origins, while losers have reasons to rely on narratives centred on faulty institutions, adverse conditions and rigid structures that are beyond their control and for the impact of which they therefore cannot be held responsible. The German–Greek conflict is the clear-cut case of a clash of these two frames. The former tends to equate observed outcomes with intentionally chosen or accepted ones, while the latter claims that we had no choice as the cards were stacked against us.

The structure of the conversation between the two sides, Greece and Germany, can be modelled as follows. The German accusation levelled at the Greek side is that 'You have decided to break the rules that apply to all of us and now you must be held responsible!'. To which the Greek response is: 'You have decided to adopt and rigorously enforce rules our compliance with which would break our neck!'. These two narratives apply to the upstream aspect of the situation: how it came into being. As to the downstream perspective applying to the future, the patterns of argument preferred by the two sides are exactly inverted. The powerful side says: 'In your own interest, you must return to the strict observance of the rules!', whereas the losers respond: 'You must, for the time being, decide to forget about the rules and grant an exception (in the form of a far-reaching debt relief)[9] until all of us have decided upon a more workable set of new rules!'.

---

[9] In fact, at the height of the crisis in June 2015, Greek finance minister Varoufakis addressed the German side with a frame of what might be called moralizing voluntarism. He reminded his German counterpart of a speech the US Secretary of State James F. Byrnes gave in Stuttgart on 6 September 1946. It was a 'speech of hope' telling the defeated Germans that they no longer had to fear the harsh Morgenthau plan of punitive de-industrialization, promising them instead that their recovery would be assisted and promoted by the victorious US. Foreshadowing the Marshall plan (effective in 1948) and the role of West Germany as an indispensable ally in the upcoming Cold War, Byrnes' speech marked a turning point towards the dramatic recovery of the 1950s. The analogy Varoufakis wishes to suggest is obvious: 'Germans', he says, 'could not have staged their magnificent post-war renaissance without the support signified by the "Speech of Hope"'. Why does not Angela Merkel, after all the benefits with which Germany and all of Western Europe were blessed as an effect of American magnanimity, now show the same attitude and deliver an analogous 'speech of hope' to the Greek people?

The plight of the Greek economy is in the dominant German perspective depicted as a matter of (mistaken) *choices* having been made by Greek actors, while in the dominant Greek perspective it is a matter of ill-construed rules and factual constraints which do not allow for making choices in the first place. In what follows, I shall concentrate on the German side of this conversation and only briefly refer to the Greek side at the end.

The core claim of the German side and its agency-focused frame (or 'epistemic regime') is that the institutional rules are not the problem. As they have served the proponents of this side so well, rules are being reified and 'naturalized' – taken for granted as unfailingly just and beneficial. The problem is some actors' failure to follow them. If they are followed, a viable social order will result. The authority of rules derives from the fact that they have been agreed upon. Some rules, such as the rule that you cannot permanently live beyond your means or that debtors must be coerced, if need be, to pay back what they owe their creditors are so evidently and universally valid that they do not even require the explicit prior consent of those to whom they apply. If social order shows signs of breaking down, it follows that this must be due to the fact that certain actors have failed to follow the rules. Excuses that particular rules are superfluous or need reform or revision in order to perform their purpose of creating order or that they were unsuited for that purpose in the first place or that actors have not voluntarily committed themselves to following those rules or that rules differ according to the cultures and traditions in which they are rooted or that rules are inherently unfair are all inadmissible. Keeping to the rules is virtuous, and their violation a clear sign of moral inferiority or of a personality defect, be it of individuals or of entire populations of nations. Wherever disturbances of the normal, rule-bound course of affairs emerge, its causes are to be assumed to be found on the spot, not in mechanisms of long-distance-causation extending in space or time. If someone is found to have violated rules, such violation must be appropriately sanctioned.[10] Unless it is sanctioned and thereby effectively deterred, 'moral hazard' is feared to set in, namely an

---

[10] The emphasis is on 'appropriately'. The enforcer can to some extent be blame-sensitive and has an interest in blame avoidance, i.e. in not being seen by others as applying disproportionately brutal sanctions. Blame avoidance is also described as a driving motive of the ECB. 'The ECB's decision to grant Greece's banks just enough funds to see them through the end of the day is part of a broader strategy to avoid having blood on its hands' (*Financial Times* 2015: 4). As the damage to the German government's reputation that it inflicted upon itself by insisting on tough conditions to be imposed on the Greek side in the July 2015 negotiations became evident (Renzi: 'enough is enough!'), the German chancellor arguably tried to make good on this damage by her ostentatiously generous gesture to open German borders to refugees in early September of 2015.

invitation of the violator to repeat the rule-breaking behaviour or a temptation of others to imitate the violations. Every single one of these tenets will not only be seen as a sign of virtue; it will, moreover, be rewarded by material and other kinds of success. These are key elements of what I call the ordoliberal mindset that is deeply ingrained in the German culture of social and economic thought and the policy-making that derives from it. Today, reliance on it and its constant invocation serves to provide a sense of good conscience for policies that imply brutal consequences for others. The folklore of the ordoliberal mindset is supported by two equivocations which are built into German everyday parlance. One is the equivocation of the moral economy of the (family) household (*Haushalt*) with that of a legislated state budget. The other is the suggestive equation of guilt (*Schuld*) with debt (*Schulden*), with the latter term easily being mistaken for a plural of the former (Offe 2016).

Somewhat more sophisticated than this rough account is 'ordoliberalism', the normative theory which fully conforms to these intuitions of economic morality. The starting point of the theory, as it was elaborated by the Freiburg School of economics in the post World War II years, is the need for a fixed set of rules (an 'economic constitution'), including rules of stability-oriented monetary policy and rules enforcing competition, which is all that is required for the sake of prosperity and economic justice. Once this order is in place, discretionary state intervention becomes both unnecessary and positively detrimental. 'Ordo liberalism is pre-eminently an ideological hybrid that appeals to creditor-state interests. It celebrates the virtues of thrift, discipline, and self-reliance that [Germans] like to attribute to themselves' (Dyson, unpublished: 8). After having been the dominant ideology of the period of Germany's 'economic miracle' in the 1950s, it 'provides a valued self-image of how Germans like to be seen. . . . It offers a sense of identity that makes Germans feel proud in the wider world' (Dyson, unpublished: 8). The debt brake, the Macroeconomic Imbalance Procedure with its one-sided adjustment pressure applied on deficit countries as opposed to export countries and on debtors as opposed to creditors more generally, as well as the banking union with its emphasis on the supervisory mechanism, are components of the EU policy tool box. They all derive directly from the economic policy doctrine of ordoliberalism which had become sufficiently hegemonic throughout the EU to by and large isolate the Greek finance minister Varoufakis in the negotiations of July 2015, while the ECB with its somewhat adventurous monetary policy innovations remained increasingly immune from the doctrine.

General policy prescriptions of this doctrine are clear enough. Roughly, they include the following items:

- current account surplus from international trade, presently (2016) amounting to more than 8 per cent of German GDP, are an unambiguous indicator of 'our' industriousness and competitive superiority, rightly rewarded by markets of international commerce; they should not be seen as 'imbalances' detrimental to others;
- inflation must always be minimized, regardless of its possible consequences for deepening a recession, in order to achieve economic and political stability;
- public as well as private indebtedness is to be avoided and budgets must be balanced, as debt is both an indicator (in public and private life alike) of imprudence and questionable moral fibre of debtors; if sovereign debt occurs, it should, following Art. 125 of TFEU, under no circumstances be mutualized through euro bonds and the like, as that would give rise to moral hazard;
- instead, budgetary imbalances must be remedied through the austerity practice of 'expenditure discipline' and, if need be, through raising indirect (i.e. regressive) tax rates, not through increasing revenues from direct taxation of income or wealth, as these would damage business confidence and competitiveness;
- political democracy, particularly if it is combined with confrontational patterns of wage bargaining (as opposed to trade unions' prudential practice of wage restraint), is public debt-prone and must, to an extent, be curbed so as to yield a 'market-conforming' budgetary process[11];
- rules (such as those laid down in the Maastricht and Lisbon Treaties) are to be strictly observed and violation is to be sanctioned.

These 'truths' are significant for both what they prescribe as 'virtuous' policies and what they proscribe as heretical and dangerous ideas. The latter include the thought that creditors (and not just debtors) must sometimes bear the risk involved in lending and pay for it in terms of 'haircuts' and 'bail-in' losses; the thought that an export surplus cannot just benefit the exporting economy but simultaneously inflict damage on others; the thought that it can be normatively as questionable to spend 'below' one's means as it is considered questionable to spend 'beyond' one's means; the thought that inflation can well be desirable in a deflationary context, as it

---

[11] On 2 September 2011, Chancellor Merkel stated in an interview: 'We live in a democracy which is a parliamentary democracy and therefore the right to pass the budget is a core right of the parliament and thus we'll find ways to design parliamentary codetermination in ways which still are conforming to markets' (author's literal translation). The careless grammar and nebulous reasoning of this statement are indicative of her appealing to a deep truth that is being summarily invoked here rather than argued for.

can incentivize time preferences of investors and consumers ('better buy today than wait') and as it, in addition, alleviates the burdens of debtors; the thought (as well as ample and incontrovertible evidence) that austerity imposed upon the losers in international competitiveness and violators of Maastricht criteria does not improve but, to the contrary, is bound to make worse their position in terms of public debt relative to GDP; and, above all, the thought that the adoption of the above macroeconomic 'truths' and corresponding policies must be left to the democratic institutions of Member States (or to a future fully democratized EU) rather than being imposed upon them by practices of paternalistic conditionalism, often perceived by target states and populations as acts of outright blackmail or 'foreign rule' (Galbraith 2015).

Once this set of normative postulates, intuitions as well as positive and negative policy prescriptions has become ingrained in everyday common-sense assumptions of policy makers, 'experts', journalists and ordinary citizens about the nature of social and economic life, it serves as an armoury of ideological warfare and interpretive struggles that targets losers and blames victims. How pervasively these ideas have impregnated the German crisis discourse became evident in the fact that a nearly unequivocal barrage of these normative claims were aimed at Greece, its people and its political elites alike, throughout the crisis in the German media ('quality' and otherwise), by German political elites and by representative speakers of economic science (Baetz 2015). All these epistemic rulers of public knowledge and dominant narratives have been forcing themselves into line during the years of the Greek debt crisis in a probably unprecedented fashion. Vehement terms of reproach and outright insults ('gambler', 'debt sinner', 'scoundrel', 'blackmailer', 'defrauder', 'ghost driver', etc.) were routinely hurled by the media at widely ridiculed Greek politicians as well as the Greek population as a whole, in humiliating ways that defy standards of civilized dispute otherwise widely observed in interaction among Member States. 'Why do we pay luxury pensions for the Greeks?' asked the *Bild* tabloid in line with a consolidated consensus by the German public – ignoring the facts that (a) 'we' did not 'pay' a penny so far and that (b) pensions in Greece are the only social security transfer that does not terminate, unlike health and unemployment insurance, after one (!) year of a person having become unemployed and which, in a large number of cases, constitutes the only source of income not just of pensioners, but of their unemployed children and dependent grandchildren as well. The question was hardly ever asked in public whether the case of non-performing loans might perhaps be due to inconsiderate *lending* (that private banks have possibly engaged in because they could rely on being bailed out if things went wrong), not exclusively to frivolous *borrowing*. And neither did any of the mainstream commentators bother to reflect on whether the draconic punishments imposed on the Greek economy – cuts of wages and pensions, harsh austerity targets, deregulation of labour law, privatization of assets at fire sale prices – were sure to render the crisis a permanent one due to giant demand gaps rather than helping to overcome it. A milder version of the German crisis discourse consisted in paternalistic and patronizing offers of advice on how to run an economy successfully and responsibly, as well as exhortations that 'you' better imitate German templates of how to do things right. These pieces of advice ignored the simple truth that 'the eurozone as a whole cannot become more like Germany. Germany could only be like Germany because the other countries were not' (Matthijs and Blyth 2011).

To be sure, the outburst of denunciatory rhetoric and punitive strings attached to the programme 'agreed upon' (if that is the right term) by the Greek prime minister in July 2015 was not just addressed to Greek elites and voters. It was also intended to demonstrate to others, namely countries like Portugal, Spain and Italy and their citizenry, what would happen to them if they allowed themselves to fall into a similarly precarious situation of insolvency. And the policy, as well as its concomitant narrative of Greeks as lazy spendthrifts deserving to be taught a severe lesson, was also addressed to the German constituency that had grown increasingly wary, under the impact of rightist populist propaganda of the new party AfD ('Alternative for Germany'), founded in 2013, gaining electoral strength, that the government overly generously spends 'our' tax money on some morally unworthy southern country. The domestic constituency was of course largely kept unaware of the facts that (a) *credits* were at stake, while not a single euro had been *transferred* so far, (b) that the major portion of the credits granted to Greece in the previous two 'rescue' programmes were intended to rescue not anyone in Greece but dangerously exposed German and French banks, (c) that the €86 billion of further credit provided by the 2015 programme was intended to prevent contagion (i.e., depositors starting a bank run in other countries, creditor banks increasing the spread applying to other debtor countries), and that (d) Germany had actually reaped a very substantial benefit[12] from the Greek debt crisis (Leibniz Institute for Economic Research 2015).

---

[12] On 10 August 2015, the Leibniz Institute for Economic Research in Halle published the results of a simulation study which found that due to the massive 'flight to safety' of Greek capital into German banks, the yield of German government bonds had decreased by 3 per cent over a period of five years. This translates into a gain of 'at least 100 bn euros', considerably more than what Germany would stand to lose if Greece were to default on all credit granted to it (Leibniz Institute for Economic Research 2015).

I hope to have shown how problematic, in both analytical and normative terms, the implications can be if we rely on categories of agency in order to make sense of complex socio-economic processes and outcomes such as the Greek debt crisis and the conflicts to which it has given rise. To account for these in terms of personality traits, virtue, prudence, discipline and lack of it, moral failure, greed, short-sighted decisions, character defects, etc., yields results and narratives of responsibility that may serve well to win support for strategic moves of one of the parties involved (the more powerful, that is) but does neither achieve an adequate causal explanation nor a promising therapy for the problem at hand. It rather results in an analytically sterile exercise in victim blaming or the moral self-aggrandizement of winners.

Much more promising (as well as honest and intellectually respectable) is an approach that Greek leaders, most prominently the social science intellectual and former minister of finance Varoufakis, have consistently taken. To be sure, there have also been voices in the Greek media which have depicted the German chancellor as the incarnation of evil. Yet in Varoufakis' numerous comments on the crisis and possible ways out as well as in a book length account of the conflict, he uses an entirely different, namely structuralist and institutionalist language, while throughout emphasizing his personal respect for his main opponent in the bitter conflict, German finance minister Wolfgang Schäuble and his analytical capabilities (Aust and Scholz 2016a, 2016b; Varoufakis 2016). Starting with the observation that 'Greece is bankrupt more than ever', from which it follows that it makes no sense to pay for accumulated and unsustainable 'debt' (which has itself become a mendacious misnomer as the term implies the *ability* of the debtor to ever pay it back to the creditor, as well as the *belief* of the latter in that ability) with ever new credit, he highlights the 'defective structure of the eurozone' and emphasizes his 'opposition to untenable conditions, not persons'. If there is blame, it should apply to faulty decisions of *former* Greek elites, such as the decision to join the eurozone in the first place, the consequences of which have resulted in 'untenable conditions' which cannot be undone. He also points to the defective institutional arrangements of the endemically corrupt Greek state and its lacking capacity for effectively making its citizens pay taxes. The practical conclusion of this analytical perspective is not to punish or re-educate people, but to change the institutional setup of the EU's monetary regime in ways for which he has proposed a set of ideas for reform.[13]

Yet institutional reforms are hardest to mobilize for and to implement

[13] Available at www.bridgingeurope.net

when the European polity is under unprecedented stress. The vast scarcity of consensus of governing elites of Member States, also exacerbated by the refugee crisis that has fuelled domestic fears (real and above all pretend ones) and populist mobilization if not the rise of populist parties to government position, seems to make any attempt at major *constitutional* change unpromising. The only force that can realistically be expected to drive a change of *policy* is not popular mobilization but the fear of (parts of) governing elites of Member States that the failure to adopt policy reforms is bound to irretrievably involve all sides in a giant and long-term negative-sum game of re-nationalization. Such perfectly rational fears of the consequences of an EU collapse are naturally greatest on the part of those who so far have gained most from EU integration and its monetary regime. Heroically assuming an adequate level of policy-elite rationality, one would assume that those who would lose most are also ready to pay most for averting the dangers that come with re-nationalization – even if the introduction of some remedial policies need to 'proceed on tiptoes, lest German voters notice' (Watkins 2014), as Europe lacks the role of an institutional opposition that would have a chance to democratically advocate positive policy alternatives that could make further integration evidently 'worthwhile'. Blueprints and proposals for such alternatives are on the table, if on tables behind technocratically closed doors. Examples are a European unemployment insurance, debt relief and debt mutualization through eurobonds, the transfer of fiscal authority to tax, spend and incur debt to a eurozone minister of finance, fiscal harmonization among Member States, and large-scale public investment programmes aimed at the most crisis-affected Member States and economic sectors. But it is certainly too early to tell whether such EU-wide policy initiatives will ever have a chance to assert themselves against the shortsightedness of self-centred German veto power which so far has refused to adopt an attitude of *rational* fear of an EU collapse.

References

Aust, S. and Scholz, M. (2016a) Schäuble war der Einzige, der einen Plan hatte, *Welt*, 15 August. Available at: https://www.welt.de/wirtschaft/article157675 904/Schaeuble-war-der-Einzige-der-einen-Plan-hatte.html

Aust, S. and Scholz, M. (2016b) Wolfgang und ich saßen da – beide hilflos, *Welt*, 17 August. Available at: https://www.welt.de/wirtschaft/article157713898/Wolf gang-und-ich-sassen-da-beide-hilflos.html

Baetz, B. (2015) Das TINA-Syndrom. Die Griechenland-Krise in den deutschen Medien. Available at: http://www.deutschlandfunk.de/skript-das-tina-syndrom-pdf-datei.media.f25cd999a9c9ceabfc2ebe4fb733aee9.pdf

CLAUS OFFE

Dyson, K. (unpublished) *The Ordo-liberal Tradition: Germany and the Paradox of Creditor-State Power in the euro Area.* Manuscript, Cardiff University.
The Economist (2015) From rage to resignation, 18 July. Available at: http://www.economist.com/news/Europe/21657836-chastened-nation-and-its-leader-face-more-hard-choices-rage-resignation
Eichengreen, B. (2015) Saving Greece, saving Europe, *Social Europe*, 14 July. Available at: http://www.socialeurope.eu/2015/07/saving-greece-saving-Europe/
European Commission (2015) Memorandum of Understanding between the European Commission ... and the Hellenic Republic, 19 August. Available at: http://ec.europa.eu/economy_finance/assistance_eu_ms/greek_loan_facility/pdf/01_mou_20150811_en.pdf
Financial Times (2015) ECB holds the trigger in Greece stand-off, 24 June, 4. Available at: https://www.ft.com/content/3dad7e5c-19bc-11e5-a130-2e7db721f996
Frankfurter Allgemeine Zeitung (2015a) Union erwägt Hartz IV für Athen, 23 May. Available at: http://www.faz.net/aktuell/wirtschaft/eurokrise/griechen-land/griechenlands-krise-hartz-iv-fuer-athen-13607568.html
Frankfurter Allgemeine Zeitung (2015b) Schäuble bringt Grexit auf Zeit ins Gespräch, 11 July. Available at: http://www.faz.net/aktuell/wirtschaft/eurokrise/griechen land/eurofinanzminister-treffen-schaeuble-bringt-grexit-auf-zeit-ins-gespraech-13697851.html
Galbraith, J. (2015) Bad faith: why real debt relief is not on the table for Greece. *Social Europe*, 18 June. Available at: https://www.socialeurope.eu/2015/06/bad-faith-why-real-debt-relief-is-not-on-the-table-for-greece/
Gordon, R.J. (2016) *The Rise and Fall of American Growth.* Princeton, NJ: Princeton University Press.
The Guardian (2015a) Greek debt crisis: deal reached after marathon all-night summit – as it happened, 13 July. Available at: http://www.theguardian.com/business/live/2015/jul/12/greek-debt-crisis-eu-leaders-meeting-cancel led-no-deal-live
The Guardian (2015b) Greece debt agreement: the eurozone summit statement – in full, 13 July. Available at: http://www.theguardian.com/business/2015/jul/13/greece-debt-agreement-eurozone-summit-statement
IMF (2015) Greece: An update of IMF staff's preliminary public debt sustain-ability analysis. IMF Country Report No. 15/186. Available at: https://goo.gl/hMdL4p
Janning, J. (2013) State power within European integration. Deutsche Gesellschaft für Auswärtige Politik. Available at: https://www.google.at/sea rch?q=janning+state+power&ie=utf-8&oe=utf-8&client=firefox-b-ab&gfe_rd=cr&ei=B4oQWMK7B4HN8geop4wY
Kindleberger, C.P. (1981) Dominance and leadership in the international economy: exploitation, public goods, and free rides. *International Studies Quarterly* 25: 242–54.
Kundnani, H. (2014) *The Paradox of German Power.* London: Hurst.
Leibniz Institute for Economic Research (2015) *Germany's Benefit from the Greek Crisis.* Halle: IWH. Available at: http://www.iwh-halle.de/fileadmin/user_upload/publications/iwh_online/io_2015-07.pdf
Matthijs, M. and Blyth, M. (2011) Why only Germany can fix the euro: reading Kindleberger in Berlin. *Foreign Affairs*, 17 November. Available at: https://www.foreignaffairs.com/articles/germany/2011-11-17/why-only-ger many-can-fix-euro

292

Minenna, M. (2015) New countdown for Greece: a bank bail-in is looming. *Social Europe*, 4 November. Available at: http://www.socialeurope.eu/2015/11/new-countdown-for-greece-a-bank-bail-in-is-looming/

Offe, C. (2016) *Europe Entrapped*, 2nd edn. Cambridge: Polity.

Offe, C. and Preuss, U.K. (2016) *Citizens in Europe: Essays on Democracy, Constitutionalism and European Integration*. Colchester: ECPR Press.

Oltermann, P. (2015) Jürgen Habermas's verdict on the EU/Greece debt deal – full transcript. *The Guardian*, 16 July. Available at: http://www.theguardian.com/commentisfree/2015/jul/16/jurgen-habermas-eu-greece-debt-deal

Reuters (2015) Italy's Renzi to tell Germany to accept Greece deal: newspaper, 12 July. Available at: http://www.reuters.com/article/2015/07/12/us-eurozone-greece-renzi-idUSKCN0PM08320150712#rlWEidmqjQC9999z.99

Schieder, S. (2014) Zwischen Führungsanspruch und Wirklichkeit: Deutschlands Rolle in der eurozone. *Leviathan* 42(3): 363–97.

Schoeller, M.G. (2016) Explaining political leadership: the role of Germany and the EU institutions in eurozone crisis management. Unpublished PhD thesis, European University Institute, Florence.

Schoeller, M.G. (2017) Providing political leadership? Three case studies on Germany's ambiguous role in the eurozone crisis. *Journal of European Public Policy* 24(1): 1–20.

Sikorski, R. (2011) I fear Germany's power less than her inactivity. *Financial Times*, 28 November. Available at: https://www.ft.com/content/b753cb42-19b3-11e1-ba5d-00144feabdc0

Streeck, W. (2014) *Buying Time: The Delayed Crisis of Democratic Capitalism*. London: Verso.

Truth Committee on Public Debt (2014) *Preliminary Report*. Available at: http://www.auditoriacidada.org.br/wp-content/uploads/2014/06/Report-Greek-Truth-Committee.pdf

Truth Committee on Public Debt (2015) *Illegitimacy, Illegality, Odiousness and Unsustainability of the August 2015 MoU and Loan Agreement*. Available at: http://www.hellenicparliament.gr/UserFiles/8158407a-fc31-4ff2-a8d3-4337 01dbe6d4/7AEBEF78-DE85-4AB3-98BE-495803F85BF6Mnimonio_ENG_1.pdf

Varoufakis, Y. (2016) *Das euro-Paradox: Wie eine andere Geldpolitik europa wieder zusammenführen kann*. Munich: Antje Kunstmann.

Watkins, S. (2014) The political state of the union. *New Left Review* 90: 5–25.

Chapter 13

The Double Crisis of European Social Democracy

Colin Crouch[1]

Social democracy is experiencing a two-fold problem in most European countries. First, the share of the popular vote in national elections by social democratic parties has often declined, while those of parties on the far left and even more on the far right are growing. Second, neoliberal policies seem to remain hegemonic despite the crash of 2008, with privatization of public services, the decline of welfare states and increasingly regressive taxation prevailing almost everywhere. A closer look at the evidence demonstrates the validity of these popular impressions, but also reveals their limitations. Social democracy as such may have lost its hold over the left side of European politics, but this is probably part of a more general fragmentation of the hegemonic blocs that often (though by no means everywhere) dominated post-war democracies. Similarly, almost everywhere neoliberal policies have had to make compromises with policies historically associated with social democracy, whether out of economic need or in order to attract popular support. Both of these elements of the decline of social democracy, and the limitations of that decline, will be discussed here.

Following my practice elsewhere (Crouch 2013), I am using 'social democracy' in its normal contemporary sense to describe political movements and parties that have as their historical mission the representation of ordinary working people, including prominently their trade unions, by seeking major changes in the operation of a capitalist economy and reductions in the inequalities and social damage that they perceive it to produce. The parties concerned are named variously social democratic,

---

[1] Note that this text was last revised on 8 May 2017, so it has not been possible to take account of the French, UK and German elections that took place while this book was in production.

labour or socialist. In the European Parliament they constitute the parties currently known as the Progressive Alliance of Socialists and Democrats, but in academic literature 'social democratic' has come to be used as something distinct from 'socialist'. Socialist movements are usually seen as seeking entirely to replace the capitalist economy and markets by a system of common ownership, meaning either the state or a co-operative arrangement. Social democrats, in contrast, accept the market and private ownership as the best means of conducting most economic business, but are deeply sceptical of the market's capacity to achieve certain fundamental social goals unaided. These goals concern: first, the need for all people to be able to enjoy a decent life, even if they cannot be very successful in the market, and with limited inequalities; and second, the need for human beings to be able to manage successfully certain shared, collective tasks. Social democrats are those politically active people who are willing to place constraints on and to shape the market, mainly, though not solely, through the use of state or local government power, and in particular the provision of public services as rights of citizenship, in order to realize those ends.

The electoral decline of social democratic parties

Discussion of parties' share of the vote in elections has to be separated from whether or not those parties are in government. The latter can be a question of the exigencies of coalition building, and parties might enter and leave government for reasons only loosely connected with their popular support. (The Dutch Labour Party was once forced out of a governing coalition even though its support in a general election had strengthened considerably.) We are here concerned only with the more substantive issue of the place that particular parties hold in the hearts and minds of voters.

Of course, parties' share of the vote rises and falls as governments gain or lose popularity. We are here concerned not with such fluctuations, but with major secular trends. In the mid-1960s social democratic parties secured between 40 per cent and 48 per cent of the popular vote in the UK, Sweden, Norway, Austria, the then West Germany and Malta. These were social democracy's core strongholds. By the mid-1980s this situation had changed only in the UK in a major way (a decline from 48 per cent to 31 per cent), though there was also evidence of decline in West Germany and of increase in Malta. Between the mid-1980s and the latest elections at the time of writing, there had been further growth in tiny Malta, but in the other strongholds decline had been considerable: to 31 per cent in Norway and Sweden, 27 per cent in Austria, and catastrophically to 5.7 per cent in the Netherlands. At the time of writing, the British Labour Party remained at around 31 per cent in 2015, but there was to be another election in June. Germany had after 1990 become a new country following its unification with the state socialist East Germany. In the first elections in the unified country in 1990, the Social Democratic Party (SPD) had achieved 33.5 per cent of the vote; by 2013 this had fallen to 26 per cent. In only two countries (apart from Malta) that had been consistently democratic since the first elections after 1945 did social democratic parties stand higher around 2010–15 than they did in the mid-1960s: the French Socialist Party rose from 19 per cent to 29 per cent, but that was before the elections to be held later in 2017, following a presidential election in which all established parties suffered major defeat; the Italian Democratic Party (PD) scored 25 per cent in 2013 where the Socialist Party of the 1960s achieved only 14 per cent. These were countries where communist parties had dominated the left until the decline of the Soviet Union, the Italian PD being itself an inheritor of reformed communists and socialists. In both countries the parties now regarded as social democratic had had far better performances at some point from the 1980s onwards than they are achieving now, but the earlier history of the decline of communism reminds us that social democratic dominance of the left has by no means been a universal feature of western European societies.

Figure 13.1a shows how social democratic parties' share of the popular vote has changed over the past three decades in all countries that have had free elections since either around the end of World War II or (in the case of Cyprus, Greece, Portugal and Spain) since the 1970s. There has been decline everywhere except Italy, Malta and Portugal and, in a minor way, Ireland and Switzerland. Decline has been particularly heavy in the strongholds of Austria and Sweden, also the Netherlands, and in two southern European countries affected by the Eurozone debt crisis after 2010 (Greece and Spain).

When the countries of central and parts of Eastern Europe entered liberal democracy after 1990, they had problematic relations with communist parties, these having dominated the dictatorships of the state socialist countries. In some cases communist parties have retained popular support as rivals to infant social democratic ones, in others they have tried to become social democratic parties, and in still others their legacy has discredited all parties advocating redistributive fiscal and social policies and the pursuit of collective goods. More generally, it has been difficult for parties of all kinds in central and eastern Europe (CEE) to establish popular roots. Organizations come and go at frequent

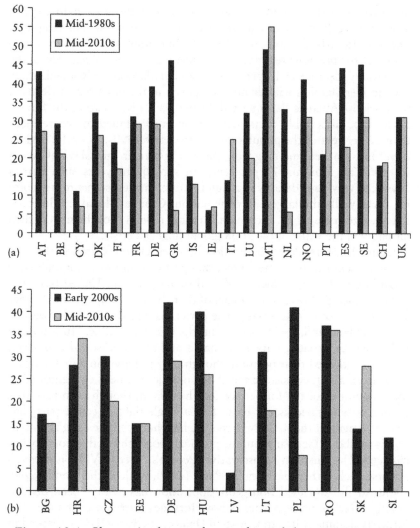

Figure 13.1: Change in shares of vote of social democratic parties:
(a) Western European countries, mid-1980s to mid-2010s; (b)
Central European countries, early 2000s to mid-2010s

Note: In part (a), DE signifies West Germany for 1987, unified Germany for
2013; in part (b) DE signifies unified Germany. For country abbreviations,
see Appendix.
Source: https://en.wikipedia.org/wiki/Elections_by_country

intervals, often (especially on the right) being little more than coteries around a wealthy individual, and support can rise and fall steeply in elections. In early elections after 1990 the Bulgarian Socialist Party, a successor to the previous regime's communist party, took 47 per cent of the vote; today it stands at 15 per cent. In similar elections in Romania there was no identifiable social democratic party; in the most recent elections the Socialist Alliance Party scored 45 per cent. Elsewhere in the former Soviet bloc discernibly social democratic parties failed to secure more than 12 per cent of the popular vote in the early 1990s. They did slightly better in countries emerging from the war in former Yugoslavia (Croatia 25 per cent; Slovenia 17 per cent). In subsequent years such parties advanced very considerably in a number of countries, sometimes becoming for a while the largest in their nation: Croatia, Slovakia, Hungary, Latvia, Czech Republic, Lithuania, Romania. Several of them were then hit badly in the wake of the 2008 global financial crisis.

Figure 13.1b tracks their position between elections around the turn of the present century (after some, though by no means all, initial party instability had settled down) and at their most recent. United Germany has been included here, since a part of that country comprises the former socialist state of East Germany. The pattern is mixed, with heavy decline only in Poland and, to a lesser extent, the Czech Republic, Hungary and Lithuania. In Croatia, Latvia, Romania and Slovakia, social democrats have strengthened their position, though only in Latvia in a major way.

Concern about consistent social democratic decline is concentrated in those countries of the former western heartland, though even here that decline does not necessarily mean that a single right-of-centre party has prevailed against them. Only in the UK has that been the case; the situation is similar in Germany, but the political geography of that country has changed. The Austrian (conservative) People's Party (ÖVP) has suffered a worse decline than the Socialist Party (ÖSP), while in the Scandinavian countries the so-called bourgeois opposition has always been divided among three or more parties, whose fortunes fluctuate over time. The formerly dominant Italian Christian Democratic Party (DC) collapsed in the general Italian party crisis of the early 1990s; the attempt to create a secular successor by Silvio Berlusconi acquiring a similar position was only able to be kept together by his personality and wealth. France today has a more or less coherent centre-right grouping in Les Républicains, but this is a recent and not necessarily durable construction, and suffered serious reversals in the presidential election of 2017. The Dutch right is split among several parties, including the major extreme-right party led by Geert Wilders.

On left and right alike across Western Europe, the decline of established parties set in around the start of the present century, but it then intensified in the wake of the 2008 financial crisis, which produced a collapse of support for governing parties in particular. More generally across Europe, from east to west, the centre-right has experienced more cases of party collapse and reconstruction, and of needing to build coalitions among rival groupings, than has the centre-left. It is, however, also possible that in several countries this greater need to assemble fractions has made the centre-right more expert at doing so.

It is unlikely that, at least for the foreseeable future, we shall see a return to the dominance of political systems by a pair of rival parties, except in the UK (and outside Europe the USA), where the voting system more or less guarantees major parties such a role irrespective of changing political identities among voters. For parties of the left this has been a hard lesson to accept, since for so much of the twentieth century and earlier they represented a class, the industrial working class, that was growing until, it was believed, it would eventually become a dominant majority within populations. The idea that the parties of this class were bound to become history's victors was a specifically Marxist one, but the belief that history was on their side affected the outlook even of social democrats with no Marxism in their origins. The working class grew with industrialization, and the conservatism that was the left's main historical enemy seemed set to decline as its main ideological support, organized Christianity, was clearly declining.

But the growth of the industrial working class started to decline in most countries of the West by at the latest the 1970s. The occupational groups of the new services sector that were replacing it in post-industrial economies lacked historical political attachments to anywhere in the spectrum, and have therefore not become reliable followers of a small number of major parties, if indeed they vote at all. Just when the Italian Communist Party (PCI) finally achieved its long awaited *sorpasso* (overtaking) over DC in the mid-1980s, both parties were about to enter terminal crises – the former through the collapse of the Soviet Union, the latter through a chain of corruption scandals – and within a few years neither existed any more as a major party. They have been replaced by a frequently changing, unstable assortment of parties. The Italian case has been particularly dramatic, but similar processes have happened in most other Western countries, and have been repeated even more rapidly in CEE.

However, while the crisis of established parties across the spectrum is general, there are two reasons why this presents particular problems for social democrats. First, since, virtually by definition, they do not represent wealthy or otherwise generally powerful social groups as do parties of the right, they depend heavily on mass support from large numbers of ordinary working people. If that support dwindles they have few resources on which to fall back. This both affects their chances to win elections and reduces the need of governments of the right and centre to take notice of the interests that social democracy purports to serve. Second, the fact that social democratic parties in office at the time of the financial crisis were punished by voters just as much as governing parties of the centre-right (Kriesi 2014) shows that the former are not perceived by voters as having had any different relationship from conservatives and neoliberals to the banking and other financial interests who caused the crisis. Whether this suggests a public unable to distinguish between social democratic and neoliberal policy stances, or that social democratic parties no longer had any particular critical stances towards such interests, their distinctive identities as the carriers of mass democracy have clearly collapsed. They are increasingly seen as just establishment parties, leaving the field for claims to represent 'ordinary working people' open to new movements.

The state of the broader left

Consistent with the overall process of party fragmentation, we find that if we look at a broader canvas of left-of-centre parties and not just those that can be readily labelled social democratic, evidence of a general decline of the left is far less strong. (A similar account could be given of the right of centre.) I am here defining left of centre as all political movements that are primarily defined by a criticism of heavy reliance on free markets, this criticism being from a perspective of seeking egalitarian redistribution and universalism. This definition is designed to embrace anti-capitalist parties to the left of social democracy, and environmentalist and feminist parties. The qualifier concerning egalitarian redistribution and universalism excludes those green parties that concentrate on protecting privileged environments, as well as xenophobic and extreme anti-business conservative parties. This definition also excludes liberal parties, though before the twentieth century it is with them that the concept of the left begins. In the complex political spectrum of post-communist societies, the relationship of liberal and ex-communist parties to the left–right spectrum is particularly difficult to disentangle. In liberal democracies, for much of the twentieth century liberal parties occupied a centre ground between conservative parties on the right and social democratic and socialist ones on the left. In more recent decades this has changed in some but not all countries, as liberals have become primarily neoliberals and therefore on the major socio-economic questions of the day constituting the right, leaving conservatives, especially Christian democrats, as the apparent centre. Because of these complexities of liberalism, liberal parties have not been included in this survey of the left, even in the Scandinavian countries where their name (*venster*) literally means 'left'.

There is some change in the identities of the parties making up this broader left. Until the 1970s (later in Cyprus, France and Italy), it consisted primarily of communist parties; more recently it has been left-socialist parties (sometimes heirs of communist parties), greens, feminists (for a time in Iceland, currently in Sweden), and perhaps doubtfully the Pirate Party.

Figures 13.2a and 13.2b summarize the situation. All the Nordic countries, France, West Germany, Austria, Italy, Malta, Spain, Sweden and Greece had more than 45 per cent of votes for left of centre parties in the mid-1980s. In Spain, Sweden and Greece it was above 50 per cent. Around the turn of the century the only CEE countries with high figures – both above 50 per cent – were the Czech Republic and united Germany. In recent years there has been a decline in overall electoral performance by the broader left, but by smaller proportions than that of social democratic parties. Some Western countries saw stability or actual increases in overall left scores by the 2010s: particularly Ireland, Portugal and the UK (despite the latter's electoral system, which punishes minor parties), but also Cyprus, France, Malta, Switzerland and Germany, if West Germany 1987 is compared with united Germany in 2013. Declines in the broad left in central Europe between the turn of the century and the most recent election were extensive in Bulgaria, the Czech Republic, united Germany, Hungary and in particular Poland, though Croatia, Latvia and Slovakia bucked the trend.

These data suggest that, like their antagonists on the centre-right in most countries, social democrats will have to become accustomed to being the leading but not dominant party among looser assemblages on the left in general. As manufacturing and mining have declined as sources of employment, reducing the size of the industrial working class, post-industrial societies with more complex class structures are emerging which do not negate the concept of a left–right continuum, but change and render more varied its content. In particular, as Oesch (2006a, 2006b), Oesch and Rodríguez Menés (2011) and Kitschelt and Rehm (2014) have shown, there is divergence over issues of authoritarianism versus liberalism (attitudes on such issues as sexuality or ethnic minorities of the classic conservative–liberal divide) as opposed to those of economic inequality (the neoliberal versus social democratic divide). A more varied party structure would seem to follow logically from this. The

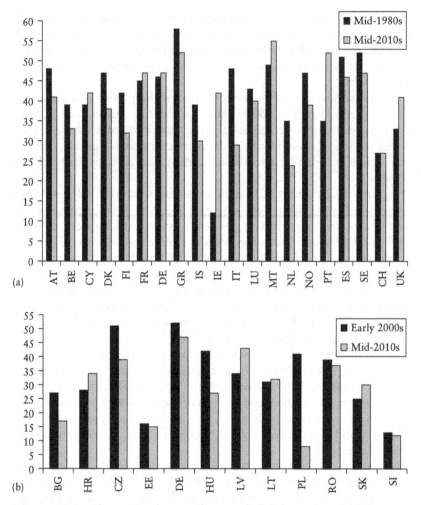

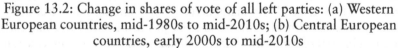

Figure 13.2: Change in shares of vote of all left parties: (a) Western European countries, mid-1980s to mid-2010s; (b) Central European countries, early 2000s to mid-2010s

Note: In part (a), DE signifies West Germany for 1987, unified Germany for 2013; in part (b) DE signifies unified Germany.
Source: https://en.wikipedia.org/wiki/Elections_by_country

formation of actual government coalitions does not always depend on ideological proximity among coalition partners. They might be based on agreement over whom parties want to exclude or the only political arithmetic that can work. However, if parties can recognize that some parties are closer to them than others, it can both facilitate coalition building and inhibit neighbouring parties from consorting with rivals.

While these developments are general, their implications for individual social democratic parties vary with differences in political history and party systems. For example, the German SPD is experienced at forming coalitions, with both Christian Democrats and Greens. It has far more difficulty with the new leftist party, *die Linken*, as while this is partly an example of the fragmentation of the left that is found in several countries, it is partly the inheritor of the party that formed the communist dictatorship of East Germany (Sozialistische Einheitspartei, SED). Many SPD politicians and voters find it unacceptable to form alliances with people from that background. Defections to *die Linken* have weakened the SPD to the point where it has little choice but to be a junior partner to the CDU/CSU – which in turn sends more voters to *die Linken*. It is difficult to see a change in this pattern until generational change phases out the SED – a process which has now begun to have effect.

Swedish social democrats have less difficulty forming occasional alliances with leftist parties, as these are not tainted by past participation in dictatorships. More problematic, ironically, is the Social Democratic Workers' Party's (SAP) own lengthy period as the dominant party of government. Other Swedish parties (apart from the far left) have therefore formed part of a so-called 'bourgeois' coalition stretching from the right to the non-SAP centre-left, whose main priority has been to exclude social democrats from government whenever possible. SAP has in turn seen them all as its enemies. These positions, if unchanged, will prevent the formation of new coalitions of a redefined left. Indeed, in neighbouring Denmark and Norway, the non-social democratic parties have recently shown a preference for negotiating deals with parties of the extreme-right in order to keep social democrats out of government.

The Labour Party in the UK, where the voting system forces an artificial duality on the outcome of elections, faces greater problems recognizing the new pluralism on the left. Worse still, the only new parties favoured by that system are geographically based ones, in particular the Scottish National Party, which tries to identify as a left party, and which has taken many votes from Labour. The Labour Party finds it very difficult to form governing coalitions with a party seeking an end to the British state, and is left with a problem similar to that of the SPD with *die Linken*, albeit for different reasons.

While theoretically it should be possible for social democrats to relocate themselves at the heart of new, broader groupings of the centre-left, history and existing structures often create major barriers to the realization of such a possibility. Two further factors must modify further any optimism: the rise of xenophobic parties on the far right, and the decline in electoral turnout in many countries.

The rise of the xenophobic right

Small right-wing populist parties have existed for several decades in a wide range of European countries, but in recent years they have acquired considerable importance in the majority of states by adopting a strong xenophobic stance, aimed partly against immigrants and partly against refugees, especially from the Islamic world. Terrorist acts by radical Islamic groups in a number of countries have assisted their progress.

Populist parties advocating a rejection of the welfare state and high taxation had been an unsuccessful feature of Scandinavian politics for several decades. More recently, their successors have acquired considerably more strength by reversing their position on the welfare state and adopting a xenophobic, in particular anti-Islamic, agenda. Since 2016 the Alternative für Deutschland Party in Germany, which began as a very small party advocating that Germany should leave the common European currency, has achieved considerable electoral traction by also becoming an anti-Islam party (particularly in the former East Germany, where very few Islamic people live). In the UK, the United Kingdom Independence Party (UKIP) began as a party mainly concerned with the apparent loss of sovereignty involved in the UK's membership of the EU, culminating in the successful campaign to have a majority in favour of leaving the organization in the referendum of 2016. During the course of UKIP's life and the referendum itself, the emphasis shifted to a major concern with levels of immigration, including that of refugees from the Middle East. In several other countries existing xenophobic parties have been strengthened in the wake of Islamic terrorism, particularly in Austria, Denmark, France and the Netherlands. The present government in Hungary has for several years maintained a policy of hostility to the country's existing ethnic minorities – Jews, gypsies, Romanians – and has now combined this stance with hostility to the EU's request that Hungary take its share of Middle Eastern refugees arriving on the coasts of Greece and Italy. A number of other governments in CEE have taken a similar position. These developments are not unique to Europe, as has been shown in the USA by the presidential election campaign of Donald Trump, with its stress on hostility towards Mexican immigrants and Islamic people. On the fringe of the democratic world, the government of Russia has adopted a strongly nationalistic position, and has attracted admiration from xenophobic movements in Europe and the USA.

A major change is taking place in global politics, with a resurgence of nationalism that has not been seen since the defeat of the Nazi and fascist regimes in World War II. Anxiety about globalization, resentment of the behaviour of global finance in the years leading up to the crisis of 2008, discomfort at the arrival of large numbers of refugees and immigrants, and fear of Islamic terrorism have come together to produce a strong climate of xenophobia. The majority of social democratic and some conservative parties have no wish to follow this path, but find their appeals to multicultural understanding losing out in rhetorical conflicts with the passions aroused by nationalism, the eventual importance of which cannot yet be predicted.

Declining electoral participation

So far we have looked at the decline in the electoral position of social democratic parties in terms of their percentages of the vote. The past 30 years have also seen a decline in the proportions of the electorate who actually vote in the established democracies, which means that the standing of these (and other) parties among citizens has declined even further. Statistics on changing turnout are presented in figure 13.3. In the Western European countries there had mainly been stability for at least 20 years before the mid-1980s, declines having taken place only in Cyprus, Finland, Portugal and Switzerland. Most CEE countries had seen very high turnout in their first elections after 1990, Estonia, Hungary and in particular Poland being the only exceptions. While decline has been on-going in some countries for a number of years, a major collapse took place across Europe around the time of the financial crisis. The only Western European countries barely affected by this trend are the Scandinavian countries, Malta, the Netherlands and Spain, while turnout actually rose slightly in Luxembourg and Switzerland. In most of CEE participation continued to drop, the only countries seeing increases being the Czech Republic and two countries where it had initially been very low: Estonia and Poland.

If we consider the votes of social democratic parties as a proportion of all citizens (i.e., of all those entitled to vote rather than of those actually voting), decline is even greater than when we examine shares of the vote (figure 13.4). Declines have been sharpest in Greece, the Netherlands, Austria and Spain. Some parties defied the trend: Italy, Malta, Portugal, and to a small extent Switzerland. In CEE the social democratic parties to suffer most from declining turnout were Poland, Hungary and united Germany. The only ones defying the trend were Latvia, Slovakia and in a minor way Estonia.

Declines in the standing among all citizens of all parties of the left have been less prominent and offset by some increases, as figure 13.5 shows.

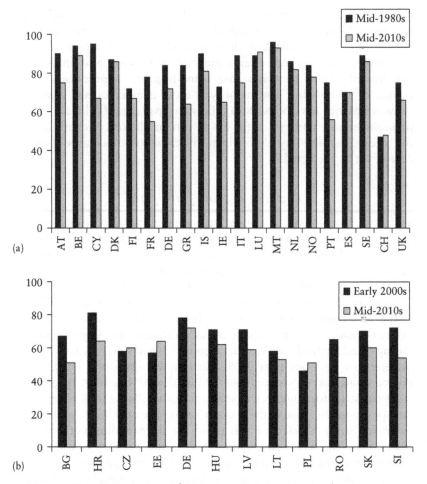

(a)

(b)

Figure 13.3: Proportion of citizens participating in elections: (a)
Western European countries, mid-1980s to mid-2010s; (b) Central
European countries, early 2000s to mid-2010s

Note: In part (a), DE signifies West Germany for 1987, unified Germany for
2013; in part (b) DE signifies unified Germany.
Source: http://www.idea.int/data-tools/data/voter-turnout

In the West there were, however, sharp declines in Greece, Austria and
Iceland, but rises in Ireland, Malta, Portugal, the UK, and to a small
extent the Netherlands and Switzerland. More striking is the fact that
since the turn of the century the broader left has strengthened its position
among citizens in general in every country in CEE except Poland.

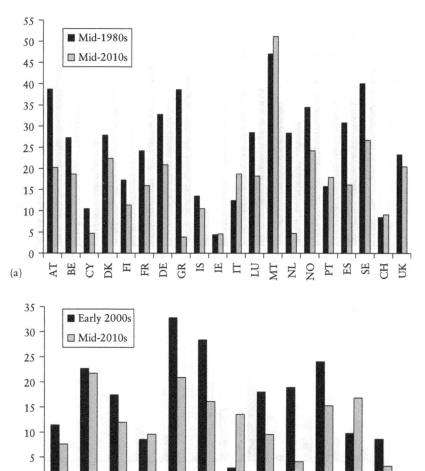

Figure 13.4: Change in shares of total electorate of social democratic parties: (a) Western European countries, mid-1980s to mid-2010s; (b) Central European countries, early 2000s to mid-2010s

Note: In part (a), DE signifies West Germany for 1987, unified Germany for 2013; in part (b) DE signifies unified Germany.
Source: https://en.wikipedia.org/wiki/Elections_by_country

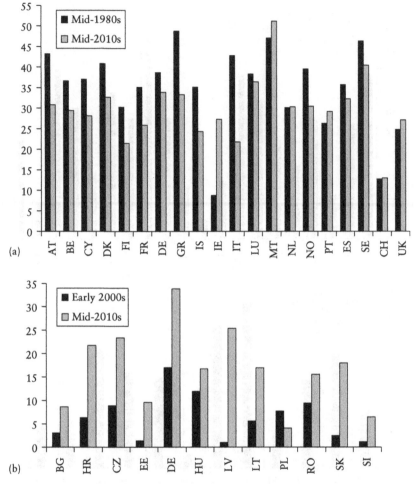

Figure 13.5: Change in shares of total electorate of all left parties,
(a) Western European countries, mid-1980s to mid-2010s;
(b) Central European countries, early 2000s to mid-2010s

Note: In part (a), DE signifies West Germany for 1987, unified Germany for
2013; in part (b) DE signifies unified Germany.
Source: https://en.wikipedia.org/wiki/Elections_by_country

The electoral decline of social democratic parties: conclusion

Overall, this analysis of voting changes suggests a more nuanced conclusion about the state of the left in Europe today than the story of simple decline. There is clear decline in social democracy's North-West European strongholds, but this is offset by recovery from a low base in CEE. There is therefore convergence towards social democracy being an important but by no means a dominant current across the continent (including its offshore islands). There is also evidence from a number of countries of growth in parties either to the left of social democracy or bearing alternative forms of left-wing politics. It is in company with these, and perhaps within a broader, liberal conception of the left that future social democrats are most likely to find their route into government. This latter shift might be particularly relevant if the rise of xenophobic parties on the far right continues.

These changes can be seen particularly prominently in the countries hit by the eurozone debt crisis: a major decline of established social democratic parties (often alongside their main centre-right rivals) in Portugal, Greece and Cyprus, and to a lesser extent Ireland and Spain though not at all in Italy; a rise in the wider left through Syriza in Greece, Podemos in Spain and Sinn Fein in Ireland. We must await elections in coming years to learn whether these sharp changes were exceptional, reversible events or have ushered in fundamental changes. Even if, as is likely, most of the new parties emerging on both left and right prove to be temporary and unsustainable, it is unlikely that classic social democratic parties will ever regain their place as the dominant representatives of society's left-leaning citizens. The political spectrum of the twenty-first century will not resemble that of the twentieth, because, mainly through the decline of industrial occupations, society itself has changed.

The neoliberal challenge to the social democratic policy agenda

Turning to substantive policy areas rather than political parties, we find social democracy in a similar position: it seems to be in retreat in many places, but retains a stubborn persistence and occasional points of growth. The reason is that it is very difficult for uncompromising neoliberal policies to be pursued in democracies. Market failures are widespread, and the inequalities and insecurities that characterize their operation create major social tensions. When governments that face elections encounter these problems, they are usually pressed into regulating

309

corporate behaviour and pursuing fiscal and spending policies to check markets and their consequences, approaches that are broadly social democratic. These are more likely to be pursued by governments dominated by, or at least including, social democratic parties, but can be found also under right-of-centre regimes. The main achievements of neoliberalism have been in the privatization of delivery of public services, rather than of the services themselves, which in the main remain publicly funded. In fact, given that most of these privatizations result in private oligopolies, they are hardly neoliberal but rather 'crony capitalist' achievements.

A major research project would be needed to evaluate the extent to which neoliberal policies have triumphed over social democratic ones, country by country. Here we must limit analysis to two areas: first, a brief examination of the extent to which EU policies have become primarily neoliberal; and second a summary look at trends in public spending.

Neoliberalism versus social democracy in EU policy-making

Overall economic regulation has mainly been delegated to the EU. European integration has always been a primarily market-making, and therefore neoliberal process, if only because, as Fritz Scharpf (1996) has long argued, it is easier to reach agreement on the negative integration involved in identifying obstacles to markets and eliminating them than on the positive one of constructing public policies. However, from the outset, the Treaty of Rome 1956 and its successors have always had built into them a commitment to 'ever closer union', an idea that transcends trade. While the significance of this phrase has been far more heavily disputed than the commitment to build open markets, it has had important consequences for policy in such areas as culture and security, some of which have been important to social democrats. There has also been major support from EU funds for infrastructure projects and structural reorganization in regions and countries with economic difficulties, especially in recent years in CEE. Not only have these been examples of a major form of social democratic collective goods provision; they have also redistributed wealth across Europe, as richer countries contribute more to the funds while poorer ones (and poor regions within rich countries) benefit most from them.

Even within the market-making arena, neoliberal approaches have by no means dominated. Trade unions and employers associations are consulted and involved in a manner characteristic of social democratic regimes. Although the strategy of labour market 'reform' launched in the 1990s had as its main target the neoliberal reduction of labour market regulation, it eventually adopted the 'flexicurity' approach, a

310

neoliberal-social democratic compromise that combined increasing flexibility through the reduction of regulation with new measures to provide workers with security that would enhance their labour market position rather than just protect it. Implementation of flexicurity measures often fell far short of these grand aims as they moved from their origins in Denmark and the Netherlands to be formally endorsed by the majority of EU Member States. Nevertheless, they constituted an important example of the continuing force of social democratic policies within the Union and the need for neoliberalism to compromise with them.

There has, however, been a major turn towards neoliberal deregulation in EU policy-making in recent years. One can point to three events in particular: the attempted Transatlantic Trade and Investment Partnership (TTIP) with the USA, the increasingly neoliberal interpretation of its role by the European Court of Justice (ECJ), and the treatment of the Southern European debtor states and Ireland, especially Greece.

The problem with TTIP from a social democratic perspective was that it envisaged a trade deal with the USA that would ease trade relations through the elimination of non-tariff barriers, and that it would establish investor–state dispute resolution (ISDR) as a means of resolving complaints against governments by corporations. The stress on simple deregulation implied a continuing neoliberal stance; a trade treaty inspired by social democracy would seek agreement on best practice, not least regulation. It is also unacceptable to social democrats (and, presumably, orthodox conservatives) to see the essential state function of judicial process handed over to private courts, as occurs with ISDR. Social democrats have not been strong enough in Europe, let alone the USA, to establish a TTIP that would suit their preferences. However, politicians of very different political colours (social democrats and protectionists) have combined to see off the original proposed treaty. When it reappears in changed form, it will be possible to discern further how far social democratic concerns will have shaped the revisions. Meanwhile, a trade deal between Canada and the EU (Canada Europe Trade Agreement, CETA), which embodies far less neoliberalism, has been agreed.

The ECJ has the primary task of ensuring that free markets agreed by Member States are not impeded. It is therefore active in limiting the powers of oligopolies and reducing tax avoidance – activities where pure neoliberals and social democrats share an agenda. The gradual extension of the Single Market into services has, however, brought it to a point of major disagreement between these two forces: the special status of public services, significantly redefined by European authorities as 'services of general interest' (Barbier et al. 2015). It remains possible for governments to reserve these services (health, education, care, policing, etc.)

311

outside the market – itself a concession to social democrats and orthodox conservatives – but the court has from time to time taken upon itself to define governments' freedom to do this when corporations seeking privatization raise objections. There may also be problems for governments wishing to reverse privatizations accepted by their predecessors. On a different matter, although European treaties entrench the rights of workers to engage in collective bargaining through trade unions, the ECJ has prevented some extensions of collective bargaining across national boundaries (Deakin and Rogowski 2011; Höpner 2008, 2014). Members of the court are appointed by Member States, but of course have the autonomy that is appropriate for a judiciary. The anti-social democrat development of the court is not therefore a direct consequence of social democracy's political decline, but of the thought processes of judges, including the particularly pro-market mentality of those appointed in the former state socialist countries.

The initial policy adopted by the European Commission (EC), the European Central Bank (ECB) and the International Monetary Fund (IMF) towards the nations caught up in the eurozone public debt crisis was a pure expression of neoliberal thinking. In particular, the first 2012 Memorandum 'agreed' with the Greek government for resolving that country's problems, placed the emphasis almost solely on the reduction of public spending, deregulation and reduction in the role of trade unions (Government of Greece 2012). Nothing was said about flexicurity or the need for infrastructural improvements if these countries were to compete in higher-value added markets. The goal was mainly to reduce direct and indirect labour costs. Even here, however, there has been a gradual modification. Despite its initial very tough stance on using monetary policy to soften the blows of the crisis, the ECB has gradually become expansive; too little, too late perhaps, but the change has occurred. Also, the 2015 Greek Memorandum, while it continues to insist on privatization, also stresses a need to end tax avoidance among wealthy citizens, strengthen the social safety net, improve vocational training and introduce employment support schemes (Government of Greece 2015). This has been a typical example of how social democracy exercises its influence today. Neoliberal policy makers and economic experts remain in the driving seat, but the sheer impracticality of their extreme measures and the social chaos they cause leads to compromises. Being reactive and non-strategic, these appear as inadequate half measures, but they continue to appear.

Public spending

It is not possible in the space available to make a detailed analysis of changes in public spending patterns, to determine the relative fates of conservative, neoliberal and social democratic policies in various countries across Europe. We can merely look at a few aggregate data. It is a central tenet of neoliberalism that the state should become 'smaller', in the sense of spending a declining proportion of national income. Social democratic parties, in contrast, are associated with the use of such spending to secure public provision and reduce inequalities. Although the trajectory varies from country to country, the rise of neoliberalism is usually dated from around the end of the 1970s. If social democracy is in decline, we should therefore expect to see an overall reduction in spending between 1980 and the present. For this purpose we can use only data from Western Europe, as the countries of CEE did not have a pre-1990 period dominated by various kinds of social compromise, nor did they have systems that enable the calculation of public spending as understood in capitalist economies. Data are missing for some countries in certain tables. It is not possible to include Germany in the general comparison, because of the impact of unification, but separate comments will be made on Germany in the course of discussion.

Figure 13.6 shows that the decline in public spending as a proportion

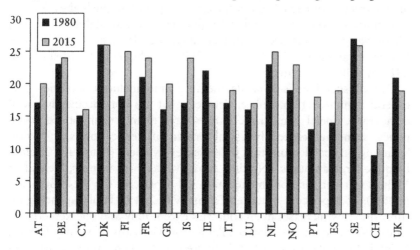

Figure 13.6: Changes in general government final consumption as percentages of national income, Western European countries, 1980–2015

Source: http://data.worldbank.org/indicator/NE.CON.GOVT.ZS

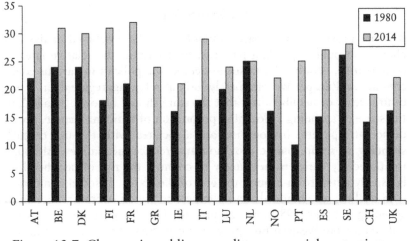

Figure 13.7: Changes in public expenditure on social protection as percentages of national income, Western European countries, 1980–2014

Source: http://data.uis.unesco.org/?queryid=181

of GDP that would be expected from neoliberal dominance is observable only in Ireland and Sweden, but the latter country had the highest level of all countries in both 1980 and 2015. (No data were available for Malta.) There was also some decline in Germany, with 1980 spending in West Germany having been 20.7 per cent of GDP, declining to 19.4 per cent in 2015 in united Germany.

Overall spending is a crude measure, and includes activities (e.g. general administration, police, defence) that are not specifically social democratic. Social democratic parties have mainly championed social policy spending, especially social protection, education and health. Spending on social protection increased everywhere (figure 13.7), often by quite large amounts. (No data were available for Cyprus, Iceland or Malta.) Germany is not an exception (21.4 per cent for West Germany in 1980; 25.8 per cent in united Germany in 2015). Public spending on education saw increases in all countries except Italy and the Netherlands (comparative data are not available for Germany, Cyprus, Greece, Iceland, Luxembourg or Malta) (figure 13.8). There were increases in public spending on health in all countries (no data are available for Belgium, Cyprus, Iceland or Malta) (figure 13.9). Germany does not seem to be an exception, with a rise to 9.4 per cent of GDP from the 1980 figure for West Germany of 6.3 per cent.

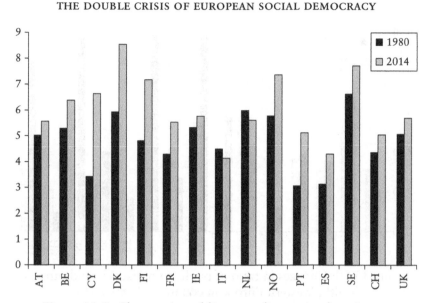

Figure 13.8: Changes in public expenditure on education as percentages of national income, Western European countries, 1980–2014

Source: http://data.uis.unesco.org/?queryid=181

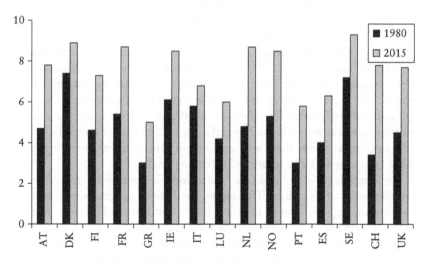

Figure 13.9: Changes in public expenditure on health as percentages of national income, Western European countries, 1980–2015

Source: http://data.uis.unesco.org/?queryid=181

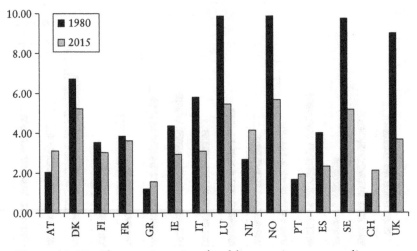

Figure 13.10: Changes in ratio of public to private expenditure on health, Western European countries, 1980–2015

Source: http://www.oecd.org/els/health-systems/health-data.htm; https://data.oecd.org/socialexp/social-spending.htm

There is, however, more evidence of neoliberal success in an increase in the proportion of spending on health that is private rather than public. Figure 13.10 shows the ratio of public to private health spending in 1980 and 2015. (The graph stops at 10 for 1980 for presentation purposes, though in fact the ratio of public to private spending in Norway in 1980 had been 53:1; in Sweden 12:1. The same data are missing as for figure 13.9.) This ratio declines in the majority of countries, showing an advance for private spending on health care in all countries except Austria, Greece, Ireland, the Netherlands, Portugal, Switzerland and the UK. In Germany, too, there was a decline in private health spending from West Germany in 1980 to unified Germany today.

Neoliberalism also seeks a reduction in taxation and in the progressivity of taxation. The aggregate figures suggest some success for this strategy on overall taxation levels, but only in Finland, Ireland, the Netherlands and Norway (not Germany) (figure 13.11). (No data were available for Malta.) However, more detailed research by the OECD shows a major decline in the progressivity of taxation in most European (and other advanced) countries during the period, mainly through reduced taxation rates on business and high incomes (OECD 2011).

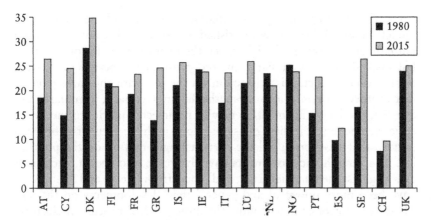

Figure 13.11: Changes in tax revenues as percentages of national income, Western European countries, 1980–2015

Source: http://data.worldbank.org/indicator/GC.TAX.TOTL.GD.ZS

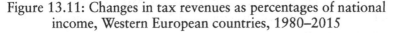

The challenge to the social democratic agenda: conclusion

After the first waves of neoliberal policies towards the welfare state in the USA, Pierson argued that few inroads had been made, because of the resilience of programme inertia (Pierson 1994). The data briefly reviewed here suggest that similar conclusions hold for European countries 20 years later. On the other hand, broad aggregates do not tell the full story, as the evidence on private health and tax progressivity suggests. As with the analysis of voting behaviour, social democratic policies emerge from this discussion reduced but resilient – though not necessarily carried by social democratic parties. Social democracy's approaches are not dominant; in fact they rarely were outside the Nordic countries. They remain important components of the overall policy mix, and have withstood much of the neoliberal onslaught, though mainly in the form of defensive protection of past achievements rather than positive strategic planning.

Conclusions

Contrary to what might have been expected, the political consequences of the crisis of 2008 and subsequent eurocrisis have not been favourable to social democrats. Because social democratic governments were in office in the UK, Greece, Portugal and Spain at the time of the crisis and shared responsibility for what occurred, they were unable to benefit from what was essentially a neoliberal crisis. Instead, new parties to the left of social democracy flourished in Greece and Spain. This could not happen so easily in the UK, given the majoritarian electoral system, but instead the Labour Party entered a prolonged period of internal tension and conflict. Dissatisfaction on the left with the early twenty-first-century economy also strengthened in Germany, Denmark and Sweden, producing again either new or resurrected parties to the left of social democracy. It is these divisions, along with the earlier rise of green parties, that have produced the current fragmentation on the political left. The xenophobic movements have, however, also been a reaction of anger against the financial crisis, and (apart from Greece and Spain) they have been more powerful and general than developments on the left. These very recent changes follow the more gradual process of electoral decline of social democracy that is a result partly of changing demography and occupational structure, partly of a more general decline of interest in voting.

If, as has been argued here, social democracy will increasingly have to accept being just one element in a group of contending political forces (something that has long been the case in the Netherlands and Switzerland, more recently also in Denmark), its relations to other political families will need to be reappraised. In addition to the historical antagonists of liberals and moderate conservatives and Christians, this now raises the issue of their relationship to the new xenophobic movements. These are usually not neoliberal, but support a welfare state (provided it is reserved for natives). While social democratic movements have in theory always been internationalist and cosmopolitan in outlook, their practical achievements have also been strongly national. As Goodhart (2013), Streeck (2015) and some other observers have pointed out, the 'universalism' of the social democratic welfare state has almost always been a limited universe that stops at the national border, as it has been based on the powerful, egalitarian concept of national citizenship, rooted in people's sense of shared membership in a national community. There has never been any reason why social democracy's ordinary voters, as opposed to its thinkers, should have cosmopolitan attitudes. The idea is expressed most clearly in the Swedish concept of the welfare state as *folkshemmet*, the place where people can feel at home. These meanings could be stretched to include small numbers of immigrants, but to how many? Is the US aversion to a strong welfare state a reflection of its cultural heterogeneity? Thinking on these lines leads some to seek a national social democracy, which requires severe limitations on immigration, a rejection of liberalism, and in the case of European countries withdrawal from the EU. Such parties could make common cause with welfare-oriented xenophobic parties. The Danish Social Democratic Party has already been exploring such possibilities.

Curiously, the rise of right-wing xenophobia is bringing social democracy into a centrist position in an evolving spectrum that runs between two different forms of what we have known as the political right. One form is neoliberal: universalist, oriented to free trade and inclusive, but rejecting strong social policy, redistributive taxation and the regulation of capital. Diametrically opposed to this is the nationalistic right, exclusionary and protectionist, supporting a strong welfare state and economic regulation. Social democrats, in the middle, share the universalism of neoliberals but the welfare orientation of at least some forms of xenophobic populism. This could develop into a position of some power in political horse-trading.

A new compromise with neoliberalism seems more logical for social democracy than one with right-wing populism. First, although the great welfare states developed under the aegis of national identity, this was a benign form, not directed against outsiders. The most advanced welfare states developed in open trading nations – Scandinavia, Germany, the Netherlands, the UK. To assert the limitation of social citizenship to 'real' nationals now can no longer be the *folkshem* of a people who just happen to be ethnically homogeneous, but becomes symbolized by the demand of the Front National that rights be limited to *français de la souche* (best translated broadly as 'true born French'), requiring active exclusion of those deemed to be outsiders. Non-aggressive nationalism is still possible in places like Scotland or Greece, where resentment against external domination does not require the victimization of immigrants and refugees. Elsewhere it has become very difficult to sustain; once it becomes common political currency to define the presence of a group of foreigners or ethnic minorities as a problem, all the running in defining increasingly hostile policies towards those groups rests with the most xenophobic party, others being dragged along in their wake but not necessarily sharing in their popularity.

Second, as noted above, economic experts in the OECD, the IMF and the European Commission are coming to realize the social limits of constant marketization and increasing inequality, motivated mainly by the risks being posed by growing US inequality to mass consumption. In the wake of the Brexit vote, some global investment advisors went further and began to worry whether growing inequality was not nourishing xenophobic resentment against globalization. Neoliberalism may be open to compromises with social democratic approaches in order to secure its own survival. There are certainly precedents for neoliberal-social democratic compromises. New Labour in the UK, the *Neue Mitte* in the SPD, the New Democrats in the USA, have all been examples, as are today the *Democratici* in Italy. These may in some respects seem uncomfortable antecedents, but arguably the largest single social change in recent times, the move towards gender equality, has also been a shared neoliberal/social-democratic, anti-conservative project.

However, that which is logical is not necessarily that which is politically the most likely. Both neoliberals and social democrats might prefer to contend for sharing the new anti-foreigner fervour that has been unleashed by far-right populism and has energized increasingly weary political systems, rather than explore their own potential for constructive compromise. Although attitudes to immigrants and refugees are governing popular feeling, the core issue is really the approach to globalization. Neoliberals are associated with unregulated, unrestrained globalization; the xenophobic right to protection against it. Here, too, social democrats stand between these two forms of the right, advocating the regulated globalization that is likely to be the only viable approach as conflict intensifies (see, e.g., Rasmussen and Bullmann 2016). Their policy stance will make a major contribution to future global policy, even if their parties are too weak to take the lead in that process.

References

Barbier, J.-C., Rogowski, R. and Colomb, F. (2015) *The Sustainability of the European Social Model.* Cheltenham: Edward Elgar.

Crouch, C. (2013) *Making Capitalism Fit for Society.* Cambridge: Polity.

Deakin, S. and Rogowski, R. (2011) Reflexive labour law, capabilities and the future of social Europe. In Rogowski, R., Salais, R. and Whiteside, N. (eds) *European Employment Policy: Labour Market Transitions and the Promotion of Capability.* Cheltenham: Edward Elgar, pp. 229–55.

Goodhart, D. (2013) *The British Dream: Successes and Failures of Post-War Immigration.* London: Atlantic.

Government of Greece (2012) Memorandum of Understanding on Specific Economic Policy Conditionality, 9 February 2012. Athens: Government of Greece.

Government of Greece (2015) Memorandum of Understanding for a Three-Year ESM Programme, 19 August 2015. Athens: Government of Greece.

Höpner, M. (2008) Usurpation statt Delegation: Wie der EuGH die Binnenmarktintegration radikalisiert und warum er politische Kontrolle bedarf. MPIfG Discussion paper 08/12. Cologne: Max Planck Institute for the Study of Societies.

Höpner, M. (2014) Wie der Europäische Gerichtshof und die Kommission Liberalisierung durchsetzen. MPIfG Discussion paper 14/8. Cologne: Max Planck Institute for the Study of Societies.

Kitschelt, H. and Rehm, P. (2014) Occupations as a site of political preference formation. *Comparative Political Studies* 47(12): 1670–706.

Kriesi, H. (2014) The political consequences of the financial and economic crisis in Europe: electoral punishment and populist protest. In Bermeo, N. and Bartels, L.M. (eds) *Mass Politics in Tough Times*. Oxford: Oxford University Press, pp. 297–333.

OECD (2011) *Divided We Stand*. Paris: OECD.

Oesch, D. (2006a) *Redrawing the Class Map*. Basingstoke: Palgrave Macmillan.

Oesch, D. (2006b) Coming to grips with a changing class structure: an analysis of employment stratification in Britain, Germany, Sweden and Switzerland. *International Sociology* 21(2): 263–88.

Oesch, D. and Rodríguez Menés, J. (2011) Upgrading or polarization? Occupational change in Britain, Germany, Spain and Switzerland, 1990–2008. *Socio-Economic Review* 9(3): 503–31.

Pierson, P. (1994) *Dismantling the Welfare State?* Cambridge: Cambridge University Press.

Rasmussen, P.N. and Bullmann, U. (2016) *The Social Democracy to Come*. London: Social Europe and Friedrich Ebert Stiftung Europe Office.

Scharpf, F. (1996) Negative and positive integration in the political economy of European welfare states. In Schmitter, P.C., Marks, G., Streeck, W. and Scharpf, F. (eds) *Governance in the European Union*. London: Sage, pp. 15–38.

Streeck, W. (2015) The rise of the European Consolidation State. MPIfG Discussion Paper 15/1. Cologne: Max Planck Institute for the Study of Societies.

Appendix: Country name abbreviations

AT	Austria	IS	Iceland
BE	Belgium	IT	Italy
BG	Bulgaria	LT	Lithuania
CH	Switzerland	LU	Luxembourg
CY	Cyprus	LV	Latvia
CZ	Czech Republic	MT	Malta
DE	Germany	NL	Netherlands
DK	Denmark	NO	Norway
EE	Estonia	PL	Poland
EL	Greece	RO	Romania
ES	Spain	SE	Sweden
FI	Finland	SI	Slovenia
HR	Croatia	SK	Slovakia
HU	Hungary	UK	United Kingdom
IE	Ireland		

Chapter 14

The Rise of the Radical Right
Michel Wieviorka

When racism concerns the dominant group within a society, and the same applies to anti-Semitism, it is easily accommodated by nationalism and the political approaches of the radical right, also sometimes known as the extreme-right or national-populist right. It is not surprising that political forces of this type have appeared and began to be established in Europe in the mid-1980s in the same historical context as that of the resurgence of racism and anti-Semitism, with precursors in the 1970s which include the Fremskridts Party in Denmark or the Parti Anders Lange in Norway. Thus in France the Front national ceased to be a marginal group and appeared as a party to be reckoned with in 1983. Jörg Haider became the leader of the Freedom Party of Austria (FPÖ) in 1986, after this party, formed in 1955, had participated in a governmental coalition for three years; he made it a party with a stronger and clearer political identity, no longer possible to ignore. And in May 2016, Norbert Hofer, the FPÖ candidate in the presidential election got 49.7 per cent of the votes; the Austrian Constitutional Court decided to call for new elections, due to too many irregularities. Another important aspect of this presidential election is that the candidates of the classical parties were totally defeated, the winner being a green leader, Alexander Van der Bellen.

The Vlaams Blok was launched in Flanders in 1978 (and became Vlaams Belang or Flemish Interest in 2004) and obtained over 100,000 votes in the 1987 election. One of the last arrivals in the arena of these radical right parties, having transcended the phase of being a small group, is the UK Independence Party (UKIP), which is also distinctly anti-immigrant and Eurosceptic, but endeavours to avoid any resemblance with a fascist force and maintains its distance from parties like the Front national whose 'visceral' anti-Semitism it does not accept. UKIP has been a key actor in the British debates and finally the vote for Brexit in 2016.

Even in Germany, a country whose Nazi past seemed to protect it from any national-populist tendencies, we have witnessed the emergence in 2012 of the Alternative für Deutschland (AfD – Alternative for Germany), which has since obtained scores which are far from negligible in the 2014 European elections (7.1 per cent of the votes cast) or in the parliamentary elections in some Länder. This party is clearly opposed to Angela Merkel's policy towards migrants.

It would be an exaggeration to say that political membership of these parties is an expression of direct and total adherence to racism and anti-Semitism: the correspondence is far from perfect. But they do afford the means of rising to the level of political systems despite the institutional, national or European mechanisms which endeavour to counter them, for example by subjecting them to legislation under which racism or anti-Semitism is an aggravating factor. This is in particular the case in Belgium, the UK and in France.

Not all national movements are of necessity racist or anti-Semitic, as we have seen with UKIP, and the idea of the nation may itself be synonymous, in some situations, with liberation, emancipation and overture – this was the case with the Year of Revolution in 1848, sometimes referred to as the 'Springtime of the Peoples'. There are still today movements of nationalist inspiration which cannot be reduced to images that portray them as forces of evil – I have in mind in particular Catalan or Scottish regionalisms, though these will not be discussed here.

Nationalist rights in Europe today: unity and diversity

Whenever the question of the radical or extremist right in Europe arises, stark images dominate public discussion, as if the threat is of a similar nature everywhere and conveys the same meanings at all times and in all places. It is true that these actors do share important commonalities. They are all nationalist and, to some extent, racist, xenophobic and anti-Semitic. They call for a closed society and a homogeneous nation and despise immigrants and immigration which they are quick to describe as 'illegal'. In instances where there is a Muslim presence in a country, or where the hypothesis has risen, they consider the threat of Islam to be a powerful factor, evoking fear and hatred – though in Hungary, the Jobbik has frequently taken pro-Palestinian and anti-Israeli (and anti-semitic) positions, and expressed some sympathy for the Muslim world. They are distinctly anti-European and constantly criticize globalization. They share a clear refusal towards any policy that would let refugees come to Europe from the Middle East or from North Africa. They shape fears and cultural as well as economic concerns, and appeal to the losers, the excluded, the forgotten or those marginalized by modernization. They turn to their advantage the tendency to discredit the political parties and their leaders. They present themselves as being on the defence, promising the self-defence of the nation, contrasting the motherland or the people with the technocratic and multicultural elites who, according to them, lead Europe.

However, there are considerable differences between countries and extreme-right movements and, within movements, between different periods in time. This is immediately obvious if one considers post-Soviet Eastern Europe and the West. In Eastern Europe these actors are classical, the more or less direct heirs of the fascists or Nazis of the 1930s. This is the case in particular for the Samobroona or Self Defence Party in Poland, the LNNK (the Alliance for Fatherland and Freedom) in Latvia, or the SRS, the Serbian Radical Party. In Western Europe, extreme-right movements are distinctly more innovative, as we shall see. For example, we cannot imagine the extreme-right in Bulgaria or Romania adopting a leader such as Pim Fortuyn, member of the Leefbaar Nederland (Livable Netherlands) who made no secret of his homosexuality and was assassinated in 2002. More specifically, it is extremely useful to consider these movements from the point of view of what differentiates them, which may be quite surprising when compared with conventional ideas. We shall do this by taking the French Front national (FN) as a benchmark for evaluation, by analysing it in depth and by examining in what ways other experiences are either similar or different.

Anti-systemic parties?

The extreme-right parties like to present themselves as being unrelated to the political system of their country and eager to undermine or destroy it. In the present European context there are several countries in which they find a favourable environment; whenever a crisis threatens the legitimacy of the institutions and parties, this can contribute to reinforcing their discourse. The crisis in the European institutions can only accentuate this tendency. When the powers that be in Brussels seem distant, technocratic and in the hands of people who are not responsible to an electorate for their actions, when the parties on the left and on the right are discredited, at best impotent, but sometimes also corrupt, the extreme-right parties can easily present themselves as anti-systemic.

But this is not the case everywhere. Let's take the FN in France. Long outside the political system, with almost no role in representative democracy, they constantly presented themselves in the public sphere as resolutely opposed to the present system. But it is also a force which has begun to penetrate the political system, intending to play a role and stand its ground there. It now comprises members at local, national and European parliament levels, makes its voice heard within the confines of democracy and presents itself as a government party. It is not the heir of the movements of the 1930s and it differs from, for example, the German neo-Nazi Nationaldemokratische Partei Deutschlands (NPD or National Democratic Party NDP), its neo-fascist Italian counterparts like Casa Pound and the Jobbik Party in Hungary (Alliance des jeunes de Droite – The Movement for a Better Hungary). Similarly the comparison with the extreme-right neo-Nazi Greek party Golden Dawn should not be pushed too far. This party, while observing the parliamentary rules, is none the less also actively violent and factional, which is not the case for the Front national today. Nevertheless, Golden Dawn, formed in 1980, is the party which is the closest to Nazism; it adheres to the idea of a link between Greek Antiquity and Aryanism, but also to neo-Nazism, with the assertion of the superiority of a white race coupled with a degree of paganism, and evokes fascism by combining electoral activity and violence.

By adopting an electoral and parliamentary approach, the Front national belongs to a political family in which we also find the Dutch Party for Freedom (the PVV), the True Finns, the Lega Nord in Italy, the Union Démocratique du Centre in Switzerland, the Danish People's Party, the Progress Party in Norway and the People's Orthodox Alarm (LAOS) in Greece. These are political forces which have all succeeded in one way or another in participating in government, in particular in governmental coalitions. And it should be noted that in Hungary and Poland, very conservative and xenophobic powers are not very far from other extreme-right forces. In recent elections (2016 and 2017), some of these political forces obtained impressive results, even if the result was somewhat disappointing for them. In Austria, the candidate for the FPÖ, Norbert Hofer, was not far from winning the presidential election, but lost in December 2016; in the Netherlands, Geert Wilders and his party made a strong progression in the legislative election in March 2017, but the result was not as good as expected, and he was not able to participate in the government. In France, Marine Le Pen gained at the presidential election almost double the votes compared with her father in 2002, but the result was also ambiguous, since it showed huge progress, but also the incapacity to get access to power. During their debates with other candidates, these kinds of leaders appear much more as protesting and criticizing the ruling elites, rather than able to promote any serious programme or vision. When they are close to power, or in power, for instance at the local level, they have difficulties in transforming electoral progress into a real ability to manage and govern. Their successes, all over Europe, indicate that populism, nationalism and some authoritarian lure are at stake; their failures indicate symmetrically that there is some capacity to resist their progress, but not necessarily due to classical political forces: in France, for example, the new President, Emmanuel Macron, does not belong to any of the established political parties.

One should be cautious and choose one's words carefully when noting that an extreme-right party, though it may participate in this type of coalition, or endeavour to win elections democratically, may nevertheless have as its goal the destruction of the political system and the establishment of an authoritarian regime in which racism, xenophobia and anti-Semitism could be central elements. But the development of a strategy that respects the institutions and democracy, even if the ultimate aim is to destroy them, is not the same thing as relying on practices of violence to access political power or move closer thereto. We must avoid any amalgamation of the forces which accept the rules of the electoral process, even if they do so temporarily and those which, from the outset, refute them. Let us add that at the European level, some extreme-right parties participate and co-operate in groups that are recognized by the European Parliament. The Front national, for instance, participates in one group that includes the FPÖ, the PVV or the Lega Nord (which recently became a national rather than a regionalist force, acting at the Italian level and not only in the north of the country). And out of the Parliament, some very radical movements such as Golden Dawn (Greece) or Forza Nuova (Italy) are members of a European party, the Alliance for Peace and Freedom (APF).

Parties that condone and use serious violence

An immediate extension of the above is to be found in the relation that exists between these forces and violence. There are two different models here. The first concerns the actors who resort directly to violence, a violence which is frequently racist and for whom violence constitutes a resource, the means of achieving an end. The second is very different. It is based on the refusal to resort to violence – a refusal which in no way exonerates the political force in question from all responsibility in the existence of certain forms of violence. We can take the case of the Front national to illustrate this second model. Today, and for some time now, the Front national considers that it is not appropriate to resort to racist violence; quite the contrary. In any event neither the political apparatus nor the main decision makers can be held responsible for extreme-right violence. When skinheads and other neo-Nazis are involved in violence, or when barbarism is on the agenda (in the Jewish cemetery in Carpentras for example, where some young extremists removed a corpse from a tomb in 1990 and impaled it), it is a mistake to immediately accuse the FN. Violence harms this party's strategy of respectability and its endeavours to advance electorally; it is a problem for the party and not a solution. But each time that the FN gains ground, it contributes to enlarging the space where hatred is fomented. It includes dimensions of racism, anti-Semitism and xenophobia which are not dissipated with the 'de-demonization' intended by Marine Le Pen. The Dieudonné affair reminded us that there are still nefarious elements within the FN, including Jean-Marie Le Pen; he has attended the comedian's shows, which have highly anti-Semitic connotations and has since never missed an occasion to remind us of his anti-Semitic obsessions, which is why he was expelled from his party in 2015. Therefore, while it does not itself organize the development of violence materially, as soon as one moves away from its most structured circles, the FN provides the elements that will legitimize those who are going to take action. It opens up new symbolic spaces; it facilitates appeals to hatred and in the last resort their translation into action.

Apparently one could make similar observations in many countries. In Norway, for example, the seventy-seven deaths caused by Anders Breijvik were set in a context in which the Progress Party was fomenting hatred, but this Party in no way endorsed the killing. This poses a very important question for general sociology: how can we avoid this version of 'sociologizing', which suggests a direct relationship between the murders and the ideas of racist hatred in circulation in a country (and which are possibly capitalized on by a national-populist force), without falling prey to 'psychologizing', which considers the perpetrators of extreme violence (such as the Breivik massacre in Norway on 22 July 2011, the Merah murders in March 2012 in Montauban and Toulouse, the Kouachy brothers, etc.) to be psychopaths, mentally ill or highly specific personalities?

Finally, regarding racist violence, we have to learn from history. A political party can advance by functioning on two registers, one being directly violent but without the party claiming responsibility for it, and the other respectful of electoral politics. These two rationales may co-exist, but may also contradict each other. The history of Nazism is instructive here; the rise of Hitler went through phases when the two approaches were complementary, but also phases when they were opposed in the mind of the Führer. This was in particular the case when

Hitler moved against the SA (Sturmabteilung or Storm Detachment) during the 'Night of the Long Knives' in 1934. The SA (the 'brown shirts') used a much more revolutionary and populist form of violence and he acted to give preference to the SS. But this did not prevent the direct, explicit violence advocated in *Kristallnacht* in 1938, which also found its place in the Nazis' strategy.

National-populism

The word 'populism', possibly qualified by the adjective 'national', has never been adequately defined, but at this point it suffices to say that it evokes powerful images, starting with demagogy, the appeal to direct democracy and the elimination of all distance between the people and authority, represented by a charismatic leader as was the case in Austria with Jörg Haider or in France with Jean-Marie Le Pen.

Now once again let's take France as an example. The FN today, under the leadership of Jean-Marie Le Pen's daughter, Marine, has a leader who is much less charismatic than he was. Above all, the aim is not to end any mediation between the people and the highest echelons of State, but on the contrary to ensure the party has an organized structure present at all levels of political life, from the town hall to Parliament and then into government. Populism has not disappeared but it is combined with other elements, and is being gradually watered down as the FN gains momentum, develops and advances step by step, election by election.

This is a reminder that these radical right-wing parties do not form a homogeneous and stable entity and that they are all liable to evolve. They may disappear, as the MSI, the neo-fascist Italian party led by Gianfranco Fini did in 1995; he moved closer to Silvio Berlusconi and entered the government. The MSI disappeared and gave way to the Alleanza nazionale which shed its references to fascism. Whether they move away from an extremism which was at the outset violent, or conversely, whether they slide into it, comparisons over time, either party by party, or within Europe, country by country are very useful here. They demonstrate that these parties range from violent neo-Nazi or fascist extremism with no institutional perspective, to being almost absorbed into the conservative right-wing parties. (On occasions it is the conservative right which merges into the radical right.) The label 'populist' eliminates the need for analysing what differentiates them.

Forces which are culturally traditional?

Let's begin once again with the Front national. Populist and national-ist, this party is very far from power and from representing a culturally inventive modernity. It is much closer to traditional values than to innovation and creativity, especially when these can be criticized as being features of the cosmopolitism of elites or of the images of the countercul-ture associated with the *bobos* or middle-class trendies. In fact, the FN is torn between rationales which confine it to tradition and even its most reactionary conceptions, and others which locate it in contemporary modernity. Male chauvinism, misogyny and homophobia can be found there, but not everyone practises these – moreover, it should also be noted that in this galaxy of radical and extremist rights we do meet examples of genuine cultural or moral overture. Pim Fortuyn, the Dutch leader we referred to above, combined extreme-right tendencies with considerable cultural modernity; similarly, Geert Wilders, the leader in the Netherlands of the PVV (Partij voor de Vrijheid, Party for Freedom), presents himself as a defender of homosexuals. This type of cultural modernity is also found in Switzerland with the Swiss People's Party, the UDC/SVP, and in Scandinavia, with the Progress Party in Norway. In France, the protest movements against '*Le mariage pour tous*' or 'marriage for all', which means primarily marriage between homosexuals, were not systematically followed, and far less supported by FN militants. Finally, while for the past 150 years France has witnessed the opposition between the Catholic church and Republican Universalism – known as the 'war of the two Frances' – the FN, in many respects heir to an anti-Semitic, national Catholicism associated with Charles Maurras, prides itself on being the defender of republican values, with secularism top of the list. Some of its arguments against Islam and Muslims originate here.

Furthermore, the FN is as adept as anyone else in the use of the Internet and modern means of communication; it is also permeated by the new IT culture which values the circulation of ideas and opinions, interactivity and the refusal of authoritarianism. The FN is in no way behind the times.

Under what conditions does a national-populist party open up to modern cultural values, even 'post-materialist' values, to use the termi-nology of the political scientist Ronald Inglehart? There is a connection here with the rapprochement of this type of party to the more traditional right-wing parties and their efforts to become more democratic and move closer to classical conservatism. When the classical right-wing is power-less, disintegrated and incapable of acquiring a strong, united vision and effective leadership, a space opens up for political rapprochements in which the classical conservative electorate turns to national-populist ideas and where the national-populists endeavour to be respectable to gain political weight in a local or governmental coalition. These endeavours may embrace a cultural opening to modernity.

The consequences of the economic crisis?

We must be wary of the rather elementary ideas which, at the stroke of a pen, link the rise of extreme and racist right-wing parties with the economic difficulties of the countries concerned. In the first instance, because an international comparison at European level contradicts anything reminiscent of summary determinism: in Switzerland and in Norway, countries which are not, or at least not deeply, affected by the crisis, impulses comparable to those which culminate in the Front national are a factor in political life. In Switzerland, for example, the UDC (Swiss People's Party) is opposed to any international opening of the country, advocates an ultra-liberal economy, is xenophobic and was politically successful in referenda which de facto threaten the participation of Switzerland in particular in the European Union's scientific and academic policies. In contrast to Switzerland or Norway, in Spain, where the economic situation is worse than in France, there is no equivalent to the Front national.

Nevertheless, the Front national is fuelled by the crisis, or, more exactly, finds therein the elements for its electoral strategy, in particular by attributing to immigrants or to Islam, the social evils of France – a form of discourse to which a large part of the working-class electorate is sensitive. This electorate comprises those who have been left behind by globalization, in the first instance the 'forgotten' and the 'invisible', those workers who are no longer newsworthy, who often live in peri-urban areas, prey to considerable difficulties with no real hope of a better future. If these parties are successful, it is not because of the economic crisis which affects these populations. It is primarily because of the shortcomings of the classical political forces, beginning with those on the left. They are the orphans of communism on one hand and, on the other, of the elements which a true social democracy backed by a powerful working-class movement should provide.

In the immediate post-war period, extreme-right networks and organizations seeking to function at the European level were constituted, so much so that there are sometimes references to 'European nationalism'. We could mention, for example, the Jeune Europe movement, associated with the name of its Walloon leader, Jean Thiriart. Movements of ideas, not strongly structured, may also have had a pro-European influence on some extreme-right parties. Europe may thus have been presented as being what had to be saved from globalization, but also in order to confront the two major imperialisms in the Cold War, the Americans and Soviet Russia, or later, to avoid the waves of immigrants (in the journal *Le Partisan européen*, for example). Similarly, the Christian identity of Europe was sometimes advanced to justify the rejection of immigrants from Muslim countries. Thus, for example, Viktor Orban, the Prime Minister of Hungary, stated in strong terms on 2 September 2005 in the *Frankfurter Allgemeine Zeitung*: 'Europe and European identity have Christian roots'. Europe has not always been perceived as something negative by right-wing extremists.

It is not only the European Union which is challenged by the rise of nationalist parties and the emergence or attraction of authoritarian powers; we have only to think of Putin's Russia, or the Tea Party and Donald Trump in the US to be convinced of this. But the European Union has entered a dialectic with these evolving tendencies from which it may well not recover. In times of economic and social crisis, the EU is rapidly and easily criticized for its inefficiency, but it is also accused of not allowing nation-states to defend their citizens and to take the steps which an independent national policy would permit. It is also accused of making the democratically elected political representatives in these same nation-states into puppets incapable of acting without the validation and implementation of decisions taken in Brussels. This all fuels the crisis of the political elites, Poujadism and populism and feeds the radicalization of the extremes, more on the right rather than on the left, given that Marxism and Communism are now permanently discredited. The greater the power of the nationalist and extremist right, the greater their capacity to highlight the shortcomings of Europe, its deficiencies, its possible structural difficulties in articulating its currency, the euro, with its political project, or of saving the Schengen free movement area and the technocratic and bureaucratic distance which it establishes between the European Commission and the grass-roots voters, the greater its capacity to render this same Commission powerless. We have witnessed this with the crisis of the migrants, which became acute in 2015 but was already very evident previously when the media published almost daily dramatic images of refugees risking death for the opportunity of reaching Lampedusa (an island to the South of Italy) or in Spain, where European leaders were pleading with the Juncker Plan for solidarity and where national selfishness largely predominated, along with fears that were racist, xenophobic and Islamophobic, and prejudices concerning the true implications of the possible reception of the migrants. Nationalist and extremist forces thrive each time terrorism strikes successfully because they demand with considerable support more security and more measures against everything that seems to come from the outside world. Now Europe can be easily incriminated there as well: in the first instance because the terrorists move around easily, as witnessed in the attacks on 13 November 2015 in Paris, organized along the axis Molenbeek (a district in Brussels) and Saint Denis (a suburb north of Paris). Then because the cooperation of the police is not very satisfactory at the European level (it is already in most instances not very satisfactory at the national level; the media like to refer to the 'in-fighting between police forces'). Furthermore, nationalist and extremist parties can focus on a national history and culture, which is more difficult when it is a question of Europe. The ever-deepening crisis in the European Union is both the horizon of these forces, which aim to intensify it, and their source, with the result that it is effectively a phenomenon that must be analysed at the European level, being envisaged country by country to take into account the specificities of each.

Conclusion

We are witnessing changes in and growth of renewed and different forms of racism, anti-Semitism, terrorism and nationalism or national-populism. As from the mid-1980s – perhaps we could say since 1984, a very symbolic date – a considerable transformation has been reflected in Europe by the growth of disturbing phenomena operating at infra-political and meta-political but also political levels. These phenomena are not necessarily specific to Europe alone; they present global, worldwide aspects and strong national specificities. But what they do share is the fact that they undermine Europe (or the old continent); they are the negation of its ethical and humanist values and its enemy on the political level. For those who wish to believe in the construction of Europe, it is extremely difficult to confront this challenge: the political crisis is patently obvious, the economic crisis prevents those in power from priding themselves on an image of success, and nationalisms can highlight, each in its own way, national narratives, languages, traditions, literatures and the vibrancy of artistic life, in areas where Europe lacks cultural resources specific to it. The main endeavour to propose cultural unity has consisted in valorizing Christianity, which in reality is only likely to divide Europeans, many of whom are atheists, agnostics and above all, anxious to separate religion from politics.

The forces of evil are also the forces of disintegration of the European Union. Europe will not emerge unscathed if it merely endeavours to redress the balance in economic affairs. As long as Europe appears to be undemocratic or insufficiently democratic, possibly non- or post-political or post-democratic, and is incapable of acquiring the military and diplomatic structures that would enable it to impose its founding values, it will be vulnerable to the forces of evil. These forces find their ideological resources and their destructive force in the spiral in which the crisis of Europe fuels Islamist violence on one hand and, on the other in response, as in a dialectic, the rise of radical extreme-right, populist and nationalist parties.

Chapter 15

From Crisis to Social Movement to Political Change: Podemos in Spain
Manuel Castells

The rise of a social movement: Spain's 15-M

The combination of a structural economic crisis, aggravated by austerity policies in Europe, with a rampant crisis of political legitimacy in parliamentary democracies, triggered a wave of social movements in Western Europe in 2011–16, albeit with variable intensity from country to country (Castells 2012, 2015; Cardoso et al. this volume). Most noticeable was the 15 May Movement (15-M) in Spain. On this date in 2011, thousands of people, the majority of whom were young, demonstrated in over 60 Spanish cities in a largely spontaneous response to a 'Manifesto for Real Democracy' that circulated on the Internet's social networks in the preceding weeks. At the end of the first day of demonstrations, hundreds, then thousands, camped in the main squares of many cities, and started a multi-thematic debate on the ills of society, on the injustice imposed on their lives, and on the potential projects to change both their lives and the world, outside the traditional avenues of institutional politics. They were at first ignored by the media, and universally denounced by the political class, right and left, as useless provocateurs. Yet, their impact on the public mind was extensive and lasting. After two months of occupations of urban space had elapsed, their protests continued on a number of fronts, particularly in a movement against evictions as a result of mortgage foreclosures when families could no longer pay their loans after losing their jobs. The collusion between banks and politicians was the main target of the protest, at the same time denouncing the dictatorship of the European Commission and of the German government over the Spanish government, at the time led by a Socialist Prime Minister. The government bowed to the direct pressure of Angela Merkel, going as far as approving a constitutional amendment, in alliance with the Conservative Partido Popular (PP), to ban public spending beyond certain limits. There was widespread agreement in the general public with the criticisms of the protesters. Between 2011 and 2014, according to a series of surveys, a large majority of Spanish citizens were supportive of the 15-M movement and subsequent protests, as the crisis deepened and led to unprecedented unemployment (up to 22 per cent general unemployment and over 50 per cent youth unemployment) and deep budget cuts in health, education and welfare.

Yet, the immediate political effect of the crisis and of social protests was to bring to power with a clear majority, in the November 2011 elections, the conservative Partido Popular, whose policies were even more prone to austerity than those of the Socialists. Punishing governments deemed to be responsible for the crisis, and betting on the opposition, regardless of its programmes, is a frequent outcome of strong social protests everywhere when there is no clear alternative in the institutional system. Moreover, opinion polls in Spain showed that the majority of citizens sided with the views of the social movement but generally thought that the 15-M would not be able to change matters because of the resistance of all political parties to their demands. Subsequently, social struggles intensified in the country. In a separate process, Catalan nationalism, whose demands were ignored by mainstream Spanish parties, radicalized its opposition to the central government. Yet, all political parties refused negotiation with the demonstrators, increasing the gap between the mobilized segments of civil society, and the political institutions. Indeed, the Partido Popular and PSOE (Socialists) answered the protesters by suggesting to them the possibility of participating in the electoral process. They were confident that the political system would be stable, as it had been since the advent of Spanish democracy in 1977, organizing the alternation in government of the two main parties, complemented by a number of smaller nationalist parties. It was the so-called 'Bipartidismo' regime, based on a dual party system that, with the exception of Catalonia and the Basque Country, had monopolized power at the national, regional and local levels, for about 34 years. At first, the different components of the social movement gave up on the chance of influencing policies from inside the system and resorted to influencing public opinion. They also used legal strategies, even calling with some success on the European Court of Justice to come to their rescue. But after years of submitting petitions to the Parliament, signed by hundreds of thousands, just to be beaten by the police as the only answer, numerous activists started to consider how to intervene in the institutional political arena, even if they were aware of the biased characteristics of institutional politics. These institutional limitations to democracy were present in the electoral law, in electoral districting, in restricted access to the media and to public finance, and in deep hostility from banks, political bureaucracies and mainstream media to any political actor that would try to sidestep the rules established by the powers that be.

As a result of this reflection, participants in the social movement formed several groups in different territories. All vowed to respect the autonomy of the social movement. Everybody was fully aware of the independence of a movement that would never accept appropriation by any party. These proto-political formations in turn asserted their own autonomy vis-à-vis the movement, and they adapted to the political legislation, playing by the rules in order to be accepted in the electoral contest. They formed a diverse geography of new politics that would appear later as components of a constellation of forces organized around the most successful of such groupings: Podemos (We Can).

Asaltar los cielos (Assaulting the skies)

In January 2014, three professors of political science at the Universidad Complutense de Madrid, Pablo Iglesias, Carolina Bescansa and Juan Carlos Monedero, decided to try their electoral fortunes to transfer the energy of the movement into political action and policy change. Four others were also part of the initial nucleus: Inigo Errejón, a doctoral student in political science in the same department, Pablo Echenique, a physicist at the Universidad de Zaragoza, Irene Montero, a psychologist at the Universidad Autonoma de Madrid, and Teresa Rodriguez, a teacher in Cadiz. This was a highly educated group with international academic experience. Monedero received his doctorate at the University of Heidelberg, Bescansa studied at the University of California, San Diego, Errejón at the University of California, Los Angeles, and Iglesias spent some time with a fellowship at the Center for Latin American Studies in Cambridge. All of them had been active in the anti-globalization movement, particularly Errejón, and in the 15 May movement, particularly Montero who was one of the leaders of the Platform against evictions in Madrid. They came from different origins on the ideological spectrum of the radical left, some from the Communist Youth, others from Izquierda Anticapitalista, still others from the neo-anarchist strand of the anti-globalization movement. They were inspired by the successful experiences of the national popular movements in South America, particularly in Bolivia (the subject matter of Errejón's doctoral dissertation), and Ecuador, and they were sympathetic to the

Bolivarian revolution of Hugo Chavez. Monedero was an advisor to the Venezuelan government, and Iglesias was consulting with the Venezuelan and Bolivian governments, although their activity in Venezuela was prior to the creation of Podemos.

They were intellectually influenced by the late Ernesto Laclau, particularly by his theory of 'empty signifiers' as a discourse that proposes a meta-ideological frame in which different sources of national identity and social protest could converge. They refused to be labelled as populist, or even as a left-wing party. Instead, they opposed the new politics to the old politics, and proposed the idea of building hegemony in society by defending the people at large against global capitalism and the domination of the 'political class', the Casta of professional politicians. Yet, they rejected from the onset being reduced to the role of a purely critical force. As in the case of the Greek party Syriza, which was also an inspiration for Podemos, their project from the very beginning was to govern Spain by winning elections, as had happened in Greece and in South America. To that end, they decided to test the waters in preparation for the upcoming elections to the European Parliament in May 2014. They elaborated a political manifesto, articulating the demands of the social movement in a broader strategy of political change, and they published it on the Internet requesting signatures of support. They had decided that they would only proceed if they obtained 50,000 signatures in one month. They received more than 50,000 in less than one week. The race was on. They multiplied their presence in mainstream television and radio (by accepting invitations to debate their ideas from journalists eager to find new faces in the dull political world), as well as on social networking sites, their natural habitat since their time as social activists. In the May 2014 European elections they received over 8 per cent of the vote and elected five members to the Parliament. They immediately organized a flexible party, both on the Internet and in territorial circles, with minimal rules of admission. By autumn 2014 they had reached over 300,000 registered members, surpassing the centenary Socialist Party, and by January 2015 reliable polls had put Podemos in first place among all parties in terms of direct voting intention for the upcoming national elections of 2015. The alarms rang frantically in the power circles in Spain, and beyond, as the threat of a new Syriza in a much larger economy loomed on the European horizon. Media campaigns denigrated Podemos, while the politics of fear was spread by the traditional political parties. Yet, with few resources, but based on an intense grassroots mobilization, Podemos engaged in the battle for the municipal and regional elections of 29 May 2015. It was at the local level that the connection was more easily made between the occupations and demonstrations of the social movement in 2011–14, and voting for local and regional governments, as shown in table 15.1. Yet, Podemos understood that the diversity of Spain, and indeed the plurinational characteristic of the country that Podemos included as part of its national-popular strategy, had to translate into local and regional coalitions of which Podemos would be a driving force, but not a hegemonic force. They thought that local leaders, independent from Podemos, but linked to the values of the movement, would make worthy mayoral candidates. This was the case in Barcelona, with the emergence of Ada Colau, the activist who created and led the platform against evictions at the national level, as a charismatic leader. This was also the case in Madrid, where a 73-year-old civil rights judge, a veteran from the anti-Francoist struggles, came to lead the Podemos-inspired municipal candidacy. The strategy was a stunning success and showed the depth of the grassroots opposition to the Conservative Party and to some extent to the Socialist Party. Madrid, Barcelona and Valencia elected independent mayors in alliance with Podemos and other forces created in the wake of the social movement. The same phenomenon took place in other major Spanish cities, such as Zaragoza, La Coruna, Vigo, Santiago, San Sebastian, Pamplona, Alicante, Cadiz, etc. Table 15.1 shows the close-knit correspondence between the cities where the May movement was most active, as measured by urban occupations, and the vote for Podemos-inspired coalitions. Furthermore, in a number of other major cities, such as Seville, and in most regional governments, the Socialist Party came to power depending on the support of Podemos.

The result was that the overwhelming municipal and regional power held until then by the Conservative PP was obliterated, with the PP losing all major municipalities and barely holding the regional government of Madrid, in alliance with a centre-right party, Ciudadanos.

In the aftermath of the resounding victory of Podemos 'and its confluences', as the variable geometry of coalitions came to be known, the ground became ready for the ultimate goal of Podemos: to win the next national parliamentary elections scheduled for December 2015. To assail the skies of government and transform the country appeared then as a reachable, albeit previously unthinkable, goal.

The transformation of the Spanish political system

The Spanish democracy was established in 1977 and enshrined in the 1978 Constitution, a Constitution that resulted from the consensus of all political parties, from right to left, based on a series of mutual concessions that would not disturb the fragile equilibrium that had been

Table 15.1 Correspondence between the cities where the May movement was most active and the vote for Podemos-inspired coalitions. Ranking of social activism – 1 is the highest

City	Population	Ranking	Party/platform	Votes (%)		Councillors (Total)		Governing	Governing with	Total votes	Participation	Autonomous community
Madrid	3,233,527	2	Ahora Madrid	519,210	31.6	20	57	Yes		1,642,898	0.6885	Comunidad de Madrid
Barcelona	1,620,943	1	Barcelona en Comú	176,337	25.09	11	41	Yes		702,692	0.6061	Cataluña
Valencia	797,028	5	Valencia en Comú	40,420	9.72	3	33	Yes	PSPV | Compromís	415,721	0.7211	Comunidad Valenciana
Sevilla	702,355	4	Participa Sevilla	28,933	8.94	3	31	No		323,731	0.5952	Andalucía
Zaragoza	679,624	2	Zaragoza en Común	80,040	24.34	9	31	Yes	PSOE	328,893	0.6551	Aragón
Málaga	567,433	3	Málaga Ahora	30,464	13.25	4	31	No		229,872	0.5434	Andalucía
Murcia	441,354	4 and 5	Es Ahora Murcia/ Cambiemos Murcia	36,483	17.97	6	29	No		203,045	0.6532	Murcia
Palma	407,648	4	Som Palma	22,346	14.57	5	29	Yes	PSIB-PSOE | MES-APIB	153,342	0.5449	Islas Baleares
Palmas Gran Canaria	382,296	3	LPGC Puede	27,127	15.91	6	29	No		170,484	0.5693	Islas Canarias
Bilbao	351,629	5	Udalberri-Bilbao En Común	13,790	8.44	2	29	No		163,362	0.5936	País Vasco
Alicante/ Alacant	334,678	3	Guanyar Alacant/ Acord Ciutadà	28,156	18.55	6	29	Yes	PSPV | Compromís	151,762	0.6328	Comunidad Valenciana
Córdoba	328,841	3	Ganemos Córdoba	18,460	12.42	4	29	No		148,639		Andalucía
Valladolid	311,501	3	Valladolid toma la palabra	22,259	13.24	2	29	Yes	PSOE	168,181	0.6781	Castilla León
Vigo	297,355	3	Marea de Vigo-SON	16,227	11.36	3	27	No		142,795	0.6006	Galicia
Gijón	277,733	3	Xixón Yes Puede	29,750	20.82	6	27	No		142,859	0.6249	Asturias

Table 15.1 (continued)

City	Population	Ranking	Party/platform	Votes (%)		Councillors	Total	Governing	Governing with	Total votes	Participation	Autonomous community
Hospitalet de Llobregat	257,057	6	Guanyem L'Hospitalet	6,962	7.42	2	27	No		93,817	0.5342	Catalunya
A Coruña	246,146	1	Marea Atlántica	36,842	30.53	10	27	Yes		120,691	0.6007	Galicia
Vitoria-Gasteiz	242,223	5	Sumando Hemen Gaude	10,390	8.56	2	27	No		121,413	0.6476	País Vasco
Granada	239,017	4	Vamos Granada	14,032	12.61	3	27	No		111,237	0.5978	Andalucía
Elche/Elx	230,587	7	Guanyem Elx	1,758	1.57	0	27	No		111,934	0.6649	Comunidad Valenciana
Oviedo	225,973	2	Somos Oviedo	20,514	18.89	6	27	Yes	PSOE,IU	108,606	0.6031	Asturias
Badalona	220,977	2	Guanyem Badalona en Comú	15645	17.41	5	27	Yes	PSC ǀ ERC ǀ ICV	89,851	0.5753	Catalunya
Cartagena	216,655	5	Cartagena Yes Se Puede	9,740	11.2	3	27	No		86,960	0.5778	Murcia
Terrassa	215,678	2	Terrassa en Comú	16,045	19.2	6	27	No		83,552	0.5449	Catalunya
Jerez de la Frontera	211,900	3	Ganemos Jerez	14,631	16.11	5	27	No		90,807	0.5475	Andalucía
Sabadell	207,938	2, 4 and 7	Unitat pel canvi-Entesa/Crida per Sabadell-CAV-PA/Guanyem Sabadell	29,119	34.4	10	27	Yes	ERC-AM	84,641	0.5515	Catalunya
Santa Cruz de Tenerife	206,965	4	Yes Se Puede	10,635	11.9	4	27	No		89,378	0.5506	Islas Canarias
Móstoles	206,031	3	Ganemos Móstoles	19,690	19.63	6	27	Yes	PSOE-IU	100,299	0.6497	Comunidad de Madrid
Alcalá de Henares	203,924	3	Somos Alcalá	18,081	19.94	6	27	Yes	PSOE	90,687	0.6602	Comunidad de Madrid
Fuenlabrada	198,132	3	Ganar Fuenlabrada	13,090	14.4	4	27	No		90,897	0.6502	Comunidad de Madrid

								Yes	EHBildu IGBAI | IE(n)		Navarra
Iruña/Pamplona	197,604	5	Aranzai-Pamplona en Común	9,701	9.43	3	27		102,916	0.6962	
Almería	191,443	4	Para la gente	5,180	6.94	2	27	No	74,683	0.5285	Andalucía
Leganés	187,125	2	Leganemos	20,148	20.89	6	27	No	96,427	0.6919	Comunidad de Madrid
Donosti/San Sebastian	186,409	5	Irabazi- Ganar Donosti	6,947	7.04	2	27	No	98,675	0.6665	País Vasco
Castelló de la Plana	180,204	5	Castelló en Moviment	10,443	12.93	4	27	No	80,771	0.6652	Comunidad Valenciana
Burgos	179,906	3	Imagina Burgos	18,579	20.34	6	27	No	91,339	0.6651	Castilla León
Santander	178,465	5	Ganemos Santander	6,029	6.73	2	27	No	89,527	0.6431	Cantabria
Albacete	172,472	3	Ganemos Albacete	13,446	15.11	5	27	No	88,959	0.6733	Castilla la Mancha
Getafe	171,280	3	Ahora Getafe	20,647	23.36	7	27	No	88,401	0.6996	Comunidad de Madrid
Alcorcón	169,308	3	Ganar Alcorcón	15,052	17.2	5	27	No	87,510	0.6995	Comunidad de Madrid
Logroño	153,402	3	Cambia Logroño	11,619	15.2	4	27	No	76,437	0.6858	La Rioja
San Cristóbal La Laguna	153,224	2	Unid@s Se Puede	12,889	18.18	6	27	No	70,889	0.5809	Islas Canarias
Badajoz	152,270	3	Recupera Badajoz	7,360	10.27	3	27	No	71,678	0.6174	Extremadura
Salamanca	152,048	4	Ganemos Salamanca	9,990	13.43	4	27	No	74,395	0.6184	Castilla la Mancha
Huelva	148,568	6	Participa Huelva	3,108	5.26	1	27	No	59,106	0.5210	Andalucía
Marbella	140,473	4	Costa del Sol Yes Se Puede …Tic Tac	3,880	8.12	2	27	No	47,790	0.5364	Andalucía
Lleida	139,834	7	Comú de Lleida	3,787	7.49	2	27	No	50,586	0.5451	Catalunya
Tarragona	133,954	8 and 9	Ara Tarragona-AD/Guanyem Tarragona	3,007	5.91	0	27	No	50,904	0.5632	Catalunya

Table 15.1 (continued)

City	Population	Ranking	Party/platform	Votes (%)	Councillors Total		Governing	Governing with	Total votes	Participation	Autonomous community
León	131,680	4 and 5	Leon Despierta/ Leon en Común	11,765	18.08	4	27	No		65,075	0.6242	Castilla y León
Dos Hermanas	128,794	2	Yes Se Puede Dos Hermanas	9,095	17.87	4	27	No		50,906	0.5118	Andalucía
Torrejón de Ardoz	125,331	2	Yes Se Puede – Alternativa Ciudadana por Madrid	9,362	16.11	5	27	No		58,116	0.6590	Comunidad de Madrid
Parla	124,208	3	Cambiemos Parla	8,746	18.25	6	27	No		47,935	0.6238	Comunidad de Madrid
Mataró	124,084	4	Volem Mataró	5,276	11.31	3	27	No		46,629	0.5382	Catalunya
Cádiz	123,948	2	Por Cádiz Yes Se Puede	18,277	27.81	8	27	Yes		65,730	0.6522	Andalucía
Santa Coloma Gramenet	120,593	2	Som Gramenet-Poble Actiu	7,852	18.42	6	27	No		42,620	0.5399	Catalunya
Algeciras	116,917	3	Algeciras Yes Se Puede	4,788	11.81	3	27	No		40,553	0.4580	Andalucía
Jaén	116,731	4	Jaén en Común	5,698	10.24	3	27	No		55,650	0.6086	Andalucía
Alcobendas	111,040	4	Yes Se Puede!ACM	5,497	10.3	3	27	No		53,389	0.6752	Comunidad de Madrid
Ourense	107,597	4	Ourense en Común	5,478	10.19	3	27	No		53,776	0.6212	Galicia
Reus	107,211	7	Ara Reus	2,476	6.32	2	27	No		39,157	0.5533	Catalunya
Torrevieja	103,720	4	Sueña Torrevieja	1,842	7.68	4	25	No		23,998	0.5061	Comunidad Valenciana
Telde	101,300	7	Se Puede Ganar	3,621	7.22	2	27	No		50,161	0.6196	Islas Canarias
Barakaldo	100,369	4	Irabazi-ganar Barakaldo	5,590	11.84	4	27	No		47,216	0.5867	País Vasco

Source: Data compiled and elaborated by Arnau Montesde, Research Group on Communication and Social Movements, Open University of Catalonia.

reached under the surveillance of the still Francoist armed forces, some-what moderated by a Franco-appointed King Juan Carlos I. The political dynamics soon evolved towards two major parties, one right-wing party, the Partido Popular (PP), that absorbed the centrist parties, and the his-toric Socialist Party, the Partido Socialista Obrero Español (PSOE). The Communists, active and influential in the clandestine resistance, became marginal as an electoral force, except, for a short period, in Catalonia. After an unstable period dominated by centrist governments in 1977–82, in November 1982 the Socialists came to power in a landslide victory and remained in government until 1996, when the PP was elected and was able to govern in coalition. This bipartisan system was called 'imperfect' because in Catalonia and in the Basque Country moderate nationalist parties were in control until the 2000s and played their cards intelli-gently by making alliances with Conservatives or Socialists in exchange for concessions of more autonomy for their 'nationalities' (as they were named in the Spanish Constitution). This skilful political architecture played a significant role in pacifying Spain and establishing on solid ground the practice of democracy. The demons that haunted Spain for 500 years since the formation of the modern nation state were tamed for all practical purposes with the membership of Spain in the European Community in 1986. The new generations were fully European and took liberty for granted. The price to be paid, however, was to subdue the con-frontation between right and left, leaving Spanish politics in the hands of a political class that became increasingly aloof vis-à-vis society and entrenched in its own privileges: what later would be called 'La Casta', that included right, left and the nationalist parties. In such a closed, endogamic system, corruption became endemic, only denounced and prosecuted for political gain. The media were fully politicized on both sides, with each media group exchanging allegiancy for political favours, and the influential public television was at the service of whomever was in government. Social struggles were confined within the limits of collec-tive bargaining between business and labour. While the trade unions (one Socialist, one Communist) remained independent and usually in opposi-tion to government's neoliberal policies (from both sides of the political spectrum), the dynamics of social conflicts were efficiently channelled in an electoral process largely controlled by the bipartisan system. Yet, the limitations of such a tightly controlled system is that when challenges arise from society they are forced to be external to the institutions, calling into question their legitimacy, and ultimately disrupting the system. Basque nationalism first, Catalan nationalism later, reacted against the accommodating politics of their leaders and mobilized for independence of their nations. In the Basque Country this took the form of a terrorist organization, ETA, that emerged under Franco but continued to operate in democracy until it was finally defeated by force in the 2000s, after hundreds of killings and thousands of imprisonments. In Catalonia, there was no violence. Instead a social movement developed in the civil society vying for independence with increasing social support that reached the threshold of 48 per cent of the population for independence, and transformed the Catalan political system, displacing the moderate nationalist parties and favouring a majority of pro-independence parties in the Catalan Parliament. Institutional confrontation with the Spanish state followed, in the judicial system, in government, and in the streets. The constitutional order started to crack. However, the absence of any Spanish political force ready to negotiate new terms of autonomy with the Catalans, let alone accept a referendum on independence as the Catalan movement was demanding, stalled the movement and radicalized its stand.

The economic crisis of 2008 (that in Spain exploded in 2010) changed everything, as the new generations, both in Spain and Catalonia, insurged outside the institutional system and distrusted the traditional parties. The corruption of political parties, particularly of the PP but extending to all parties, reached new heights and began to be exposed by a new generation of judges, and publicized by media competing for audience. It is in this context that, in the wake of the social movements, Podemos appeared as well as a number of organizations created by activists from the movement in various territories. This was the case with Barcelona en Comu, and later En Comu Podem in Catalonia; of the Mareas Gallegas in Galicia; of MES in the Baleares Islands, of Compromis in Valencia. They formed a constellation of about 20 political groupings that came to be known as Podemos 'and its confluences', but that were largely autonomous from Podemos leadership. Suddenly, the new generations (younger than 35 years of age) could feel represented by political forces participating in elections with chances of making a difference. The detailed studies by political analyst Jaime Miquel on the voting behaviour of Spanish citizens by age show that Podemos-like parties received the majority of the votes of those under 40. Meanwhile, the Socialists and the Conservatives have an overwhelming presence in the votes of those older than 60, and a slight advantage among those between 40 and 60. This is what authorizes Miquel to assert that the main political divide is not between right and left, but between old and new politics (Miquel 2015).

Furthermore, while social movements induced the growing presence of political forces engaged in social change, the new generations of middle-class professionals also became disappointed with the corruption and bureaucratization of the bipartisan system. But they were not revolutionaries. In fact, in their majority they are in favour of a modernized global capitalism, and fully immersed in the promise of a prosperous Europe. Liberal in politics and neoliberal in policies, this distinct social group found its own political expression in a new party, Ciudadanos (Citizens) that came to play a significant role in Spanish politics. It started in the early 2000s in Barcelona to oppose in the most direct terms Catalan nationalism and the independence project. But they did not want to merge with the PP, which was considered an expression of the old Spain. They soon received the discrete support of the Spanish and Catalan financial institutions. Ciudadanos incarnates the attempt by the financial elites to create a modern, liberal party that could be present in the new globalized economy without the burden of the Francoist past still alive in the PP. Led by a charismatic leader, Albert Rivera, Ciudadanos found some support among the in-between generation, college graduates in the 35–50 age bracket, employed and well-paid in the managerial economy. Unlike the Conservatives, they are progressive in social issues, such as women's rights or gay and lesbian rights, and they are not in the hands of the Church as conservatives are. Here again, following Miquel's analysis, the relevant dimension is not right/left, but new/old. However, Ciudadanos is part of the political establishment, unlike Podemos, that clearly aims at being a transformative force in the institutional system.

The emergence of new political actors and new constituencies in Spanish politics became fully revealed in the general election of December 2015. Table 15.2 shows the results of this election compared to the previous one in 2011. The table also shows the results of the June 2016 election, but my analytical commentary on this last election will come later in the text.

What has to be noted from the results of 2015 is that the two-party system that dominated Spanish polity since 1977 has been transformed into a four party system. To be sure, the weight of each party is different, which shows the resilience of the old politics (PP and PSOE) in the face of the challenge of the new politics (Podemos and Ciudadanos). But the critical matter is that no party has enough parliamentary support to govern by itself (with absolute or relative majority), thus breaking down the dominance of the two parties that were alternating in government. This four party system, according to all indications, is going to remain for the foreseeable future. Furthermore, the radicalization of Catalan nationalist parties under the influence of the independence movement has prompted an alliance of the self-labelled Constitutionalist parties (that is PP, PSOE and Ciudadanos) to bar any negotiation with the Catalan nationalists, thus losing the margin of security that both parties used in

Table 15.2   Results of the General Elections in Spain in 2011, 2015 and 2016

Participation	26 June 2016	20 December 2015	20 November 2011
Voters	24,161,083	25,438,532	24,666,441
	(69.84%)	(69.67%)	(68.94%)
Non-voters	10,435,955	11,073,316	11,113,050
	(30.16%)	(30.33%)	(31.06%)
Votes			
Void votes	225,888	227,219	317,555
	(0.93%)	(0.89%)	(1.29%)
Blank votes	178,521	188,132	333,461
	(0.75%)	(0.75%)	(1.37%)

Parties and coalitions	2016		2015		2011[a]	
	Votes	Deputies	Votes	Deputies	Votes	Deputies
PP	7,906,185	137	7,236,965	123	10,866,566	186
	(33.03%)		(28.71%)		(44.63%)	
PSOE	5,424.709	85	5,545.315	90	7,003.511	110
	(22.66%)		(22.00%)		(28.76%)	
Podemos[b]	5,049,734	71	5,212,711	69	—	—
	(21.1%)		(20.68%)			
IU[c]	—	—	923,133	2	1,811,346	12
			(3.67%)		(7.43%)	
Ciudadanos	3,123,769	32	3,514,528	40	—	—
	(13.05%)		(13.93%)			
ERC[d]	629,294	9	601,782	9	256,985	3
	(2.63%)		(2.39%)		(1.06%)	
CIU[e]	481,839	8	567,253	8	1,015,691	16
	(2.01%)		(2.25%)		(4.17%)	
PNV[f]	286,215	5	302,316	6	324,317	5
	(1.20%)		(1.20%)		(1.33%)	
Bildu[g]	184,092	2	219,125	2	324,317	7
	(0.77%)		(0.87%)		(1.33%)	
CC[h]	78,080	1	81,917	1	143,881	2
	(0.33%)		(0.32%)		(0.59%)	
UPyD	50,282	0	155,153	0	1,143,225	5
	(0.21%)		(0.62%)		(4.70%)	
BNGa[i]	44,902	0	70,863	0	184,037	2
	(0.19%)		(0.28%)		(0.76%)	

Table 15.2   (continued)

Notes:
[a] In 2015, there was also parliamentary representation of the Basque nationalists of Geroa Bai (42,415 votes (0.17%) and 1 seat) and of conservative Foro de Ciudadanos (99,473 votes (0.41%) and 1 seat).
[b] In 2016 Unidos Podemos is the coalition resulting from the alliance between Podemos and Izquierda Unida. It includes the votes for En Comú Podem (Cataluña) (848,526 votes (3.55%) and 12 seats), Compromís-Podemos-EUPV: A la Valenciana (Valencia) (655,895 votes (2.74%) and 9 seats) and Podemos-En Marea-Anova-EU (Galicia) (408,370 votes (1.63%) and 6 seats). In the 2015 electoral results of Podemos are included the convergent alliances with En Comú Podem (Cataluña) (927,940 votes (3.69%) and 12 seats), Compromís-Podemos-És el moment (Valencia) (671,071 votes (2.67%) and 9 seats) and En Marea (Galicia) (408,370 votes (1.63%) and 6 seats).
[c] In 2016 Unidos Podemos coalition of Podemos and Izquierda Unida. In 2015 Unidad popular (Izquierda Unida, Unidad Popular En Común). In 2011 includes Izquierda Unida-Los Verdes: La Izquierda Plural (1,686,040 votes (6.92%) and 11 seats) and Bloc-Iniciativa-Verds-Equo-Coalició Compromís (125,306 votes (0.51%) and 1 seat).
[d] In 2016 and 2015 Esquerra Republicana de Catalunya-Catalunya Sí.
[e] In 2016 Convergència Democràtica de Catalunya. In 2015 Democràcia i Llibertat. Convergència. Demòcrates. Reagrupament.
[f] Euzko Alderdi Jeltzalea-Partido Nacionalista Vasco.
[g] In 2016 and 2015 Euskal Herria Bildu. In 2011 AMAIUR.
[h] In 2016 and 2015 Coalición Canaria-Partido Nacionalista Canario. In 2011 Coalición Canaria-Nueva Canarias.
[i] En 2015 Nós-Candidatura Galega (BNG-CG-FOGA-PCPG-PG).

Sources: Ministerio del Interior. Subsecretaría. Dirección General de Política Interior 2015 and Ministerio del Interior. Subsecretaría. Dirección General de Política Interior 2016.

the past to complete their majority with the support of moderate Catalan nationalism.

On the other hand, as mentioned above, Podemos is based on its conception of Spain as a plurinational state, and this has made possible an organic alliance with Catalan, Basque, Galician and Valencian nationalism, bridging Spanish politics and the politics of nationalities that coexist under the same nation-state. If we consider the variable geometry of this emerging political system, I think it would not be fanciful to say that Podemos has transformed the Spanish political system, as a result of the challenges emerging from the 15-M movement and from the nationalist movements in Catalonia, as well as other nationalities. This new complexity, amounting to the loss of control of the two-party system over the country, has choked the automatic reproduction of the social and economic order, so cherished by the financial elites and by the powers that be in the European Union. An institutional crisis followed, ultimately leading to new general elections in June 2016. The transformative project of Podemos disrupted the political order, but at the same time it was stalled in the labyrinths of parliamentary politics, opening a new phase of political change full of interrogations. Yet, before studying the confused interaction between renovation of the system and the institutionalization of Podemos, it can be analytically meaningful to reflect on the factors that underlie the initial political success of Podemos. Indeed, we can speak of success when a party created in January 2014 by a small group of politically inexperienced activists, without resources and in the midst of the general hostility of the financial and political elites, in December 2015 obtained the support of 5,212,711 voters (almost 21 per cent of the votes) while the PSOE lost 2.3 million votes since 2011, and the PP 3.6 million. The two mainstream parties, counted together, went down from 73.3 per cent to 50.7 per cent of the popular vote.

Thus, Podemos' dreamers could not conquer the skies in their first assault, but they transformed the structure of the political system, and created a new style of politics, stalling the machinery of domination, and bringing the voice of the voiceless to the forefront of the political debate.

Lord of the media: Podemos and political communication

In the background of Podemos' blitzkrieg on the Spanish political system loomed the dramatic social condition of many, and particularly of the youth, as a result of the disastrous management of the economic crisis, as well as of the impact of the 15-M on the consciousness of millions. Yet, other groups emerging from the social movement had tried to enter the political arena with scant success. There is consensus among the observers of Podemos (including Podemos leaders themselves) that the differential factor was the masterful management of media (old and new media alike) by Podemos leaders, and particularly by Pablo Iglesias, the visible face of Podemos. To the point that in the European election of 2014, the first one that Podemos took part in, the ballots corresponding to Podemos included a photograph of Iglesias, so that the voters, largely unaware of the new party, could identify the ballot with the face they had come to know (and for many, to like) on television shows. If power largely relies on communication, as I have argued elsewhere (Castells 2009), the effective communication strategy of Podemos was essential in conveying their message, and in mobilizing support out of nowhere. Instead of separating the territorial organization of the party and the presence of the new politics in the communication sphere, the two processes worked hand in hand, reinforcing each other. Active and savvy presence on social networks was the easy part of this communication strategy, as Podemos emerged from a social movement that was originally born on the Internet. Social networks are the natural environment of the new generations, and even more so the daily practice of social activists. So, Podemos brought the political debates onto the Internet and found a receptive ear in the largely young crowd that participated actively in the discussion. The social space Agora, with excellent computing design, facilitated the modular incorporation of thousands into the deliberations, and into the decision-making process leading to action. Viral campaigns, based on the use of multimedia platforms, with creative use of videos, music, and a sort of cultural guerrilla, found a large echo in the younger generations of Spaniards, precisely the people suddenly plunged into unemployment, and precarious survival in spite of their college education. The echos of the never extinct 15-M reverberated in the initiatives undertaken by Podemos on social networks.

However, the very same reason that made the Internet population prone to empathize with Podemos limited its reach to older age groups who used the Internet less and were not skilled enough to participate in chats. This is why Pablo Iglesias focused the Podemos effort on television and radio presence in mainstream media. He knew well the language of media, as a professor of political communication. First, he was solicited by radio and TV shows in relation to the demonstrations of the 15-M, and soon the journalists realized that his presence on a show could animate discussion and raise audience interest. Thus, even conservative media, such as Radio Intereconomia, invited him frequently as did mainstream television networks, particularly La Sexta and Cuatro. He spoke clearly and directly, confronted the views of professional politicians and did not hesitate to engage in sharp, but polite debates, with the plethora of right-wing commentators of Spanish media. He often dominated the debates and his arguments were then taken up on social networks and amplified in numerous chats. He also created an IPTV program La Tuerka as early as 2003, and produced the TV show Fort Apache, broadcast by Hispasan, an Iranian government-supported station. In La Tuerka he invited political and cultural personalities to deal in-depth with major issues of life and power in extensive interviews that he opened to the entire ideological spectrum. As he once said, 'Podemos is not only television, but without television Podemos cannot be explained.' After the electoral successes of Podemos and its confluences in 2015, the entire leadership, as well as local leaders, such as the mayors of Madrid and Barcelona, made a point of appearing on all the shows they were invited to, in spite of often being submitted to the hostility of the journalists and politicians on the panel. While this open communication policy took a toll on the image of the least-skilled

Podemos members, overall it introduced the party and its proposals to a larger audience, without confining them either to the Internet or to their youth constituency.

The second major factor behind the impact of Podemos is of a deeper, structural character. It is the putting into practice of its conception of Spain as a plurinational country by forming a confederation of various organizations rather than a centralized organization typical of the Communist tradition from where some of the Podemos leaders came. Particularly revealing was the fiasco and reconstruction of Podemos in Catalonia. In the Catalan elections of September 2014, Podemos presented a candidacy built in a hurry, and clearly orchestrated from Madrid. Although they obtained a handful of seats, it was clearly a defeat that forced Podemos to re-think its Catalan policy, extended later to other nationalities and regions. The result of this strategic re-thinking in Catalonia was the formation of a municipal coalition around the figure of an independent charismatic activist, Ada Colau, who became Mayor of Barcelona. More to the point, Podemos committed to defend a referendum for independence in Catalonia, although Iglesias said he would campaign against independence and for greater Catalan autonomy. This subtle position actually coincided with the opinion of 80 per cent of Catalans who support the notion of the referendum but then split on the issue of independence. By combining organizational autonomy and support for the referendum, En Comu Podem (a coalition around Podemos) became the major political force in Catalonia in the general elections of 2015 and 2016. Similar processes took place in the Basque Country, Navarra, Galicia, Valencia and Baleares, with similar positive electoral results. In contrast, Podemos could only make limited inroads in Andalucia, the largest and one of the poorer regions of Spain, and which traditionally submitted to the clientelistic control of the Socialist Party. Podemos paid a price in the more traditional regions of Spain for its support for Catalan nationalism, but this position became an integral part of its programme, and in fact a key factor in winning electoral support in the more dynamic areas of the country.

At an even deeper level, Podemos planted strong roots among those who harbour the progressive ideals of the twenty-first century, beyond traditional politics, such as women's rights, gay and lesbian rights, advocacy for the disabled, international solidarity, human rights, animal rights, pacifism, cultural freedom, asylum for refugees, prosecution of police brutality, etc.

In this sense Podemos has the potential to federate the new political culture and provide a platform for its expression in the institutions. On the condition of not becoming lost in its labyrinths, as I will discuss in the following section. This could be one of the manifestations of a broader strategy at the core of the socio-political reflection of Podemos: the construction of ideological hegemony in society, in a truly Gramscian perspective, adapted to modern times.

Indeed, Inigo Errejón, considered by many the most creative and intellectual of Podemos' leadership, has followed in the footsteps of Laclau and some intellectuals of the Bolivarian revolution, including Bolivia's Vice-President Garcia Linera, to argue for opening the political frame of reference of Podemos, superseding the old dichotomy of right/left. He goes even as far as to propose the defence of the Patria (the Motherland) as the unifying motto against the forces of global capitalism and the political domination of the European Union, led by Germany. Without hinting at an exit from the euro (after the hard lesson of Syriza) in the formulation of Errejón and others, the common cause of the people of Spain is to protect their interests against the foreign forces of globalization. Here we can see the trace of the anti-globalization movement and of the national popular movements in Latin America that inspired Podemos. Interestingly enough, this defence is related to the defence of the welfare state, abandoned by the social democracy in the context of neoliberal hegemony. While these theoretical reflections appear to be far away from the mundane concerns of politics in a country in crisis, in fact it brought Podemos in line with the idea of broad, non-ideological alliances among all those who give priority to the needs of Spaniards over the requests of macroeconomic forces, starting with the financial elites. Thus the traditional class confrontation scheme is replaced by the opposition between the people and the elites, precisely the motto of Occupy movements around the world. These are the aspirations that Podemos tries to translate in parliamentarian initiatives, and ultimately implement by government programmes.

This pragmatic, yet self-reflexive elaboration allowed Podemos to live through the contradiction between reform and revolution that devoured many of its predecessors, thus enhancing their chances of political success. Yet, once Podemos entered into the halls of power, they discovered a universe for which their readings and travels had not prepared them.

Game of Thrones: Podemos' conundrum

Pablo Iglesias is a fan of the television series *Game of Thrones* to the point that he wrote a book of political commentary on the series (Iglesias 2014a). Furthermore, the first time he met the new king, Felipe VI, in the European Parliament, he gave the monarch as a gift a set of DVDs containing the complete *Game of Thrones* series. After the breakthrough of Podemos in the December 2015 elections, Iglesias and his fellow political activists found themselves immersed in real life politics very close to the world of *Game of Thrones*: power hunting without reference to electoral promises, manipulative manoeuvres between parties and against parties, double talk in political negotiations with different potential allies, media campaigns to influence public opinion, selected exposure of corruption, outright lies, and the whole range of disgraceful political practices that have induced, in Spain and in much of the world, the crisis of legitimacy of parties and institutions. The political lessons from *Game of Thrones* for Pablo Iglesias were summarized in the title of his book: 'To Win or to Die'. Yet, his practice showed that matters were more complicated.

The key factor of the new political situation was that no party could govern by itself. Moreover, the centre-right, even in the case of an alliance between PP and Ciudadanos, could not obtain enough votes for the investiture of Rajoy, the PP leader, as Prime Minister. Ciudadanos was not interested in the first instance in appearing too close to a party that had become rotten by corruption. Thus, when the king, following the constitutional procedure, proposed that Rajoy attempt to form a government, the conservative leader declined the offer. Then Felipe VI turned to Pedro Sanchez, the leader of the second party, the Socialists, to take the initiative of submitting himself to the vote of the Parliament. There was a real possibility of forming a majority that would vote for the Socialist leader, Sanchez, on the basis of an alliance between PSOE and Podemos, counting on the abstention of the Catalan pro-independence parties in the vote. Podemos was ready to make such an alliance but on conditions of quasi-parity in the programme and in the formation of the government, accepting Sanchez as premier but claiming the vice-premier position for Iglesias, as well as key ministerial appointments. Their argument was that while the difference in seats was significant (90 to 69) this was due to the biased districting system, while the difference in votes was small (22 per cent for the Socialists, 20.68 per cent for Podemos).

But as the bargaining process started, Sanchez was submitted to tremendous pressure from inside and outside his party by powerful actors opposing any alliance with Podemos (considered to be a disruptive force inspired by Venezuela). The regional bosses of the PSOE, staunch Spanish nationalists and determined to keep their share of public funding, were opposed in the strongest terms to any agreement with the Catalan parties, fearful as they were of their demand for independence. Among the opponents to this strategy of an alliance with Podemos were Felipe Gonzalez, the historic Socialist leader that governed Spain for 13 years, bringing the country to Europe, and Susana Diaz, the president of Andalucia, in control of the most important Socialist contingent in Parliament, vying to displace Sanchez from his post as secretary general. Outside the party, the financial elites, and the European Commission, worked backstage to block Podemos. They suggested instead that the Socialists should abstain in the vote for investiture, letting the conservatives form a government. Rajoy's strategy, supported by Juncker and Merkel, was to form a 'grand coalition', German style, with Ciudadanos and the PSOE, to unite against 'radicalism' and 'separatism'. Sanchez resisted because he had always in his mind the collapse of the Greek Pasok after accepting a similar coalition to manage the crisis. So, he attempted to outmanoeuvre both PP and Podemos by making first an alliance with the liberals of Ciudadanos, the darling of the financial elites, then proposing that Podemos join the alliance on the basis of the programme signed with Ciudadanos. Podemos refused on the grounds that the programme (marked by neoliberal policies) was in contradiction with its own programme of deep policy change. Ciudadanos also rejected the acceptance of Podemos because of Podemos' position in favour of a referendum in Catalonia, anathema for Ciudadanos that was born precisely to fight Catalan nationalism. Under these conditions the investiture of Sanchez was rejected in the Parliament by the negative vote of both PP and Podemos.

This convoluted process of true negotiation and fake negotiation looking into future electoral confrontations sparked acrimony between PSOE and Podemos, making difficult future alliances. In one episode during the debate in the Parliament, Pablo Iglesias accused Felipe Gonzalez of manipulating the PSOE leadership. In addition, he directly accused Gonzalez of being responsible for the assassinations of Basque separatists carried on in the 1980s by a rogue police gang known as GAL. This blatant provocation of the most important Spanish leader of the new democracy impacted negatively the image of Podemos among many Socialist voters who still revere their historic leader. The contradiction between this vitriolic, public attack and the offer to build a strategic alliance with the PSOE led many to conclude that Podemos (or at least Iglesias) was simply trying to posture itself as being for the unity of the left in view of the next election. Sanchez would never forgive Iglesias for the missed opportunity to unseat Rajoy.

As a result of reciprocal exclusions between different parties, the Parliament was dissolved and new elections were called for in June 2016. Iglesias devised a new strategy in order to reach his most cherished goal: to overtake the Socialists in the popular vote. For this, he approached United Left, a front organization for the old Communist Party, that was still receiving about one million votes. These were critical votes in

Table 15.3   Summary of the results for the coalitions in the General Elections of 2015 and 2016

Parties and coalitions	2016			2015		
	Votes	%	Deputies	Votes	%	Deputies
Podemos	3,201,170	13.37	45	3,198,584	12.69	42
En Comú Podem	848,526	3.55	12	929,880	3.69	12
Compromís-Podem	655,895	2.74	9	673,549	2.67	9
En Marea	344,143	1.44	5	410,698	1.63	6
Unidad Popular	—	—	—	926,783	3.68	2

a number of districts that could bring Podemos into second place. So, an electoral alliance was made between Podemos and its confluences and United Left, whose image had improved under a young Communist leader, Alberto Garzon, who had been active in the 15-M movement. There was a heated debate in Podemos about the convenience of this alliance. The chief of the campaign, Errejón, argued (behind the scenes) that joining with the Communist Party would tarnish the image of renovation that Podemos had obtained, because Communists represent the old politics in a leftist version. The results vindicated his position. Instead of obtaining over 6 million votes that the two parties gained in the 2015 election, they received barely over 5 million. These missing votes went to abstention. They included about half of the Communist vote, distrustful of these young intruders in their political space. The other half appear to be from Podemos voters who were lost in the tactical manoeuvres of Podemos during the weeks of byzantine negotiations between parties, with the ultimate result of preventing the fall of Rajoy.

Table 15.3 shows the results of the 2016 elections. In essence the stalemate was confirmed, with the Socialists falling further down, yet still ahead of Podemos, and the PP recovering some of the vote they lost at the expense of Ciudadanos that was reminded by its constituency that the privileged ally should be PP, not the Socialists.

After the Conservative leader, Rajoy, failed twice to be invested as president, only supported by Ciudadanos and his own party, pressure was again on the Socialist Party to abstain in the vote of investiture to avoid a third round of elections by facilitating a new government of Rajoy supported by Ciudadanos. The powers that be had succeeded in isolating Podemos from the rest of the political system, together with the Catalan nationalists that were punished for their independentism, although they remained significant in Catalonia.

However, the attempt by the power elites to regain control of the political system found an unforeseen obstacle. Pedro Sanchez, the Secretary General of the Socialist Party, elected in the primaries of the party by a mobilization of its grassroots, refused to betray the slogan of the Socialists in the campaign, 'No is No', addressing the request by the Conservative leader to obtain their abstention, rather than a negative vote, 'for the good of Spain'. Sanchez reiterated his intention to block the investiture. Furthermore, he discreetly started negotiations to form an alternative government with Podemos, counting on the abstention of the Catalan nationalists. So doing, he crossed the two red lines that had been marked for him by the old guard of the party, and by Felipe Gonzalez, in alliance with the financial elites and the European powers.

As the clock ticked towards the last chance to avoid new elections by 31 October 2016, a conspiracy was organized by the presidents of the Socialist regional governments led by the President of Andalucia, Susana Diaz, an ambitious woman aspiring to be the next Secretary General of the party, as a platform to becoming Prime Minister, and to build a stable grand coalition with the Conservatives, German style. All the while forgetting it would be highly unlikely that she would be the senior partner in the alliance. In any case, the conspirators succeeded in calling a special meeting of the Federal Committee of the party, reversing the majority favourable to Sanchez by a combination of promises and threats, and ultimately forcing the resignation of Sanchez. Under these premises, most Socialists abstained in the decisive vote under the threat of disciplinary measures in case of a negative vote, and Rajoy became prime minister for another four years, after one year without an elected government. The Catalan Socialists voted against it, in a joint decision that prompted a major crisis in the relationship between the Catalan Socialist Party (PSC) and the PSOE. Pedro Sanchez, in a rare example of honesty and coherence in the political world, did not want to break the discipline of the Party, so he resigned as MP and was unable to vote. He then began to campaign, as a simple militant for a new Congress of the Party in which he could run again for Secretary General with a programme of alliance with the progressive forces of the country. Thousands of Socialist militants joined him in his crusade, and the public opinion at large acknowledged his dignity and the exemplary character of his decision.

Yet, the mainstream media, and particularly *El Pais*, influenced by Felipe Gonzalez through his friend Carlos Slim, the Mexican billionaire who owns a large share of *El Pais*, condemned Sanchez as irresponsible for accepting the dialogue with Podemos and the Catalan independents, precisely the two political expressions of the social movements that had shaken the Spanish political landscape. The Socialist *caciques*, and particularly Susana Diaz, the self-proclaimed saviour of the Spanish nation, were despised by the public, as the new political generation became even more distant from the Socialists, digging deeper the gap between the agents of social change and the political system.

As for Podemos, while it had been close to sharing government with Sanchez's Socialists and influencing government policies, suddenly it had to withdraw and regroup, to strategize political change in the long haul. In spite of a media campaign to destabilize Podemos, most of the internal debates were not about personal power between Iglesias and Errejón. They were mainly about serious questions of how to proceed with social change in the hostile territory of institutions built to confine projects of change within the boundaries of the Parliament. The strength of Podemos was to have tapped into the outrage of millions in the Spanish society and to project the possibility of real democracy. This requires an active presence in the social struggles as well as putting forward new policies in the local and regional governments in which Podemos was a force. But in the horizon of these revolutionaries bound to be reformists, the main lever of change was still national elections, now four years away. Should Podemos become a 'normal party' after its emergence as a force of social change? Could it limit itself to being the left of the system without truly challenging the financial and political interests against whom they had insurged? Did they have to choose between integration in the institutions they had denounced and political marginality? Could the highly decentralized Podemos constellation resist the tensions of these internal debates without disintegrating?

The answer to their conundrum appeared to depend on their capacity to articulate the dynamics of social movements with parliamentary initiatives in order to gradually construct political hegemony in the civil society. However, this is the most difficult practice to implement in everyday politics. The path between social movements and political change is as treacherous as it is engaging. Podemos has been a pioneer in twenty-first-century transformative politics, in the aftermath of the economic crisis in Europe. But the limitations of the possibility of real change built into the institutions became apparent, forcing Podemos to reassess its identity and to redefine its project. Its promise is still unfolding, while its fate is uncertain as of yet.

References

There is abundant literature on Podemos in spite of the fact that it was born as recently as 2014. This is a sign of the widespread interest in

Podemos around the world. Following are selected references that have been used in my analysis in this chapter. However, the main source of facts and interpretations has been my own observation in Spain in 2014–16. Most of this observation has been published in my book: Castells, M. (2016) *De la crisis economica a la crisis politica*. Barcelona: Libros de Vanguardia.

Selected references on Podemos

Alvaro García, D. and Fonseca Porras, E.A. (2015) *El Método Podemos: Marketing marxista para partidos no marxistas*. Madrid: Última línea, S.L.
Dominguez, A. and Giménez, L. (2014) *Claro que Podemos*. Barcelona: Libros de Lince.
Errejón, I. and Mouffe, C. (2015) *Construir Pueblo. Hegemonía y radicalización de la democracia*. Barcelona: Icaria.
Fernández Albertos, J. (2015) *Los votantes de Podemos. Del Partido de los indignados al Partido de los excluidos*. Catarata: Fundación Alternativas.
Guedán, M. (ed.) (2016) *Podemos, una historia colectiva*. Madrid: Akal.
Iglesias, P. (2013) *¡Abajo el régimen!* Barcelona: Icaria.
Iglesias, P. (ed.) (2014a) *Ganar o Morir. Lecciones políticas de Juego de Tronos*. Madrid: Akal.
Iglesias, P. (2014b) *Disputar la democracia. Política para tiempos de crisis*. Madrid: Akal.
Iglesias, P. (2015) *Una nueva transición. Materiales del año del cambio*. Madrid: Akal.
Ignacio Torreblanca, J. (2015) *Asaltar los cielos. Podemos o la política después de la crisis*. Barcelona: Debate.
Monedero, J.C. (2013) *La transición contada a nuestros padres*. Madrid: Catarata.
Müller, J. (ed.) (2014) *Podemos: Deconstruyendo a Pablo Iglesias*. Barcelona: Deusto.
Osuna, O. (2015) *Momentum: Entrevistas a Pablo Iglesias, Ada Colau, Alberto Garzón, David Fernández*. Barcelona: Icaria.
Peribáñez, J. (2015) *Descubriendo el laberinto rojo*. Barcelona: Larmbooks.
Rivero, J. (2014) *Conversación con Pablo Iglesias*. Madrid: Turpial.
Rivero, J. (2015) *Podemos. Objetivo: Asaltar los cielos*. Barcelona: Planeta.

Additional references

Castells, M. (2009) *Communication Power*. Oxford: Oxford University Press.
Castells, M. (2012) *Networks of Outrage and Hope: Social Movements in the Internet Age*. Cambridge: Polity.
Castells, M. (2015) *Networks of Outrage and Hope: Social Movements in the Internet Age*, 2nd edn. Cambridge: Polity.

Chapter 16

Italy: Autumn of the Second Republic

Pierfranco Pellizzetti

The famous 2011

New social movements began worldwide in 2011, the year of indignation (Castells 2012). These movements stretched from *Puerta del Sol* to *Zuccotti Park*, perhaps alongside the Parisian Place de la République (and newcomer *Nuits Debout*). They signified the discovery that, for a long time, the *nomenklatura* of political parties had mutated into a self-referenced *Caste*. These movements have accused the *Caste* of using political careers as social elevators to improve personal, business and professional prospects. The protests have unfolded along the axis of dislike – indignation – rebellion.

This wave created new parties (*Podemos* in Spain and *Syriza* in Greece) or radically changed old ones. While mainstream politics tends to label these new movements as 'anti-politics' (i.e., pure and irresponsible destruction), a more accurate interpretation of these entities characterizes them as a search for 'alternative politics'.

In Italy, however, the field of 'anti/alternative politics' had already been thriving for approximately two decades, when the First Republic declined and fell under the weight of corruption and scandals, a short trip back in time.

A country such as Italy can serve as a paradigm of an evident Europe-wide decline. This downward spiral becomes evident in the form of disorientation and frustration manifested by public opinion, partly due to the sharp shrinkage of labour incomes. The growing awareness that public sector inefficiency and corruption are becoming systemic only aggravate this malaise.

At the end of 2014, a poll conducted by the *Demos* Institute for the newspaper *la Repubblica* clearly revealed a growing sense of collective hopelessness:

- Only 15 per cent of respondents trust the Government (down 15 per cent compared to 2010 and down 4 per cent since 2013). Regional and municipal governments do not fare much better: less than 20 per cent trust the former and less than 30 per cent of respondents trust the latter, respectively. Italians perceive European institutions as more distant than ever, since slightly more than one in four trust them.
- The distance from standard politics is on the rise as well. Only 3 per cent of individuals polled show consideration for parties. This share is remarkably close to statistical error in surveys. Distrust involves even the traditionally symbolic role of the President of the Republic: consensus shrank from 71 per cent in 2010 to 44 per cent in 2014 (down 5 per cent since 2013).
- People are growing increasingly tired of party-based democracy. Half of respondents argue that they can fare pretty well without parties. While 66 per cent deem democracy the least negative form of government among available options, in 2008, democracy was supported by 72 per cent of respondents.
- Distrust in government (both at the central and local levels) and corruption scandals highlight the degeneration of politics and parties, but do not help improve the image of other institutions. The judiciary suffered a sharp decrease in credibility: it was 50 per cent in 2010, but only 33 per cent in 2014 (down 7 per cent since 2013). Also, trust in the police, while still strong with two in three Italians, was also sliding downwards (down 7 per cent since 2010 and 3 per cent since 2013).

In almost every Western country, polls consistently point at democracy's decline in attractiveness. While in other countries this phenomenon is largely attributable to governments' inability to cope effectively with the economic crisis, in Italy, it is the result of corruption and political parties' loss of legitimacy.

Even more striking than the pervasiveness of distrust is the speed at which it developed. In less than five years, Italians have withdrawn their moral support for any authority. These unprecedented dynamics have far-rooted origins, even though the process has accelerated over the past five years, spurred by the impoverishment of the middle and lower classes. As a result, in many instances, relative poverty has become absolute.

PIERFRANCO PELLIZZETTI

The birth of the Casta

As mutual trust between citizens and government is a major pillar of well-functioning democracies, some scholars trace the roots of the Italian political system's decline back to the post-World War II period. However, others identify the origins of the detachment between citizens and institutions in the first moments of the national unification process, the reason lying in its elitist roots. Namely, the input for unification came from liberal and freemasonic ruling classes, whose plan was carried out by the armed wing of the military caste of the Kingdom of Piedmont.

Italy's unification process never enjoyed widespread popular support. Moreover, after 1870, when the Italian Kingdom incorporated the territory of the Church by militarily occupying its lands, the Papacy was explicitly hostile to unification. In a country where Catholicism is deeply rooted in people's traditions and mentality, the ruling class was left with no other choice but isolation. In 1868, in his encyclical containing the famous 'Non expedit', Pope Pius IX openly invited Catholics to boycott the government and engage in passive civil resistance against Italian authorities. Such a situation determined a psychological 'siege syndrome' in the political classes, whose flip of the coin developed into the tendency to be self-referential.

After the 20-year anomaly of the Fascist era, the division of the world into spheres of influence in 1948 perturbed political equilibria in the country, since the border between the two blocks passed through Rome (the other border was Belgrade). International dynamics influenced political mentalities, as well, because Italy was a NATO member and part of the Western block. First, politicians realized that a change of the ruling coalition in every electoral period was unacceptable, since the bipolar system consisted of the Christian Catholic Democratic Party (DC) and the Italian Communist Party (PCI). Alliances were not an option. The Christian Catholic Democrats had to stay in power to prevent the USSR from becoming excessively influential in the country. Indeed, the Soviet Union maintained concrete ideological and financial ties with the PCI, which benefited from large donations from the USSR. Anomalies in the party financing system pertained to both sides. While the 'Moscow gold' abundantly flowed into the coffers of the PCI, the Western coalition generously contributed to the financial well-being of the DC, which headed the majority coalition in the Parliament. Moreover, the DC enjoyed the support of the Vatican and its backbone, i.e. parishes and other Catholic organizations. However, other parties of the ruling centrist coalition also thrived financially through external aid.

The PCI maintained strong veto power for at least two reasons. First, it directly administered three central regions in Italy (Emilia-Romagna, Tuscany and Umbria), in which it enjoyed an uncontested majority. Second, in the Parliament, Committees were the place where parties ultimately decided the destiny of bills. In Committees, Communists exerted veto power. Hence, subterranean agreements and behind-the-scenes negotiations constituted the only viable option to let the otherwise jammed political system work. Thus, the post-World War II years marked the advent of a long process towards the strategic convergence between the two parties, the PCI and the DC. This process culminated in a radical turning point, namely the establishment of openly admitted tight relationships between communist and Catholic political forces (the so-called 'Historical Compromise') at the end of the 1970s. This process, which ended the period of hidden cross-party agreements in favour of more openly declared grand-coalition strategies, was steered by the secretary of the PCI, Enrico Berlinguer. However, the season of the Historical Compromise was rather brief and did not translate into any bipartisan government.

From connivance to collusion

Secretive practices hinged upon a consolidated tendency in the political class to consider itself as an entity separate from society. The political background of the two leading parties in the arena influenced such well-interiorized mentality: Catholic paternalism moved members of the DC. This framework idealized notables as 'shepherds of the flock' and conceptualized political action as a form of charity. In the PCI, some sort of Leninist elitism emphasized the role of party leadership. The party culture of the PCI viewed cadres as depositaries of the right course of action and regarded political militancy as a pedagogical pursuit.

Under the growing tendency of party self-referentiality, the latent, but convincing idea that societal control is the ultimate duty of politics gained increasing support. At the same time, the actors increasingly ritualized the political game, simulating interparty clashes and giving the false impression of imminent equilibrium changes looming in the background. Obviously, the actors themselves knew very well that any sort of change was impracticable. Such political stagnation offered public administrators countless daily opportunities to hoard public money, in order to either benefit the party and/or serve private interests. The first goal is not substantively different from the latter, since favouring the party increases the odds of personal political promotions. As a result, bribery and corruption spread rapidly.

Such moral degradation became a priority on the political agenda with the failure of the attempted revelation of 'consociational' practices that had been achieved by the Historical Compromise. A dramatic event abruptly stopped the process of convergence: on 16 March 1978, Red Brigades (BR) terrorists kidnapped Italy's former Prime Minister Aldo Moro and killed him after a long sequestration. Moro had been Enrico Berlinguer's main interlocutor while he was President of the DC. Hence the tipping point: during its 14th convention, in February 1980, the Christian Democrats swapped their support from the Communist Party to the Socialist Party, firmly excluding the possibility of any agreement with the Communist Party. Thus, the DC established a stable alliance with the Socialist Party, whose positions were firmly anti-communist, in line with the positions of its leader, Bettino Craxi. This was the first explicit sign of awareness of a *genetic mutation* inside the Italian political body.

The *moral question* was the political slogan of the last Berlinguer campaign in denouncement of the so-called *Casta*, the untouchable transversal constituency group of power (similar to a medieval *guild*) that is dominating Italian society nowadays. The journalists Gian Antonio Stella and Sergio Rizzo, in an investigation that soon became a best-seller, minted the term (2007). The elements emerging from this inquiry are discomforting, considering both the ethical quality of political life and the increased costs of politics. Malpractices are on the rise: on 15 February 2012, in his speech at the opening of the judiciary year, the President of the Court of Auditors, Luigi Giampaolino, quantified the annual direct cost of 'illegality, corruption and frauds' as €60 billion.

The *Casta* is an *untouchable* social class – hence, oriented to think about itself as unquestionable and invulnerable. Stella and Rizzo calculate that its members number 179,485, if we include in the count not only MPs, but also the periphery of the political system. To these costs, we should add 'the salaries of the various administration staff, drivers, underlings, external collaborators, and the honoraria given to almost 150,000 consultants. Additionally, the stipends of the C-level managers of more than 6,000 public and quasi-public companies, seats that often serve the purpose of placing friends and failed politicians' (Stella and Rizzo 2007: 22).

The same phenomenon led to the collapse of the First Republic in the mid-1990s, when the muted power equilibria enabled the judiciary to identify and punish those individuals involved in malfeasances. Two of the most active public prosecutor's offices were Milan and Palermo. The former focused on the pathological spreading of bribery and corruption; the latter on the relationships between politics and the mafia.

At the same time, in Lombardy, the unexpected rise of the Lombard League was instrumental in weakening the pernicious grip of parties on society and the reduction of political vetoes to judicial inquiries on certain uncomfortable issues. The League was a new locally focused party with a marked anti-political footprint. Almost openly advocating for the secession of the North from the rest of the country, it contests the colonization of Northern Italy by the politics of Rome and pursues forms of increased political autonomy (*devolution*). The success of this outsider in Lombardy, the region of Milan, which had been the electoral core of the Socialist Party until then, determined the collapse of a major pillar of the cabinet. This provided the green light for judiciary actions.

The operation *Mani Pulite* ('Clean Hands') began on 17 February 1992 with the investigation of a quite small extortion against a cleaning company by the socialist manager of a public hospice. Yet, it rapidly spread like wildfire, quickly reaching the national level and unmasking the involvement in the illegal financing system of many individuals active in the politics, economy and institutions of the country. The scandal did not spare anyone: ministers, deputies, senators, well-known entrepreneurs and managers were all affected. The inquiry ended up with 2,565 defendants! Some of the indicted committed suicide, and the former Prime Minister Bettino Craxi fled to Tunisia to avoid arrest. Overwhelmed with public indignation, the historical parties vanished or underwent substantial downsizing.

However, the *Casta* initiated a strategy to get rid of the judiciary's grip. The decisive move to escape the siege of indignation was inherently communicative and mimetic at the same time. It consisted of shifting the attention from the *moral question* to the *institutional* one. The argument was that the solution involved changing the rules, and not sanctioning ethically reprehensible practices. Thus, the focus was concentrated on the passage from the current proportional electoral system to the majoritarian one. Purportedly, such mechanism would have granted more control and a more direct relationship between elected officials and their constituents.

Thus, the country gradually transitioned to the Second Republic, dominated by the personality of an old partner and intermediary of Craxi, the multibillionaire TV tycoon Silvio Berlusconi. The origin of his financial and entrepreneurial fortune is still shrouded in mystery. He entered the political arena with his new political formation, *Forza Italia* ('Go Italy', as the football chant goes), on 26 January 1994. *Forza Italia* is a party conceived like a business (a company-party). The advertisement company Publitalia, which Berlusconi owned, created *Forza Italia*, which was largely staffed with Publitalia employees. Two months later,

Berlusconi won the elections on 27–28 March 1994 with 42.9 per cent of the votes, and became Prime Minister, obtaining the vote of confidence by the Parliament on 18 May 1994.

Personal parties, company-parties, star system

Silvio Berlusconi's Italy forcefully enters the realm of spectacularized politics (*politainment*).

The so-called Second Republic is deeply marked by the personality and biography of its dominating figure, the TV tycoon Berlusconi, who introduces marketing methodologies into political communication. This transformation of politics into post-democracy has been widely studied (Crouch 2000: 598; Manin 1997; Mazzoleni and Sfardini 2009):

- Elections boil down to *beauty contests* between political brands, rather than opportunities for citizens to give feedback to their representatives on the quality of their performance. Hence, elections cease to trigger processes of actual political change.
- Parties centre on their leaders and distance themselves from society, while the electorate assumes the position of passive spectator of a political scene that comes closer and closer to a show. Casting a vote becomes more similar to a round of applause than to the expression of an informed judgement.
- Politics presents its stories and its protagonists through *pop codes* – a pop style of storytelling – and becomes *politainment*. Unsurprisingly, its primary channel becomes TV, a blender of reality and fiction, news and commentaries, reasoning and emotions.

In the Italian version of *audience post-democracy*, the tendency of the political class to eschew society translates into self-referential and uncontrollable behaviour. It mixes with mimetic practices, which are necessary to shroud images tainted by scandals and suspects.

The 2015 Transparency International report confirms the sensational dimensions of this phenomenon: Italy ranks first in corruption among EU Member States. At the same time, the *spectacularization* of politics, which focuses its attention on its main characters regardless of any evidence of trustworthiness or credibility, makes connotative discourse and distinctive categories useless. In fact, at the beginning of 2014, a survey conducted by SWG showed that 60 per cent of the Italian electorate chooses their candidate exclusively by his or her personality (SWG-Agorà 2013). Antagonism between different parties becomes more and more

364

simulated. Since 'right' and 'left' become labels looking for a target, the real goal is the division of the electorate to achieve a higher purpose, namely to determine the division criteria of public sector organization charts between the various *cliques and gangs* of *Caste guild* members.

These lexical categories have been further pushed towards an indistinct entity, especially starting from the left of the political spectrum. The restyling operation began in the Anglo-Saxon area under the name 'Third Way' (Giddens 1998).

Third Way policies offered an important and appreciated ideological coverage to the concrete dynamics of anthropological unification of the political class and embodied a timely defence of their own corporate privileges. Thus, they achieved the goal of becoming autonomous from society. This happened in three phases:

1. Connivance (subterranean agreements to circumvent a jammed political scenario).
2. Collusion (shadow bargains to pursue unscrupulous business).
3. Homologation (the transformation of the political class into an undifferentiated *Casta*).

This sequence isolates politicians in the magic circle of a privileged status and is bolstered by the current evolution of the European Union, which is transitioning from the social market economy paradigm to the neoliberal one. The latter tightens the alliance between post-democratic leaderships, techno-structures and business or financial circles in promoting antisocial agendas of austerity and deregulation. This happens notwithstanding the recurrent denunciation of the effect of these policy choices: because 'austerity kills' (Stuckler and Basu 2013).

In public opinion, a growing conviction is spreading that the system is unamendable through competition from the inside. Hence, new movements appear in the political arena. Contrary to the status quo, these political formations reaffirm the direct relationship with society to promote the so-called alternative politics or anti-*Casta* movement. In Italy, this phenomenon goes hand in hand with electoral abstentionism. Approximately, only half of the electorate votes in a country where, traditionally, electoral participation reached over 80 per cent.

Indignation before indignation

At the beginning of the third millennium, the recurrent incursion of movements that blatantly challenged the course taken by *berlusconized* politics deeply characterized the Italian political arena. What these movements particularly criticized is the tendency, in Berlusconi's party, to bow to their leader's personal interests. Parties' frequent attacks on the democratic and antifascist Constitution of 1947 are under the new movements' spotlight, as well. The ruling political class considered the Charter as an intolerable obstacle to the project of a new post-democratic order, even though the critique of the Constitution has never been explicit. Instead, it has been aptly shrouded within appeals to efficiency and modernization.

Numerous independent media network initiatives flourished after the tough *No-global* contestation during the G8 meeting in Genoa on 19–21 July 2001. Specifically:

- On 26 January 2002, the so-called *Ring a Ring-o'Roses* movement (*'Girotondini'*), promoted by the film director Nanni Moretti and the director of the *MicroMega* magazine Paolo Flores d'Arcais, made its first appearance around the Court of Milan. The name of the movement stems from its non-violent protest technique, which consists of forming human circles around those institutional landmarks under threat of *normalization* by the ruling political class.
- 'Violet People' is the denomination of a self-convened aggregation via social networks on 5 December 2009. It was largely driven by university students, who organized with mass participation the *No-B-Day* meeting. During the demonstration, they asked for the resignation of the Berlusconi cabinet, which they accused of being 'a threat to democracy'.
- On 23 February 2011, there was the last protest initiative of this kind with the feminist initiative 'If Not Now, When?', which led over one million women to demonstrate in 230 Italian towns for the inclusion of women's rights issues in the political agenda.

That very social energy appears worn out right at the beginning of 2011, when protests spread worldwide against the financial world order, to which the various political classes increasingly appear subordinate in their role of social consensus Pied Pipers. Civil mobilization exploded in 950 cities and over at least 80 countries across the globe. Yet, in that very moment, in Italian society the field of social and electoral indignation was occupied by another protagonist: The Five Star Movement (*'Cinquestelle'*) (Pellizzetti 2015).

Promoted by Beppe Grillo, an Italian comedian, the Five Star Movement is deeply influenced by *politainment* and *star system* models that are a big hit in the Second Republic. Gianroberto Casaleggio, a

Milanese computer consultant keen on science fiction, was a supporter. Casaleggio, who died in 2016, could be portrayed as a 'grey eminence in the shadow' for Grillo (in a similar way as Cardinal Mazarino in the French *ancien régime*). Despite presenting itself as the standard-bearer of direct network democracy (*click-democracy*; Chiusi 2014) and spearhead in the anti-*Casta* battle, the M5S manifests its evident dependency on the Italian context, which has been colonized by *berlusconism*:

- The predominance of politics as a show, which simulates a continuous recall to grassroots participation, while inner deliberations take place under the strict control of Casaleggio & Associates staff.
- The proprietorial nature of the movement, whose trademark is the property of Beppe Grillo and registered with a notarial act. Hence, the owner may freely expel the members based on his unquestionable discretion.
- The strict control of the political stance and of the representatives' selection by Grillo and Casaleggio promotes unconditional obedience among followers. The dominating logic is an 'Us versus Them' dichotomy, where the Movement stands against 'the rest of the world', which is accompanied by politically isolationist choices that make it impossible to make alliances.

In February 2013, however, at its first attempt in national elections, M5S earned more than a quarter of the votes (about 8.7 million). This is an unprecedented achievement for a political actor facing its first electoral test: 54 senators and 109 delegates proclaim M5S the actor in pole position to obtain national consensus (25.5 per cent, against the 25.4 per cent of the Democratic Party). Moreover, the Members of Parliament of the M5S are the youngest of the Italian Parliament, with an average age of 33 years. This marks an important shift in Italian politics, which is traditionally characterized by gerontocracy. This outcome was traumatic for mainstream politics (Laudonio and Panarari 2014).

Phenomenology of the Five Star Movement

It all started on 8 September 2007 in Bologna, where Beppe Grillo brought together 50,000 people to collect signatures for an anti-*Casta* popular law initiative. From here unfolded an evolution in three phases:

1. Incubation on the Web (2005–7). In January 2005 the blog *beppegrillo.it* was inaugurated and in the following July *Meetup* became

the platform of connection among the local groups, which currently number 1,300.
2. Visibility (2007–8). Public and media appearance is achieved through large public events.
3. Elections (after 2008). In October 2009 the official Five Star Movement was born. The newly formed movement gains a promising success in the 2010 regional elections, thanks to the iconic role of Beppe Grillo.

Is it just star-system politics or alternative politics? The answer requires the consideration of two crucial aspects: the absolute duopoly at the top (Grillo and Casaleggio) and the impenetrable secrecy of its organization, which embodies the 'original sin' of Italian politics (Pellizzetti 2014).

Notwithstanding the fact that the M5S presents itself as a proponent of hyper-democracy, it is precisely Italy's Second Republic paradigm, which is characterized by star-system politics and personal/company parties, that exerts a deep influence on the organizational pattern of the M5S. Accordingly, the movement's leadership imposes absolute obedience on political militants and punishes members who voice criticism of M5S's stances.

This is demonstrated by the systematic loss (expulsions or defections) of the movement's own elected officials. By the end of 2015, 37 out of 163 had exited the party, the cause generally being internal dissent within the party (Istituto Cattaneo 2012). In particular, the expulsions depend on the unquestionable judgement of the top management (Grillo and Casaleggio) and the sentences are published on Grillo's blog.

These practices prevent the building of alliances with other parties to gain the majority of seats in Parliament and forces the movement to follow the utopian aim of the 50 per cent vote threshold to gain power. This M5S policy, while commendable from a public morality perspective, reveals the belief of M5S representatives that the Italian democratic system would fall soon, giving the chance to Grillo's movement to replace the *ancien régime* and lay the foundations of a new political system. Hence, in the eyes of Grillo's militants, the staying power of mainstream parties would speed up the faltering of Italian politics. As a result, the dominant belief is that, in matters of Italians' electoral choices, 'the worse, the better'. This vision is probably inspired by Isaac Asimov's science fiction 'Foundation' trilogy, of which Gianroberto Casaleggio was an avid reader.

The fascination of direct democracy as 'click-democracy' facilitates the manipulation of people's opinions. This provides further confirmation that media-politics and politainment are effective tools to achieve success in elections, but are not a guarantee of government quality. Nevertheless, the opinion polls routinely confirm that the electoral consensus for M5S is fairly stable, hovering around 25–30 per cent, which represents a sizable minority of the electorate. This result indicates that the Italian 'indignation area' continues to be significant and embodies a constant threat for the *Casta*.

The old politics counterattacks: Matteo arrives

The particular threat embodied by the Five Star Movement does not consist of the credible menace of an alternative government, but of a thwarting element for institutions. For this reason, the establishment (the *Casta* and its supporting business community) has favoured the entry into the scene of a fierce competitor: Matteo Renzi, the young mayor of Florence, who conquered the leadership of the Democratic Party in the primary election of 8 December 2013. This event facilitated the path towards the position of Prime Minister in the Italian Government, which Renzi attained in February 2014.

The aggregation of forces that enabled the irresistible rise of this political outsider is unclear. Supported by the President of the Republic Giorgio Napolitano, who acted as a bulwark of mainstream politics, and in fact was never legitimized by elections, Renzi grew up in the Catholic political sphere, in a family where his uncle did business with Berlusconi (Nicola Bovoli, the brother of Renzi's mother, in the 1990s was the producer of *Quizzy*, a remote device that enabled viewers to participate from home in quizzes broadcast on Berlusconi's networks). Bovoli candidly admitted to having pressured Berlusconi's entourage to let Matteo Renzi participate as a competitor on *The Wheel of Fortune*, a show hosted on Berlusconi's TV where Renzi won the extraordinary amount of 48 million lira in September 1994). Renzi maintained linkages with the Freemasonry, of which Florence, in Tuscany, is the Italian capital. Tuscany was even the incubator of coup attempts concocted by deviant branches of Freemasonry, as judicial investigations revealed. Most notably, Renzi's political task was to destroy the dangerous political aggregation of indignation. He has been invested of this task due to his unquestionable qualities as a communicator, which were built on the experience of previous world-famous political leaders:

- The strategies of Tony Blair and Gerhard Schroeder in the early 2000s, according to which the 'Third Way' to economic governance entails freeing the hands of capitalists.

369

- The Italian ideology of unbounded and strongly self-centred leadership.
- The rhetoric of the New as 'Rottamazione' of the Old, which is a political metaphor that is used in everyday language to refer to the demolition of wrecked cars. In Renzi's discourse, the New is Renzi's innovative, change-driven politics, while the Old is represented by the political class that has ruled Italy for decades, bringing the country to the brink of financial collapse and of ultimate political stalemate. Following this rhetoric, several members of the *Casta*, both in politics and in big business circles, have recently joined Renzi.
- The traditional paternalistic approach that involves barter between consensus and money (an €80 tax break in Italian workers' wages promised before the 2014 European elections and delivered as soon as the political victory was achieved).

In fact, the peak of his experience as a Prime Minister was the European election of May 2014, where Renzi's Democratic Party (PD) won with 40.8 per cent of the votes. This result marked a big success for the PD, especially considering the M5S defeat (21.1 per cent). This political outcome stemmed from the novelty of Renzi's political offer, but also from the use of a well-experimented electoral technique of the DC tradition: the widespread use of political 'bribes' as elections approach, an example of which was the €80 tax break policy, which was targeted at PD swing voters.

Over time, however, public opinion surveys and polls signalled increasing loss of popularity and suspicions of corruption, which were confirmed by several scandals. In April 2016 Federica Guidi, Italian Minister of Economic Development, had to resign over charges of conflict of interest, and the father of another Minister, Maria Elena Boschi, was sentenced to a heavy fine for the failure of the bank Etruria, of which he was vice president. The levels of personal popularity of the Prime Minister were in constant descent, but Renzi retained his leadership given the absence of alternatives. Meanwhile, the rebellious mood of Italians against the political class was turning into a jaundiced sense of impotence and frustration. Episodes of cronyism and bribery involving elected officials came to light with impressive frequency, revealing often scandals of unprecedented magnitude (e.g. the case of Mafia Capitale in 2015, which revealed a strong corruption network that ruled over Rome, and led to the resignation of Rome's mayor).

Distrust was increasingly becoming the dominant mood, as confirmed by the current decrease in voter turnout in Italy, which has reached 50 per cent. This phenomenon infected every institution, including the European

Union ones. A decade ago, Italians were still the most euro-enthusiastic on the continent, while now they have turned into Eurosceptics.

In the meantime, the original change-driven policy agenda of the Renzi cabinet had lost momentum, and the power-oriented goals had been revealed. The priority was maintaining law and order, especially through 'top-down' reform projects in the labour market and in the school system. The goal was to win elections by targeting the support of conservative constituencies, which constituted the traditional voter base of the progressive electorate. This strategic objective had its own label: the 'Party of the Nation', which was supposed to reconcile the right and the left under a single leadership.

The municipal elections of June 2016 in the main Italian cities (Rome, Milan, Turin, Naples and Bologna) and the other 1,337 municipalities (17 per cent of total) represented a very important test for this strategy, since in Italy, administrative elections usually have national relevance in indicating general voting patterns. The election results, which came in two rounds (5 and 19 June 2016, when runoff voting took place), were very negative for Prime Minister Renzi. In fact, M5S conquered Rome and Turin and won against Renzi's PD nineteen runoff votes out of twenty. Moreover, it did so by a large margin: in Italy's capital, Virginia Raggi (M5S) beat Roberto Giachetti (PD) with 67.2 per cent to 32.8 per cent; in Turin, Chiara Appendino (M5S) defeated the incumbent mayor and Democratic Party founder Piero Fassino (PD).

Foremost, these elections showed important modifications in M5S's strategy:

1. The emergence of a new politics centred on local leadership that was more flexible and attributed more importance to women's role.
2. Beppe Grillo temporarily (and tactically) stepping behind the scenes (Gianroberto Casaleggio died on 12 April 2016) reduced the aggressiveness of the communication style and increased the efficacy in targeting the non-ideologically motivated electorate.
3. The widening of the M5S's core constituencies (in the Turin runoff vote, Appendino almost doubled her votes, going from 118,000 to 202,000. On the contrary, Fassino, her opponent, did not enjoy a broader consensus, since his votes went up only slightly, from 160,000 to 168,000).

The Cattaneo Institute of Bologna University calculated that the bulk of M5S's new voters in 2016 relinquished their political identity in favour of vote choices based on the actual programmatic content of the parties' political offering. For every 100 new voters, 46 came from centre-right parties, 21 from centre-left ones, and 33 did not vote for any party. This was an important turning point that could pave the way for winning control of key national government electoral posts in the near future.

The rise to power of the M5S might have come sooner than previously expected: in a political survey at the end of June 2016 about voting intentions, 32 per cent of subjects indicated that they would have voted for the M5S, but only 30 per cent would have voted for the PD (Indagine Demos 2016).

The ongoing political struggle for power between M5S and PD, however, was still in its early stages. The June 2016 administrative elections marked only the first step in a political fight that would culminate on 4 December, when the referendum on Constitutional reform took place. The Constitutional reform had been introduced side by side with a new electoral law, with the declared goals of legislative simplification as well as a more efficient and speedy decision-making process.

If approved, the Constitutional reform would have increased the power and influence of the Executive branch of government by giving a large majority bonus (54 per cent) to the party that received at least 40 per cent of votes or won the election ballots and by permitting the parties' top management to exert strict control over electoral rolls. The enactment of these reforms would have thus concentrated significant powers in one person, namely Matteo Renzi, who was simultaneously the head of the Democratic Party and Italy's Prime Minister.

The proposed reform represented two sides of the same coin: for Renzi's supporters, it introduced a necessary post-democratic modernization, while for Renzi's opponents it embodied an evident step towards Counter-Reformation against alternative politics.

The last crash or the umpteenth delusion?

The arm wrestling between alternative politics and the post-democratic re-establishment, i.e. M5S versus Matteo Renzi, reached its final clash in the second half of 2016. In light of a long campaign marked by a series of embarrassments, gaffes and faux-pas by both contestants, there was strong evidence suggesting the irreversible decay in the quality of the national public discourse after the First Republic catastrophe and the missed rebuilding opportunity in the Second. As a result, we observe the further impoverishment of civil ethics and the reduction of public debate to a talk show.

Specifically, we could consider these stylized points:

- In the communication campaign preceding the referendum, Matteo Renzi transformed the mix of Constitutional reform and the new electoral law into a plebiscite about his personal leadership in the Cabinet. The goal was presumably to win support for a complicated reform thanks to his extraordinary popularity. In hindsight, this move backfired. After the initial momentum – the unexpectedly large victory in the European elections of May 2014 – the honeymoon with the electorate started fading away. Several scandals and/or policy failures overshadowed the feeble progress made in growth-oriented reforms, thus creating dissatisfaction. Key issues included the record-high youth unemployment, migrant crisis management and scandals in government procurements. In addition, the old-school left-wing minority in Renzi's own party took a firm stance to vote against Constitutional reform in the referendum.
- The unprecedented experiment of M5S's ruling in the major big cities produced mixed results. M5S easily gained power in the face of PD's defeat because of a civic rebellion in Turin and Rome. In Rome, M5S's victory was spurred by outrage against widespread corruption that paralysed the municipal government. In Turin, it was due to the insufficient governance of the post-industrial transition which occurred after Fiat's internationalization. Yet, especially the landslide victory in Rome turned out to be a hindrance for the aspirations to conquer the national government. In Rome, Mayor Virginia Raggi failed to choose collaborators that were untainted by judicial investigations, which had plagued previous municipal administrations as well. Some of the new council members of the majority M5S maintained worrisome proximity to environments of the previous business policy. In Turin, Mayor Chiara Appendino kept buying time to fulfil the promises of her election campaign. Meanwhile, however, the city was losing important events such as the Book Fair, which was moved to Milan, and other events on which it had centred its rebranding into a capital city of culture. Meanwhile in Parma – the first large electoral M5S stronghold since 2012 – Mayor Federico Pizzarotti defected from the movement, after experiencing years of ostracism by the M5S top management for reasons that are still unclear.

In light of the complexity of the issues that pertained to the referendum, which made its substance rather obscure to most citizens, the electoral challenge was increasingly more focused on psychological attitudes than on policy options. In fact, no matter contained in the referendum text covered issues relating to the concrete problems of citizens (unemployment, impoverishment, land degradation, etc.). In other words, it was a dilemma between the drive to oust an unfit leader – Renzi – and '*horror vacui*', i.e. fear of the political void that would have resulted after the fall of the Renzi Cabinet. Neither option was especially appealing. Hence, deep uncertainty has dominated the political climate. While polls predicted a high turnout, about one in three voters were uncommitted to either option until a few days before the vote.

The substantial stalemate urged Renzi to frantically look for illustrious endorsements for his Constitutional reform project, which included President Barack Obama, past Italian President of the Republic, Giorgio Napolitano, mainstream media, and large portions of the Italian and European financial system.[1] These moves were aimed at countervailing the growing disenchantment among the mass public about the actual progress made in jump-starting Italy's economy after the Great Crisis.

Despite these rebounding efforts and the mistakes made by M5S, indignation against mainstream politics has remained diffuse, putting the stability of the Renzi cabinet at risk. As a result, whatever the outcome of the December referendum, it was assumed that in the Italian political landscape nothing would be the same as before. Meanwhile, during the long months of the campaign, behind the mask of propaganda, the face of an overall political project began to appear, of which the referendum was only the consecration. A comprehensive project that involved large areas of society and institutions (labour market, school, business and competitiveness, governance of Italian ports, autonomy, etc.) traced to a centralizing decisionistic post-democratic logic. If in recent years studies on the quality of institutions were based on the paradigm of 'rational choice', this was also the basis being pursued by the Renzi Government's reform (Pellizzetti 2016: 117).

The historian of Economy of the University of Salento, Guglielmo Forges Davanzati, says: 'there are good reasons to believe that the public decision maker is captured by interest groups. The only predictable result of the reform is greater governance for the benefit of the interest groups that the Government defends. And these ones aren't the employees, retirees or small enterprises' (Davanzati 2016). The general picture illuminated the difficulty in witnessing unconventional political actors take the centre stage, a problem which is common to many Western democracies.

In the West, democratic political systems are showing signs of

---

[1] A notable exception in Europe is the *Financial Times*, where Tony Barber dubbed Renzi's Constitutional reform project 'A bridge to nowhere', https://www.ft.com/content/5430f982-8a28-11e6-8cb7-e7ada1d123b1. In Italy, former Prime Minister Mario Monti voiced his strong opposition to the reform: http://www.corriere.it/politica/16_ottobre_18/mario-monti-perche-votero-no-referendum-costituzionale-8546db02-94b6-11e6-97ea-135c48b91681.shtml

exhaustion. Voters have to choose between *the well-known* mainstream politicians (e.g. Rodham Clinton, Merkel, Sarkozy, Rajoy, Renzi, etc.) and newcomers who are evident demagogues ('populists' in the current lexicon of 'Newspeak', as in George Orwell's *Animal Farm*, created by the present 'dominant cultural codes') (Castells 1996). The American general election of 2016, where Donald Trump prevailed over Hillary Rodham Clinton, provides a paradigmatic example of these dynamics. Neither type of politician seems able to give an answer to the prolonged political and economic crisis of our times. Simultaneously, democracy slips from post-democracy into 'democratorship' (*democratura*), a government coated in a formal shell of a democracy which hides substantial authoritarianism. In this view, 'democratorship' is the other side of a coin of the stagnation that pervades the Western model; one which Fernand Braudel named 'the autumn season of financial capitalism' (Arrighi 1994).

In this climate the 'poker player' Matteo Renzi decided to stake everything on the December vote and he transformed the referendum into an ordeal.

The political earthquake of 4 December 2016

The first exit polls on Italian TV, aired at 11 p.m. on Sunday, 4 December 2016, signalled in real time that the referendum on Constitutional reform promised by the Renzi cabinet had had a largely unpredicted outcome. On the days preceding the vote, when Italian law bans the diffusion of opinion polls, rumours suggested that the 'No' vote was leading by a margin of 3 percentage points, a gap in the realm of statistical error. Nobody imagined that, in the end, the 'Yes' campaign would have been lagging 19 percentage points behind (40.89 vs. 59.11): 19,419,507 'No' votes, 13,432,208 'Yes' votes; the Government's proposal won only three regions out of twenty (Tuscany, Emilia-Romagna and Trentino Alto Adige). At midnight, Matteo Renzi announced during a press conference that the next day he would resign as Prime Minister to the President of the Republic Sergio Mattarella.

This was a seemingly inevitable epilogue to the voters' sentence. Turnout was unprecedented for a referendum: 69 per cent. This was evidence that there was more than the Constitutional laws at stake: the Prime Minister's future was at stake, as he had transformed the road to the referendum into a 'one-man show', pushing the personalization of the vote beyond limits. His tactic, based on frenetic activism in public speeches, press statements and TV appearances, did not achieve the strategic intent of labelling his opponents as the '*Casta*'. Public opinion rejected this illusionistic operation, since the coalition in favour of the 'Yes' vote was composed by financial institutions, the confederation of industrials, State television and large newspapers; in other words, 'the establishment'. Judgement confirmed by the support given to Renzi by all major foreign leaders, from Merkel to Obama: a boomerang in the eyes of indignant public opinion.

Nevertheless, there was every indication that the electorate had paid attention to the internal crisis conditions of the government's policies; while the relationship with Brussels and the EU had remained on the sidelines, because Renzi in the last months had taken care to tactically mark his distance from the Union, so that comments like that of Nigel Farage ('This vote has the air of being more on the euro than on constitutional reform') only seem premature. Therefore, the EU/euro theme had been sterile and made electorally irrelevant, if only for instrumental and demagogic reasons.

In these historical times, electorates tend to use the vote to punish the elites, considered predatory, from Brexit to the US presidential elections. Thus, if the actual object of the referendum was the alternative between ousting Renzi and the fear of a political void, the first alternative won. The coalition in favour of the 'No' vote, which Renzi had arrogantly defined as a 'rabble', brought together positions that were not reconcilable and was not capable of expressing a credible political alternative.

What has happened so far is the defeat of a political project which disguised the restoration of the *ancient régime* as a rationalization of the political system. As a result, the political leadership has been erased and has now to be rebuilt via a new electoral law. The President of the Republic, Sergio Mattarella, pushed for this solution, to remedy another Italian anomaly: the last three cabinets (Monti, Letta and Renzi) were not direct expression of the popular vote, but nominated by then President of the Republic Giorgio Napolitano.

But what is shaping up is a long transition, as the results of 4 December did not indicate the emergence of political alternatives to Renzi's PD, which also emerged with broken bones and at risk of internal divisions.

At this stage only electoral engineering could provide some governance, because the two prevalent poles (PD and M5S) are both around 30 per cent, and none clearly prevails. Two parties that are not able to provide quality of governance: PD is preparing a settling of scores between factions, first submitted to the Premier's leadership; the Grand Chief of M5S Beppe Grillo betrays the desire to collect the electoral advantage of the political crisis without assuming responsibility. Meanwhile, he lets leak that he would continue to ride the protest in a referendum on the euro: an uninterrupted campaign as an escape from the problems?

In their strange 'parallel lives' Renzi and Grillo would both like to go to the people as soon as possible in elections, with the aim of cashing in their respective electoral capital (although the most accredited observers, first President Matttarella, do not feel it is realistic to have an election before late spring 2017). But no political leader can consider captive the votes gone from its line. As stated in the newspaper *Il Fatto Quotidiano*:

> the 40.05 per cent of YES in the referendum are not votes for Matteo Renzi and neither for Democratic Party. So, it's not from there that the Prime Minister can allocate, as supporting, several members of the majority. For the Ipsos Institute in Milan, the picture is quite clear: YES arrived at 80.6 per cent of the votes of the Democratic Party in the European elections; 48.7 per cent of those Ncd-UDC [the right party allied in Government with Renzi]; 23.8 per cent of those of Forza Italia [Berlusconi]; 16.4 per cent of those on the left; 10.9 per cent of the League's voters, 10.4 per cent of FDI [ultra-right] and 9.9 per cent from well M5S. (Roselli 2016)

Pure tactics. In particular, a direct referendum on the euro is in practice impossible: the Italian Constitution prohibits such consultations on international treaties. Moreover, M5S is ambiguous about how they will vote (and they do not explain how an exporting country like Italy could buy the essential raw materials for its productions with a devalued lira).

An equal tactic seems to be the solution to the government crisis: President Mattarella appointed Premier Paolo Gentiloni, the former foreign minister; a Catholic politician loyal to Renzi who should allow him a quick return to the track (in the days following the referendum, 52 per cent of PD voters declared they wanted Matteo Renzi as leader of the government; meanwhile, he kept the post of National Secretary of the Democratic Party). In fact, Gentiloni is supported by the political majority of his predecessor and he leads a ministerial complex that is almost a duplicate of the previous team.

Meanwhile, emerging transversal uncomfortable areas (intergenerational and social) are not attributable to any camp: the first investigations say that no party can regard themselves as winners of the result of the referendum. Thus the vote has been a hard reaction against the government (and not against the questions of a referendum that few people understood), young people with no future (7 out of 10 in the age group 25–35 voted 'No') have voted like the reflective middle classes against the centralist restoration, de-industrialized North and the impoverished South (with the 'No' vote around 70 per cent), and the publicly employed, hostile to privatizations, and manual workers, outraged by a leader of a leftist party that promotes job precariousness.

The real tragedy is that this deep social unease is currently not producing any focal point for aggregation and representation.

An Italian 'molecular' condition, translated into resentment against the power elite, which, in the absence of political synthesis, promises only instability. While the economic decline, an aging population, the lack of communication between institutions and social issues are heavily advancing. There is real prospect of a systemic crisis.

This is Italy, as usual; that which the 'divine' poet Dante described in the sixth song of Purgatory: a 'ship without a helmsman in a mighty storm'.

Acknowledgements

The author wishes to acknowledge the assistance of Alessandro Del Ponte, a PhD student at the Center of Behavioral Political Economy at Stony Brook University. He has worked for New York's and Italy's top government officials and conducted research for the European Commission.

References

Arrighi, G. (1994) *The Long Twentieth Century*. London: Verso.
Castells, M. (1996) *The Rise of the Network Society*. Oxford: Blackwell.
Castells, M. (2012) *Networks of Outrage and Hope*. Cambridge: Polity.
Chiusi, F. (2014) *Critica della democrazia digitale*. Torino: Codice.
Crouch, C. (2000) *Coping with Post-democracy*. Cambridge: Polity.
Davanzati, G.F. (2016) Nel nome di J.P. Morgan. Le ragioni economiche della controriforma costituzionale. *MicroMega*, 2 June.
Giddens, A. (1998) *The Third Way: The Renewal of Social Democracy*. Cambridge: Polity.
Indagine Demos per l'Atlante Politico di Repubblica (2016) June.
Istituto Cattaneo (2012) http://www.cattaneo.org/AnalisiCattaneo_Parlmentarie. M5S_19dicembre2012pdf
Laudonio, M. and Panarari, M. (2014) *Alfabeto Grillo*. Sesto S. Giovanni, Mimesis.
Manin, B. (1997) *The Principles of Representative Government*. New York: Cambridge University Press.
Mazzoleni, G. and Sfardini. A. (2009) *Politica pop*. Bologna: il Mulino.
Pellizzetti, P. (2014) *La Vanguardia Dossier*, no. 50.
Pellizzetti, P. (2015) *Società o barbarie*. Milan: il Saggiatore.
Pellizzetti, P. (2016) *Fenomenologia di Matteo Renzi*. Rome: Manifestolibri.
Roselli, G. (2016) Dimissioni di Renzi, verso le elezioni?, *il Fatto Quotidiano*, 7 December.

Stella, G. S. and Rizzo, S. (2007) *La casta, così i politici sono diventati intoccabili*. Milan: Rizzoli.
Stuckler, D. and Basu, S. (2013) *The Body Economic*. London: Allen Lane.
SWG-Agorà (2013) Survey, 13 September 2013.
Transparency International (2015) *The 2015 Corruption Perception Index*. Berlin: Transparency International.

Chapter 17

Brexit: The Causes and Consequences of the UK's Decision to Leave the EU

Geoffrey Evans, Noah Carl and James Dennison

Introduction

On 23 June 2016, the United Kingdom held a referendum to gauge public support for continued British membership of the European Union, with a majority voting for Leave. This outcome represents a radical departure from over 40 years of British involvement in European integration, and a vote of no confidence in the European project itself. As such, understanding the causes of Britain's momentous decision, as well as its potential ramifications for the UK, the EU and their future relationship to one another, is of central importance. Regarding the causes of Britain's decision to leave the EU, we seek to answer two questions: why Britain rather than any other country?, and why now rather than at any point in the past? Regarding the implications of the decision, we consider the future of Britain's territorial integrity, its political and economic prospects, and its relationship with the EU, before then speculating on its effects on EU institutions and the wider European project.

The chapter proceeds as follows. First, we argue that as the EU moved closer towards political union and immigration into the UK proceeded apace, Britain's weaker sense of European identity meant that Brexit was increasingly likely. Second, we show that, in the two decades prior to the EU referendum, Britain's major political parties coalesced around a socially liberal, pro-immigration, pro-European consensus, which – combined with the country's majoritarian voting system – suppressed the socially conservative preferences of many British citizens, especially those from working-class and less educated backgrounds. We argue that, amongst these groups, Euroscepticism took on additional resonance as the European Union became increasingly associated with unprecedentedly high levels of immigration from Eastern Europe after the 2004 enlargement. Third, we outline what sorts of individuals made up the Brexit majority, and how they came to their voting decisions. Finally, we discuss the referendum's effects on Scottish independence, the constitutional status of Northern Ireland, Britain's party system, its economy, and its evolving relationship with the EU. We then consider its possible effects on the political direction of the EU institutions, the prospects for deeper fiscal and monetary integration, the likelihood of further enlargement, and the possibility of a European defence union.

Historical background and integration into the EU

This section explores the historical preconditions to the UK's EU referendum. As the EU grapples with three major on-going crises – the sovereign debt crisis afflicting Southern Europe, the military conflict in Ukraine, and the large influx of migrants into Italy and the Balkans – it is noteworthy that the first and only referendum on leaving the EU took place in the UK, a country that has been mostly unaffected by these crises. Indeed, the UK has long been considered one of the most – if not the most – Eurosceptic country in the EU. It has opt-outs from four major EU projects – more than any other Member State: the Schengen agreement; the euro currency; the Area of Freedom Security and Justice; and the Charter of Fundamental Rights (Curtice 2016a). Moreover, in social surveys, Britons consistently rank among the least favourable towards further EU integration, among the most mistrustful of EU institutions, and among the least sanguine about their country's membership of the EU overall (Fitzgerald and Sibley 2016; ORB 2014).

For illustration, we examine data from the Eurobarometer – a public opinion survey that has been administered to a nationally representative sample of each EU country's citizens annually or biannually ever since 1973. In each year between 1973 and 2011, the Eurobarometer asked EU citizens whether they thought their country's membership of the EU was a good thing or a bad thing (European Commission 2016). This question was also asked in the 2012–16 Parlemeter surveys (European Parliament 2016). Figure 17.1 plots the percentage answering 'a good thing' in each of the EU9 countries (the six founders, plus Denmark, Ireland and the UK) from 1973 to 2014.[1] Although Britons became notably more positive about their country's EU membership during the 1980s, by the late 2000s they were as gloomy as they had been in the years following the

---

[1] We do not examine data from the 2015 and 2016 Parlemeter surveys, in order to avoid contamination from campaigning effects during the lead up to the EU referendum itself.

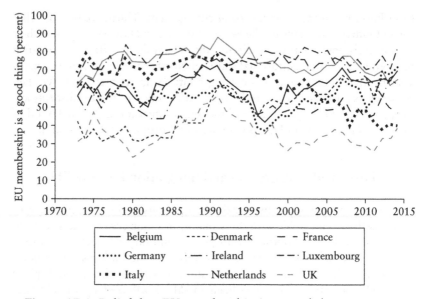

Figure 17.1: Belief that EU membership is a good thing over time

Source: Authors, based on data presented in the text

1975 EU referendum. In 2011, only 26 per cent of Britons answered 'a good thing'. This had ticked up to 39 per cent by 2014 – most likely because of the greater salience of the EU, following David Cameron's pledge to hold an in/out referendum in 2013, as well as the fact that the sovereign debt crisis had cooled by this point.[2] Furthermore, when considering all EU countries – including those that joined after 1973 – with respect to the percentage answering 'a good thing', the UK is the lowest ranked country in approximately 45 per cent of years, and is the lowest or second-lowest in roughly 83 per cent of years.

Why, then, do Britons tend to be more Eurosceptic than their counterparts from other Member States? An important proximal cause is that they have a weaker sense of European identity (Dennison and Carl 2016). In recent years, the Eurobarometer has asked EU citizens whether they see themselves more as members of their nationality or more as Europeans (European Commission 2016; and see Ormston 2015). Figure 17.2 plots the distribution of responses to this question for all 28 EU Member States, using data from the autumn 2014 wave of the survey.

---

[2] The uptick may also be due, at least in part, to differences in survey methodology between the Parlemeter and Eurobarometer surveys.

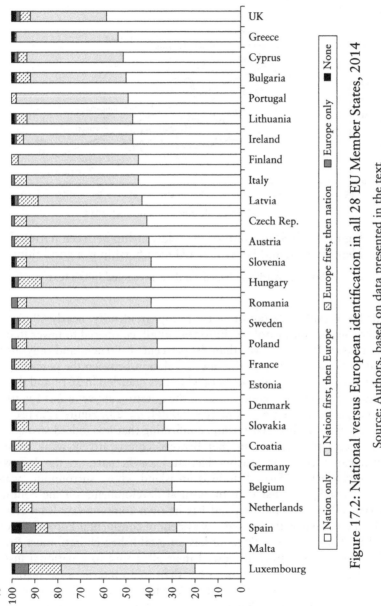

Figure 17.2: National versus European identification in all 28 EU Member States, 2014

Source: Authors, based on data presented in the text

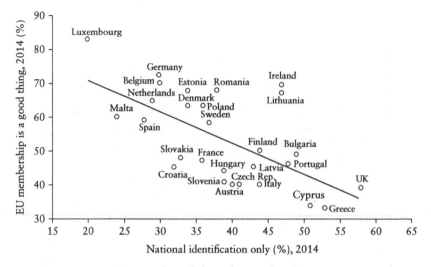

Figure 17.3: Scatterplot of the relationship between national identification and belief that EU membership is a good thing

Source: Authors, based on data presented in the text

The UK is ranked 28 out of 28 for European identity: nearly 60 per cent of Britons do not identify as European at all, compared to fewer than 50 per cent of Italians, fewer than 40 per cent of French, and only 30 per cent of Germans. In fact, the raw correlation between the percentage of respondents answering 'nation only' to this question in 2014 and the percentage answering 'a good thing' to the question above in 2014 is strong and negative, namely $r = -0.63$ ($p = 0.0004$, $n = 28$). Figure 17.3 provides a scatterplot of this relationship, confirming that it is indeed strong.

It seems plausible to us that Britons' comparatively weak sense of European identity is attributable, at least in part, to the following historical factors. First, Britain is an island whose surrounding waters have partially isolated it from cultural developments on the continent (Grant 2008). Second, England has its own common law legal system, which contrasts with the civil law system of continental Europe (Scruton 2015). Third, because England has an established church, most British Christians have historically owed their allegiance to a national institution headed by the monarch, rather than to an international institution headed by the Pope (Scherer 2014). And fourth, Britain is the only allied European power not to have been occupied during World War II.[3]

[3] Note that, of the Western European countries that are not EU members: Iceland is

By itself, of course, Britons' strong sense of national identity was not sufficient to take the UK out of the EU. After all, the country had been a member for over 40 years before the referendum was called. What changed was that the EU went from representing a comparatively small number of wealthy countries to representing 28 countries of varying levels of development, and went from being an organization based primarily around trade to one headed for much deeper political integration (see Kahanec and Zimmermann 2010; Geary 2012). Of particular importance to many Britons was their belief that the UK no longer had control over its borders, following the large influx of migrants from Eastern Europe that began in 2004 (Evans and Mellon 2016a). Indeed, 'sovereignty' and 'immigration' were the two most frequently cited concerns among those who voted Leave (Lord Ashcroft 2016; Prosser et al. 2016). Thus, it was the *interaction* between Britons' strong sense of national identity and the enlarged EU's movement towards political union that arguably took the UK out.

In addition to its strong sense of national identity, the UK is one of the least well-integrated EU Member States: it has a lower percentage of emigrants living inside the EU than any other country, and is ranked among the bottom two or three countries for percentage of trade with the EU, and percentage of foreign direct investment (FDI) to and from the EU (UN 2012, 2015; Eurostat 2015a).[4] Moreover, the percentage of UK trade that is done with the EU has been declining in recent years (ONS 2015). In our view, the UK's comparatively limited integration into the EU is unlikely to have had a major *direct* impact on voters' decision-making during the referendum – in contrast to the twin issues of sovereignty and immigration – but it probably did serve to keep Brexit within the Overton window (the range of ideas that are politically acceptable). For example, it would have been much harder for leading Leave campaigners such as Boris Johnson and Gisela Stuart to make the economic case for Brexit if the UK still did the great majority of its trade and investment inside the EU.

Overall then, as the EU moved closer towards political union and immigration into the UK proceeded apace, Britain's weaker sense of

---

an island, has a state religion and was not occupied by Germany; Norway has a state religion; and Switzerland has its own political system and was also not occupied by Germany.

4   The fact that Britain does relatively more of its trade and investment outside of the EU is due at least partly to the size and economic development of its former empire, the status of English as the global business language, and its particularly close ties with the United States. Britain's colonial past surely explains why relatively fewer of its emigrants choose to resettle in the EU; several former British territories today have large British-descended populations.

European identity meant that Brexit was increasingly likely. Note that our argument accounts for why the UK exited the EU rather any other Member State, as well as why the UK exited now rather than at any point in the past. This is in contrast to other prominent explanations for Brexit that have been put forward since the referendum result was announced. For example, Ford (2016), along with Goodwin and Heath (2016a, 2016b), argue that the result was driven by so-called 'left-behind' voters: older, white, economically disadvantaged individuals who had turned against a political class they regarded as privileged and out-of-touch. While 'left-behind' voters did indeed drive the result, such individuals can be found in countries across the EU; Britons are not even the least trusting of their politicians or parliament on average (Colborne 2014). An appeal to British exceptionalism is needed to explain why it was the UK in which 'left-behind' voters chose to express anger and disillusionment against the political class through a vote to leave the EU. Similarly, Bernstein (2016), along with Dorling (2016), attribute the referendum result to fiscal austerity policies, and the economic inequality that they helped to cement. Yet once again, fiscal austerity policies have been implemented in a number of EU countries, often more severely than in the UK (OECD 2015). The explanation fails to clarify why it was the UK in which austerity gave rise to a vote to leave the EU.

The political contest:
electoral exclusion and EU immigration policy

Any explanation of Brexit must not only account for Britain's relative Euroscepticism compared to other Member States, but also why the British people were given a chance to express their desire for 'Brexit' via referendum at all. It is notable that no other Member States have held 'in–out' referendums whereas Britain had already held one in 1975, two years after its initial accession. This referendum, held to appease Labour's primarily working-class voters and parliamentary party, resulted in a strong majority in favour of 'Common Market' membership, yet set a precedent for legitimizing Britain's EU membership *post facto* via referendums. Furthermore, the 'renegotiate-referendum' strategy successfully employed by Harold Wilson suggested that, with sufficient party pressure in an age when parties still carried considerable influence, and the idea that Britain had obtained a 'better deal', the electorate would put their anti-Europeanism to one side in the name of 'pragmatism'. However, whereas in 1975 the British electorate were willing to give the still nascent, optimistic EEC the benefit of their still considerable doubts and relatively few priors, by 2016, individual attitudes to Europe had become far more stable, entrenched and unforgiving.

The precedent set by 1975 was echoed repeatedly throughout the next 40 years of British politics as, at various times, the Conservatives, Labour, the Liberal Democrats, UKIP and the Greens all held manifesto commitments to a binding in–out referendum on EU membership or immediate withdrawal. These became more commonplace as British misgivings over EU membership increased and, under Tony Blair, referendums became increasingly seen as a legitimate way to resolve constitutional controversies. After the 2010 General Election, and in the context of a seemingly endless eurozone crisis, sections of the Conservative parliamentary party – driven by a mix of genuine anti-Europeanism and worry over the growing threat of UKIP to their seats – put Cameron, a moderate Eurosceptic, under increasing pressure to hold a referendum of his own. In early 2013, Cameron announced that should the Conservatives win the next General Election, which at the time seemed unlikely, he would pursue his own 'renegotiation-referendum' strategy. After his surprise 2015 General Election victory, Cameron, highly confident after referendum wins on electoral reform and Scottish independence, announced that he would not renege on his promise.

Just as the UK's use of referendums to legitimize EU membership *post facto* made it unique amongst Member States, its majoritarian voting system – in which a limited number of parties have in recent years competed for the liberal centre-ground at the expense of traditional support bases – makes the UK an electoral outlier. This has also played a role on the path to Brexit. Though there has been much post-Referendum discussion of Brexit and its creation of social divisions, this is misplaced: Britain is not now more divided than hitherto; it is the EU Referendum that has given these divisions the chance to be expressed. This has occurred because the electorate has, unusually, been presented with a clear choice between two opposed and competing alternatives. For the first time since the political transformation of the Labour Party from representing the interests of the working class to a centrist party aimed at the new middle class, this choice has allowed the voice of the working class to be expressed effectively through the act of voting.

How has this happened? Arguably the key architect of Brexit is the same individual who played a pivotal role in marginalizing the working class electorally by moving Labour politics onto common ground with parties of the liberal, centre-right: Tony Blair. Though New Labour's policies were sometimes redistributive (e.g., significant public spending and public sector employment increases in the North of England, Wales and Scotland in the period 2001–8), the party's liberal social agenda and its explicit attempt to attract the middle classes meant that, from the mid-1990s onwards, it engineered the electoral marginalization of the working class by rebranding itself as a centrist, middle-class party in both ideological position and social composition (Evans and Tilley 2017; Heath 2015). The Conservatives also moved to the socially liberal centre, with their adoption of policies such as the legalization of same-sex marriage. As a result of this depolarization, the electoral choices available to socially conservative voters became restricted. Consequently, class divisions in mainstream party voting declined, and working-class non-voting increased (Evans and Tilley 2012, 2017). But restricting representation does not necessarily change people's preferences. It merely leaves them without a viable electoral outlet. Blair's decision to enable immediate immigration to Britain from the new accession countries of Eastern Europe in 2004 provided the conditions under which some of those preferences became increasingly salient. No other major 'destination country' in the EU allowed this option. They maintained the decision to have a five-year period of exclusion prior to accepting immigrants from accession countries. As a result, Britain received a historically unique inflow of migrants from the EU accession countries. Since 2004, the yearly rate of increase of migrants born in EU accession countries has been close to 120,000; by 2014, there were nearly 1.5 million such workers living in the UK (Vargas-Silva and Markaki 2015).

This unprecedented inflow (for Britain and, specifically, England) led to a growing link between public concern about immigration and negative attitudes towards the EU. Analyses of the relationship between immigration rates from different origins, attitudes towards immigration and month-on-month changes in the strength of the relationship between concern about immigration and attitudes towards the EU show that concern about EU immigration evolved to become a key influence on attitudes towards it (Evans 2016; Evans and Mellon 2016a). There was only a moderate relationship between the two in 2004 when EU immigration from accession states was minimal. Over time, the correlation increased in line with the flow of EU immigrants, their growing prevalence, and their increasing relative prominence in the public's mind as other forms of immigration declined following the Coalition government's attempt to reduce net immigration to less than 100,000 per annum, primarily by targeting immigration from other areas of the world. This miscalculated promise never really had any chance of being realized whilst Britain remained within an EU for which freedom of movement was sacrosanct. Of course, Cameron's other miscalculation was to not realize that the Conservatives would gain an absolute majority in the 2015 General Election and thus not need coalition partners who could veto his promise. He was, ironically, a victim of his own electoral success.

The significance of the tightening bond between concern about immigration and attitudes towards the EU becomes even more apparent when one considers that one of the few indisputable facts in the fractious campaign leading to the EU Referendum vote was the EU's commitment to freedom of movement. Staying in the EU would mean that Britain could not exclude EU citizens from migrating to Britain – however many, on whatever grounds, regardless of any level of language or other skills. This was reinforced by the EU itself when David Cameron attempted to arrange a change of policy on aspects of free movement that might well have facilitated victory in the referendum. All other issues were disputed, contentious, at times over-played, but not this basic fact about immigration. The upshot is that although, historically, opposition to EU membership was not motivated by concerns over immigration – at the time of the 1975 referendum, support for leaving the EU was actually lower among those who believed that too many immigrants had been let into the country than among those who did not – this had all changed by the time of the 2016 referendum. The gap in approval of EU membership between those who say immigration is the most important issue and those who do not has been steadily rising since the early 2000s. By 2015, support for leaving the EU was an astonishing 40 percentage points higher among those who believed that too many immigrants had been let in (Evans and Mellon 2016a).

The referendum vote

The decisions of politicians provide the context for Brexit, but how was the outcome decided on the day by individuals? We now examine what sorts of people voted for or against Brexit and why they did so.

Since 23 June, many commentators have argued that the incendiary character and perfidious tone of the Leave campaign played a disproportionate role in the outcome of the referendum (Lewis 2016; Yeung 2016). However, systematic analyses of longer term surveys appear to contradict this idea. Clarke et al. (2016) applied a technique called dynamic factor analysis to the results of 121 Internet and phone polls carried out between 11 January and 22 June 2016, and found that Leave may actually have had the lead throughout the entire campaign, which belies claims that provocative statements made by Nigel Farage or Boris Johnson exerted decisive sway over prospective voters. Indeed, the balance of support for Leave versus Remain changed comparatively little during the two years prior to the referendum; both hovered at around 40 per cent until the summer of 2015, when opinion began to crystallize, and the fraction answering 'don't know' assumed a downward trend (Evans and Prosser 2016). In the end, despite both of the two main party leaders – David Cameron and Jeremy Corbyn – advocating Remain, nearly 40 per cent of Labour supporters and nearly 60 per cent of Conservative supporters voted for Leave (Lord Ashcroft 2016). Compared to the remarkable *volte face* executed during the 1975 referendum campaign by Labour's supporters at the behest of Harold Wilson and the party (Saunders 2016), the marked decline in voter attachment to the main political parties accompanying the rise of 'the volatile voter' (Fieldhouse et al. forthcoming) weakened the impact of party-led cues on voters' decisions.

So how *did* voters come to their decisions? Rather than coolly weighing the prospective costs and benefits of leaving through an assiduous examination of the competing claims and counter-claims put out by each campaign, most voters appear to have acted on their own prior convictions, which they then rationalized after the fact. Individuals' stated opinions were largely an expression of their prior beliefs and underlying values. Evans and Prosser (2016) analysed data from the British Election Study on what consequences Brexit would be likely to have in areas such as unemployment, international trade, immigration, terrorism and British influence. Consistent with the notion that individuals tend to rationalize their pre-existing convictions through a process of *post hoc* motivated reasoning (Kahan 2015), they found that beliefs about the consequences of Brexit were highly uni-dimensional: individuals who thought Brexit would have a positive impact in one area also thought it would have positive impacts in other areas, and *vice versa*. Moreover, this dimension was strongly predicted by attitudes towards the EU measured in earlier waves of the survey – in some cases up to 6 years earlier – and provided only limited explanatory power over and above the effects of these earlier attitudes. Further work will doubtless unravel any nuances in these processes, but the idea that the campaign was crucial can probably be discounted.

The demographics of the referendum vote are in contrast quite well-established. In one of the first such studies, Goodwin and Heath (2016b) conducted a constituency-level analysis. They linked data on turnout and the percentage voting Leave in each local authority to socio-demographic information from the UK Census. Turnout was positively associated with the percentage aged 65+ and the UKIP vote share in the 2014 European elections, as well as turnout in the 2014 elections; it was negatively associated with the percentage with no qualifications, and the percentage non-white. The percentage voting Leave was positively associated with the percentage aged 65+, the percentage with no qualifications, and the UKIP vote share in the 2014 European elections; it was considerably lower in London and Scotland than in the rest of the UK. Interestingly, the percentage voting Leave was negatively associated with the non-white percentage and the percentage of EU migrants, which suggests either that ethnic minorities were less likely to vote Leave, that migrants tend to select into constituencies with more cosmopolitan residents, that contact with migrants makes residents more 'cosmopolitan' and thus pro-European, or that socially conservative residents tend to select out of constituencies once migrants arrive. On the other hand, the percentage voting Leave *was* positively correlated with change in EU migration: constituencies that had experienced a recent influx of EU migrants tended to be more pro-Leave.

These aggregate patterns fit well with individual level analyses. Opposition to immigration divides the working class and particularly the less educated from many others to an even greater degree than the traditional core-issue of economic redistribution, and has done so for some time (Evans and Tilley 2017). This is in part because, compared to the university educated, they tend to be more rooted in their local and national communities – as opposed to the regional or global community – and tend to face stiffer labour market competition from migrants (Dustmann et al. 2013; Nickell and Saleheen 2015). These attitudes, in combination with those towards sovereignty, account to a large degree for the various social divisions in EU Referendum voting. Thus, according to Lord Ashcroft's poll conducted on the day of the referendum, 52 per cent of respondents in the lowest social grade said immigration is generally a force for ill, compared to only 33 per cent of those in the highest social grade. And, of those who said immigration is a force for ill, 80 per cent voted to leave the EU (Lord Ashcroft 2016). Evans and Tilley (2017), analysing data from the British Election Study Referendum Survey, also found substantial differences in vote choice by occupational class and education. Seventy-two per cent of people with no educational qualifications voted to leave, compared with only 35 per cent of those with a degree. Similarly, 63 per cent of the working class voted to leave, compared with only 44 per cent of the middle class. Even when the effects of age, region, race, religion, sex and housing tenure were held constant, there was still a 10 percentage point gap between the working class and the professional middle class, and a remarkable 30 percentage point gap between those with low versus high education.

Moreover, it was not simply that different groups expressed different preferences. There was an increase in turnout, especially among groups with Leave preferences. In recent decades, Britain has become ever more like the USA, where the electoral participation of the poor and less highly educated has been low for decades (Leighley and Nagler 2014). But Brexit shows what can happen when such preferences are represented on a level playing field, where choices are clear-cut and relevant. As Evans and Tilley (2017) document, using data from the British Social Attitudes Panel Pre-Referendum Survey, the participation of the working class and less highly educated increased between 2015 and 2016. Moreover, it did so to a greater degree than the participation of the middle class and highly educated. These changes in levels of turnout are exceptional. Following the nadir of electoral participation in the 2001 General Election, increases in participation have been far more pronounced among the middle class and highly educated than among the working class and less educated. The disproportionate increases in participation for the EU Referendum among the working class, poor and less educated mark a possibly unique reversal of this trend.

So one message to be taken from the EU Referendum is that when people are given meaningful choices, they turn out to vote. Removing the suppression of choices by ideologically convergent parties allows voters to shape political outcomes in the most fundamental way. There is a puzzle, however: when the demographic divisions in vote were so clear, why did the result not go in favour of Remain? After all, one of the factors underlying the move to the centre by the Labour Party in recent decades is the idea that the 'new middle class' composition of the electorate renders working-class politics electorally non-viable. To understand the referendum outcome, we also need to consider the extent to which changes in the distribution of educational qualifications have actually altered the social and electoral landscape – not least because without the 'middle-class' Leave vote there would be no Brexit (Dorling 2016). As with UKIP's recent successes (Evans and Mellon 2016c), substantial numbers of middle-class Brexit voters were necessary for the outcome given the relatively small size of the occupational working class.

One reason for this is that education is more strongly associated with support for Remain than any other social characteristic. The expansion of higher education has been the touchstone for the up-skilling of modern Britain before and since Blair's famous three-part sound-bite – 'education, education, education' – in 1997. Yet Labour and many others have probably failed to appreciate its still limited reach in terms of the demographic composition of the population. Most people do not have degrees – even among the young, and far less so among the old: the increasing likelihood of voting for Leave among older cohorts is in part a reflection of their differing educational composition. Given that the composition of the electorate is increasingly weighted to older age cohorts – through longer life expectancy and the tendency to have fewer children in recent decades – the demographic impact of the relatively recent upsurge in higher education enrolment will take many years to reach a tipping point.

It is not only the limited demographic penetration of higher educational qualifications that weakens its impact on the distribution of attitudes for issues such as immigration and the EU. The impact of educational qualifications on having a sense of being middle class has been weakening as participation in higher education has been expanding. More people are receiving higher education, but this is not associated with having a middle-class identity to the same extent as it once was (Evans and Tilley 2017). Far more people perceive themselves to be working class (around 60 per cent of the electorate; Evans and Mellon 2016b) than are typically allocated to such a position on the basis of their occupational class. Middle-class people who see themselves as working class are far more like the working class in their attitudes to immigration and social issues than are those who perceive themselves to be middle class. This might reflect the diminishing social distinctiveness of having a degree, or the experience of 'just getting by' – the target electoral category identified by the new Conservative Prime Minister – spreading ever higher through the educational pecking order. It might also reflect the diversifying nature of the composition and experience of higher education: analyses of recent British Election Study panel surveys indicate that people who attended newer universities associated with the expansion of higher education were more likely to be pro-Leave than those who attended long-established institutions (Evans and Mellon 2017). It seems more than likely that the main political parties over-estimated how well-established the liberal consensus on social issues – immigration in particular – has become. There is still a long way to go before the educational composition of the electorate is at a level that mirrors the values expressed by the main political parties. Moreover, expanding higher education may well dilute its consequences for these liberal values; a liberal consensus might never be attained.

In summary, these initial individual- and constituency-level analyses of referendum voting reveal the following: contrary to the common presumption, the Leave and Remain campaigns themselves are unlikely to have exerted much effect on voters' decision-making. Up to two years before the date of the referendum, most Britons had already made up their minds, and their preferences were apparently influenced more by prior convictions than an impartial assessment of the costs and benefits of leaving. Voting patterns were highly stratified demographically: older voters, working-class voters, those identifying as 'white British', and those with few educational qualifications were more likely to vote Leave; and constituencies with high proportions of residents with these characteristics were more likely to have a Leave majority. And as commentators such as Curtice (2016b) have argued, the referendum was to a large degree not a judgement on the role of the state as a moderating or equalizing force within the economy; rather, it was about national sovereignty, and – in particular – how much control the UK should have over its borders. Brexit appears to have occurred because concern about immigration was intensified by the unprecedented inflow of EU immigrants following the 2004 accession, which gave this issue a far higher profile and, importantly, linked it closely with attitudes to the EU. The adoption of direct democracy prevented parties from restricting the supply of policies favoured by the working class, the less educated, and those who generally did not feel part of the liberal, pro-EU consensus of the three established political parties. These groups are demographically more substantial than had perhaps been assumed. When the chance was presented, they were able to 'bite back' and, for the first time for many years, shape an important political outcome.

The implications of Brexit

So far we have considered the causes of Britain's vote in favour of withdrawing from the European Union. We now move on to the likely consequences of the UK's referendum on EU membership, looking at the implications for both the United Kingdom and the European Union, as well as the future relationship between the two.

British national integrity was called into question in the immediate aftermath of the vote. The Scottish First Minister Nicola Sturgeon proclaimed that it was 'democratically unacceptable' for Scotland to be taken out of the EU against its will and that a second Scottish independence referendum was now 'highly likely', just two years after a large minority (45 per cent) of Scottish voters had voted in favour of leaving the United Kingdom (BBC News 2016a). However, although 62 per cent of Scottish voters were indeed in favour of the UK remaining in the EU, Sturgeon has also said that she would only hold a second independence referendum if there were sustained evidence of a pro-independence majority. Polling evidence after the vote suggests that attitudes to independence have remained fairly stable (e.g. Khomami 2016) and by April 2017 began to appear more Unionist still, reinforced by the revived Scottish Conservative Party. Furthermore, Sturgeon will be aware that over a third of her party's voters were in favour of Brexit. Indeed, attitudes to European integration and Scottish independence have only a weakly positive relationship: $r = 0.11$ ($p < 0.001$; British Election Study 2016). Moreover, two-thirds of Scottish trade is with the rest of the UK, meaning that, if Britain were to leave the Single Market as well as the EU – as seems likely – Scottish independence would be even more economically disruptive than it would have been in 2014. Additionally, the greater sense of economic uncertainty caused by the vote, weak oil prices, Spanish opposition[5] and the precondition for new EU members to join the euro all pour cold water over the notion that Brexit will significantly affect the *already high* chance of Scottish independence at some point in the coming decades.

The future of Northern Ireland, which has the UK's only land border with another EU Member State and whose peace process is built on the premise that all parties would remain in the EU, is less clear. In particular, there are thus far no obvious methods whereby the UK could halt free movement of European citizens into Britain without erecting border controls with the Republic of Ireland or between Northern Ireland and Great Britain. In spite of these seemingly higher stakes and a clear majority in favour of EU membership (56 per cent), post-referendum polling has suggested that over two-thirds of Northern Irish citizens are in favour of remaining in the United Kingdom (Bell 2016). Somewhat similarly, Gibraltar will also face issues of free movement following the referendum, but given the current lack of Common Travel Area with the UK, will find it easier to retain free movement of persons with the EU.

Britain's party system was immediately struck by the referendum result, which surprised most commentators due to both the high turnout and the non-trivial margin of victory for Leave. The Prime Minister, David Cameron, quickly announced his resignation and, following a Conservative Party leadership election in which Theresa May was the last candidate standing, a new government, committed to executing Brexit, was installed. This position is likely to damage the ability of UKIP – the Eurosceptic, anti-immigration party – to raise funds and retain unity, given the loss of both their *raison d'être* and their charismatic former leader Nigel Farage, who resigned following the completion of his long-term political mission. Instead, the party's new leader – Paul Nuttall – seems keen to complete the reinvention of UKIP from a Conservative anti-European splinter group into a fully-fledged member of Europe's radical right party family, by focusing on immigration and cultural

[5] Following the referendum result, the Spanish Prime Minister, Mariano Rajoy, declared that Spain would oppose any talks with Scotland over its possible future membership of the EU. Presumably because he would not want to create a precedent that might increase that likelihood of Catalonia seceding from the rest of Spain.

identity issues. The opposition Labour Party were also thrown into disarray after many in the party's centrist, pro-European parliamentary party publicly admonished their radical, leftist leader, Jeremy Corbyn, for his 'half-hearted' pro-EU campaign, which they argued lead to traditionally Labour areas supporting Brexit (McTernan 2016).[6] Despite initial signs of turmoil within the party, Corbyn went on to win the resulting Labour leadership contest comfortably, underscoring Labour's transition into an electorally unattractive, left-wing party unlikely to pose a serious threat to May's promise that 'Brexit means Brexit'.

Similarly, in spite of economic turmoil and a dramatic drop in the value of the pound in the days following Brexit, the months afterwards saw shares return and then surpass their pre-referendum values, while government yields reached record lows, suggesting that investors still see the UK as a safe haven. Surprise election results are usually followed by market instability, and it seems that the economic fall-out of Brexit will not be sufficiently acute to prompt a rethink by either May or the electorate before Article 50 is triggered. Ironically, it was only the EU referendum that was able to bring the value of sterling – in recent years described by the IMF as the most overvalued currency in the world – closer to levels needed for an export-led rebalancing of the British economy, an aim of successive governments (Giles 2014). Indeed, the 8 per cent fall in the value of sterling is unlikely to be offset by an increase in trade barriers with the EU, even in the most pessimistic scenario. However, the fall in sterling, itself the primary driver of the FTSE 100's rapid recovery, only highlights the overwhelming view of financial markets that Brexit – and the resulting uncertainty, regulatory wrangling, risk of contagion, and potential to empower economically illiberal political forces – is more likely to be a net negative for the British economy than a net positive, at least in the short to medium term. For now though, the economic future of the UK seems relatively calm. Indeed, institutions such as the UK Treasury, the European Commission and major banks revised their economic forecasts for the UK upwards within the first six months after the vote, while official growth figures from late 2016 were also revised upwards by the Office for National Statistics.

Britain's future relationship with the European Union remains uncertain. However, following the British government's triggering of Article 50 of the Lisbon Treaty in March 2017, the UK will certainly leave the EU two years after that date. Prime Minister May will be under pressure to

---

[6] Though, as we saw earlier in this chapter, Labour was able to ally many more of its supporters to the Remain ticket than were the Conservatives, which suggests that this criticism was mainly a strategy for anti-Corbynists in the Labour Party to justify the leadership contest.

ensure that either a transitional deal or, probably less likely, a permanent deal is in place by that date to reduce the economic and social uncertainty of a 'cliff-edge' effect. The resultant deal is likely to boil down to two contradictory desires – the British government's desire to retain the right to trade freely with the tariff-free, single-regulatory framework Single Market (not least in order to protect the financial services industry on which UK public accounts are heavily reliant), and the British electorate's desire to halt high levels of European (and, indeed, non-European) immigration. Many British officials would see the optimal outcome for the UK as the retention, or even deepening, of three of the four freedoms – movement of capital, goods and services – combined with an opt-out from the free movement of persons. By contrast, the EU and its Member States are wary of encouraging a 'pick 'n' mix' approach to integration – which would necessarily weaken the EU as a solution to the collective action problem – and so will be keen to retain the notion that the Four Freedoms are indivisible and that access to the Single Market requires acceptance of them, not least as a means to prevent Brexit from appearing too attractive to other Eurosceptic Member States, especially those that (like the UK) are net contributors.

Despite the deadlock appearing to be unbreakable, domestic elected governments – both British and European – will come under considerable pressure from exporters to minimize disruption to trade, which combined with the fragile state of the eurozone, probably means that calls for 'punishment' from European officials and commentators are unlikely to be heeded. Instead, the negotiation may result in substantial limits concurrently imposed on both single market access and free movement of persons – perhaps replaced in Britain with a fairly liberal work permit system that prioritizes EU citizens and offers permanent residency to those already settled in the UK – alongside the loss of British presence in the European institutions and, perhaps, the retention of the sizeable British contribution to the EU budget (Buiter et al. 2016). Rhetorically, all involved will be keen to emphasize that Britain was always a special case and an 'awkward partner' – which our earlier analysis thoroughly supports – in order to facilitate a speedy conclusion to negotiations and to preclude the possibility of other, smaller Member States following Britain's path out of the EU.

The most immediate effect of the referendum for the EU is the shock that comes with receiving the most severe vote of no confidence in the organization's history – reflected in drops in the values of European stock exchanges after the vote – and for the first time a European electorate expressing a desire not only to impede further integration but to reverse and even abandon the process altogether. Although the United Kingdom was always a peculiar member, increasingly vocal Eurosceptic forces can now be found in most EU Member States. Indeed, some pro-EU commentators have expressed concern that, if the UK were to thrive after Brexit, there may be a contagion effect whereby other Eurosceptic states sought to leave the Union – with Denmark, Sweden and Austria identified as the most at risk (Patel and Reh 2016). However, should there be such a domino effect, it would likely only come after the future of the UK's relationship with the EU has become clear and discernibly positive for the country, precluding the possibility of other states leaving during this decade.

Furthermore, as we noted above, the UK is one of the least well-integrated Member States with respect to trade patterns, emigration destinations and capital flows. In addition, there would be far greater material difficulties for any Euro members that sought to leave the EU, making exit a harder sell in most other Member States. Finally, polling in a number of EU countries documented an increase in pro-EU sentiment following the British referendum result, as voters rallied around the perceived security of EU membership, and eschewed the alarming short-term economic and political instability that the Leave result precipitated (Oltermann et al. 2016). That being said, should the single currency experience further difficulties, particularly in fringe European states such as Greece and Cyprus, Brexit would offer a blueprint for full EU withdrawal. Overall, insofar as we see Brexit as the result of a combination of factors that are somewhat unique to the UK, it is unlikely to have a large positive effect on the chances of analogous decisions elsewhere.

Following Brexit, the EU will lose one of its three largest members, which had continuously espoused a *laissez-faire*, intergovernmental, broad-and-shallow vision of the EU. Might we now expect to see a more corporatist, protectionist, explicitly political and, ultimately, federal EU? The three EU institutions responsible for producing European legislation and thus the single market's regulatory regime – the European Commission, the European Parliament and the Council of Ministers – will all lose their British delegations. With nearly 60 per cent of current British MEPs belonging to centre-right or Eurosceptic party groups, Brexit will strengthen the position of leftists in the European Parliament, who will now be able to form majorities without the centre-right European People's Party (Patel and Reh 2016). In the Council of Ministers, the current voting equilibrium, in which both the protectionist bloc of southern states and the liberal bloc of northern states hold blocking minorities, will be broken. Certain recent policy initiatives that had been strongly supported by the UK, such as TTIP and the Capital Markets Union, may now be abandoned or significantly altered (Wright

2016). Furthermore, the practice whereby smaller states have sought to protect competitive advantages or pursue controversial domestic policies by allying with the persistently anti-federal UK, such as Maltese resistance to tax harmonization and recent Polish resistance to European interference in its constitutional courts, will end. In this sense, Brexit may lead to a more homogeneous Union in which more powerful states, particularly Germany, are better able to dominate smaller ones (Patel and Renwick 2016).

One area in which the British government had recently expressed support for 'more Europe' was the fiscal integration of eurozone countries, on the condition that safeguards for non-euro members are in place (Osborne 2012). It therefore seems unlikely that the EU will be able to more easily fiscally integrate without the UK 'standing in the way', primarily because the electorates of creditor nations, particularly Germany, remain opposed to transfers to ostensibly 'fiscally irresponsible' Southern European countries (Carl 2016). On the issue of safeguards for non-euro members, such countries will now be even more heavily outnumbered by eurozone members, which some have argued will create pressure for them to join the single currency (Patel and Renwick 2016). While it is likely that David Cameron's previous demands that the EU proclaim itself to be a 'multi-currency Union' will now be dismissed, a number of important barriers are likely to hinder any expansion of the eurozone. Following the eurozone crisis, the barriers to entry – including compliance with the Six-pack and Two-pack fiscal regulations – are now considerably higher than the original and widely flouted Maastricht criteria. Furthermore, electorates in Northern Europe, such as in Denmark and Sweden, are considerably less likely to see the economic value of joining the euro following the recent crisis. Moreover, those states that sought to join the euro as a way to tie themselves to the Western security umbrella – namely the Baltic states – have already joined, whereas other non-eurozone governments, such as Poland and Hungary, currently have governments keen to protect national sovereignty against further European integration.

As recently as 2013, a British Prime Minister outlined a long-term vision for the EU to spread as far as Kazakhstan, in stark contrast to the more narrow-and-deep vision for European integration of France and Germany (Watt 2013). Brexit may hold back, or even preclude, the possibility of the Western Balkans, Turkey or the Caucasus from acceding to the Union. Having said that, domestic misgivings over European immigration, particularly after the 2004 and 2007 enlargements, may have already veered the British government away from its historic pro-enlargement position.

One area in which there has been a consistent divide between the UK and other large EU Member States is European foreign policy, defence union and, ultimately, a single armed forces. Efforts to create such a force have thus far been confined to the Common Security and Defence Policy – a late 1990s Franco-British attempt to give the EU a more significant strategic world role within the NATO framework, which thus far has only applied to limited training, advisory and sub-strategic outputs (Smith 2015). The disappointingly minor outcomes of this endeavour, coupled with the loss of one of the two major military powers of the EU, would seem to suggest that Brexit may further damage the EU's defence potential. However, robbed of the 'British excuse' to do nothing – and in the context of the United States pivoting towards the Pacific, political chaos in much of the Near East and parts of North Africa, deepening and growing migration flows from much of the Global South, and an openly irredentist Russia – there are incentives for almost all remaining EU Member States to engage in the creation of some form of meaningful European common defence policy (Dumoulin 2016). The emergence of the European Union as a more significant regional military power may be one of the great unforeseen long-term consequences of Brexit.

Overall, Brexit is unlikely to put the grand political ambitions of the EU into reverse because, as we have argued, the UK always occupied a somewhat anomalous position among Member States. Indeed, despite half a century of existence, the EU remains a union of states, rather than of people, and so continues to derive its powers from international treaties that preclude any reversal of integration (Tuori 2015). Consequently, when faced with the UK's obvious misgiving about membership during the pre-referendum renegotiations – particularly regarding immigration – other Member States had no choice but to uphold their treaty commitments to the Four Freedoms. On the one hand, the EU's institutional inflexibility could be seen as a weakness, given that it precipitated a likely breakdown in the organization's territorial integrity and the probable loss of one of its largest budget contributors. On the other hand, it could be seen as a strength, given that – by binding the hands of the other Member States – it may have helped to avert an even greater crisis than the loss of a single Member State, namely the first major reversal of the EU's foundational commitments, and therefore a potential unravelling of the EU's entire politico-legal framework.

Conclusion

In this chapter we have explored the historical preconditions to Brexit and offered an explanation for why it was the UK – rather than any other Member State – that left the EU, and why the country did so now – rather than at any point in the past. In particular, the *interaction* between Britons' strong sense of national identity and the enlarged EU's movement towards political union arguably tipped the balance towards Leave. Political decisions shaped the context of the EU referendum, especially in relation to immigration, and we have argued that any liberal consensus on immigration and internationalism that might have been obtained in British politics was illusory. Tony Blair's rebranding of Labour as a centrist liberal party in the 1990s restricted working-class voters' electoral choices, but did not do much to alter their underlying preferences. Consequently, when they were once again offered a clear choice between two alternative visions for the UK, they opted for the one that accorded with their comparatively nationalistic and socially conservative preferences.

We have also considered the potential consequences of Britain's EU referendum result. We suggest that although the referendum highlighted differences between the British home nations, a complete break-up of the United Kingdom remains relatively unlikely; Brexit could in fact reduce the likelihood of Scottish independence. Given the clear motivations of many pro-Leave voters, any future deal between Britain and the EU will probably require limits on European migration, thereby ending freedom of movement. To do this, while minimizing economic disruption, the UK will be forced to offer significant concessions to the EU, perhaps financial. All parties are likely to coalesce around the argument that the UK was always 'a special case', not least in order to quash any attempts by other Member States to replicate the UK's referendum. Within the EU, Brexit is likely to have some, though not radical, effects on the policy outputs of the European institutions – primarily away from a *laissez-faire*, inter-governmentalist approach. That being said, steps towards fiscal integration of the eurozone are unlikely to be affected by Brexit and the pressure for remaining non-eurozone members to join the single currency may not be overwhelming. Finally, contrary to what many have argued, Brexit may actually increase the likelihood of defence integration and, in the long run, the EU's military capabilities.

References

BBC News (2016a) Brexit: Nicola Sturgeon says second Scottish independence vote 'highly likely'. BBC, 24 June. Available at http://www.bbc.co.uk/news/uk-scotland-scotland-politics-36621030

BBC News (2016b) Brexit: Theresa May to trigger Article 50 by end of March. BBC, 2 October. Available at http://www.bbc.co.uk/news/uk-politics-37532364

Bell, J. (2016) Survey: Majority say 'No' to Ireland border poll and 'Yes' to staying in UK. *Belfast Telegraph*, 28 September.

Bernstein, J. (2016) The Brexit and budget austerity: What's the connection? *The Washington Post*, 27 June.

Buiter, W., Rabbari, E. and Schulz, C. (2016) The implications of Brexit for the rest of the EU. *Vox EU: CEPR's Policy Portal*, 2 March.

Carl, N. (2016) Can the Eurozone survive? *Positive Net Result*, 14 June.

Clarke, H.D., Goodwin, M. and Whiteley, P. (2016) Why Britain voted for Brexit: an individual-level analysis of the 2016 referendum vote. Paper presented at EPOP Conference, 10 September.

Colborne, M. (2014) Political disengagement and trust in Europe. NatCen Social Research report.

Curtice, J. (2016a) Brexit: behind the referendum. *Political Insight*, September: 4–7.

Curtice, J. (2016b) Not the end, my friend: Labour, the referendum result and the challenges that remain. *Juncture*, 23: 18–21.

Dennison, J. and Carl, N. (2016) As the EU moved closer to political union, Britain drifted away. Brexit became inevitable. LSE Brexit blog. Available at http://blogs.lse.ac.uk/brexit/2016/07/21/xenophobia-austerity-and-dissatisfaction-with-politics-may-have-contributed-to-the-brexit-vote/

Dorling, D. (2016) Brexit: the decision of a divided country. *British Medical Journal*, 354: i3697.

Dumoulin, A. (2016) Brexit and European defence: an in-depth analysis. Royal Higher Institute for Defence, 8 June 2016.

Dustmann, C., Frattini, T. and Preston, I. (2013) The effect of immigration along the distribution of wages. *The Review of Economic Studies*, 80: 145–73.

European Commission (2016) Public opinion: Eurobarometer survey. Online database: http://ec.europa.eu/public_opinion/index_en.htm

European Parliament (2016) Parlemeter surveys. European Parliament, available online: http://www.europarl.europa.eu/atyourservice/en/20150201PVL00077/Parlemeter-of-the-European-Parliament

Eurostat (2015) International trade in services. *Eurostat Statistics Explained*. Available at http://ec.europa.eu/eurostat/statistics-explained/index.php/International_trade_in_services

Evans, G. (2016) The people are perceptive: immigration and the EU. In Cowley, P. and Ford, R. (eds) *More Sex, Lies, and the Ballot Box*. London: Biteback Publishing.

Evans, G. and Mellon, J. (2016a) Blair's blunder: from accession to UKIP to Brexit. EPOP Annual Meeting, University of Kent, 9–11 September.

Evans, G. and Mellon, J. (2016b) Identity, awareness and political attitudes: why are we still working class? *British Social Attitudes*, 33: 1–19.

Evans, G. and Mellon, J. (2016c) Working class votes and Conservative losses: solving the UKIP puzzle. *Parliamentary Affairs*, 69(2): 464–79.

Evans, G. and Mellon, J. (2017) University challenge? Higher educational diversity and the Referendum vote. *British Election Study*.

Evans, G. and Prosser, C. (2016) Was it always a done deal? The relative impact of short and long term influences on referendum voting. EPOP Annual Meeting, University of Kent, 9–11 September.

Evans, G. and Tilley, J. (2012) The depoliticization of inequality and redistribution: explaining the decline of class voting. *The Journal of Politics*, 74: 963–76.

Evans, G. and Tilley, J. (2017) *The New Politics of Class: The Political Exclusion of the British Working Class*. Oxford: Oxford University Press.

Fieldhouse, E., Green, J., Evans, G., Mellon, J., Prosser, C., Schmitt, H. and van der Eijk, C. (forthcoming) *The Volatile Voter: Shocks, Constraint, and the Destabilization of British Politics*. Oxford: Oxford University Press.

Fitzgerald, R. and Sibley, E. (2016) The United Kingdom in the European context: top-line reflections from the European Social Survey. European Social Survey report. Available at https://www.europeansocialsurvey.org/docs/about/United-Kingdom-in-the-European-Context.pdf

Ford, R. (2016) Older 'left-behind' voters turned against a political class with values opposed to theirs. *The Guardian*, 25 June.

Geary, M.J. (2012) The process of European integration from The Hague to Maastricht, 1969–92: an irreversible advance? *Debater a Europa*, 6: 6–23.

Giles, C. (2014) IMF says 'overvalued' pound preventing rebalancing. *Financial Times*, 28 July.

Goodwin, M. and Heath, O. (2016a) Brexit and the left behind: a tale of two countries. LSE Brexit blog. Available at http://blogs.lse.ac.uk/brexit/2016/07/22/brexit-and-the-left-behind-a-tale-of-two-countries/

Goodwin, M. and Heath, O. (2016b) The 2016 Referendum, Brexit and the left behind: an aggregate-level analysis of the result. *The Political Quarterly*, 87(3): 323–32.

Grant, C. (2008) Why is Britain Eurosceptic? Centre for European Reform. Available at http://www.cer.org.uk/publications/archive/essay/2008/why-britain-eurosceptic

Heath, O. (2015) Policy representation, social representation and class voting in Britain. *British Journal of Political Science*, 45: 173–93.

Hix, S. (2015) Is the UK marginalized in the EU? *The Guardian*, 19 October.

Kahan, D.M. (2015) The politically motivated reasoning paradigm. In Scott, R.A. and Buchmann, M.C. (eds) *Emerging Trends in the Social and Behavioural Sciences*. New York: Wiley.

Kahanec, M. and Zimmermann, K.F. (2010) Migration in an enlarged EU: a challenging solution? In Keereman, F. and Szekely, I. (eds) *Five Years of an Enlarged EU*. Berlin: Springer.

Khomami, N. (2016) 'No real shift' towards Scottish independence since Brexit vote – poll. *The Guardian*, 30 July.

Leighley, J.E. and Nagler, J. (2014) *Who Votes Now? Demographics, Issues, Inequality, and Turnout in the United States*. Princeton, NJ: Princeton University Press.

Lewis, H. (2016) How the Brexit campaign lied to us – and got away with it. *New Statesman*, 30 June.

Lord Ashcroft (2016) How the United Kingdom voted on Thursday . . . and why. *Lord Ashcroft Polls*, 24 June.

McTernan, J. (2016) Jeremy Corbyn sabotaged the pro-EU campaign, and is doing much worse to Labour. *Daily Telegraph*, 8 August.

Nickell, S. and Saleheen, J. (2015) The impact of immigration on occupational wages: evidence from Britain. Bank of England Staff Working Paper No. 574.

OECD (2015) *Government at a Glance 2015*. Paris: OECD Publishing.

Oltermann, P., Scammell, R. and Darroch, G. (2016) Brexit causes resurgence in pro-EU leanings across continent. *The Guardian*, 8 July.

ONS (2015) How important is the European Union to UK trade and investment? Office for National Statistics, 26 June.

ORB (2014) European attitudes towards the EU: Britain stands out. End of Year 2014 Global report. Available at http://www.orb-international.com/article.php?s=european-attitudes-towards-the-eu-britain-stands-out

Ormston, R. (2015) Do we feel European and does it matter? NatCen Social Research report. Available at http://whatukthinks.org/eu/wp-content/uploads/2015/10/Analysis-paper-2-Do-we-feel-European.pdf

Osborne, G. (2012) This is injury time, Europe has to act now. *The Sunday Times*, 20 May.

Patel, O. and Reh, C. (2016) Brexit: the consequences for the EU's political system. UCL Constitution Unit Briefing Paper.

Patel, O. and Renwick, A. (2016) Brexit: the consequences for other EU Member States. UCL Constitution Unit Briefing Paper.

Prosser, C., Mellon, J. and Green, J. (2016) What mattered most to you when deciding how to vote in the EU referendum? *British Election Study*, 11 July.

Saunders, R. (2016) A tale of two referendums: 1975 and 2016. *The Political Quarterly*, 83: 318–22.

Scherer, M. (2014) The religious context in explaining public support for the European Union. *Journal of Common Market Studies*, 53: 893–909.

Scruton, R. (2015) Nexus Masterclass 'Brexit: Yes or No?' with Roger Scruton. Nexus Institute.

Smith, K. (2015) Would Brexit spell the end of European defence? LSE EUROPP, 2 July. Available at http://blogs.lse.ac.uk/europpblog/2015/07/02/would-brexit-spell-the-end-of-european-defence/

Tuori, K. (2015) *European Constitutionalism*. Cambridge: Cambridge University Press.

UN (2012) Bilateral FDI statistics, United Nations Conference on Trade and Development, online database: http://unctad.org/en/Pages/DIAE/FDI%20Statistics/FDI-Statistics-Bilateral.aspx

UN (2015) International migrant stock by destination and origin. United Nations Population Division, online database: http://www.un.org/en/development/desa/population/migration/data/estimates2/estimates15.shtml

Vargas-Silva, C. and Markaki, Y. (2015) EU migration to and from the UK. Migration Observatory Briefing, COMPAS, University of Oxford.

Watt, N. (2013) EU should extend further into former Soviet Union, says David Cameron. *The Guardian*, 1 July.

Wright, W. (2016) The potential impact of Brexit on European capital markets: a qualitative survey of market participants. *New Financial*, April.

Yeung, P. (2016) Brexit campaign was 'criminally irresponsible', says legal academic. *The Independent*, 2 July.

Chapter 18

Social Movements, Participation and Crisis in Europe

*Gustavo Cardoso, Guya Accornero, Tiago Lapa and
Joana Azevedo*

A worldwide wave of contention

In the context of the current economic crisis there has been an increase of social mobilization in almost all European countries and worldwide. This escalation of various forms of conflictual politics – demonstrations, occupations, grassroots meetings – has been addressed by several authors (Bermeo and Bartels 2014; della Porta 2015; Giugni and Grasso 2016). Some scholars sustain that 'There have been periods in history when large numbers of people rebelled about the way things were, demanding change, such as in 1848, 1917 or 1968; today we are experiencing another period of rising outrage and discontent, and some of the largest protests in world history' (Ortiz et al. 2013: 2).

Although it is difficult to establish an automatic link between this outbreak of mobilizations and the economic crisis – since there is clearly a whole series of factors which should be analysed, connected to political opportunities, resources, networks – it is undeniable that the two processes are fully interlinked. This emerges from a study on protest activities between 2006 and 2013, held in 84 countries, involving 90 per cent of the world's population (Ortiz et al. 2013). These authors state that, in the context of crisis, 'there is a major increase in protests beginning 2010 with the adoption of austerity measures in all world regions' (Ortiz et al. 2013: 2).

The study by Ortiz et al. also indicates the main subjects addressed and the target of the protests: issues linked to economic justice and to austerity measures account for the majority. However, the reasons related to the breakdown and failure of the traditional systems of political representation and of the actual political systems follow in second

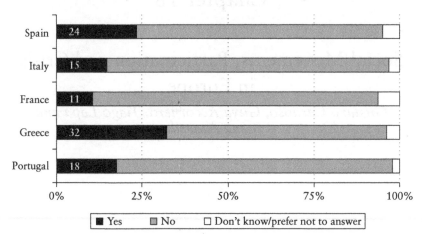

Figure 18.1: Participation/presence in global protest actions or
demonstrations against austerity (%)

Source: Networked Cultures Survey 2016

place. This shows how the elements connected to political representation
and the loss of confidence in institutions have also performed a very
important role in triggering the protest. The political crises which have
arisen in many countries have also paved the way for mobilization and,
on the other hand, it is also true that the frontiers which separate political
spheres from economic and financial spheres are increasingly less clear.

In Europe, it was above all the countries of the South that witnessed
a greater upsurge of protests. Our own transnational survey[1] found that
approximately one third of Greek respondents participated or were
present in global protest actions or demonstrations against austerity, followed by 23.8 per cent of Spanish respondents, as shown by figure 18.1.
This may well reflect in Greece and Spain the sustained period of struggles closely related to austerity and the ability of relevant new parties
(Syriza and Podemos) to capitalize on discontent and their involvement
in the anti-austerity movements.

An important feature of those protests is the role played by the new
technologies as instruments of mobilization; the combination of material, political and identity claims, and the fact of proposing new forms

[1] The data in the present study, regarding political engagement both off- and online, were
obtained through a self-administered online survey during the second trimester of 2016
($n = 500$ respondents per country). Country selection aimed, among other criteria, at the
inclusion of countries with economic hurdles such as Southern European societies.

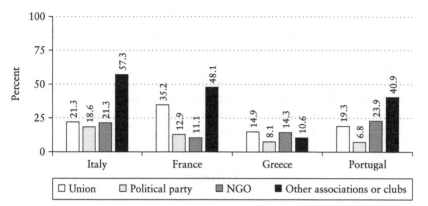

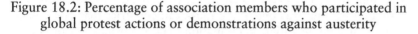

Figure 18.2: Percentage of association members who participated in global protest actions or demonstrations against austerity

Source: Networked Cultures Survey 2016

of organization, especially horizontal, and new modes of decision-making and representation. All this falls under the name of 'new social movements' (Alberich Nistal 2012; Feixa et al. 2009). At the same time, various authors have also highlighted the return of more traditional forms of protest, first and foremost the general strike (Accornero and Ramos Pinto 2015; Campos Lima and Martin Artiles 2011, 2014; Gall 2013; Hamann et al. 2013; Kousis and Karakioulafi 2013). In this emerging ecology, the borderlines between the different types of protest have become less defined and this leads to a growing collaboration between different actors, such as new movements and syndicates (Accornero and Ramos Pinto 2015; Kousis and Karakioulafi 2013). This claim seems to be supported by our data shown in figure 18.2. A relevant finding is the weight of respondents that participated in demonstrations that are members of other associations or clubs.

The data presented above suggests that significant proportions of demonstrators, especially from Italy, France and Portugal, were not mobilized through more traditional political institutions (unions, parties and NGOs). Furthermore, the crisis and austerity have also had dramatic effects at the level of institutional politics, mainly in the case of the group of countries referred to as the PIIGS. In 2011, Portugal, Ireland, Italy, Greece and Spain, the countries most affected by the crisis, changed their governments before the end of the parliamentary term. Early elections were called in Spain, during which the party in government, the PSOE, suffered a major defeat, in benefit of the PP. The prime ministers of Ireland and Portugal also stepped down and elections were held. Neither

Greece nor Italy held elections, but two 'technical experts' were called in, Loucas Papademos and Mario Monti, to form new 'unity' and 'coalition' governments, after the resignations of Georgios Papandreu and Silvio Berlusconi.

These two processes, the emergence of strong anti-austerity movements and political crisis, overlapped, contributing to changes in the political landscape – party and political systems – of these countries, as will be analysed in the following sections.[2]

Portugal

According to the European Social Survey (ESS) data, Portugal, along with Spain and Ireland, was one of the European countries that saw a major increase in demonstration participation. The intensification of contentious actions is also demonstrated by a study developed by the Portuguese Public Security Police (Polícia de Segurança Pública, PSP) which shows that in Lisbon alone the number of demonstrations increased from 244 in 2010 to 298 in 2011 and to 579 (an average of one every 15 hours) in 2012 (Elias and Pinho 2012). The analysis of protest events between 2010 and 2013 carried out by Accornero and Ramos Pinto also shows the development of a protest cycle during this period, which started when the first austerity measures were implemented (Accornero and Ramos Pinto 2015). This has been the strongest cycle of protest to occur in Portugal since the first phase of democratic transition, during the so-called Revolutionary Process Underway (*Processo Revolucionário em Curso*, PREC) between 1974 and 1975 (Accornero 2015; Accornero and Ramos Pinto 2015; Baumgarten 2013).

The first austerity measures began to be implemented in Portugal in 2010. From 2011 onwards, these measures were strengthened and increased in the context of the agreement agreed with the so-called 'Troika' (EU, IMF and ECB) through the Memorandum of Understanding (MoU). This had harsh effects on the economic and social conditions in the country and severe consequences for the life of Portuguese citizens. The first action against these measures was the general strike called on 4 March 2010, which was followed by various demonstrations, organized by the trade union federation CGTP (General Confederation of Portuguese Workers) in early July.

---

[2] The detailed analysis of Spain is left out of this chapter, since it is already covered by Manuel Castells' chapter in this volume ('From Crisis to Social Movement to Political Change: Podemos in Spain').

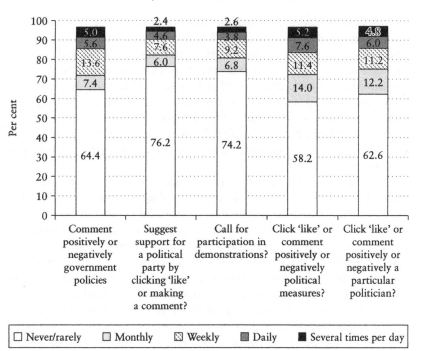

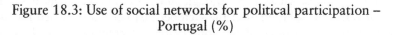

Figure 18.3: Use of social networks for political participation –
Portugal (%)

Source: Networked Cultures Survey 2016

The peak of this first phase of the protest cycle was the demonstration organized by the social movement organization (SMO) *Geração à Rasca* (GaR) on 12 March 2011. This was the first 'new, new' social movement to appear in Portugal and emerged independently from institutionalized actors, such as trade unions or political parties. The success of the demonstration, which attracted around 200,000 protesters (Accornero and Ramos Pinto 2015), mainly organized through a Facebook page, suggests a special relevance of social network sites and the importance of a networked political culture (Lapa and Cardoso, 2016), based on the personalized content sharing and appropriation across social media, among new contentious actors. As shown by figure 18.3, the use of SMS for political participation among Portuguese users has some expression but is not customary for most respondents. Nevertheless, the experience of *Geração à Rasca* indicates that the networked political action of a minority can have great communicational impact and influence the agenda setting of mainstream media (Accornero 2017).

409

This demonstration marked the starting point of the redefinition of the Portuguese contentious arena. The protest cycle showed two further peaks after the 2011 elections, in the latter half of 2012, and between March and June 2013. The main events in those phases were the demonstrations that took place on 15 September 2012 and 2 March 2013, both organized by a new movement that evolved from the 'Desperate Generation' protests: the *Que se Lixe a Troika* ('To Hell with the Troika: We Want our Lives Back!' – the QSLT). With even more participants than the GaR demonstration, these have been the largest demonstrations in Portuguese history.

Just like the *Geração à Rasca*, and being a partial evolution of it, the QSLT defined itself as apolitical in its slogans, announcements and propaganda. Nevertheless, its left-wing position is clear, evinced by the important presence of BE (Left Block) militants, organizations such as the *Precários Inflexíveis* (Inflexible Precarious) and by the occasional alliance with the trade union CGTP. Moreover, different institutional actors – such as sectors of the socialist Lisbon Municipality – openly supported the large demonstration that took place on 2 March 2013.

The Portuguese anti-austerity cycle of protest seemed to wane as of 2013, but not without leaving important changes on the left-wing political landscape of the country, as a result of the interactions among different players. These new strategic alliances have been the basis of the government solution after the October 2015 elections, when for the first time in the history of the country the Communist Party (*Partido Comunista Português*, PCP) and the Left Block (*Bloco de Esquerda*, BE, the non-communist left) agreed to support a government of the centre-left Socialist Party (*Partido Socialista*, PS). While in Portugal the cycle of protest did not result in the emergence of a new political party in the mould of *Syriza* in Greece or *Podemos* in Spain, we can consider this parliamentary alliance as an equally relevant consequence, and as the main specificity of the relation between economic crisis, austerity, and contentious and institutional politics in Portugal.

Greece

The Greek socialist PASOK government signed an agreement with the so-called Troika in May 2010 and received the largest loan ever provided to a single country (€110 billion), in return for implementing a drastic structural adjustment programme. The country had experienced a strong cycle of protest already in 2008, when Alexandros Grigoropoulos, a 15-year-old Greek student, was killed by two policemen. From 2010 onwards, protests started to increase, this time strongly underpinned by the anti-austerity issue. As in Portugal, in Greece too the trigger-event of the anti-austerity protest cycle was a general strike. It took place in May 2010 against the spending cuts and tax increases announced by Prime Minister George Papandreou following the country's bailout. The strike culminated in a large demonstration in Athens and an attempt to storm the Greek Parliament.

In 2011, the Greek government announced new austerity measures, in a context of further economic contraction, growing unemployment and increasing public debt. The crisis and the austerity started to affect not only the working class, but also the middle stratum. Consequently, in 2011 the mobilizations not only continued, but became larger and more conflictual compared with those in 2010. On 23 February 2011 the first attempt to occupy Syntagma Square (Constitution Square) took place, which failed due to the small number of participants and to the violent police reaction. On 25 May large demonstrations occurred in 35 Greek cities, and in Athens a group of demonstrators decided to occupy Syntagma Square, remaining there during the night. This initial occupation continued for months, becoming one of the leading centres of mobilization all over Greece. Even if the occupation was not a new action in the Greek contentious repertoire, the occupation of Syntagma Square showed some important innovation. First of all, the specific space in itself played an important role at a symbolic level, since the square represents, in Greek contemporary history, the fight for democracy. Moreover, the occupation not only was important as a centre of coordination of the protests, but it also was an opportunity to apply and develop new forms of horizontal participation and direct democracy.

This was the starting point of the Greek Indignant Citizens Movement (*Aganaktismeni*, the Indignant), which started to play a role as the principal actor of the fight against the Troika and the austerity measures. It adopted as its slogan 'Direct Democracy Now!', inspired by the Spanish '¡Democracia Real YA!' and also its social media-centred approach towards organizing protests and mobilizing protesters, but insisting on the specific element of the 'direct democracy', which was, from the beginning, one of the most salient characteristics of the movement (see figure 18.4).

On the other hand, unlike the Spanish Indignados and the Occupy movement, the Greek anti-austerity movement did not have a unique collective identity. If left-wing demonstrators were the majority, right-wing militants too participated in an active way in the protests. The heterogeneity of the social and political identities of the people involved (Rüdig and Karyotis 2013; Simiti 2014) significantly differentiates the cycle of

411

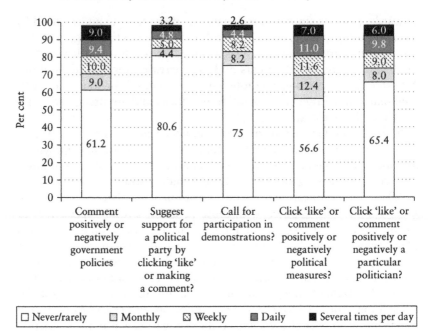

Figure 18.4: Use of social networks for political participation – Greece (%)

Source: Networked Cultures Survey 2016

protest started in Greece in 2010 compared to the previous period of strong mobilization in Greek history (Simiti 2014).

Demonstrations strongly intensified in June. The largest event during this period was the demonstration on 5 June, in which half a million demonstrators took part. On 15 June, during a general strike, demonstrators tried to surround the Parliament. On 28 and 29 June a new set of austerity measures were to be presented to Parliament for approval. The trade unions called for a general strike during both days and activists of *Aganaktismeni* surrounded the Parliament, prevented deputies from entering and appealed to those within the Parliament to vote against the measures. This action was strongly repressed, with violent scenes between demonstrators and police. In the meantime, the new austerity measures were approved.

Protests continued in the following weeks, but the number of participants gradually decreased: demonstrations became smaller, more fragmented and less disruptive. At the same time, grassroots activism got stronger: militants stopped waiting for top-down political change and started to involve themselves in a dense network of social solidarity at the local level. Grassroots organizations, more or less institutionalized associations, formal and informal groups and networks expanded significantly. An interesting case is the increase in the number of solidarity purchase groups that aimed, on ethical grounds, to supply citizens' essential needs, whose satisfaction had been strongly compromised by the economic situation. This revitalization of civil society has been one of the most relevant consequences of the Greek anti-austerity cycle of protest (Simiti 2014, 2015). As stressed by Athina Arampatzi: 'solidarity structures act as spaces where alternative modes of economic conduct and social relations are narrated, imagined and experimented with through everyday practices grounded in neighbourhoods and spanning across the city of Athens and beyond' (Arampatzi 2016: 2) and 'Grassroots responses to austerity that have emerged across Athenian neighbourhoods can be understood as practical alternatives to tackle social reproduction needs of impoverished social groups. An indicative record of such initiatives currently active shows more than 300 solidarity economy groups and networks operating across the metropolitan area of Athens' (Arampatzi 2016: 10).

On the other hand, the mobilization has also had a strong impact on the Greek party system and activated processes which changed the consolidated political landscape. The left-wing soul of the protest was mostly composed by activists with previous experience in the global justice movement and in the anti-Iraq War movement. This is the same political background at the origin of Syriza, which, along with the left-wing party Antarsya, played an essential role as the 'umbrella organization' of the movement. Created in 2004 as a coalition of different groups, organizations and little parties, Syriza was transformed into a party in 2012.

In 2011 the Greek Prime Minister George Papandreou resigned and a coalition government was created, composed by Pasok (socialist), New Democracy (conservative) and LAOS (extreme-right). The two general elections which followed in May and June 2012 radically changed the Greek established system of parties: New Democracy obtained the majority of votes in both cases, immediately followed by Syriza which moved from 4.59 per cent of votes in 2009 to 26.89 per cent in 2012. This was an impressive result which showed the role played by this party in the cycle of protest and its capacity to channel and express the great discontent with the management of the crisis and failure of national political systems. The success of Syriza continued at the 25 January 2015 elections, when it won 36 per cent of votes, and established itself as the leading party.

France

Even though France has been affected by the economic crisis and austerity – with relevant cuts especially in public health and social benefits – the country did not experience the same dramatic situation as in Spain, Portugal and Italy. According to some scholars, this is the reason why the French *Indignés*, which emerged in 2011 in the wave of Spanish *Indignados* and the Occupy movement, were not able to create a mass and durable movement (Chabanet and Royall 2014). The first mobilization of the *Indignés* took place at the end of May 2011 in more than 20 French cities. The mobilization took the form of weekly meetings focused on humanitarian claims such as the defence of refugees, immigrants and the Roma community, as well as environmental issues and the Palestinian cause. The economic matters relating to the effects of the crisis – such as social rights or unemployment – were not as dominant as in the case of Spain, Greece, Portugal and Italy. By the end of 2012 the French *Indignés* movement had practically disappeared.

However, a new wave of contention emerged in France recently. In a context of general demobilization in the other countries, youth mobilization surprisingly exploded in France in the spring of 2016 and, this time, with a specific focus on the French economic situation and labour rights. The movement, called *Nuit Debout*, appeared on 31 March 2016 as a reaction against the labour reform package known as El Khomri law, named after the French Minister of Labor who proposed it.

This protest channelled the discontent with the Hollande government, accused of not being able to tackle the increasing unemployment rates, which, in the case of younger people, had risen up to 25 per cent. With the aim of reactivating the labour market, Hollande undertook a programme of labour liberalization, the El Khomri labour law. This law, approved in the Parliament on 9 August 2016, introduced radical modifications in the labour code, making layoff easier, restricting the limitation of working hours and reducing workers' compensation in case of redundancy.

The measures were strongly opposed by youth organizations and trade unions, which undertook a series of mobilizations across the country. The largest protest took place on 31 March with about 390,000 participants at the national level and with the occupation, in Paris, of Place de la République. The occupation continued in the following days, challenging the ban on demonstrations introduced through the state of emergency declared by the government after the November 2015 terrorist attacks in Paris. Demonstrators continued to meet in the square every evening at 6p.m. to take part in a popular assembly. On the morning of 11 April, the

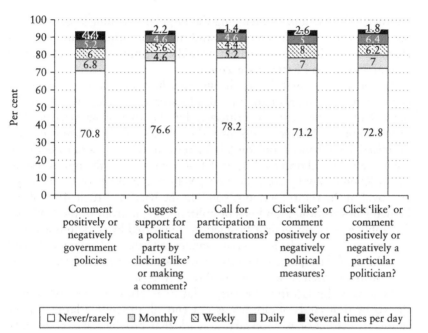

Figure 18.5: Use of social networks for political participation –
France (%)

Source: Networked Cultures Survey 2016

police evacuated the square, removing the structures created by the demonstrators, who returned to occupy the zone in the evening. On 14 April, President Hollande declared, in a TV interview, his intention to move forward with the labour reform. Subsequently, a group of demonstrators moved to the Élysée Palace, the official residence of the French President, an action which ended in violent confrontation with the police.

After some weeks, the organizers tried to expand the mobilization to the suburbs of Saint-Denis and Saint-Ouen, but with insignificant results. The same occurred in Marseille. In the meantime, along with the initial issue related to labour reform, other matters started to be discussed, such as universal basic income, amnesty for undocumented immigrants, solidarity with the refugees and gender discrimination.

As in the case of Spain, Portugal and Greece, the French movement strongly used new digital tools to expand itself and communicate and organize events (see figure 18.5). On the other hand, *Nuit Debout* militants also created their own radio and TV channels, distributed via the

Internet, with the aim of divulging the popular assemblies organized in the square, along with interviews and analysis. Other communication channels created by the movement were the bulletin *20 Luttes mille*, and several Twitter and Facebook accounts.

At the institutional level, during the first month the movement encountered the support of several left-wing politicians, while on the other hand being strongly criticized by the right-wing parties. The Prime Minister Manuel Valls met the leaders of the movement and promised some concessions on labour reform, with the aim of defusing the protest. In addition to this, on 10 May, faced with the opposition to the El Khomri law by some deputies, Valls declared he would force the approval of the reform without vote, on the basis of Article 49.3 of the French Constitution. Hundreds of militants met in front of the National Assembly protesting against this action, supported by trade unions. The government proposed a motion of confidence to the parliament and won, and the draft law passed directly to the Senate for the debate and, as previously threatened, was approved on 9 August.

As stressed by Geoffrey Pleyers, 'a latent frustration, even when it is shared by thousands of citizens, is not enough to ignite a large mobilization. A detonator is necessary, a spark that provides an opportunity for a first sequence of mobilizations. The labour rights reform package presented by the French government in February was a perfect spark', but, at the same time, 'what distinguishes a social movement from any other kind of mobilization is the fact that it does not focus on a specific claim (such as labour reform) but challenges some of the core values of a society' (Pleyers 2016). And this was what happened in the case of the *Nuit Debout* movement, as in the case of the other indignant movements in Southern Europe.

Nevertheless, the French situation is completely different from that of Spain, Portugal, Greece and Italy. Though the economic situation is not comparable with that of these countries, France is strongly disturbed by terrorism and the dramatic affirmation of populist parties which exploit the general sense of insecurity diffused in French society. At the same time, the divisions and internal fighting on the left front compromised the possibility of channelling left-wing discontent through a reliable political solution. As the recent presidential elections have shown, discontent had the effect of so-called 'cartel parties' losing a large share of their traditional votes (as happened in Greece, Spain and – even if to a lesser extent – Portugal) and was capitalized on by the centrist Macron and far-right Le Pen, both of whom advanced to the second round of the presidential elections.

On the other hand, conflict increased for everyone in the summer and autumn of 2016, with a strong involvement of trade unions and violent confrontations with the police, and the results of this wave of contention are hard to predict, as it is a recent phenomenon still in development.

Italy

While movements directly linked to austerity have emerged in Spain, Portugal and Greece, the case of Italy appears to be different, a difference that is also reflected in institutional politics, as we shall see below. In an article whose title is emblematic of this particularity – 'Why don't Italians occupy? Hypotheses on a failed mobilization' (2012) – Lorenzo Zamponi examines, and in part questions, this difference. In fact, the panorama seems more complex. Italy experienced the first of the 'anti-austerity' movements of the period under review, that is, the great student movement – but also involving researchers with precarious contracts – which swept turbulently through secondary schools and universities between the autumn of 2008 and spring of 2009 under the banner 'We don't pay for the crisis!' (Caruso et al. 2010). During 2010 a major demonstration was held about public water, and the largest and most violent protest, the 15 October 2011 international demonstration, was organized in Italy (Zamponi 2012). Nevertheless, it is evident that these mobilizations did not give rise to a single (albeit multifaceted) and major anti-austerity movement, such as the case of the Spanish *indignados*, the movements that appeared in Portugal or the intense waves of anti-Troika protest in Greece. Indeed, although issues linked to the crisis and austerity were present in the aforesaid Italian movements, they are more characterized by the identity of the actors (e.g. students) and by the type of claim (e.g. public water as the single issue). It was only at the demonstration of 15 October that the different instances united around the common denominator of the struggle against austerity. On the other hand, as in the case of Greece, various scholars have detected also in the case of Italy a revitalization of civil society in the context of crisis and austerity (Bosi and Zamponi 2015; Forno and Graziano 2014; Guidi and Andretta 2015). As stressed by Bosi and Zamponi, 'Italy in the last number of years has seen the visible emergence of various DSAs [Direct Social Actions]: forms of economic activism like purchasing groups, boycotts, critical consumerism, time banks and mutual cooperation have been significantly increasing, broadening their audience and evolving in a direction that is increasingly related to the satisfaction of material needs, in the context of the economic crisis' (Bosi and Zamponi 2015: 375).

That said, it is undeniable that at the level of institutional politics the

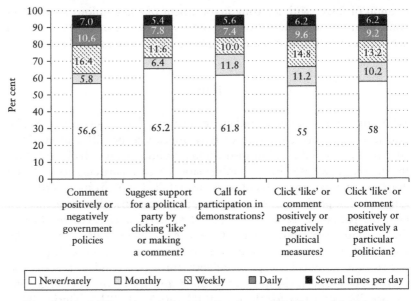

Figure 18.6: Use of social networks for political participation –
Italy (%)

Source: Networked Cultures Survey 2016

Italian landscape is completely different compared to the other Southern European countries. This difference, as has been flagged, is reflected in the institutional political scenario. While in both Greece and Spain the new parties that have made themselves the spokespersons of the discontent related to the crisis and austerity (Podemos and Syriza), managing to shake the very roots of the political systems of the respective countries, are firmly grounded in the anti-austerity movements, the case of Italy is different. In fact, the new party which has embodied this discomfort – M5S – has no connection whatsoever with the Italian movements of the last few years, apart from, and merely partially with, the movement on public water. Nevertheless, it did adopt social media practices both from similar political protest movements in other countries and developed endeogenous social media strategies based on the previous experience of its leaders and members in social media marketing (see figure 18.6). M5S never participated in the movements, nor have the activists of this party, the vast majority of whom have no previous experience of activism, and nor in general have the citizens who voted for M5S, as can be seen from the profiles of its electors (Bartlett et al. 2013; Bordignon and Ceccarini 2013).

Although Syriza and M5S have some affinities, since they are all cases of new parties which very swiftly ascended in elections called in the context of the economic crisis, disturbing political and party systems, and channelling the disquiet aroused by the management of the crisis, they are in fact very different. Apart from not having a clear political positioning on the left–right spectrum – after the European elections, M5S joined forces with the Europe of Freedom and Direct Democracy (EFDD) parliamentary group, to which other parties belong, such as the English UKIP – this party has to a large extent constructed its specific political discourse based on extremely harsh criticism of professional politicians (Bobba and McDonnell 2015; Tronconi 2015). Hence, none of the 108 deputies and 54 senators elected through M5S, most of whom are less than 40 years old, have previous political experience, neither at a national level nor a local level. M5S refuses any ideological label, insisting on its actual civic nature. This is clearly reflected in the source of its votes: the voters of M5S are almost equally divided between citizens who position themselves to the left/centre-left, to the right/centre-right and those who refuse to place themselves politically (Bordignon and Ceccarini 2013).

For all these reasons, the relationship between crisis, austerity, protest and political change appears to be very different in Italy when compared to other countries of Southern Europe. In Italy we do not find a joint and prolonged anti-austerity movement – such as the 'new, new' social movements – but rather many sectoral movements that are of a more 'traditional' type. The new party which has emerged and suddenly imposed itself in the electoral contests, embodying the discontent linked to the economic and political crisis, has no links – neither amongst its militants nor electors – with the world of social movements. This new party cannot be placed on the left–right spectrum while, at the same time, the left-wing instances and claims matured and rooted in movements do not have or have lost, in Italy – with the quasi disappearance of *Rifondazione Comunista* (RC) and *Sinistra Ecologia Libertà* (SEL) – channels of political representation. In Spain and Greece, in contrast, there has been a sustained period of struggle closely linked to austerity, and the parties which have emerged and whiplashed through the political systems are directly connected to these struggles. The case of Portugal, where the consequences of the cycle of protest can be detected in the unusual government coalition after the October 2015 election, is also different.

G. CARDOSO, G. ACCORNERO, T. LAPA AND J. AZEVEDO

Networked autonomy and political change in Southern Europe

Although the ongoing processes of political change in Southern European countries may be shaping up in different ways, one common background condition can be distinguished, namely, the growing importance of modes of engagement through connective types of action (Bennett and Segerberg 2012), that might generate original alternatives to exercise (individually or collectively) autonomous action. The argument here is that communicational changes, specifically in the current context of the networked communication model (Cardoso 2007), also strongly contribute to political transformation (Cardoso et al. 2016; Rahaghi 2012; Shirky 2011).

As indicated by Ortoleva (2004), communication models have cycles of social affirmation. Society shapes communication between actors, giving rise to different ways to communicate in different historical times. The socially shaped networked communication model (Cardoso 2007) articulates and binds together mass communication practices, auto-mass communication, one-to-many mediated communication and interpersonal communication in a multimedia environment. Networked communication combines and connects other communication models, by giving them new features and above all by allowing the use and combination of different possibilities of communication by linking them in a single network.

By connecting together offline and online networks, individuals and movements have built networking cultures that are today a fundamental trait of reflexivity and political action. An indicator of that is the data in figure 18.7, which shows that around a third of respondents to our survey in Spain and Italy, and a quarter in Portugal and Greece, use social network sites to mobilize others.

Looking at Southern European societies, what might be happening is not lesser participation, but changes in citizens' liaisons with traditional political institutions and participatory patterns (Juris and Pleyers 2009), which have intensified in recent years. Therefore, the multidimensionality of the construct of 'participation' should be acknowledged by differentiating a set of participatory patterns (de Zúñiga et al. 2012) but also a possible shift in civic and political cultures in countries like Greece, Italy, France or Portugal.

This entails analysing how new media reflects such shifts and alters participatory forms and even facilitates or supports new ones (Bennett and Segerberg 2012; Castells 2012; Rahaghi 2012; Vissers and Stolle

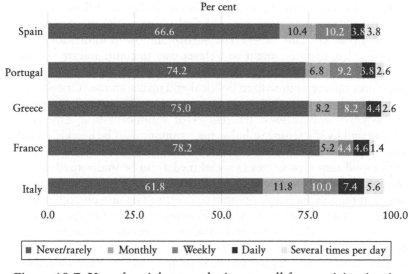

Figure 18.7: Use of social network sites to call for participation in demonstrations (%)

Source: Networked Cultures Survey 2016

2013). In this context, Bennett and Segerberg (2012) make the distinction between collective action, associated with high levels of organizational resources and the formation of collective identities, and connective action based on personalized content sharing across media networks that fosters changes in political action dynamics. In turn, one may link this logic of connective action with nascent forms of social agency, especially of the so-called 'alter-globalization activists' (Pleyers 2010) or anti-austerity protesters, that is, those who contest neoliberal globalization or austerity policies, and propose alternative policies such as horizontal and participatory organization models or call for reforms in political institutions.

If mass communication fostered the exercise of power through the integration of the individual in the existing institutions of society, networked communication, along with connective action, fosters the building of new institutional settings of power through the networking of individuals. At the same time as people are appropriating social media, governments, traditional political actors and institutions seem unable to communicate properly with citizens at large, because they are still very much shaped by the mass communication model, rather than by the networked communication model adopted by the majority of those protesting.

The transformation of power relations in the 'space of flows' must also consider the interaction between political actors, social agents and media business (Castells 2007: 254). The horizontal flow of information, often involving live updates, might be a clever way to communicate without a trace and create an aura of veracity in contrast with the information that populates the institutionalized political and media arenas (Castells 2007: 251). This horizontal flow and non-restriction of content has, however, less positive implications: the danger of misinformation, especially if propagated by the strongest hubs, since rumours can be quickly repeated and amplified if generated or shared by the most connected members. Still, mobilization processes in social media can be understood as forms of heterodox collective action, not necessarily radical or confrontational, aimed at mobilizing public opinion to exercise pressure on policy makers (della Porta and Diani 2006: 165). What the protests of recent years seem to exhibit is the clash between dissimilar conceptions of communication power: one shaped by the power of mass communication, in the case of governments and legacy political parties, and another moulded by networked communication, in the case of demonstrators and the newly arrived political parties. During the austerity years, protesters increasingly built a representation of governments and political institutions in an analogy of the search engine's role in the network society. Protesters expect that governments and political parties work as receptors of different queries to which the 'political search engine' must answer, giving the suitable responses – and swiftly, so people can click and check if they found what they were looking for. But given that there are always multiple answers available, this means that governments and political institutions are less perceived as the keepers of solutions, but instead as the ones that should produce the links towards them, bridging institutions and multiple constituencies.

Another common feature of the protests is the motivational basis of engagement and mobilization in the southern European countries, namely the 'affective investment' (Dahlgren 2009) related to awareness of the effects of austerity. The perception of injustice that turns into protest (Cardoso et al. 2016; Castells 2012; Pleyers 2010) can be regarded as the affective investment. Figure 18.8 clearly shows that, on average, respondents of our survey agree that the economic crisis brought the impoverishment of the population, the decrease of purchasing power, wages, pensions and social benefits provided by the state, the enrichment of the rich, the increase in political and financial corruption and the increase in emigration.

The adoption of social media by the protesters permitted the creation of gathering places online that, in turn, connected people with similar

	The impoverishment of the population in general	The decrease in the purchasing power of citizens in general	The enrichment of the highest social classes	The increase in political corruption	The increase in financial corruption	The reduction of wages and pensions	The decrease in social benefits provided by the State	The increase in emigration
◇ Italy	3.47	3.38	3.27	3.38	3.40	3.04	3.15	3.16
□ France	3.30	3.37	3.32	3.19	3.20	3.08	2.93	3.15
▲ Greece	3.62	3.54	3.38	3.42	3.48	3.51	3.43	3.48
✕ Portugal	3.44	3.34	3.38	3.45	3.51	3.14	3.16	3.35
✳ Spain	3.48	3.30	3.29	3.39	3.37	3.25	3.18	3.09

Figure 18.8: Impact of the economic crisis in own country, by type and country (average) (1 = totally disagree; 4 = totally agree)

Source: Networked Cultures Survey 2016

affective investments against austerity. New media appropriation helped to create ties between individuals' ideas, views, calls for action and demonstrations on the streets. Despite the risks of populism, platforms such as social network sites became a locus where people's representation of their own ability to exercise autonomy is built since it both enhances the power of individual choices and the awareness of one's role as part of a network. Following Castells, the conversion from individuation to autonomy through networking 'allows individual actors to build their autonomy with likeminded people in the networks of their choice' (2012: 231). In this sense, networked autonomy of individuals can be argued as a new modality of power. Social media becomes an integral organizational part of contemporary social movements, allowing flexibility across various conditions, issues and scale, and, through the formative element of 'sharing', enables individualized public engagement and personalized collective action formations (Bennett and Segerberg 2012).

Social media, and ICTs in general, constitute themselves as the elected tools that strengthen ties between individuals within political protest, but they have not been particularly good at connecting political institutions and individuals. They might connect individuals in institutions of power with individuals in counter-power movements, yet that implies that individuals in power also share the same networked cultures and learn how to incorporate, in their thinking and action, the same cultures as their citizens. The majority of present-day European governments have not yet understood that they increasingly live in an era in which 'networked individuals are the message', meaning that if people don't agree with policies, they will make it clear by communicating through networks and will, eventually, propose the redesign of policies and post it online in order to get the support of others.

The public appeal for change, and non-conformity to the existing rules and norms, occurs because people sense that their own perception of themselves in relation to their social environment has changed. Individuals do not merely act in the network; they think and perceive their actions as networked. The cultural innovation brought by the Internet, along with the appeals to morality or justice, the assertion of democracy, and the non-violent contestation of various methods of domination (Wieviorka 2012), is sustaining the emergence of many social movements. Taking inspiration from Touraine (2000), it can be stated that through ICT, many citizens started to perceive the need to assert publicly their individual and collective right to become free actors, to be able to constitute themselves as subjects, to use creative freedom against social statuses and social roles and to be capable of changing their environment and, therefore, of reinforcing their autonomy. The way people seem to increasingly think about social liaisons, institutions, power, social transformation and autonomy as based in networks is, perhaps, the fundamental novelty brought by new media to social mobilization in regions like Southern Europe. This is something that new political parties that rose or shared momentum with the protests against austerity, such as M5S, Syriza or Podemos, have understood and incorporated into their political practices. The question remains as to what will be the transformative power of those experiments: will they be able to go viral within the political landscape and transform the political institutions or will they be confined and locked to the fringes of protest politics? The answer will also define the future of the crisis in Europe.

References

Accornero, G. (2015) Back to the revolution: the 1974 Portuguese Spring and its 'austere anniversary'. *Historein*, 15(1): 32–48.

Accornero, G. (2017). The 'Mediation' of the Portuguese Anti-Austerity Protest Cycle. Media Coverage and its Impact. In *Media Representations of Anti-Austerity Protests in the EU: Grievances, Identities and Agency*, ed. by Tao Papaioannou and Suman Gupta. London: Routledge.

Accornero, G. and Ramos Pinto, P. (2015) 'Mild mannered'? Protest and mobilisation in Portugal under austerity, 2010–2013. *West European Politics*, 38(3): 491–515.

Alberich Nistal, T. (2012) Antecedents, achievements and challenges of the Spanish 15M Movement. In Tejerina, B. and Perugorría, I. (eds) *From Social to Political: New Forms of Mobilization and Democratization*. Bilbao: Argitalpen Zerbitzua, pp. 78–92.

Arampatzi, A. (2016) The spatiality of counter-austerity politics in Athens, Greece: emergent 'urban solidarity spaces'. *Urban Studies*, doi: 10.1177/004 2098016629311.

Bartlett, J., Froio, C., Littler, M. and McDonnell, D. (2013) New political actors in Europe: Beppe Grillo and the M5S. *Demos UK*. Available at: http://www. demos.co.uk/files/Beppe_Grillo_and_the_M5S_-_Demos_web_version.pdf? 1360766725

Baumgarten, B. (2013) Geração à Rasca and beyond: mobilizations in Portugal after 12 March 2011. *Current Sociology*, 61(4): 457–73.

Bennett, W.L. and Segerberg, A. (2012) The logic of connective action: digital media and the personalization of contentious politics. *Information, Communication & Society*, 15(5): 739–68.

Bermeo, N. and Bartels, L. (eds) (2014) *Mass Politics in Tough Times: Opinions, Votes and Protest in the Great Recession*. New York: Oxford University Press.

Bobba, G. and McDonnell, D. (2015) Italy – a strong and enduring market for populism. In Kriesi, H. and Takkis Papas, T. (eds) *Populism in the Shadow of the Great Recession*. Colchester: ECPR Press, pp. 157–74.

Bordignon, F. and Ceccarini, L. (2013) Five stars and a cricket: Beppe Grillo shakes Italian politics. *South European Society and Politics*, 18(4): 427–49.

Bosi, L. and Zamponi, L. (2015) Direct social actions and economic crises: the relationship between forms of action and socio-economic context in Italy. *Partecipazione e Conflitto*, 8(2): 367–91.

Campos Lima, M. and Martin Artiles, A. (2011) Crisis and trade union challenges in Portugal and Spain: between general strikes and social pacts. *Transfer*, 17(3): 387–402.

Campos Lima, M. and Martin Artiles, A. (2014) Descontentamento na europa em tempos de austeridade: Da ação coletiva à participação individual no protesto social. *Revista Crítica de Ciências Sociais*, 103: 137–72.

Cardoso, G. (2007) *The Media in the Network Society: Browsing, News, Filters and Citizenship*. Lisbon: CIES.

Cardoso, G., Lapa, T. and Di Fátima, B. (2016) People are the message? Social mobilization and social media in Brazil. *International Journal of Communication*, 10: 3909–30.

Caruso, L., Giorgi, A., Mattoni, A. and Piazza, G. (2010) *Alla ricerca dell'Onda: I nuovi conflitti nell'istruzione superiore*. Milan: Franco Angeli.

Castells, M. (2007) Communication, power and counter-power in the network society. *International Journal of Communication*, 1: 238–66.

Castells, M. (2012) *Networks of Outrage and Hope: Social Movements in the Internet Age*. Cambridge: Polity.

Chabanet, D. and Royall, F. (2014) The 2011 Indignés/Occupy Movements in France and Ireland: an analysis of the causes of weak mobilisations. *Modern & Contemporary France*, 23(3): 327–49.

Dahlgren, P. (2009) *Media and Political Engagement: Citizens, Communication, and Democracy*. Cambridge: Cambridge University Press.

de Zúñiga, H.G., Jung, N. and Valenzuela, S. (2012) Social media use for news and individuals' social capital, civic engagement and political participation. *Journal of Computer-Mediated Communication*, 17(3): 319–36.

della Porta, D. (2015) *Social Movements in Times of Austerity: Bringing Capitalism Back into Protest Analysis*. Cambridge: Polity.

della Porta, D. and Diani, M. (2006) *Social Movements – An Introduction*. Oxford: Blackwell.

Elias, L. and Pinho, P. (2012) Reuniões e manifestações – Os desafios das novas formas de contestação social [Meetings and demonstrations: the challenges of new forms of social protest]. *Polícia Portuguesa*, 4(3): 37–53.

Feixa, C., Pereira, I. and Juris, J. (2009) Global citizenship and the 'new, new' social movements: Iberian connections. *Young*, 17(4): 421–42.

Forno, F. and Graziano, P. (2014) Sustainable community movement organisations. *Journal of Consumer Culture*, 14(2): 139–57.

Gall, G. (2013) Quiescence continued? Recent strike activity in nine Western European countries. *Economic and Industrial Democracy*, 34(4): 667–91.

Giugni, M. and Grasso, M. (eds) (2016) *Austerity and Protest: Popular Contention in Times of Economic Crisis*. Abingdon: Routledge.

Guidi, R. and Andretta, M. (2015) Between resistance and resilience: how do Italian solidarity purchase groups change in times of crisis and austerity? *Partecipazione e Conflitto*, 8(2): 443–77.

Hamann, K., Johnston, A. and Kelly, J. (2013) Unions against governments: explaining general strikes in Western Europe, 1980–2006. *Comparative Political Studies*, 46(9): 1030–57.

Juris, J.S. and Pleyers, G.H. (2009) Alter-activism: emerging cultures of participation among young global justice activists. *Journal of Youth Studies*, 12(1): 57–75.

Kousis, M. and Karakioulafi, C. (2013) Labour unions confronting unprecedented austerity in Greece, 2010–2013. ECPR General Conference 2013, Sciences Po, Bordeaux.

Lapa, T., and Cardoso, G. (2016) (Social) Media isn't the message, networked people are: calls for protest through social media. *Observatorio (OBS*) Journal*, 10 (Special Issue): 202–19.

Ortiz, I., Burke, S., Berrada, M. and Cortés, H. (2013) *World Protests 2006–2013*. Executive Summary, Working paper, Initiative for Policy Dialogue and Friedrich-Ebert-Stiftung New York.

Ortoleva, P. (2004) O novo sistema dos media. In Paquete de Oliveira, J.M., Cardoso, G. and Barreiros, J. (eds) *Comunicação, Cultura e Tecnologias de Informação*. Lisbon: Quimera.

Pleyers, G. (2010) *Alter-globalization: Becoming Actors in the Global Age*. Cambridge: Polity.

Pleyers, G. (2016) 'Nuit Debout': citizens are back in the squares in Paris. *openDemocracy*, 8 April.

Rahaghi, J. (2012) New tools, old goals: comparing the role of technology in the 1979 Iranian Revolution and the 2009 Green Movement. *Journal of Information Policy*, 2: 151–82.

Rüdig, W. and Karyotis, G. (2013) Beyond the usual suspects? New participants in anti-austerity protests in Greece. *Mobilization: An International Quarterly*, 18(3): 313–30.

Shirky, C. (2011) The political power of social media: technology, the public sphere, and political change. *Foreign Affairs*, January/February, 28–41.

Simiti, M. (2014) Rage and protest: the case of the Greek Indignant movement. GreeSE Paper No. 82, Hellenic Observatory Papers on Greece and Southeast Europe.

Simiti, M. (2015) 'Social need' or 'choice'? Greek civil society during the economic crisis. GreeSE Paper No. 95, Hellenic Observatory Papers on Greece and Southeast Europe.

Tronconi, F. (ed.) (2015) *Beppe Grillo's Five Star Movement: Organisation, Communication and Ideology*. Farnham: Ashgate.

Touraine, A. (2000) A method for studying social actors. *Journal of World Systems Research*, 6(3): 900–18.

Vissers, S. and Stolle, D. (2013) The Internet and new modes of political participation: online versus offline participation. *Information, Communication & Society*, 17(8): 937–55.

Wieviorka, M. (2012) The resurgence of social movements. *Journal of Conflictology*, 3(2): 13–19.

Zamponi, L. (2012) Why don't Italians occupy? Hypotheses on a failed mobilisation. *Social Movements Studies*, 11(3–4): 416–26.

Conclusion

There can be little doubt that the European Union is facing a crisis as serious as anything it has experienced since its origins more than 60 years ago. As we have sought to show in this book, the current crisis is not a single crisis but rather multiple crises that have different origins and different consequences, but they have overlapped and amplified one another, creating a self-reinforcing process that threatens to spin out of control. The Old Continent of Europe appears to be quite incapable of stemming the spiral of disintegration and powerlessness.

Some may be tempted to attribute the deepening of the crisis in Europe to specific factors or events that stem from or lie outside of Europe itself, such as the catastrophic conflicts in the Middle East that have nourished new forms of extremism and terrorism which have spilled over into the streets of European cities and created new pressures in terms of migration, as many millions of people are displaced by the wars in Syria and elsewhere. They might also point to the fact that the EU is not alone in experiencing a crisis of legitimacy, that the deepening distrust of established political elites is not unique to Europe and that the rise of alternative social movements, both on the left and on the right, is evident elsewhere: these are social and political phenomena that can be seen in many Western societies and are to some extent emblematic features of our time. But while there is some truth in these observations, they don't explain the specificity of the crisis that engulfs Europe today, nor do they help us to understand the extent to which Europe's crisis is a crisis of its own making.

As we have tried to show in this book, the crises that have plagued Europe since the eruption of the economic and financial crisis in 2008–9 are structural in the sense that they stem from flaws in the institutional construction of the European Union and in the sense that they have often been exacerbated by the ways that the EU has responded to events. They are therefore crises that have deep historical and institutional origins, dating back to times when key decisions were taken about the institutional construction of the EU. This is particularly evident in relation to the economic crisis: the seeds of this crisis were planted many years ago, in the 1980s and 1990s when the plans for monetary union were being drawn up. True, the proximate source of the financial crisis in Europe in 2008–9 was the crisis in the subprime mortgage market that began in the US in late 2006 and grew ever-more calamitous during the course of 2007 and 2008. But when the repercussions of this crisis hit Europe, they hit institutions that were structurally weak and vulnerable: under the reign of the single currency, the eurozone had experienced highly heterogeneous development and European institutions had accumulated high levels of public and private debt. Moreover, the political responses to the crisis, and especially the tough austerity packages imposed on Member States who found themselves in need of bailouts as well as the unwillingness (or inability) to write off debts that even the IMF regarded as unsustainable, served in many ways to exacerbate the crisis and to intensify the social costs in terms of human suffering. The priority given to financial and budgetary stability – a priority that reflected the normative economic principles that have become ingrained in the practices and policies of the EU's most powerful player, Germany – had serious social consequences in terms of producing high levels of unemployment and deteriorating public health, especially in the countries of southern Europe. The suffering of a large number of people is not so much the outcome of the financial crisis as such, or of the financial crisis alone: it is in large part due to the measures that were aimed at ending it. So while the crisis in the subprime mortgage market in the US may have played a role in triggering the economic and financial crisis in Europe, the latter crisis is directly linked to and strongly shaped by structural flaws that were part and parcel of the process of monetary union, and the character and consequences of this crisis are the outcome of political decision-makers in Europe. Austerity was not the only policy option available to EU leaders when faced with a severe economic crisis; when faced with a comparable situation in the US, President Obama made a different choice.

The crisis in Europe is multi-dimensional: it is economic, financial, social and highly political. And as we have seen in this volume, it is also cultural, intellectual and moral, reaching to the very heart of the values that define Europe. This is why we speak of the *crises* of Europe – multiple crises, each with their own specific conditions, characteristics and consequences. For example, the resurgence of racism, anti-Semitism and terrorism – three 'forces of evil' that represent a profound challenge to Europe's humanist values – are complex processes that are rooted in specific historical developments that can be traced back to the 1970s and before; they are not new and they are not unique to Europe, but on European soil they have found fertile ground, and the inability of the EU to deal effectively with them – e.g. by integrating their police forces and intelligence services – has weakened European institutions and provided succour to the forces of nationalism which promise to respond more effectively, thereby reinforcing tendencies towards fragmentation. Similarly, what is referred to as the 'radicalization' of young people who wish to join radical Islamist groups is at least partially the outcome of a failure to integrate populations of immigrant origin in Europe. So while the multiple crises have their own histories and specificities, they are also connected to one another, they overlap and feed into one another in complex and shifting ways. Hence we must avoid the temptation to think of the crisis in Europe as a set of processes in which one episode leads to another, as if it were a sequence of falling dominoes. It is true that the various facets of the crisis – or, more precisely, the different crises – appeared at different historical points in time. But it was not the financial crisis, for example, or not this alone, which produced a social crisis and a deepening sense of distrust and discontent, and not this (or this alone) that produced a growing crisis of legitimacy – there is no single, simple logic or causal sequence of this kind. The issues are much more complex, and each of the many crises that have plagued Europe over the last decade have their own conditions and consequences. But it is precisely the interconnections of these crises, and the fact that they do not occur in isolation but rather in relation to one another, bumping up against one another and reinforcing one another rather than cancelling one another out, that makes their multiple occurrence and cumulative effect so significant and consequential.

Europe's crises are therefore part of a cumulative process that is strong enough to challenge the core institutions of the European Union, institutions that are already threatened by a growing lack of legitimacy. This lack of legitimacy has its own distinctive historical roots, stemming from the fact that the EU was always a top-down project driven by political elites who shared a particular vision of a unified Europe and pushed this project forward without trying too hard to bring citizens along with them. There has always been a gulf between the decision-making institutions of the EU and the citizens of the Member States, and a resentment in some quarters about what are seen as edicts imposed by a remote bureaucracy in Brussels. Moreover, as more and more powers have been transferred from national parliaments to the European level without a commensurate development of mechanisms of representation and accountability, the deficit in terms of democratic accountability has grown.

The lack of legitimacy was exacerbated by the enlargement of Europe, which made it increasingly difficult to unite around a strongly asserted common policy and made it increasingly likely that decision-making processes would be impeded by conflicting interests. This hindered the ability of the EU to act decisively and flexibly in the face of looming crises and increased the tendency to succumb to market forces that undermined a shared political vision.

The European Union is sometimes credited with a capacity for action which it does not always actually have. This became clear at the time of the migration/refugee crisis. This crisis stemmed from an external shock: a large influx of migrants and refugees fleeing the war-torn regions of the Middle East and North Africa. While the crisis stemmed from beyond Europe, it was exacerbated by the institutional flaws of the EU – in particular, by the fact that, with the Schengen Agreement, internal borders within the Schengen area were abolished but a common European external border, with a properly funded and trained border force, was not created, so that the entire area was only as secure as the weakest link, a point that was ruthlessly exploited by the people traffickers. When the migrants and refugees began arriving in large numbers via the Greek islands that were closest to Turkey, EU leaders responded slowly and at times inconsistently, and they struggled to come up with coherent and effective policies to which all Member States would assent. Policy was made on the hoof, and statements made by some leaders were contradicted by others. When the European Commission eventually proposed that a quota system should be introduced so that migrants could be distributed around Europe, the proposal was rejected by many Member States, some of whom were experiencing a rise in support for extreme-right movements and parties that were strongly opposed to immigration. In several countries, European legislation was flouted, the frontiers were closed and fences were erected – fences which should never have been built. The idea that Europe could speak with a single voice on an issue of fundamental importance for all Member States, and in a way that reflected a core set of common European values, was in ruins. As so often in the face of a looming crisis, the EU's response was slow, faltering and inadequate – too little, too late. We don't have to look further than the migration/refugee crisis to see how different elements are woven together to create a crisis that draws on and feeds into other related crises and that brings the institutional weaknesses of the EU into sharp relief: flawed institutions, weak governance structures, slow and ineffective policy-making, xenophobic fears, security fears, the deepening hardship stemming from economic crisis and austerity, the growing crisis of legitimacy – all combine, collide and feed on one another to create a crisis that threatens to spin out of control. Although Europe does have its own frontiers, its own diplomacy and its own capacity for military action (largely the military capacity of its individual Member States), it appears to be powerless and incapable of protecting its citizens, and frequently it relies on the US to provide military and security support, for instance in transportation and surveillance (which is why NATO seems so important for most European countries).

From the outset, therefore, European institutions were not fit for the purpose of European construction. The EU embarked on an ambitious project of political construction, seeking to create institutions that had many of the characteristics of a state, but in practice the institutions it created did not have the capacity to act as a state. It was, and remains, a state more in aspiration than in reality. Some of the institutions were not well designed and not well thought through, and they were not sufficiently robust to deal with the challenges that came their way, some of which could have been (and should have been) anticipated. This was the case with the euro: economic considerations were overshadowed by the political goals of reigning in a reunified Germany and locking in the members of the monetary union to a new and irreversible cycle of European integration. But this is not what happened – quite the contrary. As the crisis in the eurozone deepened, it brought into sharp relief the weaknesses in the original design, the institutional failings of the EU and the deleterious consequences of the policies adopted to deal with the crisis, thereby fuelling the crisis of political legitimacy rather than facilitating a new cycle of political integration.

So on the one hand, these crises are specific to Europe, and on the other hand they are part and parcel of crises that are operating at other levels, both national and supra-European. Some crises are specifically European, or European and American – this is the case, for instance, with the financial crisis. Other crises are global, or at least not restricted to Europe and the US – this is the case, for instance, with the crisis of legitimacy of political systems and of the traditional institutions of representative democracy, a crisis that we observe in many countries around the world. These crises are both objective and could potentially be tackled as something real and material, and at the same time they are subjective, a combination of representations, beliefs, feelings, emotions and fears, something that is much harder to pin down but which at the end of the day is fundamental, since ultimately this is the basis on which citizens express or withdraw their support.

There is a very real risk that Europe could break up. Many of the most fundamental problems that have shaken the EU in recent years remain unresolved, including the economic crisis that continues to threaten stability in the eurozone. Nation-states could leave the EU one by one: Brexit has opened a door through which others could choose to pass. The EU could split into a Europe of the North separate from a Europe of the South, or a Core Europe separate from a Peripheral Europe. There is also the possibility of a two-speed Europe or even a multi-speed Europe, which some analysts consider the only way of avoiding the pure and simple break-up. But the worst may not come to pass. Specific measures could be introduced to deal with the most pressing issues and the EU could pull together and, once again, muddle through. As always in a time of crisis, long-term visions tend to be dissolved into short-term goals, as those responsible for managing institutions focus on the exigencies of survival. This makes it difficult for political and social actors to deal with the crisis of legitimacy in Europe by proposing substantial and realistic measures in order to reconstruct or re-launch the Old Continent. But it's possible that the crises of recent years could have the beneficial effect of re-focusing minds on the core issues at stake and on what could be lost if the EU were to fall apart.

Our aim in this volume has not been to speculate about the future of Europe or to provide a blueprint for the reconstruction of the European Union – there are too many uncertainties at this point in time to be able to project future developments with any degree of confidence. Our aim instead has been to look back at the process of European integration, with a particular focus on the period from 2008 to the present, and to seek to understand the distinctive features of the multiple crises that have convulsed Europe over this time period. Our primary aim has been analytical rather than normative, retrospective rather than prospective. It is for others to create the future but our hope is that they will learn from the failures of the past, that they will recognize the extent to which the crises that have plagued the EU are the result of flaws in its construction, that they will be sharply attuned to the fact that ill-conceived and inflexible policies can have unintended consequences that exacerbate rather than resolve problems and undermine the very institutions you are trying to build, and that they will seek to create a Europe that embraces its citizens and actively involves them in the process of institution building rather than treating them as a reluctant partner that needs to be dragged along by an aloof and technocratic elite. European integration is more likely to be effective when it is carried out from below, through active forms of collaboration and participation in different spheres of life (as schemes such as the Erasmus Programme illustrate so well), rather than administered from above and imposed on populations. And the future of Europe, whatever that turns out to be, is a future that will endure only if its institutions are constructed in ways that attend more carefully and respond more effectively than the EU has done so far to the wishes, needs and views of its people.

Appendix: Country abbreviations

AT	Austria	IE	Ireland
BE	Belgium	IS	Iceland
BG	Bulgaria	IT	Italy
CH	Switzerland	LT	Lithuania
CY	Cyprus	LU	Luxembourg
CZ	Czech Republic	LV	Latvia
DE	Germany	MT	Malta
DK	Denmark	NL	Netherlands
EE	Estonia	NO	Norway
ES	Spain	PL	Poland
EU28	EU Average	PT	Portugal
FI	Finland	RO	Romania
FR	France	SE	Sweden
GR	Greece	SI	Slovenia
HR	Croatia	SK	Slovakia
HU	Hungary	UK	United Kingdom

Index